D1030220

Orange Empire

Orange Empire

CALIFORNIA AND THE FRUITS OF EDEN

Douglas Cazaux Sackman

UNIVERSITY OF CALIFORNIA PRESS

BERKELEY LOS ANGELES LONDON

Frontispiece: "I Grow These Myself in California": Uncle
Sam naturalized as a California orange grower on a
Riverside Navel Orange Company crate label from circa
1900. This item is reproduced by permission of The
Huntington Library, San Marino, California.

The following chapters were published earlier in different
form: chapter 2 as "Inside the Skin of Nature: The
Scientific Quest for the Golden Orange," in Stephen
Tchudi, ed., *Science, Values and the American West* (Reno:
Nevada Humanities Committee, 1997): 117–45,
reprinted by permission of the Nevada Humanities
Committee; part of chapter 3 as "'By Their Fruits Ye Shall
Know Them': 'Nature Cross Culture Hybridization' and
the California Citrus Industry, 1893–1939," *California
History* (Spring 1995): 82–99, 139–40, reprinted with
permission of the California Historical Society; and part
of chapter 4 as "'Nature's Workshop': The Work
Environment and Workers' Bodies in the California
Citrus Industry, 1900–1940," *Environmental History* 5,
no. 1 (January 2000): 27–53, reprinted by permission of
the Forest History Society.

University of California Press
Berkeley and Los Angeles, California

University of California Press, Ltd.
London, England

Library of Congress Cataloging-in-Publication Data

Sackman, Douglas Cazaux, 1968–
   Orange empire : California and the fruits of Eden /
Douglas Cazaux Sackman.
      p.   cm.
   Includes bibliographical references and index.
   ISBN 0-520-23886-9 (cloth : alk. paper)
   1. California—History.   2. Orange industry—
California—History.   3. California—Economic
conditions.   4. California—Environmental conditions.
I. Title.
F861.S225 2005
979.4'053—dc22   2003024225

Manufactured in the United States of America
14   13   12   11   10   09   08   07   06   05
10   9   8   7   6   5   4   3   2   1

The paper used in this publication meets the minimum
requirements of ANSI/NISO Z39.48–1992 (R 1997)
(Permanence of Paper). ∞

TO MY PARENTS, GEORGE AND VALARIE

CONTENTS

PART THREE

RECLAIMING EDEN

ILLUSTRATIONS

ACKNOWLEDGMENTS

As I was editing this book in the drizzly Pacific Northwest, I received a box of oranges in the mail. Crates of oranges used to bear colorful labels, often picturing the sunny landscape of California. My oranges were wrapped in plain brown paper, but the package was nonetheless evocative of sunnier climes. The oranges inside recalled a landscape I knew well, for they were from my mom's trees in the town of Fair Oaks, near Sacramento. All my life, I had taken these fruits for granted. But there was more to them than I realized, for they had become symbols of health, wealth, sunshine, and much else besides. My mom's trees are remnants of an earlier time. Though my town was named after acorn-bearing trees, neighboring enclaves christened themselves Citrus Heights and Orange Ville in honor of the fruit they thought would make their communities grow. Once, they had dreamed of becoming an orange empire, but that was to be the destiny of Southern California. My parents grew up in the southern part of the state, but moved to Northern California at a time when that meant getting out of the smog-besmirched metropolis and back to nature. In writing this book, I went back to Southern California and an earlier time when Los Angeles portrayed itself as the most natural spot on earth—as close as you could get to the original Garden.

While writing this book, I received many other packages with gifts inside—references, articles, pictures, suggestions, invitations. Midway through my research for the dissertation that formed the basis of the book,

I received a call from Hal Barron, who asked me to participate in a conference on Southern California citriculture at the Henry E. Huntington Library. Up to that time, I had thought that I was working on an odd topic; certainly, it was understudied. But at the conference I got to meet several other people doing good work on citrus, including Gilbert González, Lisbeth Haas, Anthea Hartig, Margo McBane, H. Vincent Moses, Ronald Tobey, and Charles Wetherell. Mike Steiner commented on the papers that Anthea and I presented, and he sounded genuinely excited by what we had come up with to that point. In the years since, I've continued to benefit from Mike's warm generosity and intellectual vibrancy. Steven Stoll and David Vaught, whose work was on California fruit but not specifically on citrus, were also at the conference. Since then their fine books have appeared, helping to continue to make California agriculture an especially rich subfield. Though Carey McWilliams published his brilliant chapter on the Orange Belt in *Southern California: An Island on the Land* almost fifty years ago, no monograph on the citrus industry had been published when I began my research. Since then, two books by Gilbert González and Matt Garcia, focusing on Mexican and Mexican American communities of the citrus belt, have appeared: each is superb and each explores different ground. One citrus grower told Charles Nordhoff in the 1870s, "People tell large stories about oranges . . . but the truth is big enough." I now add mine to the collection, and there is room for still more—though this one is large, it is not big enough to cover it all.

My dissertation advisor at the University of California at Irvine, Spencer Olin, was my ideal mentor. He gave me room to play with ideas and trusted that I would, by and by, put some solid history onto the page. Spence has blazed trails to a vantage point from which one can get a clear view of the forces that shape life in modern California and the West; I can only hope that I have followed in his footsteps in this project. Nina Dayton and Jon Wiener were exemplary committee members, helping keep me on track and making invaluable suggestions along the way. A host of others at Irvine shaped my outlook and work, including Marjorie Beale, Stan Beyer, David Bruce, Ian Carter, Pete Catapano, Jacques Derrida, Colin Fisher, Dorothy Fujita-Rony, Karl Hufbauer, Kyle Julian, Dean MacCannel, Morag Martin, Ken Pomeranz, Mark Poster, John Rowe, Gabriele Schwab, Amy Stanley, Sally Stein, Tanis Thorne, and Steve Topik. At Irvine I also had the great pleasure of getting to know Robert V. Hine, whose literary grace and graceful life serve as inspirations. When I gave Bob drafts to read, I learned to use a larger font. In return, Bob—who sees the world and the word differently and with more insight than most of the rest of us—helped me clarify my prose and my project.

Since leaving Irvine, I've been lucky to work with wonderful colleagues at two superb colleges. My thanks go to the entire Oberlin community for making my stay in Ohio so enjoyable and productive. The University of Puget Sound has been a supportive environment in every way. I'd like to first thank Ted Taranovski, who graciously introduced me to my new academic home, and my historian colleagues—Suzanne Barnett, Bill Barry, Bill Breitenbach, Nancy Bristow, Terry Cooney, Chris Gerteis, Matt Greene, Mark Largent, John Lear, Walter Lowry, Jeff Matthews, Eric Orlin, and David Smith—for making UPS a welcoming and invigorating home. Some U.S. historians, used to larger universities, might think twice about joining a department with only two other Americanists; but if they knew Nancy Bristow and Bill Breitenbach were to be their colleagues, they could have no second thoughts. Special thanks to Mark, who generously shared his research on Luther Burbank, and Terry, who helped me better "read" some of the visual documents from the 1930s. I would also like to thank the university for providing release time that enabled me to make revisions, and for a grant that made it possible for me to secure the illustrations for this book.

For historians, every day at the archives is like Christmas (though, to be sure, sometimes it's like those years when you don't get that longed-for present). To the staffs of the following institutions, who have brought me all those drably wrapped but usually exciting packages, I send my thanks: the Oral History Program and Special Collections at California State University at Fullerton; Special Collections of the University of California (at Los Angeles, Davis, Santa Barbara, and Riverside); the Bancroft Library; Occidental College Library; the Prints and Photographs Division of the Library of Congress; the Oakland Museum; and the Henry E. Huntington Library. At the Huntington, Jenny Watts was especially helpful in locating images for the book.

Hal Rothman and Ted Steinberg were supportive at critical times during the genesis of the book, as were Mike Davis, Dan Kevles, Anthony Lee, Patricia Limerick, Virginia Scharff, and Greg Woirol. Gordon McClelland was most generous in his help with orange crate labels. My thanks also go to Janet Brodie and Claremont Graduate University for the opportunity to present my work. It was wonderful to come back to Claremont, where I have taught a few graduate courses, and present my work beneath a snowy Mount Baldy (uncharacteristically in clear view from town that day).

Questions and suggestions from Robert Dawidoff and other people in the audience helped me improve the book. Gabriela Arredondo, my good buddy from our days at Reed, generously plowed through a complete draft of the manuscript, and her insights helped me improve it considerably. My thanks to her for all of her support over the years. I was also fortunate to have two scholars whose work I greatly admire read the book for the University of California Press: Elliott West and Bill Deverell. In my revisions, I tried to improve the manuscript by following their direct suggestions; I also aspired to live up to the high standards of narrative grace and scholarly analysis exhibited in their own work. I would also like to thank Vicki Ruiz, whose penetrating reading for the Press led to several important changes. Monica McCormick, my editor, showed enthusiasm for the manuscript from the beginning and helped me get through the long revision process without losing faith in the project. Thanks also to Randy Heyman, who answered all of my questions about illustrations and permissions; Jan Spauschus, who expertly copyedited the manuscript; and Laura Harger, who guided it through the production process.

Incarnations of parts of this book have been previously published. Earlier versions of chapters 2, 3, and 4 appeared in *Science, Values and the American West; California History;* and *Environmental History,* respectively, and are reprinted here by permission.

A pivotal chapter of John Steinbeck's *The Grapes of Wrath* contrasts the vibrant abundance of California's fields and groves with the destruction of "surplus" oranges that took place while people starved. When I moved from the Pacific Northwest to Southern California to begin graduate studies, I wanted to know more about the citrus landscape, and this is the account of my explorations. In the process, I found out that my great-grandfather was an orange grower in Santa Ana, and I gained a greater appreciation of the taken-for-granted fruits on my mom's trees. Oranges have been imbued with all sorts of meanings, have played a key role in California's economic history, and have become one of the most alluring fruits consumed by Americans.

I personally owe a lot to them. I first shared oranges from home with my wife when she was but a friend. She says they are the best in the world, so perhaps they played some role in our first kiss, which led to our now long embrace. Mythologically, we know that all sorts of trouble starts when women offer men fruit, but if Adam had given Eve the apple, maybe things would have turned out differently. In my case, at any rate, I have been blessed with an amazing and beautiful wife, Sonja, and two beautiful and amazing daughters, Zoë and Iris. They have sweetened my life daily. Sonja, whom I also thank for her steadfast support over the years, also brought into my life Karin Debelius and Bill and Sophie Seltzer—my appreciation to them for giving me all kinds of familial and intellectual support, for this project and for much beyond.

Finally, I thank my mom and dad, Valarie and George, for taking me across the verdant fields, down the rushing rivers, through the green forests, and over the golden hills of California (often to Grandmother's house, it turned out). They took me to these places through stories as well, opening my eyes to the words and worlds of Steinbeck and Snyder and many others. My parents passed on to me their twin loves of language and landscape, and this book is dedicated to them.

An Allegory of California

THE GODDESS OF FRUIT

IN THE SPRING OF 1931, a most unlikely figure could be seen in the new Luncheon Club of the San Francisco Stock Exchange. By all accounts, he went about his business with as much alacrity and stamina as the most ardent trader. But this man did not deal in stocks. A devoted Marxist, he considered such financial speculation the work of "parasitic exploiters." In any other circumstances, this brown-skinned Mexican would not have gained access to the exclusive club. But his name was Diego Rivera, and he was considered by many to be the second-greatest living painter (and Picasso was not available). In this inner sanctum of an economic system he abhorred, Rivera was covering the walls with his *Allegory of California* (see figure 1).[1]

In creating the mural, Rivera acted on his belief that art should relate to the conditions of life of its audience. He drew inspiration from the work of pre-Columbian artists, which "had been intensely local: related to the soil, the landscape, the forms, animals, deities, and colors of their own world." In envisioning the mural while in Mexico, Rivera knew he wanted to "represent California with the three bases of her richness—gold, petroleum, and fruits." As a stranger to this land, he would have to find some way to immerse himself in California's actual and symbolic landscape. At first, however, it looked like Rivera's entry into the Golden State would be denied. The FBI had a file on the artist, but the lobbying of San Francisco's

Figure 1. Diego Rivera's 1931 fresco *Allegory of California* represented the state as a Mother Earth figure offering up an array of fruits, but she is enveloped by technology. (San Francisco, Pacific Stock Exchange. Photographer: Dirk Bakker. Photograph © 1986 The Detroit Institute of Arts.)

elite convinced the State Department to open the way for him. When Rivera finally arrived, he hit San Francisco like El Niño—creating a storm of controversy, he was perceived as both a loveable and a destructive child. The painter Maynard Dixon, expressing an artistic nativism, charged that Rivera was an "inappropriate" choice to paint the mural because he had "publicly caricatured American financial institutions." The *San Francisco Chronicle* fueled the speculative fire with a "composite photograph": on the space Rivera was to paint, it superimposed a detail from one of his Mexican murals "showing Ford, Rockefeller and Morgan trying to lure 'Miss Mexico' from the paths of communism to the fallen ways of capitalism." "Will Art Be Touched in Pink?" the *Chronicle* asked.[2]

As it turned out, Rivera tinged his mural with orange and other colors he gleaned from the California countryside. He took trips into the field to look at the landscape: down the coast to Monterey and east across the great Central Valley and into the foothills of the Gold Country. As one friend explained, these excursions were his way of "sizing up California, getting the feel of its people, the curve of its hills, the color of its air, sea, fields and sky, the nature of its activities, soaking up like a thirsty sponge the flow of unfamiliar life around him, trying to decide . . . what should go into the quintessential distillation of the land and its people."[3]

At the center of his mural, Rivera painted what another friend called "the heroic figure of California, the mother, the giver." Wheat, the staff of life, encircles her neck. With her left hand she offers up peaches, pears, apples—and the signature fruit of California, the orange. With nature personified as fecund mother, this might seem to be a universal image rather than one created specifically to embody the California landscape. But at the time, Rivera's California struck many observers as too *particular*. In this generalized Madonna they saw the specific features of Helen Wills Moody, tennis champion. "Soon a cry was heard," Rivera explained. "California was an abstraction and should not be an identifiable likeness of anybody." But to Rivera, Moody represented "California better than anyone I knew—she was intelligent, young, energetic and beautiful." With her intelligence, youth, and "Grecian features," Moody embodied Rivera's understanding of California as a Mediterranean land, "a second Greece." In this, he was simply reflecting the image that boosters had been projecting of California since the nineteenth century. Greece and Italy were famous for their fruits, and California promoters had long used icons of the fruit goddess Pomona, with her horn of plenty or overflowing bowl of fruits. The colorful labels of orange crates often featured Pomonaesque women holding up a sample of the golden fruit, ripe for the consumer's taking. Female icons of fertility had long since taken on local attachments. Rivera's *Allegory* is thus grounded in the particular soil of California, and it allows us to see the place of fruit between heaven and earth.[4]

Rivera explained that "California itself is symbolized by a large female figure—a woman of tanned skin and opulent curves modeled after the rolling hills of the landscape, with one hand offering the subsoil to the labor of the miners, and with the other offering the ripe fruits of the earth." His fruit-bearing symbol is heavily laden: she is at once rolling hills, wheat fields, fruit-bearing trees, the mother lode, the eternal maternal mother, *and* a new woman ("intelligent, young, energetic"). And, of course, she is nature. We might aptly put the words of Walt Whitman into the mouth of this multifarious embodiment of California: "I am large, I contain multitudes."[5]

She is also surrounded by multitudes. A whirl of men and machines are remaking the landscape around her. Nature's cornucopia stands amidst icons of industrialization—oil derricks, ocean liners, refineries, a crane, a dredging machine, an airplane. Above ground, a redwood has been sawed through. An engineer—holding a primary emblem of science, the compass—is formulating a plan (no doubt for the control of nature). To Rivera's eye, the United States represented industrial, scientific, and mechanical forces, while Mexico embodied agricultural, mythic, organic ones. Although California "is more agricultural than industrial," he explained, "its agriculture is highly advanced and mechanized." He also detected the Mexican past sedimented under California's Yankee present. California thus represented a hybrid landscape, part north, part south, part pastoral, part industrial.[6]

California appears to have what Rivera called "metallic nerves." Though the redwood stump may evoke wanton destruction, Rivera's goddess, despite her staid expression, assures us with her fruits that the earth remains fecund. A verdant orange tree grows before her. Three decades earlier, Frank Norris, in his novel *The Octopus: A Story of California,* had created an indelible image of the rapacious nature of the machine. Norris's version of the Southern Pacific Railroad was an "iron-hearted monster" with "tentacles" spread across the land. He described a map of California "sucked white and colorless," while the railroad as a "monster stood out, swollen with life-blood . . . a gigantic parasite fattening upon the life-blood of an entire commonwealth." In Rivera's *Allegory,* the land seems all the more alive and colorful because it is crisscrossed by a technological network. The *Allegory* is a positive view of the hybridization of the mechanical and the organic, of culture and nature.[7]

It is no accident that California's famous plant hybridizer has a prominent place in the *Allegory.* The white-haired figure kneeling to the right of the orange tree is Luther Burbank, grafting two plants together. The creator of countless new fruits—giant plums, white blackberries—Burbank was seen as a horticultural wizard, the Edison of the plant world. He described himself as "a specialist in the study of Nature for the definite purpose of producing new forms of plant life, for the better nourishment, housing, and clothing of the race." This nurseryman-utopian appealed to Rivera, who used him as a symbol of the illimitable benefits of hybridizing culture with nature. Rivera also wanted his art to participate in both the "control of nature" and the harmonizing of "man with earth and man with man." In the *Allegory,* the pastoral is infused with the technological; Mother Nature is enveloped in an industrial whirl, a "growth machine."[8]

But California's actual growth machine worked toward ends opposed to the artist's vision of social and ecological harmony. As defined by sociologists, a growth machine is an "apparatus of interlocking progrowth associations and governmental units" that makes "great fortunes out of place." Growth machines may use tractors, derricks, railroads, telephone lines, and the like, but they are not simply technologies. They are made up of interlocking social institutions such as newspapers, chambers of commerce, and corporations. Motivated by the promise of profit, growth machines work to transform place into things that can be bought and sold. Land becomes real estate; real estate is made scarce and desirable; prices rise. In California, the growth machine turned the land into factories of fruit.[9]

From the 1880s through World War II, the citrus industry was the primary engine of the growth machine in Southern California. The machine manifested itself in the millions of evergreen citrus trees scintillating in the sun beneath the snow-clad San Gabriel and San Bernardino mountains. But it showed itself as well in the infrastructure of the built environment, in train tracks and packing houses, in worker camps and growers' mansions, and in the downtown Los Angeles office building of the California Fruit Growers Exchange (the cooperative, founded in 1893, that created the Sunkist brand). The Los Angeles Chamber of Commerce, a vital component of the growth machine, created an image for a promotional brochure that revealed this landscape perfectly (see figure 2). As William McLung observes, at the center of the scene is a flower-bearing goddess "dressed in the color of the

Figure 2. Framing the scene with arches evoking former empires, this image from a Chamber of Commerce promotional brochure (1929) celebrated Los Angeles as the capital of an agricultural empire built on citrus. (This item is reproduced by permission of The Huntington Library, San Marino, California.)

magic fruit, the orange." The machine and the garden—intermixed landscapes in Rivera's mural—are here conveniently separated. On the left is a view of the citrus landscape, with a single orange tree peeking around the edge of the archway ruin. To the right is the bustling metropolis of Los Angeles. This bifurcated scene should be seen as a unity, for the horticultural landscape was intimately shaped by the machine, while the organic fruits of nature made the rise of the cityscape possible.[10]

The mountains stretching across the horizon are the San Gabriels and San Bernardinos, and we are looking into Los Angeles from the south. But the artist would have been more accurate to place the groves to the east of the city. By 1929, the city had grown up over many citrus acres, but groves still stretched beneath the mountain ranges eastward all the way to Redlands and Riverside. In any event, the picture opens a vista on the heart of the citrus industry. Though oranges were grown as far north as Corning (115 miles north of Sacramento and 500 miles from the Mexican border), most of the state's oranges were grown in the Los Angeles basin. Composed of the valleys and foothills south of the San Gabriels and San Bernardinos, the basin stretches 110 miles inland and 50 miles from its northern to its southern reach. With the protective mountain wall to the north, three watersheds, the moderating effects of the Pacific ocean, and its Mediterranean climate, the region enjoys natural advantages that made it ideally suited to citrus growing. By the 1930s, some 170,000 acres were growing citrus; over seven million trees yielded almost 80 percent of California's oranges. As one geographer observed, "No other horticultural industry . . . is so compactly situated and no fruit district is more intensively cultivated or more productive of wealth." This was the place that was called the Orange Empire.[11]

One might wish to write off this Orange Empire as merely a hyperbolic title invented by boosters such as the Southern Pacific Railroad's *Sunset* magazine. Real empires exercise effective social and political control over far-flung territorial expanses and the people who inhabit them; they hold the kind of pervasive power political theorists call hegemony. Southern California, like the American West at large, was colonized by the United States to join the political domain Jefferson called the Empire of Liberty. But just how does this Orange Empire, an apparent *imperium in imperio,* fit in? Though it was something less than a "supreme and extensive political dominion" (the *Oxford English Dictionary* definition of an empire), the Orange Empire was more than just an industry. It established hegemony over peoples and places. It recruited and managed thousands of laborers from across the globe. It also created millions of consumers, colonizing public and private spaces across the country to convey its alluring advertisements. The Orange Empire's spheres of influence stretched over nature as well as culture. As we will see in part 1 of this book, earth, water, trees, and fruits all were transformed under its governing hands. Lacking the right to demand tribute, the Orange Empire filled its coffers by selling the fruits of the earth. Images and words worked to legitimize the regime, as if the order it created had been anointed by God or nature itself. But like all empires, it found its power contested on a number of fronts.

NATURE'S LABOR

Beginning in the 1870s, the Orange Empire took control of a landscape boosters had described as Edenic and made improvements. The Orange Empire, its proponents claimed, augmented and democratized the fruits of Eden to create a landscape of abundance that could be enjoyed by all. Utilizing science, technology, and marketing acumen, growers covered the hills and valleys with productive trees and created a lucrative industry. Though the empire marketed oranges like a mass-produced commodity, it advertised them as pure products of nature. They were the fruits of Eden, unmediated by culture. Having been kissed by the sun, the orange was often presented to the consumer in the hands of a country maiden or earth goddess. Such iconography masked the hand of the worker. But the industry relied on a workforce—a workforce whose position at the bottom of California's social scale was reinforced by images placing its members in the kingdom of nature, like the plants and animals under Adam's command.

Such ideological sleights of hand made a public appreciation of farmworkers unlikely, but Rivera wanted to restore workers to the consciousness of the public. "I painted the fruits of the earth which enrich and nourish because of the productive labor of workers and farmers," Rivera explained. In the Stock Exchange, an Oz of economic growth, Rivera wished to draw back the curtain to reveal that all value ultimately comes from labor and the earth. He wanted to show the financiers "that what they eat and what enriches them are the products of the toil of workers and not of financial speculation—the natural beauty of California, fertilized by the vigor of workers, farmers, and scientists." But we might question how effective his mural is in conveying a "labor theory of value." Even though Rivera remembers painting "representative working men and women," we might wonder where they are. Where are the workers in the fields? Where are the women in the factories, who largely did the jobs of sorting and packing fruits? On the left there is the image of the eggheaded engineer instructing—perhaps scientifically managing—the tool caster, with his enormous hands. Down below, there are two hardrock miners. But on the right, where Rivera intended to paint "the lush agriculture, its workers and heroes," we see only a placer miner and John Marshall, the man who saw something glint in the American River and set off the Gold Rush. And there is Burbank.[12]

Perhaps Rivera felt that the wizard of horticulture—an indefatigable worker, a man of science, and a cultivator of crops—embodied in his one person the grower, the scientist, and the worker. But some people saw him more as a plantation master, employing, as legend had it, gangs of Chinese laborers to blow pollen, by the bucketful, into the flowers with bellows. Burbank employed no such gangs, although he did have Chinese gardeners work for him, one of whom he considered excellent, for "he, too, had learned to explain to the plants what was desired."[13] Nevertheless, Burbank was a supporter of the Chinese Exclusion Act of 1882. On the authority of his work with plants, Burbank became a leading light in the eugenics movement. Others would graft onto this new science the ideas that helped create and maintain California's racialized division of agricultural labor. Such thinking was key to the transmogrification of workers into racial others biologically suited to stoop labor, manual labor, labor in the heat, any labor that white workers could not or would not stand for. Under this ideology, their brown or yellow hands had been provided by nature to serve its crops and be guided by the white man's brains. So what is gained by this economy of representation—having Burbank stand in for agriculture—comes at the expense of revealing the important divisions within California agriculture, as well as the ways in which those divisions were fostered by racial ideas rooting the contingencies of a cultural and economic construct in the solid ground of nature.

Elsewhere, Rivera had more visibly represented the racial divisions of California agriculture. He did so in a mural called *Still Life with Blossoming Almond Trees,* painted just south of San Francisco for a private patron immediately after completing the *Allegory.* It portrays an almond orchard in full white bloom. In the background, a tractor blazes between the trees, half hidden. In the midground, workers of different races are clearing weeds. In the foreground, three children reach for fruit overflowing from a bowl. Two are modeled after the patron's own Anglo children (one of whom would go on to become a vice president for Levi Strauss). But a mestizo child is among them, reaching for an equal share of the fruit. The mestizo child was modeled after one of the actual children's imaginary friend "Dega." By showing the mixed children reaching for the bowl, Rivera envisions a future where all will grow up together on nature's engineered abundance.[14]

Though Rivera fantasized communal harmony at the point of consumption, the landscape of production was a place in which divisions were routinely made. To follow the journey of the orange as it makes its way from the tree to the marketplace is to see the active construction of race and gender. Field workers tended to be organized in racially homogenous groups, and men worked outside, close to nature, while women took over in the packing *house,* where the fruit was cleaned, sorted, and packed for presentation to the consumer. The orange was reshaped by this process; so were the laborers, as we will see in part 2. The workers' experience of California's nature can be revealed by looking at how oranges passed through their hands. And the fact that the fruits of their labor passed out of their hands and into those of consumers and growers shows that they were tributaries of the Orange Empire.

The *Allegory* was meant to remind the financial elite that "the productive labor of workers and farmers" went into the "fruits of the earth." The growth of the economy was based on the labor of workers, the power of technology and, ultimately, the fertility of the earth. In California, these elements had been forged into an imperium that naturalized social inequality and commodified all of nature, from sun and water to soil and seed. Bolstered by a powerful ideology legitimizing its regime, the Orange Empire's hegemony reached its height by the 1920s.[15]

THE SYMBOLIC USES OF FRUIT

But the world the growers made was nearly brought to the ground during the Great Depression. In 1934, Upton Sinclair ran for governor, fulminating against the want that flourished amidst plenty. Envisioning a new world in which workers would partake directly of the fruits of labor, Sinclair promised to "End Poverty in California" (EPIC). With its legitimacy being challenged, the Orange Empire spearheaded the campaign to defeat Sinclair. In this it was successful. But EPIC had turned the fact of poverty that existed despite continued natural abundance into an indictment of the growth machine, setting the stage for what anthropologist Victor Turner calls a social drama. In such dramas, a transgressor of social norms is put on trial before the public. Redress, reform, and even revolution become possible. This social drama, which almost turned out to be the fall of the Orange Empire, is the subject of part 3 of this book.[16]

On the surface, Rivera's *Allegory* does not contain any dramatic challenge to the system that his comrade Sinclair would traumatize with EPIC. But it does contain subtle portents of revolutionary change. The smokestacks of the ocean liners are marked with dollar signs, and the needle on the safety valve (just above the redwood stump) is dangerously above the red line. However, Rivera probably did not mean to condemn the mechanization of nature with these signs. He was fond of quoting Emiliano Zapata's imperative to "exploit the land and not the man."[17] A great admirer of America's technology, he saw the machine in the garden as a potentially liberating presence. But Rivera viewed the earth as enslaved by the oppressive force of capitalism. This would change when workers took control, Rivera believed. But his essentially optimistic representation of the "natural interconnection of agriculture and industry" may have underestimated the power of modern science and technology, whether operating under socialism or capitalism, to rationalize nature and, in the bargain, kill all local deities, including the earth goddesses.[18]

During the Dust Bowl years, many American artists and intellectuals would lose this kind of faith in technology. In the wake of the coincidence of the economic collapse of the Depression and the ecological collapse of the Dust Bowl, visions emerged that saw the growth machine as exploiting both people and land. Pare Lorentz's 1936 film made for the New Deal's Resettlement Administration, *The Plow That Broke the Plains,* juxtaposed tractors plowing the land with military tanks blowing it up. The painter Alexandre Hogue, in *Erosion No. 2—Mother Earth Laid Bare* (1938), tried to represent the destruction of the land in a way "that will make the observer not only see the Dust Bowl, but also feel its heat, its despair, its anguished death, the tragedy of the farmers." With a phallic plow in the foreground of a landscape eroded to reveal a prostrate Mother Earth, *Erosion* presented a stark vision of exhaustion, barrenness, even rape by the machine.[19]

Confronting the Dust Bowl, some artists and intellectuals became convinced that capitalism must be challenged on ecological as well as social grounds. Picking up on Sinclair's political vision but pushing it further was a group of "agrarian partisans" (including Paul Taylor, Dorothea Lange, Carey McWilliams, and John Steinbeck) who saw capitalism as a system that manhandled land as it uprooted dwellers on the land. Dorothea Lange's 1936 photograph of a migrant mother—America's white Madonna thrust onto the road and exposed to the elements—drew attention to the plight of those who had been driven off the land and opened up the larger issue of the social relationship to the land. From the perspective of the agrarian partisans, the Orange Empire was representative of the larger problem of modern agriculture. It was an economic and moral failure, for it partitioned nature into private property and then withheld its bounty from deserving citizens. In order to keep prices up, the agrarian partisans charged, the fruits of Eden were going to waste. In their hands, as we will see in this book's final chapters, the orange became an incandescent political symbol.

In Isabel Allende's novel *The Infinite Plan* ("based on a true story"), an itinerant preacher and occasional mural painter wanders the fruit-growing regions of Depression California, using an orange as a central prop. "We must know our place in the cosmos," Reeves says, and then he points to an orange dangling on a string and invites "people from the crowd to study the orange and describe its appearance." "Invariably," Allende writes, "they would describe a yellow sphere, that is, a common orange, whereas Reeves saw the Soul." In *The Dharma Bums,* Jack Kerouac put an orange to similar use, employing it to explain the Buddhist doctrine that "all things are empty." But what about this orange in my hand? a skeptic asks. "Your mind makes out the orange by seeing it, hearing it, touching it, smelling it, tasting it and thinking about it but without this mind . . . the orange would not be seen or heard or smelled or tasted or even mentally noticed."[20]

Reeves and Kerouac act not unlike the leaders of Los Angeles's Utopian Society, who in the 1930s made technological artifacts into religious symbols for their initiation rituals. What Allende's preacher fails to recognize is that he has suspended from the ceiling not nature's unmediated soul, but a reconstructed object already full of meanings. Reeves ties the orange to a string, but the orange is suspended in other "webs of signification." Scientists have prodded it for its secrets and attempted to reinvent its nature; advertisers have inscribed its skin with messages; workers have handled it, leaving behind remnants of themselves. Neither pure products of nature nor pure mental creations, the fruits of Eden can be seen as artifacts, what Karl Marx called "social hieroglyphics." A multitude of minds and bodies, as Kerouac would put it, have made the orange what it is. But unlike Kerouac, I will maintain that these minds and these bodies were working with "real" nature to transform oranges into objects of their liking.[21]

To unpack the orange is to restore the social, cultural, and environmental strata of the citrus landscape, a landscape well masked by orange crate labels of Edenic California. If only historians could set up cameras equipped for time-lapse photography at select sites—say, an orange grove being picked in Pasadena, a citrus laboratory in Riverside, a grocery store window being filled with oranges in Chicago, a family at home in Rochester reading *Life* or *The Grapes of Wrath*—the growth of the Orange Empire could be revealed in action. But we will have to rely on more conventional methods to look at how these oranges were grown: at what knowledge was brought to bear on the natural world to make them grow more perfect and abundant; at the labor power that brought them from tree to consumer; at what meanings and values were attached to them and how these accumulated within California's economy and flowed through the culture at large; and at how, amidst the want of the Depression, the spectacle of the fruits of Eden in flames seemed almost apocalyptic, prodding many Americans to look with new eyes upon their culture's relationship to nature.

People mean many things when they use the terms *nature* and *culture*. They are notoriously difficult words to define, and my use of the terms will shift in different contexts to reflect the meanings attached to them by different actors. But I generally take *culture* to mean the web of stories that shape members of our species into human beings. It is the human-made stuff of being and identity. *Nature* is everything else, including plants, animals, soils, and air, as well as our own bodies. But the boundary between nature and culture, as a close look at oranges reveals, is constantly being crossed. *Orange Empire* explores the symbiosis of nature and culture by following the Sunkist orange on its journeys across that boundary. Its history is an allegory of California, a way of recovering lands and peoples not quite lost to us—like paradise itself.

PART ONE

Fabricating Eden

IN 1878, the enterprising Luther and Elizabeth Tibbets saw their dream come to fruition: two ripe oranges dangled from trees in front of their Riverside home. During the subsequent land boom in southern California, legend has it that real estate sharks caught their share of greenhorn Yankees in a bold trompe l'oeil: plots of desert land were made seductively abundant by dangling oranges from Joshua trees. What juxtaposition—fruit hanging artificially from an unlikely parent tree and a real orange tree naturally bearing its own fruit—could be more complete?

But a look at the origins of the Tibbetses' tree complicates this division between nature and culture. The progenitors of sweet oranges most likely originated in the Malay–East Indian Archipelago some twenty million years ago. Orange trees were then taken into human hands and were cultivated for centuries by the Chinese and other Asians before Europeans began to grow them in the artificial environments of orangeries. Citrus then followed the colonial expansion of Spain and Portugal into the New World, with Columbus, on his second voyage in 1493, importing citrus seeds as part of the complex of plants, animals, and humans used to implant Castilian culture on Hispaniola. In *El naranjo (The Orange Tree)*, Carlos Fuentes uses the linkage between citrus and Spanish culture to tell the story of the reunion of Hernán Cortés and Jerónimo de Aguilar, who had been lost among the Indians for eight years. Looking as if he had gone native, Aguilar proves that he is still among the *gente de razón* (men of reason) by eating an orange he had grown from seeds. "I had the sun in my hands," he says. "Could any image verify a Spaniard's identity better than the sight of a man eating an orange?" Along with grapes and wheat, the Franciscans brought oranges into Alta California when they began establishing missions along El Camino Real in 1769. Along this "royal road," the Spanish imposed new forms of nature as well as culture on the Native Californian landscape. The missionaries tended to see their fruit, like their culture, as a gift from God offered up to California's Indian peoples. This view was captured by a French visitor, Eugene Duflot de Mofras, who drew a sketch of a padre's arm reaching out from the cultured space of the mission to the wilderness landscape of the Indian child. A gift of fruit, held liminally between two figures and the two spaces, symbolized the Franciscans' missionary work. In 1804, the fathers at San Gabriel Mission directed their Indian "children" in the planting of some four hundred orange trees, creating the first large-scale grove of the exotic tree that would come to symbolize California.[1]

Meanwhile, in the 1820s, a mutation in a grove in São Salvador de Bahia, Brazil, created a new and more succulent variety of orange. These seedless and delectable fruits were actually two oranges in one: an embryonic orange developed within the body of the larger orange, forming a navel. The reputation of the new orange soon spread. An American missionary tasted these fruits and in 1870, at the request of William Saunders of the U.S. Department of Agriculture, shipped twelve seedlings to Washington. In the nation's capital, these plants—the "fruit of Yankee perspicacity," one Brazilian scholar has called them—were grafted onto new rootstocks and rechristened the Washington navel. Three seedlings were then sent to Eliza Tibbets in Riverside; before she had moved west in search of health and a new life, Eliza had lived next door to Saunders in Washington. Sometime after two of the trees had been nursed to maturity with Eliza's legendary dirty dishwater (one tree was trampled by a cow), the Washington navel became a widespread symbol for sun-kissed California. Thus the mutant fruit from the Far East via South America, first inscribed with the name Washington, was now stamped Sunkist.[2]

The myth of California as some kind of tropical paradise—America's Eden at the end of the westward course of empire—was cultivated by boosters who put their distinctive stamp on nature and used it to advertise California's attractions and imperial potential. The first chapter of this book looks at how myth and imagery were used to drive a succession of changes in the California landscape as it was taken out of the hands of Indian horticulturalists and Mexican pastoralists and given over to wheat barons and, finally, fruit growers. Boosters then used the garden Anglo-Americans had created to legitimize the uprooting of Native Californians and Mexicans. The fruits of Eden became signs of an empire in the making.

If California was an Eden, it nonetheless would require some improvements in order to fulfill imperial ambitions. Focusing on the work of Luther Burbank and the Citrus Experiment Station scientists, chapter 2 examines the creation of a technological cornucopia. The scientists dreamed of fashioning the perfect fruit. To find and control such golden oranges was a Herculean task—the eleventh, to be exact, in which these fruits, the gift of Gaia, had to be stolen from the Hesperides, the goddesses of an island to the west (as California citrus growers took great delight in pointing out). Though growers never achieved complete control over nature, they did turn their groves into efficient fruit factories.

But abundance alone did not guarantee success. As a glut of oranges reached the market in the 1890s, prospects for the industry looked bleak. Chapter 3 examines how immense marketing challenges were overcome by the California Fruit Growers Exchange. Launching the Sunkist trademark, the CFGE created a culture of consumption for mass-produced oranges. Sunkist, which would eventually market three out of four oranges grown in California, organized and expanded the territorial and cultural reach of the citrus industry. It was the driving force behind the rise of the Orange Empire.

ONE

Manifesting the Garden

THE GARDEN OF WORLDLY DELIGHTS

A GIRL RUNS THROUGH row after row of blossoming orange trees. The air is densely fragrant. But this is no dreamy scene of sun-dabbled Arcadia. The girl is not some Pomona or queen regally gazing over her citrus landscape, like the images adorning so much promotional literature (see figure 3). She is furtive and desperate; she is a fugitive. Her pursuers wish to capture her and thereby redeem her. In their eyes, she is wild and uncultivated. She is the desert, and they are the rain. They have the know-how to make her bloom and train her growth, like they have done with the orange trees around her. They want to take her back to the Sherman Institute in Riverside, a boarding school established at the turn of the century to "improve" the lives of Indian children. Part of the institute's mission was to show the land's conquered peoples the marvelous ways whites could improve the desert. As Los Angeles nurseryman and Indian agent Horatio Rust put it, "They cannot help but gain some ideas, when they go to Riverside or other thrifty towns by seeing what industry can accomplish." After studying the garden schools of Europe in which "pupils obtain an intimate knowledge of nature," Rust urged that every Indian student be taught to "make, and care for, a garden . . . so that when he leaves school he shall be competent to perform all the varied labors on a farm or a garden."[1]

20

Figure 3. This 1893 piece of booster literature called Southern California the "Land of Sunshine" and used a Pomona-like figure to impress the scene with a sense of mythological destiny. This promised land would not languish under the sun, for its products could be shipped out by the steamship or railroad in the background. (This item is reproduced by permission of The Huntington Library, San Marino, California.)

The girl darts across a road and makes her way into an ornate garden within this larger garden landscape. The orange trees give way to eucalyptus, lilacs, and then a trimmed yard with ornamental plants—plants she has never seen before, from Asia and South America, from Europe and Africa. There are peonies, dianthus, cosmos, roses, scarlet hollyhocks, and red dahlias. A Victorian house rises at the center of this garden, and a greenhouse, an essential adjunct to the entire floral enterprise, stands to the side. All the world is here in this strange place: the garden embodies exoticism.

Crawling beneath the immigrant shrubbery, the girl is at last discovered. Linnaeus's gaze fixes upon her. Linnaeus is a monkey, brought back from the Amazon after an orchid-collecting trip by the plant hunter Edward. The monkey had saved Edward's life, so he honored it with the namesake of the Swedish botanist who created a taxonomy for all of creation. At that moment the girl becomes fixed in an imperial system not of her own making.

Edward is a quintessential Enlightenment figure—a man conquering the global unknown, seeking out new organisms and expanding the horizons of knowledge. Done in the name of objective science, this penetration of the dark worlds of the Amazon—or, for that matter, the deserts of the American Southwest—amounted to a global appropriation of the variety of nature as means of production. Consider the orange trees in the grove the young girl has run through. They were the Washington navels—those "fruits of Yankee perspicacity" imported by the USDA from Brazil and then planted by the Tibbetses in Riverside in 1873. By 1910, over a million Washington navel trees, each grown from a bud derived from these original seedlings, grew in Riverside alone. In 1923, at a ceremony in which a gavel fashioned from the wood of one of the original parent navels was given to Sunkist president Charles Collins Teague, USDA citrus scientist A. D. Shamel said, "Two small and apparently insignificant plant immigrants arrived in southern California 50 years ago," yet they were "the beginning of the commercial growth of the citrus industry in California."[2]

The girl, the monkey, and Edward are fictional characters from Leslie Marmon Silko's novel *Gardens in the Dunes* (1999).[3] The space they meet in is fictional as well, though it is thoroughly grounded in history. Silko carefully researched the gardens and culture of Riverside. She has also brought to life the kind of gardening practiced by the girl's people, the Hia C'ed O'odham, or Sand Papagos. Silko's Edward, confident in the Enlightenment project, does not realize he is but an agent of empire appropriating the world's wealth of plants and peoples. In the novel, Silko can punish him for this arrogance, and she does, with poetic justice. In the end, Edward's mind and body come apart as if some Cartesian curse had been put upon him: poisoned by his will to plunder the earth, the rational man of science descends into madness, losing the power to think and therefore be. Silko counterpoises those people who have nourished a symbiotic relationship with the natural world (the O'odham, as well as English pagans) and a system of capitalism whose agents penetrate every corner of the globe, seeking plants that, as if by bio-alchemical magic, may be turned to gold. Silko's novel is a deeply historicized parable, an anticolonial account of the struggle between cultures that live with nature and those that work to exploit both nature and people.[4]

Exposing a kind of ecological imperialism, *Gardens in the Dunes* provides a provocative entrée into the garden landscape created by Anglo-Americans in Southern California. Southern California was very proud of the garden, or at least Southern California's promoters were. They appropriated the world's store of garden literature and used it to coat their region with an Elysian luster. The booster literature—Southern Pacific Railroad and California State Chamber of Commerce pamphlets, guidebooks, postcards, articles in magazines like *Sunset* and *Land of Sunshine*—perfected the genre of Edenic travelogue cum real estate brochure. With its mountains and sun, ocean and soils, Southern California was the most perfect garden—"emphatically the land of fruits and flowers, always fresh and fascinating. If not the first, it is the second edition of the true Garden of Eden," one writer enthused. Thus was Southern California made out to be a simulacrum of Eden, more perfect than the original. For here, one could have one's fruit and eat it too.[5]

Gardening became a source of livelihood and pride. Southern Californians grew fruit trees and they grew ornamental trees. Their identity, and economy, became fixed to plants. Each bustling enclave—Pasadena or Ontario, Pomona or Anaheim—vied for the title of "the garden spot of earth."[6] The region's inhabitants, many of them newcomers who had been drawn by the pictures of its lush landscape, took up gardening in earnest. They planted for beauty as well as for the market and remade the landscape in Eden's image. But aesthetic delight was ultimately subordinated to a drive to turn place into profit, for the remaking of the landscape was driven by a growth machine. Charles Saunders, who much admired the gardens of Southern California, wrote that "Los Angeles has been a marvel of urban growth." *Growth* and *Los Angeles* seemed near synonyms. The city's growth rate rivaled that of Jack's beanstalk, one writer mused.[7]

Though the name Los Angeles now evokes sprawling smog that damages the environment and creates an "ecology of fear," the city initially portrayed itself as the most natural one on earth. The fact that Los Angeles is now considered toxic to nature seems all the more monstrous—even matricidal—given that the growth of Southern California was congenitally linked to Mother Nature's unique beneficence. Though all places are ultimately natural, the identity of Southern California has been exceptionally entangled with nature. The ecology of the region created abundant possibilities: an inviting climate, varied microclimatic zones, and a rich range of soils in which all manner of plants could be grown. But the ecology did not determine the creation of the garden. In order for the Anglo-American garden to grow, that ecology had to be rearranged—water controlled and channeled, native flora and fauna uprooted, older claims on the land dissolved, new property lines demarcated, and so on.[8]

The legal and material changes in the landscape were underwritten with a vision of the proper arrangement of nature, a vision whose ultimate purpose was shrouded by all the greenery. The ideology was circulated in a barrage of booster literature inviting readers to fall into a semitropical paradise of the imagination. But this second edition of Eden was not meant to be a sacred place, walled off from the world of commerce. The gardens would have economic functions, becoming either factories turning nature into commodities or places of conspicuous cultivation delineating social rank. The landscape of Southern California became deeply infused with market forces and bound up in a web of economic, political, and ecological exchanges that spanned the globe. Plants from the four corners of the earth were transplanted to California, along with people to harvest the crops. The growth of plants and the growth of the economy were linked in one vast "material dream," a garden of the most worldly delights. And the most delightful of all of the garden's fruits, tourists, boosters, and growers agreed, was the orange. It contained the seeds of empire.[9]

FROM EL DORADO TO CORNUCOPIA

Gardens are anthropogenic landscapes, the result of humans' shaping nature into patterns that they find hospitable and desirable. The human work of design, selection, exclusion, and cultivation that goes into their creation makes gardens hybrid zones of human enterprise and natural expression.

Gardening is "a way of bringing wildness to heel by sending it to school." Any gardener knows that gardens are hardly inevitable, but the making of Los Angeles's garden around the turn of the century was often portrayed as an outcome ordained by natural evolution, and an outcome with lessons for the nation.[10]

It is tempting to wonder whether Frederick Jackson Turner, that famous theorist who linked wilderness to American identity, felt any need to revise his frontier thesis to apply to the lush environs of Southern California as he enjoyed his thrice-daily glass of orange juice at home at 23 Oak Knoll Gardens in Pasadena in the late 1920s. Did he feel remiss for having failed to theorize the "fruit frontier"? Turner's 1893 essay "Significance of the Frontier in American History" provided a powerful explanation of how American character and institutions were forged on a frontier, which he defined as the "meeting point between civilization and savagery" and "the line of most rapid and effective Americanization." As Turner had it, contact with the pure nature of aboriginal America stripped Europeans of all cultural baggage, including their clothes. Environmental challenges forced a kind of cultural molting: discarding the skins of their former selves, Americans emerged on the frontier. Turner's environment becomes a kind of body snatcher. But the plot runs in reverse of the 1950s sci-fi classic: those who are snatched become not soulless drones but willful, independent, industrious Americans. But as in the film, there is a colonial theme in Turner: the new Americans immediately go about implanting their culture on the landscape that gave them new life. Miners make a mining landscape; farmers an agrarian one; and so on, up to the city builders.[11]

Turner has been roundly criticized on a number of fronts, including the neat progression from one stage to another. William Cronon has noted that the city builders of Chicago essentially preceded the farmers of the Midwest, and a similar reversal of Turner's stages holds for Los Angeles and its environs.[12] Yet there is something to his way of looking at history as a succession of landscapes, each bearing the inscription of a dominant economic actor and activity, and each written over by the next as if the land itself were a palimpsest. If we could hold this landscape palimpsest of California up to the light, we would be able to identify several distinct layers. The first, predating sustained European colonialism, was the horticultural landscape of Native Californians. Though this place has often been imagined as a wilderness where nature alone ruled, Native Californians actually played a large role in its creation. Through a variety of land management practices, including fire and harvesting techniques,

California's Indians had created a garden in which a variety of useful plants were grown.[13] With the Spanish *entrada* in the 1760s, that aboriginal garden was pushed back to make way for the complex of plants and animals that the Spanish imported and sponsored, including wheat, cattle, sheep, the grapevine, and the orange tree. During the Mexican era beginning in the 1820s, the economy, still very local in orientation, became ever more pastoral as immense flocks of sheep and herds of cattle overran the native garden. In 1848, California became an American frontier. First, of course, was the rush for gold, which created a mining landscape. The advent of El Dorado was closely attended by the expansion of cattle ranching and the rise of bonanza wheat farming (but already, citrus was being sold to miners in the camps to stave off scurvy). Toward the end of the 1870s, a new order emerged, the landscape of intensive horticulture. California was remade into a new garden, with oranges as the emblematic fruit.

The succession of landscapes from native gardeners to American growers can be portrayed as an inevitable expression of progress, and it often was. Americans put together such a fable of progress to justify their conquest. At first, the story went, the landscape was rich and beautiful but languishing under the hands of lazy Californios. This was the landscape as it appeared from the perspective of Manifest Destiny, a nationalist narrative that "implied the domination of civilization over nature, Christianity over heathenism, progress over backwardness, and, most importantly, of white Americans over the Mexican and Indian populations that stood in their path."[14] Mexicans, the story went, locked up land in idleness, while Americans put it to the best and highest use. But in Anglo-American hands, the land would become better, for American agency alone could do God's will on earth and create a flourishing agrarian republic.

But the promoters of horticulture also criticized the devastation of Gold Rush mining and bonanza wheat farming. They argued that the American promise of improvement had not been fulfilled, for miners had merely robbed the land of its wealth, and the great grain ranchers were simply "mining for wheat" in a way that would leave "the great, beautiful valleys of our State as treeless, verdureless plains."[15] They believed that creating a way of life centered on fruit would be supremely rewarding—fiscally, physically, and culturally. In this potent vision, California as cornucopia would be the highest and most perfect stage in the succession, a landscape that would manifest the American dream itself.

In a speech at the Southern California Horticultural Fair of 1878, fruit advocate and University of California professor Ezra Carr made out gardening to be a motor of social evolution. "Love of country," he argued, "could not exist till cave and wigwam were supplanted by the hut, the permanent abode around which the vine might clamber." Man reclaimed the "sour bog" and "reclaimed the wildness of his own nature in the process, until he grew sweeter with the grasses, less savage and more generous with the fruiting fullness of his trees." Instead of natural selection, Carr saw horticulture as the key factor in the ascent of man and origin of the state. "The gradual transformation of the savage into the citizen," he theorized, "may be traced in the changes in the animal and vegetable world which have accompanied it and we may look for the greatest improvement where the close and constant relations of man and Nature are the most agreeable and permanent."[16]

In his widely read book *The California Fruits and How to Grow Them* (first published in 1889), E. J. Wickson argued that the fruited garden, not the frontier, was the space of the most rapid and complete Americanization. Fruit growing was a "token of our advancement in one of the highest of the agricultural arts . . . [and] a demonstration of the quality of our agricultural citizenship." With an experimental outlook "free from tradition and prejudice," citrus growers in particular had created "an industry characteristically American." Many reformers believed fruit was good not just for the growth of the economy and population, but for cultural growth. Fruit would even eliminate the need for a cheap and nonwhite labor force. Since fruit growing would be so profitable, Wickson claimed, it would enable growers "to compensate the high-grade American labor which is employed in their growth, packing and marketing." He was excited by the prospect of producing "an American orange for Americans." According to this garden variety of nativism, citrus would be "the motive force . . . drawing into horticulture the class of people which constitute the most desirable element in the upbuilding of a great State."[17]

Orange growers, having been assured that they were agents of national progress, felt that their handiwork was almost divine. As one Riverside grower explained, their job was to "redeem sage and sand and glorify it." Having "wrought the evolution," this grower was proud to be able "to have a hand in creation, . . . to say 'let it fruit'; and it was done." *Horticulture* meant much more than a branch of agriculture devoted to the production of fruits, vegetables, trees, shrubs, and flowers. The term also "entailed a moral dimension."[18] The California Fruit Growers' Convention would sum up a generation of rhetoric in a pamphlet entitled "Hand in Hand Go Horticulture and Civilization," which outlined the fruit grower's version of Manifest Destiny. Under the hands of such an enterprising people, the natural and cultural landscape would be improved by a genesis authored by citrus growers, the Southern Pacific, and other boosters.

In their writings appears a variation of social Darwinism, one designed to explain and legitimate the succession from the primitive Native landscape, to the colorful yet idle regime of the padres and vaqueros, through the energetic yet profligate years of El Dorado and the wheat bonanzas, to, finally, the beautifully balanced and progressive cornucopia. Enthralled with the gardens of Southern California, Helen Hunt Jackson wrote of the "record of successions" that they were "not the result of human interventions and decisions so much as of climatic fate . . . successions through which the country has been making ready to become what it will surely be, the Garden of the world."[19] But instead of fulfilling a script authored by evolution or destiny, these successions were in fact accomplished through a series of "human interventions" that could be called conquests. Each landscape—the horticultural landscape of Indians, the pastoral landscape of Mexican ranchers, the market-oriented gardens of Anglo-Americans— had been a co-creation of a dominant social group and the environment. In each, natural space had been made into a territory, a place with a set of rules governing human-natural relations. The succession of landscapes did not arise from a calm, evolutionary transition. It involved a violent process of deterritorialization and reterritorialization. Territories—particular plants and the people who derived power from them—were uprooted, and new ones, sanctioned by authority, were established in their place. In the implanting of new empires in the place of old, nature was used twice: first, as it was shaped into new forms for gaining wealth and power, and then it was reshaped as those new forms were used to legitimate the new regime. A reinvented Eden would represent this crowning glory for the Orange Empire.[20]

A grand narrative of social and ecological improvement was told to legitimate the rise of the Orange Empire. The story, in short, was the second oldest one in the book: the quest for a recovery of Eden.[21] But Southern Californians put a twist on the myth, finding a way to meld the Protestant work ethic with the garden idea. God had only provided a *potential,* in the form of Southern California's geography, soil, and climate. But the Indians had been content to live simply off the land, and the Californios had been too idle to act on the divine possibilities. At the State Agricultural Society meeting in 1887, one delegate argued that the "face . . . of nature it is the high prerogative of man to change." He declared that agriculture was "the only vocation upon which it is put the high honor of finishing and improving the Creator's work. It was the skill and labor of man that made Eden what it was, and so when Adam was ejected for trespassing it went back to wild land again. . . . But labor restores to man the Eden he has lost." God had only made fruits "in the rough"; people could and should train "them into lusciousness and largeness." California's horticultural boosters felt that they could go beyond a simple return to the garden: they could fabricate Eden itself and improve it in the process.[22]

OUT OF THIN AIR:
THE CLIMATOLOGY OF CITRUS

In the making of this new Eden, geography and climate were invaluable, and malleable, materials. Like gold, they could be shaped into new forms valuable as exports and as lures for immigrants. As *Sunset* put it, Southern California had no gold but "eastern prospectors discovered an inexhaustible supply of twenty-two karat climate." Guidebooks told would-be orange growers that fantasies could materialize in California, that the state was simply supernatural. "When the land within the Orange Belt of Southern California is planted with skill and cultivated with care," the Semi-Tropic Land and Water Company claimed, "the dreams of the Orient will become realities of the Occident, and the fables of Mythology be made the facts of History." Yankee ingenuity would make the most of nature's gifts, which were prodigious: "Nature here runs a boom that is permanent. It is founded on Mountain, Sea, Soil and Sun, giving us a region where Flora's reign is continuous, where Spring and Summer are the only seasons, with a Harvest of grain, nuts and fruits absolutely perennial."[23]

In 1874, Major Ben C. Truman, who would go on to head the literary bureau of the Southern Pacific, called the region "Semi-Tropical California." A magazine called *Semi-Tropic California* pictured a verdant landscape of palms and tropical foliage, as if Southern California were another Hawai'i. But the tropical metaphor ultimately proved counterproductive because it "allowed nature a wild, defiant luxuriance which could never be subdued by industry." Convinced that there was a direct relationship between climate and racial advancement, many potential immigrants might be put off. Would they undergo racial declension in such balmy climes? they wondered. Charles Dudley Warner offered an attractive alternative, writing that "this land of perpetual sun and ever-flowing breezes, looked down upon by purple mountains . . . is our Mediterranean! Our Italy!"

"For more than a century," Mike Davis notes, "this Mediterranean metaphor has been sprinkled like cheap perfume over hundreds of instant subdivisions, creating a faux landscape celebrating a fictional history from which original Indian and Mexican ancestors have been expunged." Nonetheless, Southern California's climate—with moderate precipitation confined to the winter, and with hot, arid summers—does share much with that of the Mediterranean (as well as parts of South Africa, Chile, and Australia).[24]

Warner boasted that Southern California "manufactures its own weather and refuses to import any other." In fact, the character of the Southern California landscape and climate is shaped by ocean, latitude, topography, and deep geological forces. About five million years ago, tectonics split Baja California off from the rest of the continent. At the same time, lands to the north were compressed, creating the Santa Monica, San Gabriel, and San Bernardino mountain ranges. Situated in the zone where the northward-moving Pacific plate and the westward-moving North American plate crash against one another along the San Andreas fault, these mountains have rotated into a very unusual east-west orientation (they are known collectively as the Transverse Ranges). The mountains have provided a picturesque background for many a postcard of citrus groves, but they have yielded much else as well. When winter storms move into the region from the mid-Pacific, the mountains fleece the clouds of their water before they drift over the desert lands of the Mojave and Colorado. The Los Angeles, San Gabriel, and Santa Ana rivers bring alluvial soils down the mountains to the plains. The watersheds charge underground aquifers, storing up a bounty of sub-surface water that citrus growers began tapping in the 1880s.[25]

Warner saw a destiny for Southern California as a revised Mediterranean landscape covered in fruit. "From San Bernardino and Redlands, Riverside, Pomona, Ontario, Santa Anita, San Gabriel, all the way to Los Angeles, is almost a continuous fruit garden, the green areas only emphasized by wastes yet unreclaimed," Warner wrote. Figs and olives, raisins and walnuts, all could be raised here, but the orange "will of course be a staple, and constantly improve its reputation as better varieties are grown." From the early 1870s, growers had been experimenting with citrus growing in a number of communities from Los Angeles in the west to Riverside in the east. The journalist Charles Nordhoff, writing a guidebook for the Southern Pacific Company, estimated that some thirty thousand trees had been planted by 1873. "The industry is yet in its cradle," he admitted.

97 ORANGE GROVE FROM SIERRA MADRA VILLA

Figure 4. The emerging citrus landscape is depicted in this photograph of, as its original caption reads, an "orange grove from Sierra Madre Villa." (This item is reproduced by permission of The Huntington Library, San Marino, California.)

But because of the unique climate and the imminent railroad links to national markets (a line would reach Los Angeles in 1876, and the southern transcontinental route would be completed in 1883, followed by the Santa Fe in 1886), this orange industry infant would jump out of the cradle in no time. There was no danger of overproduction, Truman and Nordhoff assured readers, since "We have the whole country for our market, from Sitka to Maine." California would even be able to compete with the Mediterranean producers on the world market. "People tell large stories about citrus," one grower told Nordhoff, "but the truth is big enough." Insisting that he was passing on the unvarnished truth, Nordhoff promised that citrus growers could make about $100 per acre, though he hinted that much higher profits were possible. One grower said that "when you have a bearing orange orchard, it is like finding money in the street."[26]

Pasadena's "millionaire row" would be called Orange Grove Avenue, but before mansions could rise, groves had to be planted (see figure 4). Promotional literature may have promised that Southern California was intended by nature to be one vast orange grove, but actually growing one was no easy matter. Climate, mountains, sea, and soil created potential, but experimentation and hard work were needed to realize it. Thomas Garey, an influential nurseryman who introduced many varieties of citrus, thought that those who walked among the "majestic trees" would be inspired to "thank the Great Author of the grand, useful and beautiful in nature for so sublime a manifestation of His works, and His good gifts to mortals." But orange growing was not all "poetry and romance," he warned. In *Orange Culture in California* (1882), Garey introduced growers to the "stern, cold facts and responsibilities of the industry." Many pitfalls lay before them. For example, they might plant trees on the lowest plains only to discover that, in the coldest days of winter, freezing air would pour down from the mountains and accumulate in the lowlands as if it were an icebox.[27]

There was much to learn about the dirt itself. Growers should find soils of a rich loam, with clay, sand, or gravel predominating. Groves planted in soil of gravelly loam produced fruit that commanded a premium price at market, Garey reported, while trees rooted in less favorable dirt bore second-rate fruit. The heavy clay soils of Redlands and Riverside could be excellent, but careful cultivation and aeration of the soil was needed. As the state commissioner of horticulture would write, "The man who cultivates a clay citrus grove must have good brain power, and must use his brains to the limit."[28] Methods of cultivation and pruning had to be developed. A grower might get stuck with an inferior variety of orange, or one ill adapted to his or her lands. Since Southern California's level of rainfall could not support the efficient growth of trees, growers had to secure a source of irrigation.

Inventing a reliable supply of the ingredient the heavens failed to provide involved growers in the complicated politics, technology, and law of water appropriation in the arid West. Native Californians, some of whom had developed irrigation technologies prior to European contact, were conscripted to build hydraulic systems for Spanish missions in the eighteenth century. Later, as they worked the fields the Spanish had appropriated, Indians could slake their thirst with lemonade made from the waterworks they had constructed and the groves they planted and maintained.[29] In the late nineteenth century, Americans continued the re-engineering of California's watersheds. Riverside became a symbol of what could be done with water. Despite its name, the town had too little water to support the growth of the citrus industry. In 1881, George and William Chaffey used concrete pipes to channel water down from the streams of the San Gabriel mountains to the dry plains of Riverside. A few years later, the preeminent citrus town built a twenty-mile canal bringing the underground river of the San Gabriel Valley basin into its orchards. The project "was the largest waterwork of its time and a forerunner of other irrigation projects that established the citrus industry."[30] With a funnel on the mountain streams and a straw in subterranean aquifers, Riverside became a well-watered oasis. Similar moves were being made elsewhere. By 1890, approximately one million acres of land were being made fruitful by the artificial water systems, and the number rose to five million by 1930. More than 500,000 pumps, 46,000 pumping plants, 4,000 dams and reservoirs, and 32,000 miles of pipelines and canals were just part of California's water technology.[31]

Citrus scientists probed the mysteries of water and growth, developing knowledge about the effects of minerals, the efficiency of different irrigation methods, the "physics of soil moisture," and the effects of climate and season. Increasing the frequency of irrigation could increase "the rate of fruit growth," but too much water could harm the trees. The 76,000 cubic feet of water orange orchards needed every year had to be applied at varying rates, with the most supplied in the dry summer months. Growers experimented with different ways of delivering water to trees, including furrows, levees, and sprinklers—"nature's method of irrigating," as one manufacturer had it. But, of course, it wasn't nature's way: water, seemingly so elemental and natural, had become "artificial . . . shaped by human enterprise and labor."[32] The juice-laden membranes of nearly every orange grown in the state had been fed by the manmade vascular system of California's "hydraulic civilization." Massive canal projects turned Owens Valley streams and the Colorado River into tributaries of the Orange Empire. Removed from the paths of natural watersheds and riparian ecosystems, water was rechanneled into the economics of growth, becoming "so many 'acre-feet' banked in an account . . . so many . . . carloads of oranges to be traded around the globe."[33]

Once he had water on hand, the grower had to take care not to drown the trees, especially if hardpan lay below the surface of the soil. Wickson explained that "the tree may not live on climate as a man may, because a tree cannot speculate; it must have a good foundation in the earth as well as a good outlook in the sky." But improvement of the soil was always possible. One could add fertilizers, and if the prospective "foundation in the earth" was that troublesome hardpan, a little dynamite could work wonders.[34]

Mary Vail, a Southern Californian who took it upon herself to deflate the equation of California with Eden, would have agreed, both about the requirements for trees and the ability of people to make a living off of thin air. She noted that many greenhorns of the 1880s, finally facing up to the fact that money didn't simply grow on trees (and that trees didn't simply grow), would go around saying, "But you can't live on climate!" "We certainly can live on climate," Vail retorted, "and climate alone, so long as those who want it, seek for it and pay us for it when they have found it." Vail put her finger on how atmospherics had materialized in Southern California. A million dollars of climate-seeking capital "tunnels the mountains and carries water to the valley, causes it to blossom like the rose, and make its people prosperous and happy. It builds churches and schools, towns and cities, and railroads." Her statement is generally accurate, save the last, which gets the order of things reversed: the railroads brought the Mediterranean climate to Southern California. To be sure, the region experienced wet winters and arid summers and had developed a Mediterranean complex of flora long before the railroad began transforming the American landscape. Nonetheless, the railroads, more than any other agent, were responsible for turning this part of America into a second Mediterranean, and more. Indeed, it would become a "second edition" of Eden whose fruits could be shipped out and sold to the nation.[35]

GARDEN SHOWS OF THE SOUTHERN PACIFIC

By the late 1880s, Southern California was crowded with communities claiming to be this second Eden. Pasadena was called "an earthly paradise in every sense which the term implies."[36] Riverside was a place where "the omnipresent orange hangs yellow with its ripened harvest . . . where Nature rejoices, birds sing and the very heart of man expands with the pleasure of living." Having made "a waste place bloom as a garden," elderly Riversiders could enjoy in their earthly surroundings a "foretaste of approaching paradise." Governor Perkins, speaking at Los Angeles's horticultural fair, resorted to neologism, coming up with a new transitive verb, *to emparadise.* Here it is in use: "Look at the wonderful array of nature's gifts spread before us, amplified and enriched by the effort of your Association. A few short years ago and these valleys, now emparadised in fruits . . . raised their upturned faces in sullen, uninviting barrenness." The governor assured his audience that heaven smiled upon their miraculous work. Everywhere "the happy results of your labor shows forth to gratify both heart and eye. The whole world lies before us here. That fig speaks to us of Syria; that luscious peach recalls to us the fertile land of Persia." One is reminded of the grapes of Irenaeus, the second-century church father who wrote of talking grapes.[37]

Boosters wanted to put this horticultural Babel on the road. Beginning in the 1880s, fruits were loaded onto thousands of railroad cars to bring Southern California's garden discourse to the nation and the world. The Southern Pacific Company, recognizing the potential to increase the value of its vast land holdings as well to reap the profit of a voluminous traffic in fruit, organized the exhibition of California as a horticultural wonderland. It started by loading preserved specimens prepared by the Los Angeles Chamber of Commerce on a train called California on Wheels. Inside were specimens of hundreds of vegetables, flowers, and fruits suspended in glass jars.[38] Well over a million people in the Midwest and South were thus exposed to a display of California jam-packed with these fruits. For the international expositions in Louisville and New Orleans in the 1880s, the SP helped organize and assemble California's displays. Charles Turrill collected specimens from agricultural and booster organizations across the state to create a thirty-thousand-square-foot exhibition described as "California in miniature." Visitors, Turrill thought, were captivated by "the prodigious variety of products, the amazing diversity of vegetable wealth." Riverside beat out Florida for the top prize in citrus, a much-touted honor.[39]

The SP also helped put together a citrus fair in Chicago in 1886. The exhibition hall featured an avenue of live olive, palm, and orange trees. The *Chicago Times* seemed fully convinced that California was a veritable Eden: "Its mountains and hillsides, burdened with millions of grapevines, may be described as dropping down new wine continuously, while its valleys and plains pour forth rich treasures of fruits and grain. . . . Travelers who have seen the world, when describing this lovely California land of which we speak, declare that of all the Almighty's works (on this earth) this is by far the best." Though such displays were carefully constructed to produce this effect, many fairgoers apparently felt that the oranges and other fruits spoke for themselves. As the *Sacramento Bee* put it, "Those silent fruits preach a sermon."[40]

The SP would continue to help create and facilitate the displays through which millions of fairgoers—at Chicago in 1893, Paris in 1900, Buffalo in 1901, and Chicago again in 1910—would get to know California by its fruits. Fairs proved perfect places to practice landscaping as a form of boosterism. For the World's Columbian Exposition in Chicago in 1893, SP sent seventy-three railroad cars full of fruits and flowers. A fabulous array of preserved fruits was put on display under glass, and fresh oranges were sculpted into spectacles of California's fecundity—a globe and a Liberty Bell composed of thousands of pieces of fruit. But these reified symbols of abundance were enhanced by living specimens. An entire garden—living orange and lemon trees, together with palms, tropical plants, and lawns—was transplanted to Chicago. "If your State can make such an excellent showing two thousand miles from home," a typical visitor surmised, "you must have an incomparable climate and splendid soil." Fresh fruit drove the message home. On California Day, some 230,000 fairgoers were given an orange as a consumable token of the horticultural empire to the west.[41]

These perishables were supplemented by something more durable: printed material. "Land of Sunshine," a pamphlet published in 1893, was filled with photographs of Southern California's garden landscapes—lovely mansions with rose gardens and palm trees, gargantuan pumpkins, and citrus groves beneath snow-covered mountains. Topping the list of reasons to move to California were climate and fruit growing that could make the immigrant rich as well as healthy. Over seventy million oranges were sold that year, bringing in $32 million in return. The pamphlet referred to the large profits of fruit growers and "the now well-established belief that the market for choice Southern California fruit . . . is practically unlimited." In fact, that very year the Southern California Fruit Exchange was formed, doing much, as we shall see, to make the market for citrus infinitely elastic. The *Los Angeles Times* and Southern California papers were impressed by the fairs and all of their enticing materials, seeing them as dynamos of growth. "It takes no prophet nor the son of a prophet," wrote the *Times,* "to foretell a growth within the next few years more rapid than Los Angeles has yet experienced." The *Times* saw into the future accurately: the population did soar and citrus continued its sprawl across the landscape.[42]

One might wonder why the SP would so generously open its coffers and tracks to spread the Edenic mythology. That railroad, after all, had been called "the Octopus." This view of the railroad as a parasite had been imbedded in the anti-railroad rhetoric of California since the 1880s. The San Francisco *Wasp,* for example, ran a cartoon that portrayed California as a cow being "sucked dry" by Stanford and Crocker. The publication called the SP a "vampire. . . . The miner digs, the farmer plows, the shepherd shears—and Stanford and Crocker take the proceeds." In its battle to secure title to lands the SP claimed, the Tulare Settlers Land League proclaimed that farmers "are endeavoring to save their homes from the grasp of a corporation . . . which now seeks . . . to appropriate the result of the labor, industry and perseverance against natural obstacles." But these farmers insisted they would not be "despoiled of the fruits of their labor."[43]

This controversy over title to the lands and control of the fruits of labor erupted in May 1880 at Mussel Slough in Central California, when a shootout between SP agents, a U.S. marshal, and farmers left seven men dead in the wheat fields. The event was most memorably commemorated by Frank Norris, whose novel *The Octopus* (1901) excoriated the railroad as a ruthless machine in the garden. In his opening scene, "The leviathan, with tentacles of steel clutching into the soil, the soulless Force, the iron-hearted Power, the monster, the Colossus, the Octopus" crashes into a flock of sheep, which wind up "caught in the barbs of the wire, wedged in, the bodies hung suspended." Having created this scene of ruminant crucifixion in the garden, Norris later describes a map in which the railroad is made out to be an octopus throbbing with the life-blood of the land, leaving it ghostly white.[44]

Yet the railroad was not simply an insatiable super-parasite. In fact, the SP did more than any institution, with the possible exception of the federal government, to encourage growth in California in the first several decades after the completion of the transcontinental line. As one historian argues, the SP was "a very constructive force contributing to the state's economic and social growth." The SP ran an immigration bureau and supported scores of county and state efforts to advertise the attractions of California. I. N. Hoag, the SP's immigration commissioner, wrote a widely distributed pamphlet called "California, Cornucopia of the World." A poster carried the message visually: with the horn of plenty yielding an overflowing abundance of colorful fruit, California, with its "climate for health and wealth," was pictured as an ideal place for millions of newcomers to make millions of dollars from nature.[45]

The SP consciously shaped people's perceptions of the California environment to encourage immigration and agricultural development. It helped gather, analyze, and publicize climatological information. Its surveyors and other personnel furnished the U.S. Department of Agriculture, the Army signal service, and the University of California with information on precipitation, weather, soil characteristics, and water sources, and one of its agents published a widely read article, "The Climate of

California" (1878). The SP transformed California from a terra incognita with a wide variety of soils and microclimates into a known landscape ripe for a new system of control and cultivation. Far from inhibiting the growth of California, the railroad was a constant cultivator of it, for such a position corresponded directly with its self-interest. But it would be growth along particular lines. The SP had the resources and incentive to focus powerful newspapers, regional booster organizations like the chambers of commerce, and the state government on growth. The railroad was not just steel and steam; it was also the engine of a growth machine that used representations of the landscapes it traversed to materially change those landscapes.[46]

More than anything, the SP wanted to see a horticultural landscape materialize. From a shipper's and landholder's perspective, fruit had intrinsic advantages over, say, wheat. The intensive agriculture of fruit growing would intensify the value of that landscape, a powerful incentive for a corporation that had been granted eleven and a half million acres (or 11.4 percent of the state). Wheat was shipped, at most, three times a year, and then only between the Central Valley and Port Costa on the San Francisco Bay. But with the advent of refrigeration technology in the 1880s, fruit could be shipped across the country. With both winter- and summer-ripening varieties of oranges being grown (and ripening at different times along the coast of Southern California, in its inland valleys, and in the Central Valley), the golden fruit could be shipped year round. When the bottom fell out of the wheat market in the 1890s, the SP pushed fruit growing as an alternative for farmers.[47] A landscape given over to intensive horticulture could optimize SP shipping. As a bonus, citrus could draw tourists. While no one would travel over the Rockies to see amber waves of grain, "golden oranges" could get people on the train, especially in winter. As commodities or tourist attractions, oranges could pay their way coming and going.[48]

By 1890, SP pamphlets were enticing prospective farmers with photographic images promising that all "fruits, including oranges, limes, lemons, berries, &c., grow to perfection and in great abundance."[49] In 1898, the SP sought to reach a larger audience by launching *Sunset* magazine. The first issue included a lavishly illustrated article on Yosemite ("Such is Yosemite Valley. The most inspiring. The most sublime. The most beautiful"). *Sunset* was a vehicle with which to promote SP interests by celebrating the nature of California and the West. On its pages, given over unabashedly to the "Propaganda of the Prune" or the "Empire of the

Orange," the railroad promoted California fruits and their uses and thereby expanded their market. It also circulated millions of copies of its pamphlets promoting "the golden orange in its glossy leaves," including "Eat California Fruit" and "Orange Primer." Since "*abundance of continuous sunshine* is a requisite of perfection," eating such "sunshine fruit" would make the consumer healthier. Indeed, those who ate oranges would find they had no need of "physical exercise." The claim was backed by voices of scientific authority, including that of Dr. J. H. Kellogg of Battle Creek Sanitarium fame. The SP had thus established the essential conditions and metaphors from which an orange empire would grow. All kinds of railroad tracts—advertisements in newspapers, the articles and images in *Sunset,* and its pamphlets to attract fruit growers to the state and create fruit eaters in the nation—would bring growers and growth to the state.[50]

In addition to showing off California's garden potential at fairs and in the media, the SP was directly involved in planting gardens on the soil. Through subsidiaries like the Pacific Improvement Company, the SP had a direct hand in establishing a number of "fruit colonies" on lands it owned. When J. Parker Whitney proposed the establishment of an "Educational Orange Colony" in *Sunset* in 1906, he was building on a long tradition. Whitney proposed a kind of school where scientific orange growing could be learned from experts. The land purchased for the colony would be irrigated, subdivided, and planted with orange trees in perfect patterns so that it would serve as a model of improvement. Taking pains to argue that there "would be nothing Utopian in such a venture," Whitney nevertheless had combined utopianism with capitalism to promote fruit culture. His proposal at once foreshadowed the state-supported Citrus Experiment Station and hearkened back to the fruit colonies that had been common from the 1870s.[51]

GROWERS AND THE CITRUS LANDSCAPE

Orange growers did not come to Southern California in covered wagons, one day declaring "this is the spot" and spending the next building a log cabin. Breaking the mold of the mythical pioneer, the citrus grower came by boat or train. Nevertheless, growers would attain a kind of legendary status, though it would be very different from that of the hardscrabble pioneer. More often than not, in the early years, prospective growers were part of a colony that had already purchased land at the proverbial end of the trail. John W. North, for example, formed the Southern California Colony

Association in 1869, recruiting Easterners who were interested in fruit. A plot of land was secured in what would become the most famous citrus town—Riverside. Along with twenty-four other middle-class families, Luther and Eliza Tibbets signed on. They had been living in Washington, D.C., next door to the USDA's superintendent of gardens and grounds, William Saunders. With the assistance of a "lady missionary" in Brazil, it was Saunders who had imported the navel and then sent three seedlings to the Tibbetses in California. The plants proved instrumental to the colony's success. By 1879, the Washington navels were winning prizes, and Riverside instantly became the model citrus landscape. It was featured in countless parables of reclamation: it was the place where God had "left his labor unfinished; left a possible paradise treeless and barren, without life or beauty—a desert." Man came, harnessed the river, and created a miracle that could be "seen today in Riverside, home of the orange."[52]

But oranges were at the center of the development of a number of communities stretching westward from Riverside and San Bernardino to Pomona, Pasadena, and Los Angeles, and, later, south into the towns of Orange County. Pasadena traces its roots to an agricultural colony, the San Gabriel Orange Association. Pasadena would come to draw tourists to its "millionaire mile" of wealthy homes with fabulous grounds stretching along the aptly named Orange Grove Avenue. Of course, not every orange grower would become a millionaire, but growers were always imagined as a refined sort of farmer who might become extraordinarily prosperous.

The grower was advertised as a different breed of farmer. Growers would not be engaged in an elemental struggle against nature in the soil, wielding axes to subdue the West. Indeed, some of them were quite frail. The stereotype of the grower was a successful businessman who had, unfortunately, succumbed to "neurasthenia" or some other ailment of the modern age that befell "brain workers." Health failing, they went to California to grow fruit and there underwent a miraculous transformation. In California, where a Committee on Medical Topography was established, climate was portrayed as a general doctor whose services were rendered daily to all residents. In *California: Its Attractions for the Invalid, Tourist, Capitalist and Homeseeker*, the SP argued that "climate and soil determine, to a great extent, the condition of health and the duration of human life." Booster stories often told how California's nature made invalids into productive citizens, and how, in turn, those citizens made California's nature productive.

As Wickson argued, "The orange . . . is an exponent of the possession of those natural characters of sky and air and soil, constituting the most desirable environments of human life—the highest desirability in the location of a home." One Ojai resident called himself a "pulmonary pomologist," and told anyone who would listen how orange growing had chased away the maladies that too much "brain work" had brought upon him. Eliza Tibbets herself was an asthmatic, but such sickness did not stand in the way of greatness. As "invalids" went about improving the landscape with citrus groves, their own health would improve as well. The land would cure their bodies, and then their minds could go back to work using their restored faculties to improve the land. The *California Citrograph* explained that the health-seekers of Riverside, with their eye for efficiency and their experience as modern managers, had "worked out great problems of profitable fruit growing, changed all old systems of irrigation and cultivation and given us far better fruit and more of it with less water and less work." By the late nineteenth century, the conquest of nature in California had been recast as a therapeutic enterprise: good for the land and good for the brain workers now working the land.[53]

The SP created the mold for California growers, portraying them as "men of large ideas. Visit a California orchard or vineyard, note the process of picking, selecting, grading, and packing, and you will be impressed with the fact that on this western coast a farmer is a man beyond his class." Those whose attention had been captured at the fairs back east were "a large number of the most valuable class of immigrants and home-seekers." Having been "induced to turn toward California" by its fruits, these new migrants had helped re-create and improve what had once been a rough "land of bachelorhood." The fairs had encouraged the "settlement of cultured, refined people . . . on all lands." According to one witness to the boom of the 1880s, "Nowhere else in the world had such a class of settlers been seen. Emigrants coming in palace-cars instead of 'prairie schooners,' and building fine houses instead of log shanties, and planting flowers and lawn grass before they planted potatoes or corn." Such images became part of a self-fulfilling mythology: Southern California immigrants were not rugged pioneers, but cultivated individuals who could jump-start California's growth, bypassing subsistence agriculture to practice a refined and profitable horticulture.[54]

The grower was a clean, efficient, gentlemanly, and yet modern businessman imbued with the aesthetic sensibility of an artist, the pragmatism of an engineer, and the spirit of a civic leader. *Out West* magazine declared, "The horticulturist combines city life with country pleasure and his occupation is one requiring rather more of brains than of hard labor." The state commissioner of horticulture wrote that "citrus fruit growers will generally be marked by refinement and culture." Possessing "rare intelligence," the grower was a man who had taken nature's awesome fertility into his own managerial hands. Others would do the manual work; he would reconstruct nature's elements and forces into a regular, efficient, and abundant factory, a factory that was still somehow a garden.[55]

Southern California's economic and population growth would be driven by citrus and horticulture well into the twentieth century.[56] By 1895, California had indeed become a "Cornucopia of the World." The horn of plenty gushed forth 8,000 tons of deciduous fruit; 3,900 tons of dried fruit; 5,000 tons of raisins; 2,800 tons of canned fruit; 5,800 tons of potatoes; 14,000 tons of beans; and 80,000 tons of oranges—all told, over 200 million pounds of produce a year. And millions of people seemed to be heading for this cornucopia. Correlating irrigation with population increase, *The Rural Californian* concluded that "rapid increase of population is evidence of prosperity." The big stars in the story were San Bernardino, San Diego, Los Angeles, Fresno, Orange, Ventura, and Tulare counties—all important or fast becoming important citrus regions. With orange growing at its core and Los Angeles becoming nature's metropolis, Southern California had become what the Los Angeles Chamber of Commerce called an "empire of agriculture."[57]

The first railroad car load of oranges, packed from the Los Angeles groves of pioneer-grower William Wolfskill, was shipped to St. Louis in 1877. By 1889, 452,000 boxes were being shipped annually from Los Angeles County alone, and some 1.2 million from the state as a whole. The 1889 crop was worth $2.2 million. A decade later, almost 6 million boxes were shipped, and by 1909 the output had grown to 14.5 million boxes worth $13 million. Centered on the Los Angeles basin, a vast citrus landscape was coming into bearing. In 1870, only 30,000 orange trees were growing in the state. Twenty years later, 1.1 million trees were producing fruit. In 1920, 10 million orange trees yielded 22 million boxes annually. Countless photographs recorded, and promoted, the appearance of these trees on the landscape. The 1910 census plotted out their existence with simple dots, each representing a grove from which came 10,000 boxes of oranges (see map 1). The dots represent much more, however, showing us just where California's nature was transformed into an Orange Empire.[58]

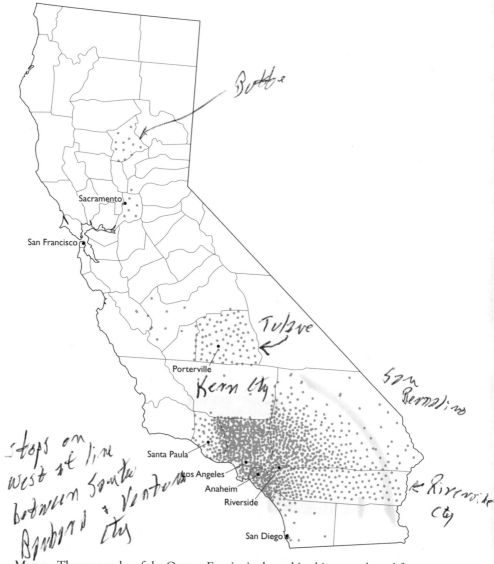

Map 1. The geography of the Orange Empire is charted in this map adapted from the 1910 census. With its protective mountain ranges to the north, its three watersheds, the moderating effects of the Pacific Ocean, and its Mediterranean climate, the heart of the Orange Empire was located in the greater Los Angeles basin in the counties of Ventura, Los Angeles, San Bernardino, Riverside, and Orange. The area around Porterville in Tulare County also became an important citrus-growing region. Each dot represents ten thousand boxes of oranges. (Adapted from Department of Commerce, Bureau of the Census, *Thirteenth Census of the United States Taken in the Year 1910*, vol. 5, *Agriculture 1909 and 1910, General Report and Analysis* [Washington, DC: Government Printing Office, 1913], following p. 734.)

But the map cannot show us how or why that empire was forged, nor does it reveal its other components. The citrus landscape involved more than oranges. Growers cultivated many other plants to reflect and confirm their place in the world, a place they envisioned as a refined and civilized garden community reclaimed from savage wastelands. They planted ornamental trees, shrubs, and flowers in great numbers, creating a leafy wonderland to match their Edenic vision. Nursery businesses like those of Thomas Garey expanded, becoming virtual factories for the production of palms or citrus to complete the manifestation of the garden.

But an expanded list of plants is not enough to complete our cartography of the citrus landscape. In "An Orange Empire," a writer in *Sunset* magazine celebrated what he called the "social fruitage" of the citrus landscape. Gardening shapes culture as well as nature. Wickson had envisioned the growth of egalitarian, and white, communities around fruit growing, and many other observers saw in the citrus communities of Southern California a society to match this image. But in fact, the work of creating and maintaining the ornamental and fruit-bearing plants required intensive labor that was supplied by a stream of Native Californians, Californios, and immigrants from Mexico, China, southern Europe, Japan, and the Philippines. These workers were often seen as others, and they were essentially barred from the Wicksonian dream of the perfect citrus community. To the extent that their real presence was rendered invisible through spatial segregation and willful ignorance, the character of the original garden could seem to have been fully achieved: it was a place removed from work. Restore these workers to our map of the citrus landscape, and we can see that citrus did not create an organic space of democratic opportunity. The gardens of Southern California inscribed social hierarchy into the landscape, yielding a "social fruitage" that was more variegated than the celebratory portraits of the empire revealed. Like any empire, Southern California had its colonized peoples.[59]

Citrus growers and other elites used plants to confirm their elevated social position. As Victoria Padilla explains, "A man's status was symbolized by the sweep of the lawn that separated his house from the street and the number of specimen trees and palms that grew thereon."[60] The invidious use of plants did not escape that sharp critic of "conspicuous consumption," Thorstein Veblen. He pointed out:

> Some beautiful flowers pass conventionally for offensive weeds; others
> that can be cultivated with relative ease are accepted and admired by the

lower middle class . . . but these varieties are rejected as vulgar by those people who are better able to pay for expensive flowers and are educated to a higher schedule of pecuniary beauty in the florist's products; while still other flowers, of no greater intrinsic beauty than these, are cultivated at great cost and call out much admiration from flower-lovers whose tastes have been matured under the critical guidance of a polite environment.[61]

According to Veblen's theory of the leisure class, such nonutilitarian plants performed their job of delineating social status with the utmost efficiency. Vast groves of orange trees were a sign of wealth, but groves of rare trees collected from around the world—trees that produced nothing that could be sold, and that required much labor to maintain—sent an even louder message about personal power. The wealthiest members of Southern California's polite society bought exotic plants in great quantities and hired professional landscape gardeners to acclimatize the plants to California and create spectacular grounds for their patrons. In Redlands, citrus growers A. K. and A. H. Smiley created a two-hundred-acre garden with "artificial lakes and planted forests." "Barren ridges have been changed into flower gardens," explained a writer for *Land of Sunshine*. "Almost every variety of tree, shrub and flower that flourishes in the semi-tropics is to be found here." More than a thousand species of trees and shrubs from around the world were grown in this private park, which the Smileys kept open for the admiring perusal of tourists and townsfolk alike.[62]

Communities also put plants to work in creating an exotic and Edenic look. By 1888, Pasadena had transformed itself into "an earthly paradise [with its] beautiful pepper and eucalyptus trees, cypress hedges and other ornamental trees and shrubs, beneath which are miles of substantial cement sidewalks, which enclose countless blocks of palatial mansions and pretty cottages of modern and unique design, which are surrounded with rare flowers and semi-tropic plants." These city gardens amounted to three-dimensional advertisements for the community, confirming that this was a place where paradise could be re-created.[63]

The garden as a place of conspicuous cultivation relied on immigrant plants. Celebrations of the world's flora, such gardens also amounted to a "public display of American imperialism." The "Columbian exchange"—the massive transplanting of biota among the continents of Europe, Africa, and the Americas following 1492—had been reshaping the world for four hundred years. By the late nineteenth century, improved steamship transportation accelerated a "Pacific exchange" between the Americas and Asia. A particularly rich traffic in biota opened up between California and Australia, with Californians planting eucalyptus and acacia trees by the thousands. Southern Californians gathered plants from the Pacific world and beyond and made them their own. The citrus landscape was a hybrid of the world's flora: Australian trees were planted as windbreaks to protect the Asian orange trees from the dry, hot, and forceful Santa Ana winds, which could turn the idyllic valleys into swirling storms that sandblasted the golden fruits.[64]

The gardens represented an imperialistic appropriation of the world's flora for the purpose of creating an Edenic aura or other marketable products. These artificial Edens of amazing biodiversity served to legitimate conquest, produce economic growth, and foster the interests of the ascendant class. Southern California itself could be sold to tourists and settlers alike as an exotic place of natural abundance imbued with exceptional therapeutic qualities. Wealthy Southern Californians wrote into their gardened landscapes stories about themselves, narratives that proclaimed their elevated status and celebrated the transformation of the landscape they now governed. The gardens also yielded fruits that could be sold to the nation as condensations of nature's goodness. At bottom, Southern California's gardens were less realms of aesthetic delight than power plants fueling the growth of the Orange Empire.

EDEN LOST?

Of course, not every garden was a sign of empire. The working class and immigrants grew plants for solace and sustenance. Mexicano workers living in *colonias* maintained their own vegetable gardens. Chinese, Russian, Italian, and Japanese immigrants developed truck gardens and sold their produce in downtown Los Angeles. These are instances where land was not turned into profit by the growth machine. In these small plots located in the interstices of empire, workers were able to use the land to secure for themselves some small piece of the agrarian dream.[65]

Gardens also could serve as places from which to challenge both the Orange Empire's emphasis on worldly gain and the spatial construction of social inequality. Telling other stories about the garden in California could challenge the cultural and natural landscape of citrus. If they were portrayed as remnants of an Eden lost instead of as the invention of grower industry, Southern California's gardens could force a reckoning with the legacy of conquest. Consider Carmelita ("little orchard-garden"), Ezra and Jeanne Carr's garden on Pasadena's Orange Boulevard. Carmelita included an impressive array of exotics like the Bunya-bunya of Australia and China's Tree of Heaven. There were forty-six grapevines, nine nut trees, eighteen varieties of deciduous fruit, and nine varieties of citrus. John Muir judged Carmelita "nothing less than an exhaustive miniature of all the leafy creatures of the globe." Jeanne Carr, for all of the exotics that were incorporated into the designed space of Carmelita, devoted herself to spreading appreciation for California's native plants. "No effort of the Landscape Gardener's art," she argued, "can equal the beauty of Nature's wild parks and gardens." Carmelita was run as a semipublic garden, open to the public for enjoyment (eventually the grounds were turned over to the city). Instead of standing as an endorsement of ecological imperialism, it became the ground that inspired a challenge to the mercurial ascent of citrus growers.[66]

That challenge came from Muir and Helen Hunt Jackson, Carmelita guests who were the twin creators of a California garden literature critical of empire. Muir melded Romanticism's celebration of the wilderness sublime with garden imagery, creating poetic portraits of the botanic wonders of mountain valleys. In defending the doomed Hetch Hetchy Valley, Muir eloquently spoke up for the "gardens, groves and meadows of its flowery park-like floor." "Garden- and park-making goes on everywhere with civilization, for everybody needs beauty as well as bread, places to play in and pray in, where Nature may heal and cheer and give strength to body and soul," he insisted. Refusing an absolute dichotomy between garden and wilderness landscapes, Muir put the gardens of the mountains on a continuum with the "poor folks' window gardens" and the "costly lily gardens of the rich." But Yosemite and Hetch Hetchy were "natural landscape gardens," and Muir sought to preserve them by investing them with all of the moral significance of the Garden of Eden. With righteous fury, he attacked the "devotees of ravaging commercialism" who wanted to dam the valley. Their "arguments are curiously like those of the devil devised for the destruction of the first garden—so much of the very best Eden fruit going to waste, so much of the best Tuolumne water."[67]

Jackson stayed with the Carrs when she was researching *Ramona,* and the story spread that she wrote the novel there in a vine-covered cabin. Though not strictly true, Hunt did draw inspiration from the Carrs' gardens. Jackson used garden rhetoric to rewrite the history of the American conquest and to question how the California landscape had been transformed after Americans took control. This may seem surprising, since *Ramona* has often been seen as a puff piece that originated what Carey McWilliams called the "Spanish Fantasy Past." The romance between the lovely señorita Ramona and Alessandro, cast as a noble Indian, captivated the attention of readers, but the garden settings created the regional aura in which the plot developed. Here is Hunt's portrait of the view from señora Moreno's veranda: "Between the veranda and the river meadows . . . all was garden, orange grove, and almond orchard; the orange grove always green, never without snowy bloom or golden fruit; the garden never without flowers, summer or winter." As we have seen, such scenes blossomed all over the booster literature of the day.[68]

But Jackson's goal was to undermine the Anglo-American talk of progress and improvement: her garden narrative was meant to manifest the violence of deterritorialization. She depicts the relationship of both Californios and Natives to the pre-American garden landscape as deep, profound, and fundamentally healthy. Against this idyllic backdrop, the fragmentation of landscape that happens with the American entry becomes all the more tragic—indeed, it is a fall out of Eden. Alessandro and Ramona, the lovers crossed by the star of empire, dramatize this tragedy. They become exiles searching in vain for a refuge. Alessandro's ancestral lands have been stolen, and greedy Americans have occupied his home. At last, the refugees find an Indian community that seems to have escaped the American land regime. Alessandro puts his hands to the plow. But before he can reap what he has sown, yet another American takes away his land. Endowed with the Adamic power to name the essences of people, Alessandro says, "That is their name—a people that steals, and that kills for money." As a last resort they retreat to the mountains of San Jacinto. Planting wheat and vegetables, they make a last attempt to re-create the garden. But having had their connections to the landscape repeatedly ripped asunder has taken its toll. Alessandro goes to pieces. Sometimes, he runs for hours, convinced that the Americans are after him. At other times, he imagines that he is back in control of the California landscape, and he shepherds vast flocks of sheep as if they were his own. This madness embodies California's history of violent dispossession. In the aftermath of conquest, only a crazy man could believe that Indians might still have rights and power in the landscape. They have been deterritorialized, Jackson makes plain. The refugees have no business driving livestock across the land or raising a garden under the new regime.[69]

Historically, the American usurpers saw themselves as agents liberating and improving a land that been locked up in languid idleness. "In the hands of an enterprising people," Richard Henry Dana had written in 1840, "what a country this might be." In an article in 1883, Jackson had already begun to probe this mythology and question the spirit of the "close-reckoning Yankee." Romanticizing what she saw as the laid-back culture of the Californios, she imagined them "shuddering, even in heaven, as they look down on [the Yankee's] colonies, his railroads, his crops,—their whole land humming and buzzing with his industries." In compensation for the "sunny empire they lost," Jackson thought, they would eventually see the Yankees undergo "a slacking, a toning-down." The languid land would colonize them and change their identity. Jackson used the stereotype of Californios to question the commercial thrust of the Orange Empire and its promoters' beliefs in the racial superiority of Anglo growers.[70]

At the time Jackson was writing, the effects of deterritorialization could not be reversed. But she hoped to create the political will that would allow Native Californians to join the agrarian republic. In 1883, she had been appointed commissioner of Indian affairs, and, along with Abbott Kinney (who was also a great garden advocate, promoting citrus culture and Australian eucalyptus and creating the Mediterranean fantasy landscape of Venice), investigated the state of California's Indians. Though Kinney and Jackson thought it was "humanly speaking, impossible to render [to Native Californians] a full measure of justice," Jackson hoped that her literary work might begin some form of redress. Jackson countered the stereotype of California Indians as "diggers," a subhuman people who had no real claim to the land, with another stereotype: Alessandro as the noble man living in harmony with creation. But unlike most of the "ecological Indians" portrayed in popular fiction, Alessandro was depicted as capable of working hard to turn nature into a garden. Responding to the situation portrayed in Jackson's exposé, the federal government did organize an Indian commission, which included in its membership the citrus grower A. K. Smiley of Redlands. As mentioned, Smiley had made of his own home an elaborate garden, but he also supported efforts through which "every landless Indian in California shall be secured the land upon which he can maintain a home." In 1909, he gathered together a group of luminaries, including Stanford University president David Starr Jordan and author Charles Lummis, to meet with Indians at Riverside's Mission Inn. At this symbolic capitol of the orange empire—Frank Miller's famous hotel evoking the Spanish Fantasy Past—plans were drawn up to redress the deterritorialization of California's Indians the empire had caused.[71]

Smiley's group may have done the groundwork, but very little land was actually given back. Nationally, much reform aimed at turning Indian communities into collections of freeholding yeomen working the soil. But because they were forced to farm small parcels of agriculturally marginal land, the ecological cards were stacked against Indian farmers. Much reform centered on modern boarding schools, which, following Richard Henry Pratt's injunction to "Kill the Indian and Save the Man," aimed to erase the culture of their Indian pupils and replace it with the dominant society's. Horatio Rust, who earned the praise of Pratt, had run such a school in Perris, yet he shared Jackson's sense of outrage at the fate of California's Indians. "In his simplicity," he wrote, "[the California Indian] believed that the Great Spirit had given him the land and water and the air he breathed alike as an inheritance for his use and his children forever." "The white man's law," he added bitterly, "took away his land and ordered him off." As we have seen, Rust had also been inspired by European garden schools.[72]

In 1901, the Sherman Institute, a model school for Indian uplift and assimilation, opened in Riverside, the heart of the Anglo garden. Rather than questioning the legitimacy of conquest, schools like the Sherman Institute trained ideological floodlights on the conquered landscape, making it appear to be an empire of light and liberty. Consider how the school was represented in the Southern Pacific's *Sunset* magazine. In this neatly kept institution of progressive education, with its mission-style buildings, Indian children would read from the schoolbook of civilization and absorb the "spirit of Americanism." The railroad is clearly linked to all of this, as an SP engine is pictured at the nearby station, which architecturally invokes the Spanish Fantasy Past. Just beyond the border of the institute's grounds, marked by palm trees and an irrigation canal, the lush orange groves begin (see figure 5). Look at the landscape, *Sunset* invites its readers. Where once was nothing but "sunshine and sagebrush" now gleams "the largest orange-growing district in the world." Its crop was worth $1.5 million. Where once were Indians living haplessly in sage and desert are now Americans in the making. But Indigo, the girl in Silko's *Gardens in the Dunes,* would have known that the oranges grown for export hung over a landscape that had once yielded mesquite beans, piñon, acorns, cactus buds, chia, and two hundred other plants useful to people and cared for by the Cahuilla for generations before Europeans arrived.

ORANGE GROVE, ADJOINING SHERMAN INSTITUTE ON THE SOUTH

Figure 5. Orange groves border Riverside's Sherman Institute, a boarding school designed to "civilize" Indians and impress them with what white Americans could do with the wilderness. (From *Sunset* [October 1901]: 155. This item is reproduced by permission of The Huntington Library, San Marino, California.)

The Orange Empire's garden was Eden razed and then remade. Dispossessed of this original landscape, the Cahuilla and other Indians would go on to toil for wages, replanting it with the Washington navel.[73]

FORBIDDEN FRUIT

Rust, the "friend of the Indian," was also renowned for his horticultural achievements in Pasadena (a German magazine printed a picture of Rust's rosebushes under the caption "Ein Rosenbusch in Californien"). But every garden has a serpent; Rust's carried a baseball bat. It seems that boys were playing ball on the street, and "ball playing is not conducive to the care of lawn and ornamental plants." Retrieving their stray balls, the boys would also pick oranges from his trees, "giving no thought to the mutilated hedge and scattering orange peel on the street." In the summer of 1906, Rust petitioned the city council for help. "I have endeavored to improve all my holdings," he complained, "and now I only ask you to protect me and all who use the streets in what seems to be our natural rights." Though Rust may have simply been a killjoy, he was also expressing a widespread belief that he had a right to enclose the garden—a right diametrically opposed to the view of nature he had attributed to Indians. The right that seemed so natural to Rust was to make the landscape into private property, a fenced-in organic richness valuable for producing an exportable crop and for elevating civic pride and land values. Such a conception of natural rights did not include usufruct, for this was a thoroughly commodified cornucopia. "No trespassing" signs went up all across the empire. As Carey McWilliams observed, the unauthorized picking of an orange "is perilous activity . . . likely to invite a blast from a shot-gun, a jolt from an electrically charged wire fence, or a sentence in jail." The stories of growers rigging guns to their orange trees to kill would-be poachers may be extreme, but they do manifest the commonplace exclusions. Though they seemed to express nature's abundance, Southern California gardens also produced scarcity. Fenced in, the garden became forbidden.[74]

The gardens naturalized social inequality and sublimated the facts of conquest, proclaiming instead that California's verdant landscape was simply a manifestation of natural evolution and American destiny. The growth machine portrayed it as the culmination of a triumvirate of improvement—of land, people, and plants. The land had been reclaimed and its fertility magnified through factory production; the people were of a better, more intelligent, and rooted class and, of course, were racially superior; the plants had been imported and acclimated and their very genetic nature improved. As we shall see, tremendous energy and enterprise went into the improvement of the orange in California so that it could become not just another of nature's products but the most perfect garden variety.

TWO

A Cornucopia of Invention

HERCULEAN SCIENCE

HERCULES HAD ALREADY COMPLETED eleven labors, including the theft of the golden apples from the Hesperides, when he challenged the river god Acheloüs for the hand of the beautiful Deianira. Hercules threw sand into Acheloüs's face, and the two wrestled in the dirt. In desperation, the river god turned himself into a fierce bull, but Hercules was not deterred. Scoffing at the god's attempt to employ "weapons that are not natural" to him, he seized the fakir bull and forced its horns into the ground. Triumphantly, he grabbed a horn and twisted it completely off. Blessed by the naiads, it filled with an ever-flowing supply of fruits.[1]

Wrestling the river god for the prized cornucopia could almost be an origin story for California's Orange Empire. It had won control of rivers, and its supply of fruit seemed unlimited. But California's agricultural heroes didn't look much like that muscle-bound cowboy Hercules. They were men such as Luther Burbank and the researchers of the Citrus Experiment Station at Riverside—that is, scientists. Their drive to conquer nature and to make it produce infinite abundance was the same, but they favored brain over brawn. Burbank was a hero for the modern world: a scientist using knowledge and technology to remake the living world. His name became a synonym for the new and improved. Scientists working at Riverside tried to build on Burbank's achievements to create oranges that would duplicate those issued from the gods' own horn of plenty. Indeed, they believed that they had the power to construct their own cornucopia of perfect fruits.

"The men who work in the experimental farms," Steinbeck wrote of these scientists in *The Grapes of Wrath*, "have made new fruits . . . selecting, grafting, changing, driving themselves, driving the earth to produce." The California Steinbeck portrayed was not a bountiful Eden naturally offering up her fruits, but instead an agroecosystem in which nature had been meticulously reconstructed. Donna Haraway calls such hybrid landscapes, produced through the crossing of human technologies with natural systems, "artifactual nature." Acting to realize the dreams of their culture, scientists tell stories about nature, producing the knowledge and techniques to change nature in their own image. As Steinbeck recognized, they "have transformed the world with their knowledge." If the citrus landscape can be seen as artifactual nature, then oranges become artifacts. We normally think of artifacts as something handmade by humans, a part of their material culture. Oranges are certainly grounded in the soil and elated by light—that is, they are objects of nature. But oranges also became objects of culture—packages wrought by science, repackaged through advertising, grown in an environment increasingly controlled by an array of biotechnologies. Technology, as we cannot overlook in our own day, when new varieties of rodents have been patented, has so deeply penetrated the organic that our categories of nature and culture, of mice and men, have themselves become shape-changers. We can find some of the important roots of our contemporary biotechnologies growing in the soil prepared by plant breeders and geneticists in California before World War II. Indeed, legalizing the notion that organic life, like mechanical technologies, can be invented, Congress passed the Plant Patent Act in 1930, largely in response to California's cornucopia of inventions.[2]

BURBANK'S MAGIC WAND

Fruit Growers' Progress: From Vallejo to Burbank

Under the auspices of the California State Board of Horticulture, the eighth California State Fruit Growers' Convention was held in Sonoma County in November 1887. At the Santa Rosa gathering, Dr. A. S. White welcomed the audience with a booster's description of his home county.

"Here," he enthused, "every fruit, every product of the climate, and of the soil, grow to the greatest possible perfection."[3]

He was stretching the truth, of course. The very purpose of the convention was for fruit growers to share information on how to improve fruit growing. Many words were given over to the myriad problems faced by growers: marketing, the use of "artificial fertilizers" in orange cultivation, the management of "inefficient and unwilling workers," the importance of packaging fruit "in bright, clean boxes," and the conservation of the mountain "armies of pine and fir, and the serried ranks of giant redwoods," which protected the valleys of "the orange and the apple." Much discussion focused on how best to handle, pack, and even gas fruits in order to make them more attractive to consumers. Insects could destroy crops; one grower believed that such pests were created by "spontaneous generation." Growers discussed the efficacy of hydrocyanic gas in controlling cottony cushion scale, which was threatening to nip the citrus industry in the bud. This insect pest, which had arrived in California in a nursery shipment from Australia in 1868 or 1869, would finally be defeated in 1889 with the introduction of a natural predator of the insect scale, the ladybug. Fruit growers called for a state agency to establish and enforce quarantines at California's borders. As one grower put it, "Eternal vigilance is the price of good fruit in California." Perfection, clearly, was a hard row to hoe.[4]

American growers felt themselves more than equal to the task, considering themselves agents who could work wonders with California's natural endowment. While the Franciscans were acknowledged as having brought cultivated fruits to the state, E. J. Wickson and others consigned the horticultural efforts in the Spanish and Mexican periods to an "old era" of little importance. But with the arrival of Anglo-Americans, the "efforts at improvement of California fruits" accelerated exponentially. "As soon as the first thought—to get gold directly from the soil—would admit the second—to get it indirectly, by agricultural and horticultural arts—there came a demand for something better than the wild fruits of the mountains, better and more abundant than the fruits of the mission orchards," he claimed. Manifest Destiny provided the plot for these fruit histories, stories that turned the dispossession and "decline of the Californios" into necessary developments in the improvement of nature.[5]

The most famous of all Californios, General Mariano Guadalupe Vallejo (the one Californio fruit grower Wickson had praised), was on hand at the 1887 convention. Vallejo had once said that the "Yankees are a wonderful people—wonderful! Wherever they go, they make improvements. If they were to emigrate in large numbers to hell itself, they would irrigate it, plant trees and flower gardens, build reservoirs and fountains, and make everything beautiful and pleasant."[6] By 1887, though, Vallejo had lost his own lands and livestock to "money-mad" thieves, retaining only a remnant of the once vast empire he called Lachryma Montis ("tear of the mountain"). The old Californio was introduced to the growers as the man who had originally "laid out this county." Vallejo told his audience that "no better climate is found anywhere." Like many a booster, Vallejo had envisioned Sonoma County, once situated in the far northern frontier of Mexico, as becoming a place full of "civilization and society." The Santa Rosa of 1887, a place of prosperous fruit groves and enterprise, "was in my mind's eye long ago."[7]

Though Vallejo could tell the growers all about fruit culture in the early days, what they seemed most eager to hear was his story of the Bear Flag Rebellion. So at the end of the conference, he described how he had been arrested by the rag-tag rebels and imprisoned in Sacramento. As he spoke, a man in the audience blurted out, "I am a personal witness . . . what you hear the General say is correct." The man, who had been one of the soldiers who had arrested Vallejo forty years before, then offered his own version of the changes that had taken place in the country. "The American comes," he said, "and he comes with his wand, and nature's face is all changed." Potatoes had once been only "as big as walnuts . . . Now look at it. The American comes and the face of nature is all changed, and the little potato is a big one." The same was true of fruit: "Now look at it. . . . It is wonderful!" "By George!" said Vallejo, suddenly recognizing his long-lost captor, "I remember you was there below Sutterville where the potatoes were no potatoes at all." Vallejo did not take the occasion to contest the man's claim about the Americans' magical effect on nature. Instead, he inflated it: "After the Americans came, that Bear Flag business was like medicine from a good doctor. He gave a tremendous emetic, and afterward that potato became bigger, and bigger, and healthier."[8]

Elsewhere, Vallejo had indicted the American occupation of California and tried to recover "the good name of my native land, the memory of our efforts in the service of civilization and progress."[9] But at the public gathering, Vallejo helped paint an image of the Americans exactly as they tended to see themselves in their westward mission—rain following the plow, fecundity delivered by the obstetrical devices of American civilization. And though they might have preferred the image of the rugged pioneer to that of the doctor, the role was well-suited to the California of the

1880s, with its numerous health seekers, self-styled physicians, and belief that growing fruit could cure any human ailment. Vallejo's emetic metaphor also played into how Americans tended to see the Mexican (and Asian) cultures that existed to their west: as torpid, idle systems on idle land. For the fruit growers in attendance, the metaphor must have added to their own sense that they were not just harvesting nature's bounty; they were liberating, invigorating, and improving nature. They were constructing a cornucopia out of which would flow fruit that was bigger, more abundant, and close to earthly perfection.

The potatoes were in fact getting bigger. The new and improved variety had been brought to California by a man who was thought to wield a magic wand: Luther Burbank. When he packed his bags for California in 1875, he had included ten "Burbank potatoes" as his "sole capital." The potatoes were "as different from the old Early Rose as the beef cattle of to-day are different from the old Texas long-horn." Burbank settled in Santa Rosa, which he thought was "the *chosen* spot of *all this earth* as far as *nature* is concerned." "I wish you could see California fruit," he wrote to his brother. But however much he was impressed with those fruits as he found them, Burbank pictured improved versions in his mind's eye. Just as "a painter is a man who can see the picture in the landscape," the plant developer was someone who could "see new varieties of future plants when he looks at old varieties." He would soon go to work "to give the farmer and gardeners of the world earlier varieties, better flavored fruits and vegetables . . . and more profitable varieties of all sorts and kinds."[10]

Burbank called himself a "plant developer," but most observers liked to think of him as an Edison-like inventor or a wizard. Governor George Pardee said that "Burbank has worked what to our lay minds, appear almost like miracles. . . . Now, like Columbus, Burbank has shown us the way to new continents, new forms of life." His name would later become synonymous with improvement, entering *Webster's* as a transitive verb: "burbank, v.t. To modify and improve (plants or animals), esp. by selective breeding. Also, to cross or graft (a plant). Hence, figuratively, to improve (anything, as a process or institution) by selecting good features and rejecting bad, or by adding good features."[11]

Burbank's "Feeling for the Organism"

Though Burbank believed in improving nature, he did not view it as just so many parts that could be rearranged at will. To him, plants possessed a kind of consciousness and were shaped by a deep natural history. In working to create the spineless cactus, Burbank even talked to his plants. "You have nothing to fear," he said. "You don't need your defensive thorns. I will protect you." As Helen Keller observed, "Only a wise child can understand the language of flowers and trees. . . . When plants talk to him, he listens." Burbank, schooled in the transcendentalism of his native Massachusetts as well as what he called "Nature's University," never established a rigid division between himself and the objects of his work. Instead, like corn hybridizer and Nobel laureate Barbara McClintock, he had a "feeling for the organism." Like his Bay Area friends John Muir and Jack London, Burbank believed that all of nature was alive. Vitalistic and mechanistic conceptions of life had been doing battle since at least the seventeenth century; Burbank, seeing himself as "one of Nature's interpreters" rather than its master, granted nature a vital essence. "All my investigations," he explained, "have led me away from the idea of a dead material universe tossed about by various forces, to that of a universe that is absolutely all force, life, soul, thought, or whatever name we choose to call it. . . . The universe is not half dead, but all alive." Burbank claimed that the "secret of improved plant breeding . . . is love."[12]

However much skepticism such statements aroused, no one could deny that Burbank's love—or whatever he wanted to call it—worked wonders. Inspired by Darwin, Burbank cross-fertilized plants in the hope of bringing together desired phenotypes in the hybridized offspring. He worked toward a desired outcome, always with an eye to the marketability of his "new creations" (as he would call them in his plant catalogue). Such a process was hardly original. Indeed, Darwin invented the concept of *natural* selection as an analogue to the kind of purposeful selection people had been doing in breeding animals. But Burbank operated on an enormous scale and had an uncanny knack for making fortuitous selections.

Burbank saw plants as organisms carrying traces of past states of nature (atavisms) as well as buds of future growth. In this, he differed from the direction evolutionary biology would take in the United States. Biologists would come to work within a "structuralist" framework; the gene would be seen as the all-powerful determinant of life, its blueprint or control tower.[13] The geneticist's plants lived in space, and their character was thought to be keyed mechanically by the structure of their genes. By contrast, Burbank's plants lived in history.

In planning a new plant, Burbank used his imagination to "look back far into the past and inquire as to the racial history of [a] fruit." "Heredity," Burbank posited, "is only the sum of all past environments." He sought in the individual plant traces of a historically developed "life-world"—each plant a text opening up to Burbank the "Book of Nature" and a horizon into which he might project the plant. As if going directly against the structuralist bent of biology, Burbank wrote, "Our search will not be a search for substances, but a search for *stored up heredities*—not a search for bricks or stone or lumber, but a search for *living traits. . . . In order to work forward a little, we must work backward ages and ages.*" Such appreciation of the living history of organisms could be used "to move forward a little," that is, to make progress.[14]

Burbank wanted to make that past usable by making plants work for the benefit of humankind. As a nurseryman Burbank drove his plants toward an end that would fulfill or create cultural needs. His creations were put on the market, and buyers made a capital investment with the plants they purchased. Burbank saw no contradiction between capitalism and plant breeding: improved vegetables and fruits could only enhance the lives of Americans—nutritionally, aesthetically, culturally, and economically. Though he was perhaps the gentlest of nature's colonizers, his work was nonetheless vital to growers' efforts to gain imperial dominion over California.

Giant Prunes and Redwoods, Little Peas

In June 1893, Burbank published a catalogue of his flowers and fruits called *New Creations in Plant Life*. Distinguishing himself from ordinary nurserymen, Burbank explained that the "fruits and flowers mentioned in this list . . . are more than new in the ordinary sense. They are new creations, lately produced by scientific combinations of Nature's forces, guided by long, carefully conducted, and very expensive biological study." Burbank then linked his work to a grand narrative of progress. The "mental light" of scientists was beginning to illuminate the "dark problems of nature." "We are now standing just at the gateway of scientific horticulture," he proclaimed, "only having taken a few steps in the measureless fields which will stretch out as we advance into the golden sunshine of a more complete knowledge of the forces which are to unfold all the graceful forms of garden beauty, and wealth of fruit and flowers, for the comfort and happiness of Earth's teeming millions."[15] His catalogue offered new and improved varieties of quinces and walnuts, berries, roses, lilies, peaches, apricots, plums, and prunes—a cornucopia of invention.

When talking directly to growers, Burbank emphasized the invented aspect of his goods. He even put aside his vitalistic philosophy to make the point. At the Fruit Growers' Convention in Sacramento in 1899, he argued that "only by growing the most perfect fruit possible could a profit be made." "The fruit grower of to-day is strictly a manufacturer, and should have the latest and best improvements," he insisted. Telling growers that "the manufacturer of pins and nails would not long tolerate a machine which failed to produce pins and nails every other season," Burbank spoke of trees that would mass-produce "good fruit with the utmost regularity and precision." Burbank's celebration of an improved and regimented nature was, of course, the setup for his commercial punch line: he had some great new fruit-making machines for sale, like those that would turn out the plums he had branded the Wickson, the Giant, and the Burbank.[16]

Burbank's varieties caught on and would have a far-ranging impact on the plum and prune industry (prunes differ from plums in that they may be dried in the sun without spoiling). In California, some seven and a half million trees were being grown by 1905. One town even named itself Prunedale. An appreciative grower wrote to Burbank that his plum tree proved to be "1. A more rapid grower. 2. An earlier bearer. 3. An earlier ripener. 4. Larger fruit. 5. Richer in sugar. 6. Its great size gives it a distinct commercial value over others." Burbank had intended to implant these very qualities in his new creations. He would cross varieties of plums, trying to combine, say, the heartiness and frost-resistance of one with the rapid growth of another, the abundance of a third, the attractiveness of a fourth, the high sugar content of a fifth, and the shipping qualities of yet another. Sometimes six or seven plants would be crossed in succession to produce the new organism. Burbank would graft seedlings thus produced onto trees, which would themselves become hybrid creatures: dozens of varieties of fruit might grow from their limbs, "presenting a curious and striking appearance as they develop on the same parent tree."[17]

Making bigger fruits was not always better. In 1905, a Colorado canner named J. H. Empson came to Burbank frustrated, hoping that the wizard would give him the secret of the French *petite pois*. But the French peas, noted for their tenderness, sweetness, and especially their petiteness, were no different from Colorado-grown peas. The proof was in the picking: the French harvested the peas early and often, then added sweeteners and used copper sulfate to bring out a vibrant green. Empson wanted a small pea that would ripen uniformly and could be harvested by machine. Through a regimen of selection—impressive in its speed and results—Burbank delivered a higher-yielding plant with peas that were sweeter, 15 percent smaller, and capable of being mechanically harvested. (The University of California would do basically the same thing with tomatoes in the 1950s.) The desired qualities were thus poured into the biological constitution of the peas, rather than into cans at the cannery. So while it might appear that the pea had been divinely made for man, it had in fact been significantly manmade. As Burbank explained, his plants' material qualities were manipulated according to "the conception of an ideal, [a] mental picture of the new plant form desired." His improved plants vivified the imagination of fruit growers dreaming of empire.[18]

When the Southern Pacific published a series of pamphlets on the virtues of California's fruits, it pointed out that "the improvements made by Luther Burbank" put the California plum in a class by itself. The SP built up the reputation of Burbank in conjunction with that of California's nature. *Sunset* ran a full-page photograph of Burbank and carried Wickson's four-part portrait of the man whose fruits had led to the "elevation and advancement of mankind." An SP subsidiary placed an advertisement in *Sunset* about the Luther Burbank Golden Jubilee. It featured Burbank's portrait next to a giant redwood, "the most perfect growths in the vegetable kingdom." To join Burbank in the redwoods in Northern California would be to grow more perfect, for nature in Burbank's California "encourages human existence at its best." If readers couldn't make the trip to California themselves, they could get a taste of that rejuvenating nature by purchasing the fruits the SP shipped eastward. "Eat California Fruit," a pamphlet instructed, for they "are important foods which are needed to make one physically and nervously strong." Sliced this way, California's improved nature provided a nutritional bounty for the nation.[19]

The Eugenics of Eden

California's most imaginative boosters envisioned the perfection of both plants and people. Some Burbank admirers claimed that his "monumental creative work . . . has been an inspiration to the multitudes to labor for the creation not only of better plants and better animals but of a better human race and better world." Burbank himself began to speak of how to apply lessons gleaned from plant breeding to human beings in the early 1900s, though he emphasized nurture over nature. "There is not a weed in the whole realm of nature that, if given the proper nourishment and sunshine, will not grow up into a beautiful and useful plant," he insisted. Nurture the "dwarfed, diminutive and broken specimens of the human kind" and they too would flourish. Burbank served with Stanford University president David Starr Jordan on the American Breeders' Association's Committee on Eugenics and wrote an essay titled "The Training of the Human Plant." Explaining how his plant breeding principles could be applied to human beings, Burbank wrote that "life itself is only growth, an ever-changing movement toward some object or ideal." By substituting a human ideal for the telos of nature, Burbank promised to put the process of evolution in the hands of human beings. He thought that "we are now standing upon the threshold of new methods and new discoveries which shall give us imperial dominion."[20]

Dreams of imperial dominion were well represented at the Panama-Pacific Exposition of 1915. Celebrating the completion of the Panama Canal, the exposition was an occasion to rehearse and update the narratives of Manifest Destiny. The fair promoted progress on a number of fronts: economic, environmental, and eugenic. The SP gave a quarter of a million dollars to the cause and constructed a pavilion on the Avenue of Progress. The architecture of the fair celebrated the "steady ascension of Progress, Technology and Civilization." The building of the canal itself had re-created landscape on a continental scale. A promotional poster pictured it as "The Thirteenth Labor of Hercules" and showed the hero parting the land. This conquest of nature was portrayed not as benefiting America alone, but as a channel toward the improvement of the whole human race. The fair was a celebration, the official guidebook maintained, of "a new race in the making."[21]

Burbank was present at the fair, both as a person and as a symbol. He embodied the dream of natural and cultural improvement as no one else could. There was an exhibit of Burbank plants and fruits and June 5 was officially designated Luther Burbank Day. He was also invited to speak under the auspices of the Second Congress for Race Betterment. While the sculpture *The End of the Trail* was on display in another part of the fair to lament the supposedly vanishing Indians, Burbank talked about his ideas for "biological improvements in the race of Americans." In his speech, Burbank spoke of "*two distinct lines* in the improvement of any race; one by favorable environment which brings individuals up to their best possibilities; the other ten thousand times more important and effective—selection of the best individuals through a series of generations. By this means and by this only, can a race of plants, animals or man be permanently or radically improved."

Was it possible to "create a new race of man?" a delegate asked. "Without question," Burbank replied. (But when pushed further on who should do the selecting, Burbank evaded the question.)[22]

The Race Betterment Foundation set up a display and hosted several events to spread its grand vision of racial reconstruction. It staged a play. In the first act, "Mankind" boasts of "his achievement in conquering the forces of Nature." Unfortunately, Man takes to leisure and neglects the development of his child. Serving up a version of the frontier anxiety that was felt by Teddy Roosevelt and others, the play expressed the deep anxiety that in an America with no more wilderness to conquer, Mankind would fall into a stupor and racially degenerate. The Californios, as Helen Hunt Jackson had suggested, might have their revenge. In its exhibit, the group presented placards arguing that such a fate could be avoided through "Eugenic Marriage," "Sterilization or Isolation of Defectives," and "Simple and Natural Habits of Life . . . Out-of-Door Life Day and Night." Controlling environment and heredity were presented as complementary paths toward the improvement of "the race" (which, in this context, meant the white race). Here was the California plan for utopian development: place an enterprising people in a natural Eden, watch them make improvements, and then allow them to apply their ingenuity to human beings themselves. Both plants and people would be burbanked toward perfection.

Plant Patents and Spineless Oranges

Burbank's garden was not just a museum of earthly delights; it was a factory for the simultaneous modification and commodification of forms of life. The next step in building an agricultural empire would be to place patents on these reinvented fruits. But in 1889, the U.S. Patent Office had decided that allowing patents "upon the trees of the forests and the plants of the earth . . . would be unreasonable and impossible." None of Burbank's "new creations" ever secured the protection of a patent during his lifetime. At first, he was "glad" that no patents could be given on plants, for "things that live and grow are a law unto themselves." But later in life, Burbank changed his tune, pointing out that "a man can patent a mouse trap or copyright a nasty song, but if he gives the world a new fruit that will add millions to the value of earth's annual harvests he will be fortunate if he is rewarded by so much as having his name connected with the result."

That would change in 1930. Indiana Senator Frank Purnell, who had been given a copy of Burbank's views on the matter by the man who had inherited Burbank's catalogue of plants, quoted the lionized scientist and pushed for the passage of the Plant Patent Bill. Thomas Edison telegrammed in his support: "Nothing that Congress could do to help farming would be of greater value than to give the plant breeder the same status as the mechanical and chemical inventors now have through the patent law," he wrote. "This will, I feel sure, give us many Burbanks." In Edison's estimation, the new law would be a means for cloning a new crop of plant developers.[23]

In its report on the issue, the Senate's Committee on Patents cited the constitutional provision instructing Congress to "promote the Progress of Science and the useful Arts, by securing for limited times to Authors and Inventors the exclusive Right to their respective Writings and Discoveries." "It is obvious that nature originally creates plants," the committee reasoned, but "man often controls and directs the natural processes and produces a desired result." Noting the use of X rays to induce mutations, the report held that new plant forms were a product of nature and culture in combination. Therefore, plant developers should be viewed as inventors and authors. Nature could be transformed into intellectual property. If passed, the committee argued, the bill would produce a nation-building bounty: the increased production of "new improved plants" will "be of incalculable value in maintaining public health and prosperity, and in promoting public safety and the national defense."[24]

Some senators were skeptical. Clarence Dill said, "The experience with the monopolization of patents . . . raises grave doubt as to the wisdom of granting patents on new kinds of plants of a food-producing nature." Senator Thaddeus Caraway of Arkansas raised an ostensibly practical question: "When are we going to lay our hand on nature and say, 'You can go only this way and that way?' How are we going to control it?" He was concerned with the problem of deciding just when in the process a new form of life had come into being. But the statement "How are we going to control it?" also pointed to moral anxieties about humanity's ability to take creation in its hands.[25]

But the Senate ultimately agreed that patenting plants would protect and fortify the body politic. The Plant Patent Act of 1930 codified the notion that people could stake claims to living matter. According to historian Jack Doyle, as a result, "Commercial interests have staked out, protected and perpetuated private ownership of some of the most crucial natural resources available to mankind: food-producing resources governed by genes."[26] Plant patents, under which living organisms could be stamped as "property," enabled a corporate colonization of nature. Instead of providing the liberation from nature that the rhetoric of improvement had promised, nature would now more efficiently be incorporated into the growth machine.

By the end of the decade, over 350 plants had been patented, among them 80 fruits, including 4 new oranges. Charles Collins Teague, the president of Sunkist, kept track of the bill's passage. By the late 1930s, nurseries were advertising new navel varieties such as the Robertson, claimed to be "California's finest winter Orange, outbearing the Washington navel every year and ripening three weeks earlier." This "improved citrus" was controlled by Armstrong Nurseries of Ontario, which held Plant Patent No. 126 on this particular scion of nature. Stark Brothers Nurseries—the inheritors of Burbank's new creations—patented seven fruits Burbank had originated and came to control a large percentage of the apple, plum, pecan, and peach patents. But they held no patents on citrus varieties. Luther Burbank achieved no great success with the orange, which he believed to be "one of the first fruits cultivated by man." Though he experimented with kumquats, grapefruit, and oranges, no citrus of agricultural significance would bear his imprint.[27]

At an appearance promoting the Panama-Pacific Exposition, the plant developer was introduced as "Mr. Burbank—you know, the man who discovered the spineless orange." Obviously, his work with cactus had been crossed with imaginary work with citrus. The Allstate Motor Club *Vacation Guide* said that he had invented the grapefruit. In his novel *The Razor's Edge,* Somerset Maugham credited the character modeled after Burbank with producing a seedless orange.[28] Burbank just had to have had a hand in creating California's most magical fruit, the public seemed to think, so it invented burbanked oranges. But Burbank had something against the citrus family. In contrast to Wickson's belief that a land of oranges is the best place to make a home, Burbank claimed that "wherever you can grow oranges you can take it from me is no fit place to live."[29] Though he had "been offered every inducement to locate near Los Angeles," Burbank refused. But Southern California growers got over it, and found themselves more successful in importing scientific knowledge from other quarters. The USDA exported scientists to the Orange Empire, and the state government tried to re-create Burbank's magic touch in an experimental garden devoted to citrus.

Storied Roots

With notable exceptions like Stanford's David Starr Jordan, university-based scientists tended to distance themselves from the horticultural wizard. They questioned whether Burbank's work was built on scientifically sound footing, and they looked down on his intuitive methods and haphazard record-keeping. Nonetheless, they shared his vision of liberating humanity by improving nature. Indeed, scientists tried to create what the public *thought* Burbank wielded: a magic wand that could change nature at will.

Citrus growers wanted the help of scientists to solve every problem nature threw their way, from pests and freezing spells to lack of water and the decay of fruit in shipping. Beginning in the 1880s, USDA and University of California scientists devoted much attention to these problems. They also established farmers' institutes to spread their expertise and encouraged experimentation by growers themselves. But growers wanted more: a state-sponsored institution devoted to citrus science.[30]

In 1903, the California Fruit Growers Exchange (a.k.a. Sunkist) passed a resolution asking the federal or state government to create such a station. The Citrus Protective League, Sunkist's lobbying arm, prodded the USDA to send G. Harold Powell to solve the problem of citrus decay during shipping. The league kept up the pressure for a station, and the California legislature responded in 1905. It authorized the construction of a Southern California offshoot of the University of California's land-grant Agricultural Experiment Station. In 1906, experiments were begun at the Citrus Experiment Station in Riverside.[31]

But when plans were made for an expansion of the Citrus Experiment Station in 1913, other communities in the Orange Empire wanted in on the action. The San Fernando Valley (newly verdant with water from the Owens Valley) emerged as the major rival. The news that Riverside had won out was received with much fanfare. Riversiders danced in the street, rang the Mission Inn bell, and let the steam whistle of the local electrical plant blow its top for fifteen minutes. "Instantly the city was electrified," reported the Riverside *Daily Express,* "and the rejoicing was most hilarious." The citizens had reason to be excited. Taxpayers from across the state would be pumping nearly $200,000 directly into the institution by the 1920s, on top of the $400,000 they chipped in for pest control, plant quarantine work, fruit standardization, and other efforts benefiting the citrus industry. The station promised to help growers with a myriad of problems, including plant diseases, the use of cover crops, the value of fertilizers, the selection of rootstocks, and methods for "maintaining old citrus groves in good productive condition."[32]

The maintenance of an old grove—or, more accurately, two old trees—became one of the station's first and most public challenges. Scientists were called in to save the Tibbetses' "parent trees," the original Washington navels. Not only were they the original examples of the variety that would dominate growing in the area, they had been used as sources of budwood to graft onto rootstocks that would be grown elsewhere in the state. These trees were not just the progenitors of offspring; they were the source from which millions of clones, each genetically identical, were cut. In a sense, the seven million navels growing across the state by 1929 and the Tibbetses' trees were one and the same organism.

But Riversiders fixated on the parental status of the Tibbets' trees, giving them a central place in the city's mythology—and geography. In 1903 they were transplanted downtown, with Teddy Roosevelt personally putting hand to shovel. Annual orange festivals included "Planting of the Navel Orange," a kind of passion play in which the original planting of the trees by Eliza Tibbets was acted out. Like totemic figures, the trees were seen by Riversiders as both the source and the embodiment of an entire way of life. Their culture, literally and figuratively, grew out of these trees.[33]

But while the trees had grown to mythic proportions in the minds of Riversiders, by 1918 the actual trees had become quite sickly. Hoping for scientific salvation, town fathers called in station director Herbert John Webber. Despite Webber's warning that "the last minute doctor makes the death statement," station scientists stepped in to try to save one of the trees. They agreed that the tree was suffering from gummosis, caused by a fungus that attacks the root system. "It was certain that the top would die," Webber explained, "unless it could be saved by some drastic operation."[34]

The scientists decided to perform an "inarching" operation to supply "a new and healthy root system." Seedlings of other citrus varieties would be grafted into the parent navel, like nine fingers reaching out of the soil and tapping into the tree about two feet up its trunk. "As the saving of this historic tree was of great importance," Webber decided that it would be best to have three station scientists perform the operation. No single scientist should bear the burden of, perhaps, killing these parents. The scientists with their "surgean's hands" performed their operation, and the patient livened up. It still serves "as a State Monument which inspires faith in the great industry it established."[35]

Though they saved the navel, the scientists simultaneously sapped some strength from the old tree. The tree was regarded by station scientists with a mixture of envy and awe; it was a source of their power as well as an obstacle to it. They sought to save the tree so that it could stand as a kind of historical monument, but they wanted to kill its significance. They hoped to end the tree's continued relevance as a supplier of genetic material by producing a new parent tree with a fruit that would be ideal. Although everyone agreed that the Washington navel was an exceptional variety, Webber insisted that "we have not arrived at perfection yet."[36]

In their work, the scientists treated the orange like an artifact that could be reinvented. They did so at the behest of Sunkist growers. In Riverside, the close personal and institutional relationship between the station and Sunkist would amount to "a virtual interlocking directorate." Scientists did not pursue pure research. Instead, "farming realities . . . obliged agricultural scientists to consider science itself as a negotiation of natural and human forces." Scientists positioned themselves as mediators between business interests and nature and worked hard to facilitate the creation of more profitable agroecosystems. Sunkist and the station formed an arm of California's growth machine that reached directly into nature to deliver new fruits.[37]

The desire for more perfect fruits and a more profitable industry was expressed at the ceremonies officially opening the station in 1918. Sunkist President F. Q. Story acknowledged "the great benefit the fruit growers of this state have received through the University of California."[38] The president's name proved apropos: that day representatives of science, the university, and the citrus industry all told narratives legitimizing the institution in which all of their interests would become ever more intertwined.

Thomas Hunt, dean of the University of California's College of Agriculture, saw the station's founding as part of an epic of Western progress. Southern Californians had built "an agriculture and a civilization" that was unequaled. The agricultural achievements of Europe, Africa, and the Orient had all been thrown into California's "melting pot." "This station has been founded to study some of the problems which this boiling mixture has created," Hunt added. The station's purpose was not only to combat mottle leaf, but to benefit humanity. "We are here today," he said in solemn tones, "to dedicate these buildings and consecrate these men to truth, justice and human advancement." Here was an update of Turner's frontier thesis, with the mysteries of biology representing a new frontier that would shape the exceptional character of the "peoples of [the] Southwestern United States." By expressing this faith in the emancipatory power of science, Hunt was telling his version of the "grand narrative of legitimation" used to justify both modern science and the modern university. University science would, as Alexander von Humboldt saw it, guide "the spiritual and moral training of the nation."[39]

As participants in the burgeoning discourse of eugenics, plant scientists of this era linked "the spiritual and moral training of the nation" to transformations of both nature and human nature. At the ceremony, D. T. MacDougal said the study of evolution was of interest to "the breeder and eugenist who seeks to use these principles in the improvement of man and the organisms he has brought into his service." The following year, Howard Frost suggested that station scientists might help solve "social problems" with the knowledge of heredity they would generate. Having linked plant growth to the growth of civilization, Hunt's words on overcoming the pathologies of the "boiling mixture" and consecrating scientists to "truth, justice and human advancement" carried the ring of eugenics.[40]

Webber was interested in genetics as well, but he spoke more directly about improving plants. A major division of the station would be devoted to plant breeding and genetics, he explained. Genes were still new words in the biological lexicon, but many were beginning to think that they were the key to controlling life. MacDougal later compared organic life to metals that could be reshaped for human uses and argued that "our handling of organisms will depend upon the intimacy of our knowledge of the fundamental unit, the gene." Webber assured growers that the station would devote itself to immediately practical concerns, such as the influence of soils, climate, irrigation, and cultural practices (such as pruning). "We are first concerned in establishing the optimum conditions for plant growth," Webber made plain.[41]

Reinventing Oranges and the Environment

Citrus scientists knew full well what problems they were supposed to solve and who was to benefit from such problem solving—Sunkist. They were working to produce a product that could be, as Sunkist boasted in its advertising, "uniformly good." Under the right regimen, trees just might be capable of making millions of oranges that were standard, identical; in a word, perfect. To gain this control over the groves, station scientists would join nature on two fronts. On what I will call the environmental front, scientists researched fertilizers, irrigation, soils, insecticides, and climate in the hope of creating optimum growing conditions; work on this front was aimed at giving scientists the power to change nature from the outside in. On the evolutionary front, scientists employed hybridization techniques as well as X rays to create new varieties; scientists pushed on this front in order to get inside the skin of nature and refashion it from the inside out.

Howard Frost, summarizing the accomplishments of the station on the evolutionary front, explained that the key question was one of the origin of difference or variation in citrus. The answer would, he hoped, lead to "improved horticultural varieties of *Citrus*." For Frost, difference lay in the genes. Finding ways to change citrus, then, meant getting into the plant's genetic material. Inducing change in the genetics of a citrus plant was easy, but the challenge lay in directing that change toward the ideal fruit. The ideal that the scientists were aiming for was, of course, determined by people. In nature, new plants, if they are to survive, must possess "growth vigor, climatic adaptation, disease resistance, and capability of seed reproduction." But under the "artificial selection of fruit varieties . . . one requirement is added, adequate production of fruit desirable for human consumption." The market was always present in the citrus lab. Frost knew that any new fruit must meet a "long list of requirements related to growing, marketing, and consumption [including] attractiveness to consumers . . . [and] convenience of use, eating quality . . . and dietary value." The fruit had to be adapted to conditions of industrial production and mass consumption. "None of the existing citrus varieties are ideal in all respects," Frost insisted. Webber was looking for "perfection." And so the quest for the golden orange was on—a quest that was at the same time aimed at penetrating and controlling life itself.[42]

One possible route to this goal was through the kind of breeding or hybridization that Burbank used. Two different varieties of citrus could be crossed to produce a new variety that might have some advantage in carving out a market niche. In making citrangekuats, for example, four different varieties of citrus were crossed to create a fruit that was frost resistant. This complicated double-cross would be adapted both to environmental conditions and market requirements.

The work was made doubly difficult by the fact that it was not easy to distinguish heritable from nonheritable traits. Was the particular size, shape, yield, or flavor of fruit on a new tree one of a kind, or could it be passed on to other trees? Nonheritable variations, Frost explained, were attributable to "difference in environmental factors." So the geneticist would have to isolate such "modification by external factors" from the deeper and truer genetic variations—those that are "inherent in the nature of the cells of the trees." At work here was a metaphysics of interiority: essential characteristics of a plant were to be distinguished from those that occur as a result of "exposure" to "environmental influences." So the genetic mapping of a territory entirely separate from the terra firma of California (the land with all of its variations of soil, climate, and sunshine) was a critical step in the creation of new orchards.[43]

Frost saw that in theory, the gene was the key to reproduction, heritability, and growth. In practice, it was quite difficult to discriminate between differences that genes made and those caused by environmental factors. To separate the organism from outside influences, controlled environments were established in which to test theories and develop a taxonomic system that could take into account the complexities of growth and development. But developing a vocabulary to name what the scientists were seeing, and developing the powers of observation to see what they wanted to name (i.e., the truth about the fruit, its genetic map), proved elusive. Citrus taxonomy was complicated; even today, there is considerable disagreement over certain aspects of it. Some taxonomists claim that there are 16 species within the genus *Citrus,* but others put it as high as 162. Still others (employing a kind of Catholic logic) say that what appear to be 162 species are really one.[44]

Taxonomy was further complicated by the wild aberrations that would sometimes appear on citrus trees. As Frost explained, "The genus Citrus is characterized by remarkable genetic variability, both in seed reproduction and with clonal varieties." Even in trees that had been clones, it was not uncommon to see bud variations and chimeras. Such chimeras were not the fire-breathing creatures of Greek mythology, but they were wild nonetheless. A chimera was the result of two varieties growing together; two buds, for example, might be grafted together and penetrate each other in the growth process, producing strange fruit indeed.[45]

Some varieties showed a perplexing instability. The Wase satsuma orange, for example, arose as a bud variation on an Owari orange tree. The Wase satsuma had a few desired characteristics, and so trees were propagated from this bud variation. But the propagated trees had a tendency to revert to the Owari. The oscillation between these two varieties confounded breeders' efforts to fix the desired form. The Wase-Owari shape-changer showed that nature escaped the naming practices of science and its techniques of control; the orange could not be fixed, in language or in practice. A wild and unpredictable nature presented serious problems for scientists and growers who were attempting to introduce their nonhuman workers, the orange trees, to the kind of scientific management advanced by Frederick Winslow Taylor.

Growers would often find that the buds they had grafted into rootstocks would grow up to be unlike the Valencia or Washington navel from which they had come. The buds had been taken from a limb that had grown genetically apart from the rest of the tree; a single cell, plant pathologist A. D. Shamel posited, had changed, perhaps because of environmental factors. Shamel devoted much attention to the growers' problem of seeing parts of their trees suddenly taking paths of their own, eventually developing a method of bud selection that would weed out the aberrant strains and give growers the efficient trees they could count on. Many growers kept careful records of the yield of each tree, as the *California Citrograph,* the industry magazine, had instructed them to do in articles explaining how to conduct "An Efficiency Analysis of the Citrus Grove." Still, bud variation was an unpredictable phenomenon that evaded the geneticists' theories of the day. Such wild growths reminded growers and scientists that citrus trees had not become mere machines.[46]

But the unexpected chimeras and other varieties also held a promise: they might be superior in some way to the parent. Through the *California Citrograph,* station scientists asked growers to be on the lookout for unusual varieties. The growers' orchards could be made into an extension of the station, just as the station was an extension of the growers' interests. Scientists would explore and track down variations in nature and claim a kind of proprietorship through right of discovery. Indeed, the plant breeder was often more a "plant explorer," as Frost admitted, than an agent creating new varieties. The patents that were awarded under the Plant Patent Act for new varieties of orange, for example, were all for found varieties. Though the language of the act implied that human agency had prodded new varieties into existence, scientists whose varieties had been awarded patents were doing nothing different than what had been done when the Bahia mutant was reclassified and Americanized as the Washington navel. They were naming what they saw in nature rather than making nature conform to the image in their mind's eye.[47]

Though not directly involved in citrus experimentation, scientists such as Jacques Loeb and H. J. Muller promised to put more agency in experimenters' hands. In 1927, Muller used X rays to induce mutations in plants. This breakthrough to the core of the gene earned him a Nobel Prize. The citrus industry shared a faith that X rays would light up a path to the absolute control of nature. General Electric and Sunkist collaborated in the development of an X-ray machine to be used in scanning fruit for frost damage: "We know they're good because we know what's inside," Sunkist assured consumers. But X rays had the power to do more than simply make the inner contents of fruit visible. Muller felt that they could disclose fruit's "inner secret," allowing scientists to chart the very character of genes. He was one of the earliest scientists who posited that the key to life—the blueprint controlling physiological and morphological properties of an organism, its growth and variation—was the gene. Yet the kind of exposure that would reveal the secret of the gene, DNA, would have to wait twenty years, for the work of Watson and Crick.[48]

Scientists were excited by X rays' power to induce mutation. As Muller explained in 1916, "The central problem of biological evolution is the nature of *mutation,* but hitherto the occurrence of this has been wholly refractory and impossible to influence by artificial means, tho' a control of it might obviously place the process of evolution in our hands." Controlling mutation would be a "keystone" of what Muller called "our rainbow bridges to power." Muller hoped his kaleidoscopic X-ray bridge would lead to the inner sanctum of the gene. "The beginning of the pathway to the micro-cosmic realm of gene-mutation study thus lies before us," he said. "It is a difficult path, but with the aid of the necromancy of science, it must be penetrated." Muller went on to encourage efforts on this evolutionary front in the name of progress: "We cannot leave forever inviolate in their recondite recesses those invisibly small yet fundamental particles, the genes." The genes withheld "those forces, far-reaching, orderly, but elusive, that make and unmake our living worlds." With X rays, necromancers of science might just have that magic wand that would allow them to control mutations, evolution, and, ultimately, life itself.[49]

"The science of biology is only at the beginning of its task, the understanding and remaking of living things," announces Dr. Patricia Storrs, a character in an Upton Sinclair play that he wrote during his run for governor of California in 1934. Many years before, Sinclair had been exposed to this grand vision when he met Berkeley biologist Jacques Loeb. Loeb had developed the technique of artificial parthenogenesis, by which embryological growth could be stimulated in unfertilized sea urchin eggs by applying inorganic salt solutions. An admirer of Burbank, Loeb echoed the plant wizard's rhetoric in speaking of "utilizing the forces of nature to bring about new combinations, creating things which have never been created outside of nature's workshop." Loeb and Muller had transformed biological science by adopting an "engineering standpoint." In their hands, biology would become interventionist rather than descriptive. If biology had hitherto described the natural world, Muller and Loeb felt that it was now time for biology to change the world.[50]

The scientists at Riverside would follow in Loeb and Muller's gene-busting footsteps. In a revealing fantasy, Dr. Howard Fawcett went so far as to adopt the pseudonym "I. C. Bigg," put on "a rubber suit," miniaturize himself, and find a way into the vascular system of a Valencia orange tree. The destination of this voyage of discovery was reached, Bigg explained, when "I pushed my way through the central tissue . . . on to the center of the ovule." In this inner sanctum, Bigg witnesses genetic processes at work. Ostensibly contrived for the readers of the *Citrograph* to help them understand some genetic mysteries, Bigg's narrative reveals the peculiarly male dimensions of scientific exploration: he wanted to penetrate the skin of nature, gain access to the inner sanctum of life, and thereby achieve control over life itself.[51]

Apart from such fantastic journeys, scientists used toxic chemicals, radium, and X rays to get inside the skin of nature and induce mutations in orange seedlings. But the absolute control of nature proved more fantasy than reality. The results were disappointing: albinism, twisted stems, bud fasciation, aberrant leaf forms. Only occasionally was there a promising result, such as a plant that flowered in its first season. The X-ray machine was no magic wand. Instead, it performed like a lottery-ticket dispenser, giving scientists long odds at creating the perfect tree of their dreams. Thousands of mutant citrus varieties were discarded like so many scratched-off lotto cards.[52]

Likewise, hybridization did little to change the character of the citrus industry. Since citrus is extremely heterozygous, few traits are determined by a single gene. In addition, since trees require five to fifteen years to mature, citrus breeding is very time consuming and complicated. Making matters worse, the strange phenomenon of nucellar embryony and the "absence of characteristic morphological marker genes" make the selection of promising hybrids very difficult (though new techniques such as isozyme analysis hold promise).[53] Nature proved an elusive and at times canny adversary in science's efforts to name it and change it in its own image.

Even when promising varieties were created, they often proved ultimately unsatisfactory. A variety might grow fast and easily and be better tasting but have a crinkled, unattractive skin. The hybridizers' best creations might be rejected because they would not fit in the standard-size box, or they would compete for a market niche that was adequately, though not exquisitely, filled by some familiar variety. Frost explained that even "small-scale marketing encounters special difficulties, particularly where, as in California, the citrus industry has standardized very strictly on one or two varieties of each main group." Ironically, the way that the citrus industry had cultivated the market reduced the possibilities that fruit genetically altered by scientists would find a place in the groves or on the tables of consumers. Frost explained that the "horticultural prospects of new hybrids depend not only on the *intrinsic excellence* of the new varieties in comparison with the varieties in use, but also on the general cultural and marketing difficulties in the way of successful establishment of new varieties in commercial production." A few hybrids did find their way into the market. Exemplary was a lime crossed with a kumquat, which was passed off as simply a lime. It presented no challenges because it did not disturb the market's established categories. While the magic wand still eluded scientists, experimenters could have shaken up the array of cultivated varieties had the market not acted as such a conservative force. Seeking to have a hand in creation, science seemed to find that the market's guiding hand was there first.[54]

But if there would be no immediate gene revolution, research on the environmental front did yield results of far-reaching significance. Work at the station led to advances in irrigation, entomology, biological and chemical controls, frost protection technology, soil science, and plant nutrition. Despite skeptics' amusement at the project of "heating the whole outdoors," the station improved the efficiency of outdoor heaters, which had been used since 1896 to keep temperatures high enough to prevent damage to trees and fruit in cold spells. A whole dietary knowledge was developed for citrus trees, determining the proper "mineral nutrition of citrus" and involving investigation into the "mechanism of nutrient absorption, . . . the effect of light, temperature and humidity on nutrition, the relation of microflora of the soil to nutrition." In addition to pitting nature against nature to foster "biological control of insects," extensive research was conducted into hydrocyanic acid and petroleum-based insecticides and their application. Whereas work on the evolutionary front sought to graft marketable fruit varieties to cold-resistant citrus strains, or find the key to fast growth with a fortuitous mutation of genetic structure, these practices all sought to modify the external environment in order to maximize desirable plant growth.[55]

The scientists never succeeded in replacing the Washington navel or the Valencia, the two varieties that dominated orange production. But their work did amount to the re-creation of the environment in which the fruits would grow. Despite the boosters' rhetoric, the environment in California had not been created by God to produce the best and most marketable citrus. In terms of "heat units"—a measure of average temperature in an area, which is strongly correlated with rate of growth and fruit quality— the subtropical climates of Florida and Brazil and the tropical climates of Trinidad and Sri Lanka were superior to California.[56] But the knowledge and techniques created at the station did much to modify the soils and the very climate in which citrus grew in order to make up for some of these deficits. The scientists would not invent a perfect orange. But by modifying the orange grove and its environs, they did reinvent California's cornucopia.

Science in the Groves

The station's research made its way into the groves through many conduits. Scientists regularly published articles in the *California Citrograph,* and Sunkist was quick to share new techniques with its growers. Scientific research helped give rise to many businesses that supplied the machinery and petrochemicals that growers would use in the groves to reconstruct their cornucopia. Emblems of science—test tubes, microscopes, scientists in lab coats—often appeared in the advertisements of such companies as Ortho and the Pacific R & H Chemical Corporation. "By grafting the chemical technology of the University with the regulatory force of the state, the spray-chemical industry became the principle dispenser of insect protection" in California, Steven Stoll explains. Fruit crops came to be protected by a "million-dollar chemical shield."[57]

Until the mid-1930s, fertilizer companies often presented a picture of science working with nature. In one advertisement, science had helped uncover a dietary régime for crops that was both perfect and naturally balanced. "ISN'T NATURE GRAND?" the company asked. "For years Science has shown that Bat Guano is of economic importance to the growers of all crops." N. V. Potash argued that "scientific analysis proves . . . [that to] produce uniform quality fruit year after year, you must fulfill the natural plant food requirements of your trees. Mother Nature knows best!"

Picturing science's ability to uncover just what nature intended in order to maximize natural growth mirrors how Sunkist would use nutritional science to claim that oranges would foster the cultural and physical growth of children. But if organically based fertilizer companies like Chilean Nitrate argued that "It's Pretty Hard to Beat Nature," the manufacturers of petroleum-based fertilizers and insecticides presented science as a tool that would allow growers to do just that.[58]

In one ad, Owl Fumigation Corporation screeched, "PENETRATION!" Underneath, the owl explained, "Years of research shows that Hydrocyanic Acid is . . . one of the most penetrating and toxic gasses known to science!" A fumigation team is depicted in the background, pulling tents over trees and pumping the insecticides into this enclosed environment; a sidebar explains that the gas can penetrate seventy layers of gunnysack to kill rats placed inside a bucket. Apparently, there was no worry that the gas would escape from the tents and harm workers, or that the gas might penetrate the fruit and harm the consumer. If there was any doubt about this last concern, an advertisement for American Cyanamid & Chemical Corporation assured the grower, "When [the consumer] slices an orange, *she prefers* fumigated fruit."[59]

A variety of scales and other insects had plagued citrus monoculture in California from the 1880s. There were citrus aphids and lice; silver mites and red spiders; red, yellow, purple, and cottony cushion scales. In fact, the "simplified ecology" created by growers "invited a population explosion among alien (nonnative) insects." The cottony cushion scale would indeed seem to explode on trees, giving them the appearance of being caked in white cotton candy. This insect pest, which had arrived on citrus trees imported from Australia in the 1860s, was controlled when the USDA went to Australia to find a natural predator. It found that *Vedalia cardinalis*—the ladybug—fed on the scale. Imported and released in the groves, the ladybug soon had the scale under control. Despite such dramatic success, fighting pests with chemicals—which had the advantage of being "new, scientific, progressive"—ultimately displaced "nature's way."[60] Citrus growers had become large consumers of insecticides and thus contributed to the growth of the agrochemical industry. By 1939, Sunkist's Fruit Growers Supply Company alone was spending $2 million on sprays, commercial fertilizers, and equipment. The Citrus Experiment Station, which had conducted extensive research on such sprays, developed the cyanide dust fumigation method and worked with the chemical industry on the standardization of oil sprays.[61]

Insecticide companies ratcheted up fears of insect infestation with pictures associating natural pests with labor activists. A 1938 DuPont ad for Hydro-Cyanic spray promised that "FUMIGATION WILL CONTROL THE RED SCALE MENACE." The red scale was pictured as a hooded, snarling, simian creature—a King Kong that embodied the growers' worst nightmare of both nature and labor out of control (see figure 6). Labor activism in citrus groves had, of course, been portrayed as a "red menace" (and had in part been fought by law enforcement and grower-sponsored vigilante groups with tear gas—one form of which, chloropicrin, was also used as an insecticide). When the Associated Farmers, an organization of growers and industrialists, outfitted a cameraman to record the faces of striking workers, it made sure to purchase a gas mask for him as standard equipment, so that he could keep the film rolling after tear gas filled the air. At the end of the decade, Carey McWilliams, whose book *Factories in the Field* exposed many of the violent tactics used to break strikes, would be targeted by the Associated Farmers as a member of the insect kingdom: "Of all the pests which the crops of California are infested with, Mr. McWilliams is Agricultural Pest Number One." So when DuPont pictured the "red scale menace" in heavy shackles, the metaphors became mixed, but the message was loud and clear: DuPont could provide the ammunition to get one's groves under control.[62]

The fumigation tent became an assuring symbol of control. The August 1945 cover of the *California Citrograph* featured a photograph of a grove covered by fumigation tents. The *Citrograph* had tended to feature an Arcadian citrus landscape, often with young white women or children amidst the trees eating oranges. Making the cover of the *Citrograph* was a sign that the fumigation tent had been naturalized as part of an increasingly mechanized citrus landscape. DuPont even turned the tent into the traditional metaphor of natural abundance—the horn of plenty. A fumigation tent with a horn extending from its center yielding an overflow of perfect fruit first appeared in a DuPont advertisement in September 1940, and by February of the next year this chemical cornucopia, spilling forth perfect oranges that would please the most discerning consumer, had become a company logo (as in figure 7).

Nature's bounty was thus seen as the product of scientific and technological control, and the groves had become battle zones. It should come as no surprise that the Food Machinery Corporation—which manufactured a long list of machines for the citrus industry, including water pumps, large-capacity sprayers and dusters, packing equipment, automatic box makers,

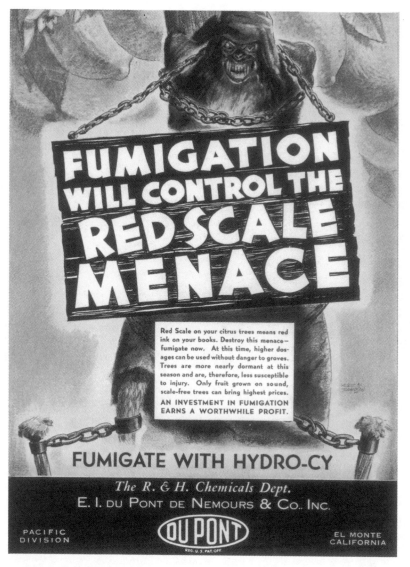

Figure 6. DuPont was a leader in producing products for citrus growers that allowed them to control red scale and other pests. (From *California Citrograph* [February 1938], inside front cover. Courtesy of DuPont.)

"HYDRO-CY" FUMIGATION

SCALE insects must be controlled if you want to produce first grade fruit—fruit that has good looks, good taste and good sales.

Fumigation is an effective method of scale control because it reaches every part of the tree, fruit, twigs, and wood. It does not impair the normal healthy growth of the tree and does not affect the fine flavor of the fruit. It leaves no residue.

Have your local fumigator inspect your grove and plan a fumigation program for you. A properly timed fumigation will help to keep

your grove in a clean healthy condition, the only condition in which it can produce an abundance of first grade fruit.

E. I. DU PONT DE NEMOURS & COMPANY
Incorporated
THE R. & H. CHEMICALS DEPARTMENT
PACIFIC DIVISION • EL MONTE, CALIF.

"HYDRO-CY" FUMIGATED FRUIT
Good Looks . . . Good Taste . . . Good Sales

Listen to "CAVALCADE OF AMERICA" every Monday
evening, 6:30 to 7 P.M. P.S.T., N.B.C. network.

Figure 7. In this DuPont ad, the fumigation tent *(lower left)* was ingeniously turned into the mythological horn of plenty, yielding Edenic fruit for the discerning consumer's pleasure. (From *California Citrograph* [June 1941], inside front cover. Courtesy of DuPont.)

fruit graders, and canning machinery—also manufactured instruments of war. During World War II, this company made "Water Buffalos . . . Big, tough, deadly . . . heavily armed and armored amphibious tanks." "Water Buffalos," the May 1944 advertisement in the *Citrograph* claimed, "*are rough on rats!* [and] the answer to Pacific warfare!" (At least as rough as Owl's fumigant had been on actual rats.) Human and natural enemies were demonized in a vicious metaphorical circle, justifying a "war without mercy" both in the Pacific and on the home front. It is ironic but not accidental that an agroindustrial company organized around the growth of food produced machines that could "ride over barbed wire, barricades and pillboxes, spraying death as they go." Their food machinery was designed to perform a not entirely different function: penetrate enemy lines, with its insecticides "spraying death as they go." The "Water Buffalo" simply reveals how much armament the Orange Empire had amassed on the environmental front of nature.[63]

The Boiling Cauldron

However these technologies were represented, they were part of the amalgamation of forces that led to the global change in agriculture known as the Green Revolution. The Green Revolution was a kind of growing frenzy in which millions of barrels of oil—in the form of insecticides, fertilizers, and gasoline-powered farm machinery—were used to create tremendous quantities of food. This revolution was made possible by approaching nature as much from the environmental as the evolutionary front. The new hybrid varieties of grains and other crops that began to be grown around the world depended upon "capital-intensive soil management practices (fertilizers, agrichemicals, irrigation) to create controlled fertile environments for these carefully selected varieties." Much of the knowledge and technologies that fueled the Green Revolution had been developed in and around California's citrus industry before World War II. Fabricated in California and in the Midwest, the hybrid creature of agribusiness—composed of improved plants, state-sponsored scientific knowledge, federal farm policies, and agrochemical corporations and their products—was exported to the world. Agricultural yields soared. But rather than emancipating the world's peoples and improving nature, the Green Revolution disrupted rural cultures, increased dependency, and degraded environments. The oil-based, interventionist, and imperialistic nature of the Green Revolution, with its drive to conquer nature, is well illustrated by the logo of "the World's largest Manufacturers . . . of Insecticides and Fungicides," Sherwin-Williams. A bucket of Sherwin-Williams's product—something it claimed "every citrus grower needs"—is tipped over the earth's north pole, and a dark sludge drips down the globe. The slogan is "COVER THE EARTH."[64]

Rachel Carson's *Silent Spring* (1962) broke the story of the unintended effects of the chemical cornucopia. She illustrated her conclusions with a striking incident from California's citrus industry. In the 1940s, it began to use DDT to control pests. Unfortunately, the pesticide did not just kill pests. It was an indiscriminate killer, and thus all but wiped out the ladybugs. In their desire to gain absolute control of the environment, growers had killed a part of nature that was working for them, and the cottony cushion scale came back in full force. When citrus experiment station scientists discovered that some scales had grown resistant to cyanide fumigation through a "survival of the fittest" mechanism, they offered a new solution: "spraying with oil emulsions . . . and numerous proprietary brands of sprays were prepared and sold to growers in large quantities."[65] Chemical technology had promised to provide growers with an ecological blank slate, a sterile environment in which to manufacture their products.

Though drawn in the Halloween spirit, the November 1936 cover of the *Citrograph* presented a revealing image of the citrus industry: a sorceress, with a full array of test tubes and other scientific apparatuses, has created in her cauldron a tree with golden oranges. During its pesticide campaign thirty-three years later, the United Farm Workers would portray the University of California, the USDA, and the Food and Drug Administration as witches combining the fruit of the vine with DDT. The alchemy of science, technology, and nature produced golden oranges as well as a dangerously toxic landscape.[66]

Scientists, of course, were not sorcerers, despite this playful imagery and Muller's rhetoric about the "necromancy of science." They could not conjure up new organisms with a spell or a magic wand, though Burbank often appeared to do so. Nonetheless, scientists working in conjunction with the citrus industry saw oranges as artifacts to be reconstructed and the California environment as a greenhouse to be improved. Donna Haraway suggests that "organisms are made as objects of knowledge in world-changing practices of scientific discourse." For her, discourse refers not to idle chatter but to a process in which scientific knowledge about the living world is inextricably bound to its transformation. California's oranges had become what Haraway calls "natural-technical entities."

The fruits had been crossed with each other, but they had also been hybridized with growers' technologies and desires.[67]

Advertisers would also have a hand in the reconstruction of oranges. Though the scientists' cornucopia of invention failed to produce the perfect orange, the goal would be accomplished by this other group of necromancers. However large the gap between California's artifactual oranges and the ideal orb remained, oranges touched by the magic of advertising began to appear before consumers' eyes as the most perfect products of nature.

THREE

Pulp Fiction

The Sunkist Campaign

IMPRINT

AT THE WORLD'S COLUMBIAN EXPOSITION of 1893, a very curious figure stood in the California State Building: a medieval knight in armor, mounted on a horse, composed entirely of prunes. As the exposition's brochure explained, this figure "metaphorically impressed the fact that the prunes of that state are being introduced victoriously into all lands, to the discomfiture of the products of other countries." Lording it over other exhibits of California's fertility—such as an "Old Liberty Bell . . . perfect in shape," composed of 6,500 oranges—this knight of prunes was a member of a most regular army: one semiotic soldier in phalanx after phalanx of images that intertwined the myth of California with fruit, and molded that fruit and its state of origin into new material and symbolic forms for the nation's consumption (see figure 8). California fruits became associated with market as well as martial conquest, and with national as well as personal growth and vigor. But this would be an empire of liberty, if we can believe the message spelled out by those 6,500 oranges. These themes neatly came together in a turn-of-the-century orange crate label from Riverside on which a strong and ruddy Uncle Sam, naturalized as a native of the Golden State, holds up the fruits of his labor—grown "myself in California," he says (see frontispiece).[1]

Figure 8. Sixty-five hundred oranges were used to compose this symbol of liberty for the World's Columbian Exposition of 1893 in Chicago. (From *Final Report of the California World's Fair Commission: Including a description of all exhibits from the state of California* [Sacramento: A. J. Johnston, Supt. State Printing, 1894], facing p. 90.)

If Uncle Sam is here the embodiment of the nation, the oranges he holds up on the label would come more and more to embody nature. As we have seen, California rooted much of its self-promotion in a vision of the land's astounding natural fecundity. Indeed, anything that could be grown under the sun seemed to be on display in the California building at the exposition, prompting one Chicago newspaper to conclude, "California proved her claim that she is the land of sunshine and flowers." But the historian Henry Adams, more taken by the machines and "dynamos" on display elsewhere at the fair, wondered if he was witnessing the birth of a modern America whose heart would be "capitalistic, centralizing, mechanical." That same year, a new cooperative was formed in California that began to provide the nation with organic symbols, therapeutic assurances that America could still be "nature's nation." The California Fruit Growers Exchange billed its oranges as the answer to the anxieties of city-bound Americans: they would restore their health, vigor, and contact with nature.[2]

But thinking of Sunkist as leading America "back to nature" is deceptive: in shaping its oranges for the market, and in shaping the market for its oranges, Sunkist participated in the retooling of America for modernity. Drawing power from images of nature, Sunkist was nonetheless part of the "capitalistic, centralizing, mechanical" forces that so worried Adams. Through what it called "scientific salesmanship," Sunkist hoped to reproduce in countless other places the feeling at least one Chicago fairgoer got amidst California's displays of overabundant nature: "The moment I enter her building I feel like eating and drinking."[3] To capture the palates of the American public, the Orange Empire sculpted oranges into Liberty Bells, claimed that they were essential to healthy growth, and branded them. Experimenting with a fly swatter and a stove at his home, Don Francisco, the CFGE's advertising manager, was the first to put his company's mark on the oranges. By 1926, the cooperative was inscribing millions of oranges with the name Sunkist. But well before that time, oranges and consumers alike had received the kiss of advertising.[4]

Paralleling the work of scientists at the Citrus Experiment Station, advertisers saw themselves as "apostles of modernity." Instead of controlling nature, modern advertisers developed techniques for getting inside the skin of culture and refashioning it from the inside out. Advertising responded to the crisis in capitalism brought about by the advent of mass production. Though not a manufacturer in the strict sense, Sunkist faced the problem of having a productive capacity that outstripped consumer demand. But its advertising manager, expressing the conventional wisdom of corporations, redefined *surplus*. Oversupplies were no longer "the result of overproduction" but were "due to underconsumption." To invent a mass consumption to match corporations' capacity for mass production, advertisers needed to transform American culture from one that celebrated thrift, self-sufficiency, and restraint to "a secular business and market-oriented culture, with the circulation of money and goods as the foundation of its aesthetic life and moral sensibility."[5]

The movement of things, advertisers found, could be greatly facilitated by the circulation of representations of things. A thing, they also discovered, was not just a thing. A product did not have a set use-value that was obvious and unchangeable. Like beauty, use-value is in the eye of the beholder. Sunkist developed brilliant ways to change the way consumers saw oranges. It created new environments for oranges, niches across the nation ideally suited for its consumer product. Just as space in the exposition's California building was carefully constructed to create a sense of spectacle (not to mention thirst and hunger), Sunkist developed ways to make the alluring displays at such fairs into moveable feasts. The imaginative use of a range of media, from magazines and radio to billboards and window displays, allowed Sunkist to place oranges before prospective consumers in both the public and private spheres. Sunkist would leave its mark in all sorts of places and make the simple act of eating an orange into a secular sacrament performed daily across the nation. Consumers would come to see oranges as a gift of nature scientifically proven to promote health and growth—the perfect antidote to all of the pathologies of modern living. Advertisements were the foot soldiers of the Orange Empire, marching forward into new territories and expanding its spheres of influence.

NATURE AND GENDER ON THE ORANGE CRATES

From the 1880s onward, oranges going east were conveyed in crates bearing colorful labels, labels that often featured California's landscape as a resplendent garden. One even turned the landscape quite literally into a brand (see figure 9). They were designed to catch the attention of buyers at auction points, but the fruit was often sold to consumers right out of these crates. As they reached for oranges, consumers would see pictures of idyllic, sun-drenched groves beneath purple mountains. Images of Yosemite's Half Dome or El Capitan abounded. In reality, the landscape they portrayed had been profoundly altered to meet human desires.

By the 1920s and 1930s, crate labels might feature a road with a motorcar making a leisurely errand into the wilderness. This crate design reflected the increased interest in automobile tourism and wilderness. *Sunset* recommended the automobile for the man "who thrills in an elemental contact with the reality of nature."[6] A striking example of the figure of the road into nature is a Big Tree label that depicts an actual site where a hole had been hewn in a giant sequoia big enough for a figure

Figure 9. To sell their oranges, growers associated their products
with the citrus landscape they created. Landscape brand label.
(Courtesy of Gordon McClelland.)

labeled "the pioneer" to drive a horse-drawn carriage through (allowing
him to pass through culture into nature and out again, in a kind of condensed performance of Turner's frontier process). In fact, Turner, who had
given his talk about the frontier in Chicago the year of the expo, could
have strolled over to the California building to do something just like this.
Not too far from the knight made of prunes was a forty-foot hull of a giant
sequoia fitted with a door. Visitors, like dwarves, could walk inside the
"big tree" and come away with the impression that nature in California
was, in truth, supernatural.

On crates and at garden shows, oranges were presented as pure products
of nature that would provide instant contact with California's therapeutic
environment. In its quest to replace oranges with nature, Sunkist's trump
card was of course the sun. Its first logo was a sunburst. Many crate labels
featured the sun as an orange globe, sometimes emblazoned with the name
Sunkist. One label depicted a spectacular "orangeset" off the Pacific coast.
Advertising copy referred to oranges and orange juice as "stored-up

sunshine." When it selected its trademark, the CFGE had made a psychological study of possible names and arrived at Sunkist as the most compelling.[7]

To chart this solar system of symbols, it may be useful to consider metaphoric versus metonymic uses of language. Metaphors establish relationships between objects that are in some way clearly separable (e.g., the lion is a king). Metonyms transfer meanings between things that are in some way contiguous. The question "Can I have the keys?" is metonymic: some part of a car is used to represent the whole. The trick of Sunkist advertising was to make metaphoric relationships seem metonymic. In bridging the gap between oranges and the sun, Sunkist made this relationship of difference more and more one of sameness. Indeed, the kiss of the sun signified that oranges really were in touch, or contiguous, with the solar body, establishing a metonymic connection between the orange and nature in its most primal and purest form. Thus, consumption of the orange would literally be getting in touch with nature, unmediated by any signs of culture; the consumer would also be sun-kissed.

In a world based on a solar theory of value, the work that growers did (or had done) would not just be regarded as valueless, it would be seen as denaturing the goods. The more hands the orange passed through, the more mediated the relationship between consumer and orange would become. The neat trick of absenting the grower and other laborers not only heightened the consumer's sense of communing with nature, it masked the working conditions from which the fruit emerged. Erasing the workers who brought the fruit to the consumer's lips made California an Eden in which fruits naturally materialized for the pleasure of people.

Women, however, were privileged as mediators between nature and consumer. One of the most frequent motifs in Sunkist advertising was of a woman's hand offering the fruit—the woman-as-Mother-Earth icon. She might be represented as a Victorian lady in the garden (as on the Lady brand label) or as a country maiden, healthy and close to the earth (as on the Sonia brand label). To heighten the association with nature, women were adorned with flowers. One label even pictured a female head growing out of the center of a flower. Such woman-flower hybrids conferred a double dose of pure nature on the oranges. One crate label featured the Shasta daisy, the perfect symbol of youth, innocence, wholesomeness, and pristine nature. Its striking whiteness underscored these attributes. But the daisy served as such a good symbol partly because what E. E. Cummings

Figure 10. If California was an Eden, it had to have its Eve—appropriately enough, one who bore some resemblance to Hollywood's Mary Pickford. California Eve brand label from the 1920s. (Courtesy of Gordon McClelland.)

called the "naughty thumb of science" had prodded nature into producing this appealing plant form. The Shasta daisy was no virgin: it had been burbanked. Flowers, however "tainted" they really were, nevertheless underscored the purity of the white lady and her associations with hearth, beauty, and family. Flowers had a special place in the private sphere, where, as Sunkist's narratives had it, women, food, beauty, and nature would commingle to create a healthy and happy environment.

But flowers and women could confer other, more robust meanings. The fruit-bearing woman was not only a maternal Gaia; she could also be sexy. Consider, for example, the California Eve label, on which a California girl named Eve sits on a wall by an overhanging orange tree (see figure 10). The orange tree is on the grounds of a mission, and in the background a padre has just come into the yard to survey the garden. This Eve (who looks very much like Hollywood's Mary Pickford) has pulled her red skirt up over her knees. She smiles into the eyes of the viewer as she reaches up

Figure 11. The motif of the woman's hand offering up oranges, and more, was common in citrus advertising. Have One brand label from the 1930s. (From author's collection.)

to pick an orange, which she will deposit with others in her lap. This California landscape rendered as a garden complete with its Eve was also alluring, a place of temptation—its fruit forbidden and for that reason all the more desirable. Condensed within the image is a message to abandon traditional restraints and join in a pleasurable world of consumption.

The sexualization of the fruit offering is taken to its furthest point on the Tesoro brand label, which features a woman dressed as a pirate—shorts ripped high, bare arms adorned with gold bracelets, a red sash around her waist—sitting astride a treasure chest on the beach of a desert island. A sailing ship displaying the Jolly Roger cuts through the waves just offshore. The woman has reached into the treasure chest between her legs and pulled out a golden fruit, seductively displaying it as an object of desire. The Have One label (see figure 11) represents a more stylized way of sexing the motif of the woman's hand. In a pamphlet on label designs, Sunkist singled out this label for special praise, noting that it is "a simple label which is suggestive of the box's contents and makes a good appeal to the consumer's appetite."[8] It was not explained just what kind of appetite was being appealed to, but the advertisement seems designed to meet more than one. The outstretched arm, adorned with a gold bracelet, offers a half-peeled orange, succulent and firm, and the consumer is urged to "have one." To have an orange is also to "have" a woman.

The motif of the woman's hand undergoes a revealing change between the crate labels (often created by individual growers) and its appearance on a billboard designed by Sunkist. On the billboard, the woman is a discerning consumer engaged in a pleasant inspection of the orange in her hand. She looks more like the New Woman of the 1920s than a neoclassical nymph. This more professional advertisement is designed to appeal to women as consumers. But if this ad is not about sex, it is still about romance—the romance of a relationship with a pastoral, wholesome nature. As early as 1916, Sunkist began to see oranges' "naturally-protected cleanliness" as "a powerful sales-compelling advantage." Explaining to growers the rationale behind advertisements placed in *The Saturday Evening Post* and other publications, Sunkist's advertising manager said, "We picture this well-liked, delicious-looking fruit in the process of being peeled by the housewife's own fingers; and we tell her 'your hands and only yours need ever touch the fruit inside Nature's germ-proof package.'"[9]

Associating women with nature and presenting oranges as if they were pure products of Eden implied that Sunkist was not a large, impersonal organization that rationalized the growing and selling of millions of boxes of oranges. Instead, it positioned itself as one that was intimately involved with the process of picking each piece of fruit and bringing it to the individual Sunkist called "Mrs. Consumer." Whether the image of the woman is naturalized, romanticized, or an object of desire, the motif of the woman's hand performs an ideological function similar to that of the sun-kissed orange: it is yet another way in which the field hands drop from sight. Again, we forget the worker in the field and the women in the factories sorting and packing fruits. But "invisible hands" have always played a large role in creating economic empires.

THE KISS OF ADVERTISING

There was of course a hand behind all of this attraction—that of the California Fruit Growers Exchange, which was created in August 1893.

Twenty-five years later, a Sunkist cartoon compared the event to the birth of the nation: like the fathers of the nation, the founders of the CFGE had met to "declare their freedom from commercial exploitation." Feeling that they were being robbed by middlemen—jobbers and packers—growers turned to cooperative marketing techniques to win freedom and gain control of a commercial empire.[10]

Like unions, the CFGE had three levels of organization: local, district, and central associations. Individual growers belonged to a local association (such as the Pasadena Orange Growers' Association). The locals were grouped into district exchanges. Above it all stood the central exchange. At first, the CFGE focused its energies on the problem of marketing in a narrow sense: How could growers most efficiently harvest their fruits and get them to market? It was actually a complicated issue. Railroads had opened the national market to Southern California by the mid-1880s, making it possible to ship oranges across the country in refrigerated cars. The picking of oranges of various sizes and grades had to be rationalized to produce a product that was, as Sunkist's advertising claimed, "uniformly good." In order to meet that challenge, the CFGE became essentially a vertically integrated corporation, developing an impressive managerial method for mapping out supply and demand across the nation. Getting the product to market was more than a challenge in physical communication. The complex operations that made the exchange of fruits possible and profitable were predicated on an exchange of words. By 1936, an estimated one and a half million words were circulated annually by teletype or telephone among Sunkist's fifty-seven sales offices in the United States, Canada, and Europe. These sales offices connected the landscapes of production in California with those of consumption in urban and rural spaces across the country.[11]

In addition to marketing upward of forty million crates of oranges each year, Sunkist also expanded the scope of its operations. In 1907, it formed the Fruit Growers Supply Company to provide packers with shooks for orange crates (about forty million board feet of wood went into crates each year). It bought a forest in Northern California for this purpose. The Growers Supply Company also offered members radios, tires, fertilizers, insecticides, and other products at wholesale costs. In the mid-1910s, Sunkist's Exchange By-Products Company developed markets for citric acid and bottled juice. The Citrus Protective League was Sunkist's lobbying arm. The league helped "obtain an agricultural college" (the Citrus Experiment Station), get higher lemon tariffs passed to protect growers from Italian competition, convince the Interstate Commerce Commission to lower railroad freight rates, and win passage of state quality standardization laws. These laws assured that higher-quality oranges were sent to the national market and put pressure on smaller growers, who were not as well equipped as Sunkist members to regulate the appearance of fruit.[12]

Sunkist's managerial practices required tremendous cooperation from individual growers. Sunkist told members in 1904 that the "citrus fruit grower is no longer independent of his neighbor as to marketing his crop, but each is dependent upon each other." Through cooperation, each grower, as an economist argued in an early study of the exchange, "can be made to feel that he is something larger than himself." Such producers' cooperatives were beginning to sprout up across the country as farmers grappled with the vicissitudes and complexity of marketing their products. To them, " 'Cooperation' became an almost mystical symbol of modern civilized life." The citrus growers who formed Sunkist were at the forefront of this movement. Sunkist soon became a much-touted success story in agricultural cooperation.[13]

The fruit growers' associations turned toward developing state- and nationwide markets for agricultural produce with the same kind of energy, expertise, and capital commanded by Ford or General Motors. Growers sang the "gospel of efficiency" and favored progressive, modernist positions over conservative agrarian ones. Sunkist managed to bring what Alfred D. Chandler called "the managerial revolution" into agriculture, and in so doing, make citrus growers indeed part of something larger than themselves—corporate capitalism. Value would be created not so much by an individual's labor in the soil but through cooperation. By eliminating waste, increasing efficiency, magnifying the scale and scope of operations, and applying scientific growing, managing, and marketing techniques, growers could also become captains of industry.[14]

In the contract between the central exchange and its seventeen districts, Sunkist explained that it was established "to encourage the improvement of the product and the package. To increase the consumption of citrus fruit by developing new markets and to aid in supplying all the people with good fruit at a reasonable price. To maintain an advertising bureau for the purposes of stimulating consumption and demand."[15] Sunkist thus committed itself to reconstructing the nature of the orange as well as the culture of its consumption. To accomplish this, it turned to "scientific salesmanship."

Traditionally, farmers had been wary of advertising; they tended to see it as an enormous con game. Images could not really add to the value of crops because all value came from labor, they reasoned. Paying money for advertising, therefore, would make about as much sense as blood-letting. Sunkist felt a need to constantly lead its individual members away from such retrograde thinking. During difficult times, growers' populist rhetoric would flash up to challenge both the value of advertising and Sunkist's cooperative organization. In the "Sunkist Courier" (a four-page section of the *California Citrograph*), the exchange was constantly justifying its advertising. Sunkist told and retold origin stories that portrayed advertising as the industry's white knight, bringing exponential growth in production while at the same time increasing or maintaining prices. To accept this story was to abandon the labor theory of value. Most growers came to accept the idea that advertising added value to their product in excess of what labor and nature had put in.

The key to its success, Sunkist maintained, lay in how it had reconstructed the orange to adapt it to market niches. As Don Francisco explained, Sunkist's first major campaign in 1907 was an "attempt to use the tools of the manufacturer on one of nature's perishable fruits." But conventional wisdom had held that "an orange was just an orange. It grew on a tree and when it was ripe somebody ate it. . . . An orange would resist any attempt to make it a particular orange." Furthermore, "Nature was a notably poor manufacturer when it came to turning out standardized fruits that were absolutely alike in size, appearance and eating quality." But since "orange growers were doing the planning," they were able to adapt nature to such industrial plasticity. Francisco insisted that nature's oranges could be reconfigured, mass-produced, and sold like any other commodity.[16]

Not only could advertisers work the magic of making the fruits of nature "a particular orange," they could make that single orange be hundreds of "particular" oranges. Francisco explained that citrus could be many things to many people: "A lemon is not one product but a group of totally different products. A lemon may be classed as a pie, a hair rinse, a cool drink, a hot drink, a garnish, a mouth wash, a vinegar or a skin bleach. The toilet and medicinal value of the lemon are alone sufficient to bring it fame." Sunkist persistently pushed citrus into the public eye, giving it a kind of celebrity status. Advertising, Sunkist argued, "creates new markets, new demands, new products, new ways of doing things, a better national life." But such magical changes would not come about if Californians simply held up their oranges. Instead, advertisers needed to learn to see such offerings from perspectives outside of California, so that they could figure out how to get potential consumers—"prospects," they called them—to re-envision oranges. "We get more inspiration from a day in New York . . . than we do in a week in the groves," Francisco said. In order to re-create "national life" through citrus advertising, Sunkist would have to both understand and re-create eastern markets—or better, eastern market *places.*[17]

Sunkist was a genius at product placement. Its iconography appeared almost everywhere: on the picturesque labels of the forty million crates of citrus shipped each year; on the sides of speedboats; on billboards, street cars, and railroad cars; in school curricula; in essay contests; in retail outlet displays; in pamphlets distributed by doctors; on the pages of America's most popular magazines, such as the *Saturday Evening Post;* and on the radio airwaves. All of these media carried new messages about oranges.

From the beginning, Sunkist emphasized that oranges weren't just luxuries, special fruit to be cherished at Christmas. The Sunkist message was that oranges should be eaten every day. Some growers wanted to establish "a national orange orgy. They would make it the duty of every one of the nation's ninety millions to dispose of at least one orange on this day." *Sunset* mused, "Imagine every man, woman, and child, unless excused by a doctor's prohibition, busily eating oranges—at home, in school, on the farm, in Wall Street, in the mines, in prison, at army posts—everywhere— all oranging themselves in great appreciation."[18] Though proposed in jest, the idea of an orange orgy enforced by authorities and health experts is nonetheless telling.

Since Sunkist cultivated relationships with doctors who saw oranges as a key to good health and efficient work (as we shall see), it is unlikely that many schoolchildren, prisoners, or mine workers would have been excused from eating a daily orange. Indeed, hospital patients in 1920 consumed one orange every three days, while people at large ate one every eight. Sunkist worked hard to make oranges standard fare at schools as well. It devised multifaceted plans to reach every possible consumer and retailer with the one-a-day gospel. Having put over $25 million into the effort by 1938, Sunkist could claim success in transforming oranges from special treasures to everyday necessities. "From veritable luxuries," Sunkist proclaimed, "citrus fruits have become necessaries of the daily diet."[19]

The omnipresence of the image of the orange prodded the nation into adopting the "orange habit." However colorful and alluring, crate labels alone could not create a national market. While many consumers did see the colorful labels in retail outlets, market research showed that less than a half a percent of them bought their oranges because of these labels. All publicity, including individual growers' labels, should be "so designed that they will 'cash in' . . . on the broad background painted by [Sunkist's] national advertising." While the labels did have "a billboard's opportunity to tell a story," Sunkist recognized that the power of its advertising campaign lay in its ability to paint, all across America, a broad background for its product.[20]

Sunkist used actual billboards to establish its presence in urban environments. "The successful advertising is obtrusive," one promoter of outdoor advertising proclaimed. Billboards, along with illustrated print ads, electrical signs, and shop window displays, were part of a "new visual media" that began to "occupy visual space through an onslaught of pictures . . . and change not only the way many people saw and understood goods but also how they lived in their society." Billboards were quite literally frames of reference. A pioneer in the field said that "sign boards are so placed that everyone must read them, and absorb them, and absorb the advertiser's lesson willingly or unwillingly. The constant reading of 'Buy Blank's Biscuits' makes the name part of one's sub-conscious knowledge."[21]

Since the late 1910s, the exchange had been filling in the blank with the name *Sunkist*. For the 1932–33 campaign, it put up 1,034 billboards in 11 urban markets. Every day thirty-five million people passed the signs, some of which occupied over a thousand square feet of vertical real estate. A million people passed the one in Times Square every day. The one at Coney Island spelled out *Sunkist* in ten-foot-high letters outlined in orange neon lights, assuring that the sign would work "day and night" and catch the attention of a hundred million people a year. "Wherever the largest groups of people congregate in Sunkist's most important markets," an in-house publication explained, "you find these great illuminated outdoor posters." Sunkist thus made itself present in the spaces of mass culture that were, as historian John Kasson puts it, "amusing the million."[22]

But Sunkist was not content to reach consumers only in their leisure time. It placed its message in streetcars to commune with commuters on their way to work. The placement of advertisements inside streetcars "permits the wide circulation of the Sunkist message." It "holds [prospects] for an average ride of 20 minutes, favoring the reading of the Sunkist message." Like the billboards, these advertisements—called "car cards"—were splashed with color, something Sunkist's market research had determined was a boon to food advertising. With its "blanket coverage . . . virtually the entire traveling public in New York and Chicago will be reached by Sunkist." Carried on half of the streetcars in the United States and Canada, such advertising had no equal for achieving "intimate contact of the Public." With twenty-one million passengers riding streetcars every day, this traffic in signs amounted to over seven billion encounters between "prospects" and the "Sunkist message" every year. Through billboards and streetcar cards, Sunkist created spaces in which to capture and hold the attention of people who seemed to be always on the move.[23]

The streetcar cards were meant to prime "prospects when they are en route to do their shopping." Once they reached the store, consumers found oranges that were carefully arranged to look alluring. Adeptly transforming the techniques used at fairs, Sunkist taught retailers to compose elaborate citrus arrangements in their store windows (see figure 12). In doing this, they were building on the work of L. Frank Baum. Before Baum became wealthy from his Oz stories (and went to California, where he bought an orange grove in Claremont), he pioneered the use of window displays. As historian William Leach argues, Baum made the Oz-like "landscape of glass" an integral part of the consumer "land of desire."[24]

Sunkist conjured the land of desire by filling store windows in cities with the vibrant colors of California's groves. In 1914, it established an Exchange Dealer Service to "educate and assist" grocery stores, restaurants, hotels, and soda fountains. Members of the service would visit outlets across the country, bringing with them display materials that would "reiterate Sunkist advertising messages in full color illustrations creating appetite appeal and suggesting varied uses at the point of consumer purchases." In 1916 alone, Sunkist representatives visited retail outlets in nine hundred cities and provided millions of pieces of display material to store operators. In its film *Partnership in Profits* (1932), Sunkist informed retailers that "nothing in food stores and markets is so enticing and colorful as large displays of California Oranges, Lemons and Grapefruit." Sunkist claimed that sales increased by as much as four times at shopping places where Baum's landscape of glass was combined with California's landscape

Figure 12. The art of window displays, pioneered by L. Frank Baum of *Oz* fame, was perfected by Sunkist. (LC H814-T01 2974-003. Courtesy of Library of Congress.)

of oranges. The efforts paid off: by 1940, half of all stores retailing citrus displayed California oranges in their windows.[25]

Sunkist quickly made alliances with the chain stores that by the late 1930s had largely displaced the older neighborhood grocery store. The older stores had operated in distinct neighborhoods, and their proprietors had been bound up in a system of moral as well as economic exchange with customers. The "Mom and Pop" in these groceries were, in a sense, the communities' fictive kin. But the chains "separated the store as commodity from its role as a community establishment." Shopping became less personal. While clerks in the neighborhood stores had procured the goods that customers wanted and had negotiated with them over price, the new stores operated on a fixed-price, self-service model. Shelves were filled with nationally advertised brands, prices often dropped but were fixed, and purchasers of food became consumers within a national market.[26]

When the *Saturday Evening Post* and the chain stores wanted to illustrate a "Parade of Progress of Nationally Advertised Grocery Products," they told a strange parable in which oranges figured prominently. The *Post* pictured two modern consumers walking into a grocery store. But something is not right. The old-time grocer is a ghostly figure, and when they ask for oranges, he is puzzled: "Oranges? We sell oranges only at Christmas time." These modern consumers have walked through a time warp and ended up in one of the old neighborhood stores, where nationally advertised brands are not available and oranges are a luxury that cannot be had year-round.[27]

Like other nationally advertised brands of food, Sunkist's mass-produced oranges sold well in modern supermarkets. Sunkist easily established its presence within these new commercial spaces. In turn, Safeway, one of the leading chains, regularly ran advertisements in the *California Citrograph* to build its relationship with growers. Safeway's "farm reporter" would tell the story of a real grower who appreciated the "genuine spirit of cooperation [that] exists today between producers and chain store distributors like Safeway." In 1936, Don Francisco (who had proved his mettle in the campaign to defeat Upton Sinclair in 1934) was put in charge of the effort to defeat a populist initiative proposing a tax on chain stores. Speaking before a group of growers, Francisco acknowledged that there had traditionally been conflicts "between producers of farm products and those who place these products in the hands of consumers." But he maintained that "the chain stores and farmers should be natural allies." Indeed, they were. Both were interested in maximizing consumption and rationalizing marketing. Chain stores, Francisco pointed out, "eliminate unnecessary handling and in-between expenses and operate a straight line between producer and consumer."[28] The chains got a steady supply of a product consumers were predisposed to buy, and Sunkist had access to the sites where their oranges would fall into the "hands of the consumers."

The chains worked with Sunkist to establish an efficient flow of oranges from groves to consumers by making it possible to extend advertising into the market place, where consumers, in picking up the orange, were entering into, and completing, a story told to them in images and words over and over again. The store was the site at which such stories, composed as they were of fantasy elements, truly came to life.

Just as displays behind glass could increase sales, Sunkist discovered that offering oranges in a glass could do so as well. In 1916, Francisco's "drink an orange" campaign began in earnest. Sunkist quickly developed its own electrically powered juice extractor and offered it at cost to fountain operators. By 1932, some 66,000 juicers were in operation and Sunkist could rightly claim that drinking orange juice "has been developed into a national habit." Marketing its juice as a superior alternative to "artificial" beverages, Sunkist was able to steal some of the lines Coca-Cola and other soft drink companies had once used to sell their mixtures. Coca-Cola, which was caught up in the scandal over patent medicines and pure foods, had been forced to cease advertising its beverage as a "nerve tonic" and all-around curative nostrum. But Sunkist, untouched by the Pure Food and Drug Act's restrictions, advertised its product as "Purity 'Bottled By Nature.'" Sunkist presented its juice extractors as veritable fountains of youth. Juice was "*good* and good for you—helps to *keep the body young!*"[29]

By creating the "juice habit," Sunkist built demand for its beverage at soda fountains, which were often decked out with an array of colorful Sunkist placards. By the mid-1930s, more than seven million boxes of Sunkist oranges were being consumed annually as juice—one box out of every five. In 1928, sales of orange juice totaled $55 million at over 100,000 cafes and soda fountains, making it second only to Coca-Cola. It was an important victory for Sunkist to establish its presence at soda fountains, which Coca-Cola, among others, had advertised as exciting places where glamorous young people met and mixed. Indeed, in the era of Prohibition, the soda fountain was an important site where youth culture took shape. Here, as elsewhere, Sunkist exported the presence of California's orange groves and secured for them an influential place in the public sphere. Sunkist's campaigns were designed to win over territory in which oranges would be represented or consumed. "Just before the heavy navel shipments came on, New York city was attacked," read one memo explaining the advertising department's colonial efforts. "Every street and avenue on Manhattan Island running in both directions was thoroughly canvassed and displays placed in 1445 retail windows."[30]

In any environment, humans will both create and seek out symbols. Symbols, as anthropologist Victor Turner observes, sometimes derive from markers used to find one's way in a dense forest. For the Ndembu people of Zambia, for instance, the word for symbol comes from the term for "to blaze a trail." Such symbolic landmarks may then take on more and more significance. Fruitful trees, for example, may become part of rituals designed to celebrate and augment female fertility, and the trees may then come to stand for motherhood, nurturance, and female solidarity. Alternatively, fruitful trees may be used in rituals designed to help hunters, since the emergence of the fruit is associated with making game "visible" in the dense forest. Symbols do more than convey meaning, for "they are determinable influences inclining persons and groups to action." In this manner, an environment full of natural objects becomes a forest of symbols, and wilderness is transformed into a public sphere.[31]

In the three decades before World War II, Sunkist's advertising campaigns created landmark symbols for people in cities across America. Competing with other advertisers, Sunkist tried to dominate the process through which city dwellers made their urban jungles into a forest of symbols, implanting a diverse crop of signs showing the way to those sites—the soda fountain and the grocery store—where wages could be exchanged for golden treasures (that is, where game became visible). Many no doubt ignored or resisted the sense of place the advertisers worked hard to create, but many others, as increasing rates of consumption attested, found themselves moving through their cities in patterns charted by Sunkist's treasure maps.[32]

A "PATH TO THE HOUSE OF THE CONSUMER": SUNKIST IN THE PRIVATE SPHERE

Sunkist's efforts to blaze trails in the public sphere were concentrated in areas where people congregated. But its larger goal was to reach all prospects, "from the illiterate mountaineer of the Blue Ridge to the College Professor in Maine and California." To touch them with the kiss of advertising, Sunkist devised an effective strategy to reach them in their homes. William Geissinger, Sunkist's advertising manager from 1925 to 1933, explained that "the producer now beats his own path to the house of the consumer through the medium of advertising."[33]

Geissinger ridiculed the "producer who thinks he can reach the consumer without a systematic and well planned campaign in advertising and merchandising." Sunkist was at the forefront of such well planned marketing. Francisco had pioneered the use of consumer surveys in 1916, when he visited Chicago and several small Midwestern towns to make what he called a "test tube analysis." He went "from door to door asking questions. He wanted to find what people ate, what they read, what they thought about, what influences affected them and why they took various publications." But Francisco's marketing sociology stopped at the door of the house. A decade later Geissinger had his researchers go right in. Inventories of household cupboards were taken; fifteen thousand families representing the "stratas of humanity" were intimately surveyed. By the early 1930s, Sunkist had collected a mountain of data reflecting not just what consumers said they preferred but what they actually did with their dollars. It developed population maps of the country containing statistics on income, literacy, car and telephone ownership, and retail outlets. Sunkist kept track of the demographics of gender and age, of rural and urban residency. It knew that women spent 71 percent of the food dollar. It knew that urban dwellers, who made up 59 percent of the total population, spent 70 percent of the $9.7 billion spent on food every year. It knew that the use of color in food advertising was particularly appealing. Like Santa Claus, Sunkist seemed to know if people were naughty or nice—and if they were pouting, it would offer oranges as relief. Holiday advertisements portrayed oranges as "Santa Claus' most *healthful* gift."[34]

Marketing had indeed become a science. Turning its analysis into maps, charts, tables, and instructive narratives, Sunkist had created for itself an "ethnography" of American culture. The sociologists of selling were able to get inside the skin of consumers, to discover how they thought, and to make oranges a part of that thinking. Sunkist was searching for ways make its orange stories meaningful to all kinds of people.

Sunkist found mass-circulation magazines an ideal medium to spread the word—and image. By 1903, *Ladies' Home Journal* had achieved a circulation of one million, and other slicks would soon follow. The success of such magazines rested largely on advertising, and vice versa. Advertising subsidized the magazines, reducing the price to a level far below the cost of production. Publishers realized that readers could give them something far more valuable than their coins: their attention. National advertisers would pay handsomely for the chance to place their pitches before the eyes of a million or more readers. In 1926, a four-color full-page ad in the *Saturday Evening Post* cost $11,500 but would reach some ten million people. The *Post* "was created to echo and reinforce in its contents the emerging concept of America as a nation unified by the consumption of standardized commodities."[35] By the mid-1910s, Sunkist had entered into a symbiotic relationship with mass-circulation magazines: they served as ideal vehicles for carrying its stories about its "uniformly good oranges" into millions of homes.[36]

Sunkist ran its first national advertisement in the *Post* in 1914. Readers learned that in California the orange trees "receive scientific soil cultivation—they are supplied with just enough water, at just the right time—the sheltering mountains, the warm sunshine and the balmy Pacific, all combine to yield an orange of royal excellence." These "perfect" products of science and nature were "never touched by bare hands" for "each picker and packer wears white cotton gloves." These "cleanest of fruits" were thus made safe to enter the home. Readers were encouraged to bring them in by the box, for eating "them for breakfast, for lunch, for dinner and in between times" would, according to a Dr. Wiley, "save many a doctor bill." Silver premiums (such as spoons) were offered in exchange for Sunkist wrappers. Sunkist wanted people to demand oranges by name, and they did so to get the premiums, catapulting Sunkist into the role of largest silverware dealer in the world. There was also an offer for a free recipe book describing "27 delightful ways to serve 'Sunkist' Oranges." In just two years, 300,000 such recipe books were delivered to American homes. Readers were thus invited to write themselves into the Sunkist story—by sending off for the recipe book, by sending in wrappers, by buying oranges, by buying the copy.[37]

Sunkist, working with the ad agency Lord & Thomas, regularly began placing advertisements in such magazines as the *Ladies' Home Journal, Good Housekeeping,* and the *National Sunday Magazine.* In the 1919–20 season, ads in eleven magazines reached a total of 119 million subscribers. In 1929, 300 million Sunkist ads ran off the presses. Sunkist designed its ads and selected its media to reach five groups: professional men, homemakers, social leaders, doctors and nurses, and teachers. The advertisements aimed at males (which tended to emphasize the positive effects that drinking orange juice had on job performance and health) might appear in the *Saturday Evening Post* or *Literary Digest,* while those directed at women (emphasizing the importance of oranges to children's health and illustrating ways to serve oranges) would run in *McCall's, Ladies' Home Journal,* or *Good Housekeeping.* The company ran ads in such publications as the *Journal of Home Economics, Normal Instructor,* and the *American Journal of Nursing* to reach educators and health care professionals. Sunkist seemed to have a call for every calling.[38]

It also put its voice on the airwaves. In 1928, it launched its first program on the NBC Red Network, reaching an audience of fifteen million. The decision to put Sunkist on the air was not reached easily, however. Paul Armstrong, Sunkist's general manager, disagreed with Geissinger's decision to go on the air. He felt that commercials on radio were an unwarranted intrusion into the haven of the home. At the time, many professional advertisers shared this opinion. In 1925, *Printer's Ink,* the advertising industry magazine, proclaimed, "The family circle is not a public place, and advertising has no business intruding there unless it is invited [as with periodicals]." But this wall between public and private spheres would crumble by the early 1930s. The attractions of radio overwhelmed moral qualms about going into the home. Radio offered the possibility of achieving mass distribution of commercial messages while creating a feeling of intimacy between the individual and the salesperson. Radio could "deny its own status as a *mass* medium" because it "carried the human voice into the privacy of the home, to the center of the revered family circle." By combining entertainment with commercial appeals, advertisers could place their products inside the home and make them part of the fabric of life.[39]

In 1929, Sunkist began sponsoring a program that used the allure of Hollywood as an entrée into potential consumers' homes. Hosted by Louella Parsons, Sunkist's show featured guest stars from the silver screen and spun out an endless stream of Hollywood gossip. Interwoven with the entertainment were Parsons' pitches for oranges. After sponsorship for Parsons' program was taken up by a soap company, Sunkist developed another program called "Hedda Hopper's Hollywood." Initially carried on twenty-eight CBS stations, the program played in Portland, Pittsburgh, and Peoria. Sunkist was delighted that it cost it only $2.91 to reach a thousand families through this broadcast. Its map of the broadcasting range showed two-thirds of the nation covered, including, as Sunkist had intended, both rural and urban places.[40]

A contest inaugurated the show. Listeners were invited to complete the sentence "I use Sunkist California Oranges because . . ." and send in their entries along with six Sunkist wrappers ("That means business!" exclaimed a Sunkist ad announcing the program to growers and retailers). The prize was a trip for two to Hollywood. With its "glimpses of Hollywood personalities together with dramatic sketches of the careers of the screen personalities," Hopper's show was "a California program for California products." By sponsoring the show, Sunkist put an ingenious twist on the notion of product placement. In 1940, the program's audience was invited to enter a new contest: to name the Sunkist orange groves owned by film star Fred MacMurray. Entrants, who again had to send in six Sunkist trademarks, made the "family circle" part of the larger circulation of oranges and images. The tissue papers bearing Sunkist's stamp were gathered up by people mailing in their names for the groves, thus quite literally writing themselves into the stories of glamour, health, and idyllic nature associated with the Sunkist product. Hedda Hopper's Hollywood, like all of Sunkist advertising, was about offering a fantasy landscape of citrus and California to people living in places far from that fabricated Eden and, for that reason, all the more attracted to it.[41]

Sunkist was proud of the mark it placed on public and private spheres. It saw advertising not as a way of shoving things down people's throats, but as a means of giving people what they wanted or enlightening them as to their true wants. It would simply present the "facts" in an "educational campaign" and increased consumption would follow. Occasionally, though, a different image would appear on the pages of the "Sunkist Courier." One cartoon, titled "Speaking of Nav(a)l Appropriations," pictured a battleship firing blasts from its guns, which were labeled "posters," "car cards," "newspapers," and "magazines." In another, a football player runs down the field toward goal posts wrapped into the shape of a dollar sign, while fellow players, labeled "Billboard," "Car Card," and "Magazine Advertising," knock down opposing players named "Sales Resistance." Usually a less rough relationship was portrayed: Sunkist pictured itself as gaining access to "Mrs. Consumer's" office while other "non-advertised brands" are forced to wait, or as dancing with a woman embodying "the market."[42]

Though Sunkist advertisers used every line to seduce this dance partner, they sincerely believed that their work was socially beneficent. If they were agents of empire, they saw themselves as working to create an emancipatory regime, for they were quite certain that the consumption of oranges would enhance people's daily lives. Proud of their manipulations, they nonetheless saw them as part of a larger educational project with a "moral purpose." Identifying with Progressive reformers, advertisers, as one historian explains, "claimed to be stabilizing a steady movement toward a secular millennium . . . [and held] the regnant fantasy that 'we' (the managerial elite in question) had acquired the capacity to predict and control 'them' (the consumers) through 'social science.'" In a Sunkist pamphlet distributed to its growers for free, Don Francisco employed this ideology to celebrate his work:

When we know specifically that cooperative advertising has widened markets, stimulated industry, stabilized selling, improved merchandise and lowered costs; when we know that it has been used to make us take better care of our eyes, live better, read more good books, put more money in the bank, and give more to the church . . . I do not think that we can doubt that cooperative advertising is not only a powerful sales force, but a social service as well.[43]

Just as Progressive reformers aimed at improving home life, and thus national life, by making the home a more hygienic and efficient place, advertisers came to see their efforts to join the "family circle" in the home as constructive visits rather than destructive intrusions. Advertising was portrayed as a "social service," part of a larger program of social engineering designed to improve American culture from the inside out.[44]

Sunkist president Charles Collins Teague, featured in an advertising campaign designed to "counteract the attempts of certain groups to destroy consumer confidence in advertising" during the Depression, explained in a spot in *Woman's Home Companion* that "advertising may appear selfish, for its purpose, of course, is to sell. But the only kind of advertising that pays . . . is the kind that benefits *everybody*."[45] The winner-take-all game of football did not really capture Sunkist's understanding of its relationship with consumers; the image of the ballroom dance serves better. Radio and magazines provided the means for Sunkist to leave its calling card in the home of the prospective dance partner. Advertisers thus cast their work of social engineering as an innocent seduction, with the consummation of the partners' attractions leading to a harmless yet exhilarating exchange—a stolen kiss.

"ORANGES FOR HEALTH"

Sunkist's sense of public mission rested on its firm faith, backed up by research it sponsored, that California's oranges improved the health of consumers and the body politic. They were, as Sunkist's director of nutritional research put it, "virtual medicines." Sunkist wanted "to increase the consumption of citrus fruits because we know we are performing a public service, a public health service to be more exact, by encouraging people to purchase our product."[46]

The association of oranges with health goes far back. Shortly after the voyages of James Cook in the eighteenth century, the British navy began issuing citrus to its sailors to prevent scurvy, earning its sailors the nickname "limeys." In the nineteenth century, some authors prescribed oranges as a remedy to a host of ailments, including malaria. E. J. Wickson was expressing the conventional wisdom when he wrote that "semi-tropical fruits are nature's demonstration of the existence in a place of a climate which promotes health, comfort and a maximum of physical and intellectual attainment in mankind."[47] But such salubrious benefits could be exported in the package of the orange.

Inheriting the booster's Edenic portraits of California's nature, Sunkist used scientific research to configure oranges as veritable fountains of youth. With urban populations swelling and the frontier officially closed, many reformers had worried that Americans, deprived of sunlight and the challenges of the frontier, might degenerate. John Muir had presented California's wilderness as the antidote for "tired, nerve-shaken, overcivilized people." "Awakening from the stupefying effects of the vice of over-industry and the deadly apathy of luxury," he wrote in 1901, "they are trying as best they can to mix their own little ongoings with those of Nature, and get rid of rust and disease."[48] One did not need to go west, though, to mix one's "ongoings with those of Nature." In the form of the orange, the curative effects of nature could travel to those suffering from the "rust" of modern life. To eat an orange was to imbibe the spirit of the land, to be lifted momentarily from the city sidewalks of Chicago or Boston and placed in the paradise of California's resplendent valleys.

In 1907, Sunkist launched its first major campaign to amplify the message that oranges were good for consumers. Sunkist's president secured from growers a $10,000 allocation—an unheard-of amount for an agricultural cooperative—that was matched dollar for dollar by the Southern Pacific. Iowa was selected as the target. Special trains crossed the state carrying banners reading "Oranges for Health—California for Wealth." With this catchy slogan linking monetary and bodily prosperity, Sunkist started to make oranges almost synonymous with health. Lantern slide shows of California orange groves were presented. Newspapers promoted the special orange train. A Sunkist cartoon showed a young girl in a sundress with flowers in her hair ("Miss California") passing on the condensed sunshine of an orange to an Iowa lad bundled up with mittens and ear muffs.[49]

The winner of a poetry contest sponsored by Sunkist in 1908 wrote of a magical place where oranges "grow amidst the peace and plenty" and where

All the brightness of the sunshine
All the glow of hidden golden fields

All the dew from healing herbs
Are by cunning nature blended
In this fruit of golden hue.[50]

The poet expressed the central themes of the Sunkist story as it would take shape in the next four decades: California's Eden-like nature imbues oranges with a special, vitalistic quality; oranges, "by cunning nature blended," are restorative; the "peace and plenty" in which they are grown may be passed on to the consumer; eat one a day and you too can experience the therapy of "this fruit of golden hue." The word *health* appeared all over Sunkist's advertisements. Some interjected *Health* in italics between *Sunkist* and *Oranges* to create an indelible ligature between the fruit and well-being. Oranges came "*fresh* from California for Vigorous Health." "Health Begins at Breakfast," the ads declared, with "Sunkist *Health Oranges* for Juice," which "Builds Robust Bodies"; oranges are simply a "Big Help to Health."[51]

Sunkist turned to medical science to back these claims and deny that it had simply invented the therapeutic character of oranges to sell them. By 1918, for example, Sunkist claimed, somewhat defensively, "That the familiar phrase, Oranges for health, is founded on medical fact and is not merely a so-called 'catch-phrase,' valuable only for its advertising appeal, is being proved almost daily."[52] Science would show that the connection to health was natural, simply there in the fruit. "Catch phrases" backed up by science proved very good indeed for producing "advertising appeal." Sunkist found ways to stretch the truth without ever making false claims. Francisco maintained, "We stuck to the truth; and if there was any doubt about a claim, we omitted it, or we waited until we could back it up. We had doctors and dieticians behind us."[53] There was nonetheless an insidious circularity to Sunkist's health claims. It often funded research in nutritional science that yielded certain findings, which Sunkist in turn promoted, inflated, and then defended by pointing to the fact that scientists had discovered them.

Between the mid-1910s and World War II, the science of foods went through a sea change. While Progressives had earlier awoken the American public to the dangers of foods that were ill prepared or impure, the "Newer Nutritionists" began to point to particular foods as being "protective" and providing positive elements for growth and health. Breakthroughs were achieved in isolating vitamins and in relating diet to biological processes. Sunkist was quick to put any of this new knowledge, or proto-knowledge, to its own use. As early as 1918, Sunkist was passing on the advice of Dr. J. H. Kellogg, who claimed that the "arrest of growth" of bottle-fed babies could be overcome by supplementing an infant's diet with orange juice. A devout advocate of vegetarianism, Kellogg's research had also linked meat-eating to masturbation. Kellogg recommended orange juice in treating fevers and advised that oranges were a good source of "vitamines." The presence of vitamin C in citrus was inferred in the early 1920s.[54]

This gave Sunkist just the thing it wanted—a new and mysterious presence in its product about which it could educate the public. Sunkist ingeniously presented educational narratives that simultaneously aroused fear of dietary deficiency and offered relief with its unique remedy. In a 1922 *Saturday Evening Post* ad, Sunkist warned, "It's You, Madam, who are most concerned with Vitamines." Hailed as the "'Health-Commissioner' of the home," housewives were informed that "according to all modern authorities [vitamins] are essentials to good health."[55] Fortunately, "Mother Nature has bottled pure water in citrus fruits in a germ-proof container." Not only is this natural mix of water and fruit "delicious" and better than "artificial beverages," "it plays an important part in the control of fevers . . . pneumonia, flu and common colds." One advertisement claimed that "Vitamin C is the anti-infection vitamin that is so important to normal growth and the development of sturdy bones and sound teeth. . . . C is needed each day." Physicians and nutritionists agreed that everyone could use a little orange juice, even infants. Transforming vitamin C into a daily requirement by linking it with a meal, Sunkist said, "Oranges are your richest practical source of breakfast-Vitamin C." When it became possible to measure the amount of vitamins in food in the early 1930s, Sunkist tested Florida oranges against its own Washington navels. It turned out that the Washington navels were "22% richer in vitamin C," as Sunkist's ad copy and billboards announced. Sunkist oranges, therefore, give "you more health for your money." But this claim outran the knowledge, since vitamin C had been proven helpful only in preventing scurvy.[56]

The new nutritionists and home economists, often supported by research money from Sunkist, "helped create a national vogue for oranges, grapefruits, and lemons." Elmer McCullom, the dean of the new nutritionists, propagated another important theory concerning the healthful benefits of oranges. He believed that consuming different foods created either acid or alkaline effects in the body. Sunkist seized on the idea, educating the American public that "acidosis" would be caused by "eating freely of such good and necessary foods as cereals, bread, fish, eggs, and meat—all of which are of the acid-forming type—without sufficient fruit, vegetables and milk to balance them." Oranges were thus sutured to such dietary staples as meat and eggs, so that the everyday consumption of citrus would become as natural as eating one's daily bread.[57]

Without balance, people might lose "punch" at the office. Good things came from being in acid-alkaline balance. Since "good health is magnetism, it wins people to you, makes it easier for you to influence others." But developing acidosis, and leaving this condition untreated, could send one down a slippery slope to bad health, bad disposition, and, ultimately, serious disease of mind and body: "Unpleasant symptoms, such as headache, listlessness, acid mouth, sour stomach, acid sweat, sleeplessness and 'sour disposition,' frequently accompany acidosis and this condition is thought to make the body more susceptible to colds, and to lead to more serious diseases." Severe cases of acidosis *can* in fact lead to serious health problems, but these cases are caused by kidney failure, the ingesting of poisons like antifreeze, or, ironically, overdoses of vitamin C. Acidosis is also a possible side effect of diabetes (but oranges would be an unsuitable remedy because the sugar in them would be dangerous to a diabetic). Acidosis is a real and dangerous malady, but diet has little or nothing to do with it. The body normally regulates acid-alkaline balance through the kidneys, lungs, and blood. The effectiveness of the advertising lay not in the accuracy of its depiction of a disease and its cure, but in how it played into people's desires for a more healthful, energetic life. Like neurasthenia, acidosis fed on preexisting cultural anxieties about loss of vigor in the modern, corporate, machine-driven world. Sunkist situated its advertising in such a way as to play into and profit from these anxieties and desires for relief within a new "therapeutic culture" fixated on personal growth.[58]

Sunkist took special care to tell stories of how citrus promoted the healthy growth of children. As Francisco recalled, "In the first years we advertised orange juice for babies, the reason for that being that a mother will probably dip deeper into her budget to buy a product that is good for her baby than she will for one that is good for herself or her husband." Ads regularly featured mothers feeding their children oranges or juice, with headlines like "Above All Else, Watch His Food," or "He'll Thank You When He's Grown."[59]

The Sunkist pamphlet "Feeding the Child for Health," which was distributed by the thousands to "parents, teachers and child health workers," recommended a child drink at least 1.6 ounces of orange juice a day for every 10 pounds of weight. In 1939, a "Home and Household" feature in *California Citrograph* pictured the properly developing child standing on a scale, arrows pointing to "muscles firm," "trunk well proportioned," and "proper weight for height-age." The accompanying article outlined all of the health benefits of oranges—promoting growth, protecting against scurvy, colds, and scarlet fever, aiding in the development of perfect teeth and bone structure, and, of course, counteracting acidosis. The following year Sunkist timed a campaign pushing the link between oranges and "normal" growth to coincide with the U.S. Children's Bureau's National Baby Week. Twenty thousand sets of posters were distributed. One pictured an infant displaying the "normal development of the body," and a second featured a "growth and health diagram." At the local grocery store, mothers encountered Sunkist displays featuring pictures of a baby standing tall on an oversized orange. "Build now for sound teeth, sturdy bones and vigorous health," they were told.[60]

Sunkist raised the specter of the ill-fed child and offered the solution: "A child that is underweight, lacking in vitality, nervous, fretful . . . is undernourished. An orange a day . . . has been found especially valuable in helping underweight children gain weight." A parent had only to buy oranges and his or her child's thinness and listlessness could be replaced with healthy bulk and vigor. Sunkist's "parable of the skinny kid" (as one historian calls this marketing strategy) disciplined parents into accepting the word of experts and deploying it as a child-rearing practice.[61] Parents were being educated to create the proper dietary, exercise, and sleep régimes for their children.

But the power, money, and desires of Sunkist and other food producers had deeply shaped the nutritional knowledge of the day. Sunkist "fostered and supported the research" conducted at the University of California and elsewhere that established the dietary value of oranges, as its advertising manager noted in his article "Sunkist Aids Science—Now Doctors Help Sell Oranges." Geissinger modestly explained, "We are only advertisers, not scientists. We can't shout these things to the world until the research workers who whisper them have tested, weighed and proved beyond doubt their discoveries." But Sunkist whispered a research agenda into the ears of these scientists and shouted its own interpretations of the results, using the legitimacy of science as a microphone and purchasable space in the media as an auditorium. Sunkist used medical authority—indeed, the endorsement of "3000 physicians"—to bolster its claims that oranges, "potent with fresh vitamines," were essential ingredients for "proper growth and health." The daily eating of oranges should be a "household rule," one 1922 ad in *Good Housekeeping* instructed (see figure 13).[62]

We asked

3000 Physicians

about

Orange Juice for Babies

WE wish at all times to give information to mothers about the value of orange juice as a baby food. But in a matter so important we don't depend on our own knowledge. We go straight to the doctors for advice, then pass it along to you.

We have lately done that—asked 3000 physicians to tell us the main reasons why orange juice is given to babies. Here is the remarkable result:

Practically all agree that there are three reasons: 1. For the *vitamine* content—needed especially where pasteurized milk is used. 2. Because orange juice is a *natural laxative*. 3. For the orange's salts and acids, which are aids to good digestion.

Many stated their views at length in an enthusiastic manner, which we will quote to you if you wish.

IF you are not feeding your baby orange juice, we urge you only to ask *your* physician if you *should*. Every sensible woman abides by the result of what her own doctor tells her.

We do want to leave this thought with you, however, on the subject of the family's food and vitamines:

Vitamines, as you no doubt know, are the newly discovered elements in food which are considered vitally necessary to proper growth and health. Children especially seem to need them, and orange juice is potent with fresh vitamines.

Heating frequently destroys vitamines, so pasteurized milk is likely to be deficient in them. Likewise some of our common foods, due to ordinary cooking. Even mother's milk sometimes is said to lack the proper content, because the mother does not eat the proper food.

Physicians for years knew that scurvy and other malnutrition diseases were due to some lack in food and they prescribed orange juice, which proved to supply the lack, in thousands of cases, long before they ever heard of vitamines by name.

Vitamines, therefore, are elements in food, which not only the baby, but every member of your family must get with the daily meals. The body doesn't store vitamines as it does certain other elements in food. You need a fresh supply every day.

There's a simple way to insure it. Serve orange juice or a halved orange at breakfast

In the days of sailing vessels scurvy was prevalent among all sailors, due to a lack of fresh, green foods at sea. An English law made it obligatory to carry lemons or lemon or lime juice on all voyages. That is why these sailing vessels of other days were often called "Lime Juicers." The ship's doctor of that day knew that lemons prevented or cured scurvy. The modern scientist has proven that it is the VITAMINES in the lemons that were effective.

or an orange salad or fresh orange dessert at lunch or dinner, orange in some form at least once daily the year 'round.

If you do you'll secure a regular vitamine supply in a most delicious form. The family will like it and be better for it, so make it a household rule.

We pack tender, juicy, practically seedless oranges under the Sunkist grade. If you want to be sure of uniformly good oranges daily, ask your dealer for this kind.

We will send on request a book of orange and lemon recipes. Also a small folder on the subject of vitamines.

Sunkist
Uniformly Good Oranges

Lemons and oranges, although known as "acid fruits," have an alkaline reaction when taken into the system and are, therefore, valuable in offsetting excess acidity due to acid-producing foods.

California Fruit Growers Exchange
A Non-Profit, Co-operative Organization of 10,500 Growers
Dept. 366, Los Angeles, California

September 1922 Good Housekeeping

Figure 13. Sunkist used medical authority to bolster its claims that oranges, "potent with fresh vitamines," were essential ingredients for "proper growth and health." (From *Good Housekeeping* [September 1922]: 144. Courtesy of University of Washington Library.)

Sunkist also used scientific legitimacy to gain access to captive consumers by establishing orange juice programs in schools. Sunkist worked hard to win over the minds of children as well. By developing school curricula and distributing it for free, Sunkist went under the heads of parents to reach children directly. Wall charts, textbooks, and coloring books for younger children were advertised to teachers in professional journals. By 1932, 800,000 copies of the text designed for younger children had been distributed, and 40,000 copies of the more advanced text were being sent to teachers annually. Schoolchildren were thus "told the story of oranges from the time the young trees are planted until the ripe fruit reaches the market." Having also absorbed Sunkist's list of "Good Health Rules," these children might very well have brought the knowledge home to their parents.[63]

The child playing with building blocks was a recurring motif in citrus ads. Sometimes parents could be seen in the background, watching over their toddler, who was learning the skills required for participating in the building of culture. Among the blocks was an orange. Through children, Sunkist's semiotic practices linked the simple act of consuming oranges to the culture's hopes of creating a healthful and vital society. Sunkist helped write a kind of bildungsroman—a parable of the skinny nation. Without oranges, Americans would be vulnerable to disease, their children would be underdeveloped, businessmen would lack the proper "punch" to get the job done, and such everyday problems as headaches might prevent Americans from performing a whole host of activities vital to both production and reproduction. By using the legitimating stories of medical science and playing on cultural fears of disease, Sunkist configured nature's oranges as a vital ingredient for the health and growth of the nation. Sunkist got people around the country to know and need its fruits through these stories, creating habitats for habits.

MAGIC KINGDOM

In the mid-1950s, orange groves in Anaheim were razed to make space for a very special landscape—Disneyland. This was a dramatic event in the postwar decline of citrus growing in Southern California, when it became more profitable to grow the new crop, houses. Disneyland is now taken as evidence that the real world has been lost, replaced with one that is immaterial, magic, "hyperreal."[64] But Disneyland's Main Street U.S.A. did not replace some authentic enclave of Arcadian farmers living off the soil, enjoying the fruits of the earth, and cultivating a Jeffersonian democracy. Entertainment and spectacle did not simply replace agriculture and substance—and besides, Sunkist put up two Citrus Houses in Disneyland, adapting the former landscape of production to consumption.

The golden fruits of California's orchards are in some ways like the fireflies in the Pirates of the Caribbean attraction: both are artifactual, meaning-laden, consumer-oriented, profit-driven, neon-enhanced, and spectacular. The real groves in California had always depended on magic kingdoms across the country: fairs of all kinds, chain stores with their window displays, Times Squares and Coney Islands, soda fountains and the colorful pages of national magazines. Disney and Sunkist were natural partners. As early as the 1920s, Donald Duck and Mickey Mouse had gotten in on the act of promoting oranges at the San Bernardino National Orange Show. In a description that seems to prefigure Disneyland, one visitor in 1939 noted the orange show's "manikins of Joan Crawford and Marlene Dietrich lolling in the lawn chairs among garden paths laid out with lemons and grapefruit, and pretty-boy Clark Gable in neat white flannels and open-throat shirt under a fake orange tree glistening with two large golden globes. . . . [The fair] showed such gorgeous taste, and yet such hybrid mixtures, that at bottom it was garish . . . largely boosterism run amuck." To top it off, Indian students from Riverside's Sherman Institute performed tribal dances daily, perhaps modifying the first acorn celebrations to herald instead the fruits of empire.[65]

If modern agriculture is a kind of imperialism, as Alfred Crosby, Donald Worster, and Frieda Knobloch have argued in different ways, then we must recognize that it has created an empire composed of both land and images.[66] Sunkist advertising created and colonized spaces in which the growers could hold the bodies of consumers. It is no accident that we call the work of advertisers *campaigns:* like the military variety, they are battles over space, designed to gain control over the *campagne,* or country. Through images and stories, the landscapes of production and consumption were colonized and connected.

When consumers reached for the oranges they had seen advertised, they were pulling images out of the world of simulation and making real connections, however misunderstood, with California's landscape. Like the growers, advertisers and consumers both had a hand in creation. Thus, the domain of the Orange Empire cannot be fathomed simply by measuring the lands that grew orange trees in California. To the some three hundred thousand acres given over to the fruit by the mid-1930s, we must add the real estate of billboards and supermarket fruit displays; to the volume of insecticides sprayed in the groves, we must figure in the radio airtime given to Sunkist; to the limbs of the fourteen million trees, we must attach the hundred million pulp pages that each year carried Sunkist's colorful stories into homes across the country.

The images created carefully for those spaces of consumption reached back to shape the landscapes in which oranges were grown. The emphasis on uniformity, purity, and "natural" beauty led to the regimentation of nature in California. The gap between advertising's representations and reality created a problem. To give the consumer spotless oranges, Sunkist committed itself to producing blemish-free fruit. "We told people that an orange should not have scars on it, 'thrip' marks and all of that," one grower explained. "It is not always possible to grow the perfect vegetable or the perfect product that we have allowed educated people to expect." To close the gap, Sunkist enforced careful handling and inspection procedures and turned to insecticides and processes like the Food Machinery Corporation's FlavorSeal—a technique that reduced moisture loss to make fruit that "looks better, tastes better, and *sells* better." Using these techniques to cosmetically enhance nature's products, growers were able to fill store windows across the country with oranges that would live up to consumers' visions of Edenic fruit.[67]

It took a lot of work to maintain the illusion of Eden. Though advertising may have masked the role of workers in the creation of Sunkist oranges, their work and lives must be explored in order to fully chart the rise of the Orange Empire.

PART TWO

Work in the Garden

INTRODUCTION

IT WAS only in the beginning that there was no work. At that time, as the legend goes, fruits of every sort appeared abundantly on the trees of Eden. Man and woman, together with the other creatures, lived lives of leisurely bliss. But some fruits were off limits. With a fateful bite, the leisure world disappeared. Having lost their right to the other fruits, man and woman would have to "till the ground" for grain. And though Adam and Eve presumably had the capacity to "be fruitful and multiply" while in the garden, it was only after they were cast out that bearing children became a labor.

The story of the garden is seeded deep within the Western tradition. It bears all sorts of lessons. Some have seen the story—in which man is given "dominion . . . over every living thing that moveth upon the earth"—as the original license for ecological destruction. Others have stressed its lessons of stewardship, for Genesis did contain an image of the peaceful coexistence of humans, animals, and plants. They spoke the same language. The fall—whether we blame the snake, the woman, the man, or the god—splits the harmony between humans and the rest of creation. Digesting the fruit of the tree of knowledge, Adam's and Eve's eyes were opened and the world was torn asunder. They were cast out of the garden, and at the gates were stationed cherubim with a flaming sword, guarding against any attempted return.

Nonetheless, the dream of a return has persisted. For some, the wild places—supposed remnants of God's handiwork in a Yosemite or a Yellowstone—are where a sublime oneness can be recovered. For others, a reconnection to the land is only possible, paradoxically, through work: outside of the garden we must work, but we must work to get back to it. That, at least, is the message contained in the georgics of agricultural literature stretching back to Virgil and Hesiod. It has been cultivated by American agrarians was well, from Thomas Jefferson to Wendell Berry. To them, work on the land is seen as a spiritual practice. To turn the soil. To love it. To break it. To work with animals upon it. To become what remains when the sun breathes in the land's wetness—the salt of the earth.

California's Indians also have a garden lore. Most tell of a mythical place and time that sounds a bit like Eden. In the Indians' "first-time," people conversed with animals and lived in a world made fruitful by a creator. There is often a fall as well: the first-time people depart, leaving the world to its present inhabitants. In the Yurok tradition, it is transgression of the sexual laws that brings an end to the first-time. The original people turn themselves into trees and animals and tell the Yurok to keep clean and keep the law. To maintain a world of abundance and assure that the abundance will be reproduced every year—to maintain the garden—the Yurok must keep strictly to the law and recognize that all of the world around them is alive. Every stone and tree and deer and salmon is intensely, relentlessly watchful. A covenant governs how nature may be consumed; transgress it, and the world might shrivel up. A watchful world created discipline and ecological respect. Everyone was watched. Everyone, even the creatures, had a hand in earth's management, were part of a common dominion, a domus, a home. Thus, the Yurok carefully performed first-fruit ceremonies, hoping to properly recognize the rest of creation and assure the earth's continued fertility.

During the Enlightenment in Europe, a new architecture was created to give people the power of watchfulness: the panopticon. Jeremy Bentham designed it for use in prisons, schools, insane asylums, even harems. The design called for a large courtyard, with a tower in the center, surrounded by buildings divided into cells. Each student or inmate or wife was always, in principle, under surveillance. A similar kind of watchfulness was key to the rise of industrial capitalism. By the early twentieth century, panoptic scientific management was a basic part of any factory.

Karl Marx saw all of this. He developed a theory about how workers' relationship to nature changed under industrial capitalism. Man was part of nature, he said, it was his body. But what happens when working people use the "sensuous external world" to make things for others?[1] They split off a part of themselves and make it available for sale, literally losing themselves in their work. Capitalist production, whether industrial or agricultural, did not, in the end, make things. It did not make clothing. It did not make wheat. It made divisions: between some people and other people, and between all people and nature. This was his story of the alienation of labor.

Managerial capitalism transformed the countryside as well. By the early twentieth century, California agriculture had largely become what Carey McWilliams called "factories in the field." Instead of growing crops in a world in which nature was alive and watchful, owners of the land arrogated to themselves the power of watchfulness. They began to see the land as a dead arrangement of matter, not a sensuous world of which they were a part; they began to see workers as units of energy that could be leveraged here and there at will. Growers themselves began to do less and less of the work on the ground. The growers would see, and the workers would work. Farmers made themselves managers, or hired them (it matters little, for *managerialism* was put in charge). A strict division was established between those who planned and figured and those who stooped and planted.

But the growers were divided in their own minds as well. Their managerial role alienated them from nature, and yet they loved their land as something more than a commodity. They sometimes thought of farming as a collective activity in which their hired men and women worked with them, not for them. They were proud of the improvements they had made to Eden, and yet they were nostalgic for it. Amidst their highly rationalized operations, they harbored remnants of a hope that agriculture was something more than a business—that it was a culture, a way of life that had given birth to democracy in America.

Perhaps the growers' use of agrarian rhetoric was a delusion, employed, consciously or not, to maintain their power. And the workers on whose labor they built an empire were naturalized as part of the landscape, not members of the body politic. Naturalization, as Roland Barthes defined it, is the process through which things made by humans come to appear as if they were made by nature. Such naturalization turned the socially constructed labor relations in the citrus industry—in which racial, class, and gender divisions were firmly wrought—into a gift of nature. Like any gift, it was something to be accepted, not negotiated.

Naturalization, most recognizably in the name of the federal bureau that handles immigration, can also mean the process of becoming American.

From its beginnings, the Orange Empire drew workers from across the globe. Once in California, hard work might have allowed them to make claims to the land. But they often faced a racism, either virulent or subtle in its expression, through which they would find themselves permanently "alienated." In California, two contradictory things happened at once: they became American and became "other."

Naturalization can also speak to the way that workers were becoming intimate with California's landscapes. They actually worked in the soil; they handled fruits and vegetables, making them flow from field or grove to packing house or cannery; they bent their bodies to the forms of nature, that the harvest might be gathered and then sent out across the nation like a miraculous gift. Growers often celebrated their workers' contact with nature. California's resplendent environment, they suggested, made work in the groves more salubrious that work in a real factory. Wages may not have been great, but the sun paid bonuses every day.

Workers often did fall in love with California's nature, in their own ways: whether hailing from China, the Philippines, Japan, Mexico, Europe, or Oklahoma, they brought with them agrarian dreams that they adapted to California soil. Those who worked the land for others dreamed of owning it, and loving it, for themselves. It is to these fields—of dreams, of work, and of living matter—that we now turn, hoping to unmask some of the many faces of naturalization.

FOUR

The Fruits of Labor

PICTURING ORANGE PICKERS

NOT CONTENT TO FEED only the physical bodies of the one-third of the nation he saw as ill-nourished, Franklin Delano Roosevelt also served up images designed to fortify the body politic. The New Deal commissioned over 1,100 murals in post offices "to develop local cultural interests throughout the country."[1] The images were to be rooted in the country-side, in the hope that they would help connect the people to one another and the land. When muralist Paul Julian saw his space on the wall of the Fullerton post office in Orange County, he did not have to look far to find his subject: *Orange Pickers* (see figure 14).

Though painted with the brushstrokes of realism, Julian's mural depicts a scene that did not correspond to any actual grove. All its elements are realistic enough, but his picture is a composite. It brings together a range of representative figures, all of whom might have picked oranges at a par-ticular time, though not likely at the same time: some white male high-schoolers; a young white woman with bobbed hair and a bright-red bikini top; a young Mexicana with long hair and bare feet, gathering oranges in the skirt of her simple sundress. To fully capture the range of peoples who worked in the Orange Empire, the artist would have had to crowd in Indi-ans, Californios, Chinese, Japanese, Filipinos, "fruit tramps" of European descent, Okies, blacks from the American South as well as Jamaica, society

Figure 14. In his New Deal post office mural in Fullerton, *Orange Pickers* (1941–42), Paul Julian portrayed an unlikely, and unskilled, orange-picking crew. (Photograph by the author.)

ladies doing their patriotic duty to glean the trees in times of labor shortage, and a host of other immigrants pushed from their homelands and pulled to California's promised land. Whatever their ethnicity or gender, such workers could not see themselves or the true nature of their work accurately represented in the mural.[2]

Julian portrays his attenuated and unlikely cast of orange pickers as happily pulling nature's bounty off the tree and transporting it to boxes below. It's a kind of picnic of production in the plein air. Like his fellow muralists, Julian envisioned work as "a communal and productive activity in which men work harmoniously with each other and with machines." This vision of harmony seems to jibe with how growers tended to remember relations in the groves. "We had no racial problem here whatsoever," explained Charles Chapman. "We never felt that they were working for us. We were all just working together."[3]

And yet, something in Julian's picture struck this longtime grower as terribly wrong. "How anybody ever imagined such a thing!" he exclaimed. There was no picking sack and the gender of the pickers was wrong. "This picture showed women up on ladders picking oranges without clippers and throwing them at the box. It is the stupidest thing. Anybody who would try it would break his back or his neck."[4] Chapman was wrong about the sack and women being up on ladders in the mural, but Julian did depict one woman picking oranges. To Chapman, the woman's position in the grove, or the artist's decision to place her there, appears downright unnatural.

Chapman was not simply being sexist. He knew full well that without the work of women, his oranges would never have made it to market. But women did not typically work in the groves. They worked inside, in the packing *houses,* washing, sorting, grading, and packing oranges at a dizzying pace.[5] Equally revealing is Chapman's critique of how the woman handles herself—or, more to the point, how she handles the oranges. He was right to call the modus operandi of the imagined picker into question. Without gloves, she risks nicking the skin of the oranges with her fingernails. Without clippers, broken-off stems would become spikes in the crate. Tossing them down would only compound the damage to the fruit's precious natural wrapping. Rather than arriving in perfect condition for the consumer in Chicago or New York, oranges mishandled in this way would be vulnerable to nature's entropic forces, quite likely dissolving on their journey east into an ash of blue mold.

Chapman also took issue with the imagined woman's position on the ladder. "Anybody who would try it," he warned, "would break *his* back or *his* neck." Having corrected the gender of the generic picker, Chapman pointed out the danger to the worker's body. Readily admitting that orange picking was arduous work, growers sought ways to make it less difficult and more efficient at every step. They wanted a steady flow of oranges from the groves to the packing plants, and workers breaking their backs and necks would interrupt the flow. In the 1925–26 season in Sunkist groves across the state, 35 workers were injured in falls from ladders, and another 52 were poked in the eye by branches or hurt by thorns. Packing house workers reported 245 injuries to the Workman's Compensation Board, including bruises (59), sprains (30), and mashed fingers (23). Sunkist's work on "accident prevention" was designed to prevent needless scrapes and falls, but its ultimate concern was the bottom line. As Sunkist instructed its managers, "Safety First Pays."[6]

Such managers would have had their work cut out for them if given the crew Julian depicted. While the vision of people working together in sun-drenched nature might resonate with the public's romantic agrarianism, a manager or a seasoned grower like Chapman would be horrified by such a scene. Imagining such a crew as this in his or her own groves, the grower would see waste clogging the line of production. Blissful though they may be, they are doing work for which they are obviously ill-equipped.

Growers would have to find employees more suited to work in what the Los Angeles Chamber of Commerce called "nature's workshop." This chapter explores the "shop floor" of this workshop, asking how, in the process of bringing oranges from the tree to the boxcar, nature was remanufactured into a commodity. Human labor was critical to the transformation of oranges into artifacts that could be bought and sold. As Richard White points out, "It is ultimately our own bodies and our labor that blur the boundaries between the artificial and the natural." The bodies of workers mediated the artificial zones of the market and the organic landscapes of the groves, and they were shaped by the physical work they performed.[7]

Their bodies were shaped by the work of ideologies as well. From the moment of recruitment, the Orange Empire marked workers' bodies with the stamp of race and explained their subordination as part of the natural order. Racialization and naturalization operated in tandem, like a couple of thieves: one lifted labor from workers while the other pushed down their aspirations. Citrus workers' contact with nature was structured by gender, too, for men and women handled the fruits in different ways and in separate spheres. Ultimately, it was the labor of those men and women that allowed nature, in the form of carefully packaged oranges, to flow to consumers. In the process, nature also flowed through the bodies of workers, though not always with salubrious effects.

NATURE'S WORKFORCE

A marketable orange doesn't simply grow on a tree. However much citrus growers came to distance themselves from the image of hardscrabble yeomen working the soil—celebrating sweat on their brows only if it came from furrowed thought—they still needed the muscle, skill, dexterity, and energy of human labor. Though it was indispensable, growers campaigned hard to assure that this labor was never dear.[8]

"Stand at the Cumberland Gap," Frederick Jackson Turner advised in 1893, "and watch the procession of civilization." From a vantage point above the Golden Gate or at the bridge over the Rio Grande at El Paso, one could witness a procession of people equally significant to the American frontier. The story of these waves of immigration has been told before, in many cases in considerable detail and with great care. Sunkist, working with other agricultural and industrial employers, influenced federal and state policy on immigration and helped construct the racial ideologies that would encircle the new peoples as they arrived in California. Though close studies of most of the groups' experience in the citrus industry remain to be written, the outline of their involvement is fairly clear. Indians provided much of the initial labor; Chinese predominated from the 1870s through the 1890s; Japanese from the late 1890s through 1910; Mexicanos from 1910 through the 1930s, augmented by Filipinos in the 1920s and somewhat displaced by Dust Bowl migrants in the 1930s. The "fruit frontier" was opened where the white fruit grower, called to California by booster literature, met the racialized worker hailed from lands further to the West or South. Without these workers, the transformation of citrus growing into an empire would not have been possible.[9]

Most observers of California agriculture agree that "cheap labor" provided by migrant groups was the fuel powering agricultural growth. But too often, race has been used casually as an explanation in itself, rather than something that needs to be explained, as in the near tautology that Chinese provided cheap labor because they were marginalized and they were marginalized because they were Chinese. We should not assume that "race" is some bounded essence that groups brought with them when they entered California, but see it instead as something that was constituted historically in relation to preexisting and ever changing economic, environmental, and ideological conditions. "Race" was something that was made in California, not found there or imported wholesale from abroad. In California, immigrant workers entered a crucible of work and identity, drawing on the resources of their own cultural traditions but adapting them to survive, and, they hoped, flourish in the new environment. But that environment was hardly a neutral space. Racial categories honeycombed the landscape, delineating niches for the new immigrants and stinging those who strayed from their appointed domain.[10]

From the 1850s, California boosters had been adding a new episode to the story of Manifest Destiny. It was about the role of workers. *The California Farmer* was sure that "California is destined to become a large grower," but wondered, "Where shall the laborers be found?" "The Chinese!" it answered, for "those great walls of China are to be broken down and that population, educated, schooled and drilled in the cultivation of these products, are to be to California what the African has been to the South. This is the decree of the Almighty, and man cannot stop it." The divine work of the Chinese was to toil in the fields; it was the white growers' burden hire them. Wage work would lift them up and prepare them for emancipation and civilization, the rhetoric implied. *The Overland Monthly* reasoned, "If society must have 'mudsills,' it is certainly better to take them from a race which would be benefited by even that position in a civilized community, than subject a portion of our own race to a position which they have outgrown." *Mudsills* was a term used to describe workers pressed close to nature, like diggers of irrigation ditches and planters of fruit trees.[11]

But growers didn't really expect their workers, caked as they were in the mud of racialism, to rise from the earth. And to assuage Jeffersonian objections to the creation of a class of permanent wage earners, some growers pushed the assumptions of racial difference. The environmentally determined character of California agriculture was perfectly suited to the biological character of its workforce, they said. One grower suggested that "the short-legged, short-backed Asiatic performs all of the stoop-over work, the squat work. He stands any temperature. He works in every sun and clime." Such stories held that Chinese were "consigned to the farm work force by a mechanism of natural selection." The basic elements of this narrative were used and adapted to explain why each wave of workers—Indians, Chinese, Japanese, Filipinos, Mexicanos (and also Okies)—could be left to wallow in the mud while the growers preserved a clear conscience.[12]

Growers tended to subscribe to a loose evolutionary theory about how nature had adapted peoples to their labor needs, and they conceived of these adaptations as racial essences. Sunkist president Charles Collins Teague explained that Mexicans "are naturally adapted to agricultural work, particularly in the handling of fruits and vegetables, for the Mexican climate is in many ways similar to that of California. Many of them have a natural skill in the handling of tools and are resourceful in matters requiring manual ability." Emphasizing workers' hands and their bodies' adaptations to climatic conditions, these fables made worker skill a product of natural selection. Even when heaping praise on their workers, growers often viewed them as simple and innocent children—primitives, even.[13]

One grower, who felt that his Filipino picking crew was "one of the best in the country," explained that "they were a small people, and they were like monkeys on these ladders. They would start at daylight and pick [all day]. They would work during the picking season and make a lot of money and then go to San Francisco, or wherever, and live it up (laughter). They were very interesting people." Though this grower clearly had a feeling of warmth toward his workers, he could not quite see them as full human beings: as workers, they were monkey-like; as people, they were "interesting." Such depictions are not surprising, given the widespread Orientalism that represented the East as exotic and Asians as "other." Visitors to the Louisiana Purchase Exposition (1904), could (after taking in California's spectacle of fruit) turn to the wonders of the Orient. An entire village of Filipinos was imported for the fair to display the "growth of civilization" from the primitive to the civilized. The Igorot Village exhibit subsequently traveled to Los Angeles, where it was advertised as "The Call of the Wild . . . the most interesting and instructive educational exhibit portraying primitive man ever made."[14]

The anthropologist behind the Igorot Village exhibit argued that "it is the duty of the strong man to subjugate lower nature, to extirpate the bad and cultivate the good in all living things, to delve in earth below and sky above in search of fresh resources . . . and in all ways to enslave the world for the support of humanity and the increase of human intelligence." This version of the white man's burden called for the civilized domination of both nature and people, a message well suited to the Orange Empire, which was drawing the human and natural resources of the Pacific Basin into its fold. When Filipino immigrants arrived in California, they were taunted by popular versions of this scientistic demonology. Carlos Bulosan heard the simian epithet so often that it became a "a chorus shouting: *'Why don't they ship those monkeys back to where they came from.'*"[15]

For growers, the construction of Asian peoples as primitive served as a trestle for their power. Making monkeys out of Asian men may have also resonated with their own visions of Eden. Western fascination with actual primates has always been linked to a search for human origins, and "the story of the Garden of Eden emerges in the sciences of monkeys and apes."[16] Having taken over the role of creator, growers could see the Eden they had fabricated as peopled, naturally enough, with primitives.

In fact, the workplace of the groves had been so effectively racialized that the appearance of whites in nature's workshop came to be seen as unnatural. At a United States Chamber of Commerce meeting in the late 1920s, Ralph Taylor argued that the Mexican "is fitted by natural environment to withstand our climatic conditions . . . and able to perform work which demands hard physical exertion." In contrast, "We are educating our Americans away from hard work and menial tasks." Not only did white workers find such labor undesirable, they were simply unable to perform it. Noting the heat of harvest time, Taylor said that "it is impossible to find American labor which can, without serious physical consequences, work in those fields and accomplish anything." California growers "must have labor that is . . . fitted to work under unusual climatic conditions, and, in addition, favorable to seasonal migration." Mexicans, who were biologically and culturally adapted to such conditions, would be the only solution to growers' labor needs "until Thomas Edison or Henry Ford develops machinery which will take the drudgery out of the harvest or until the idealist becomes amenable to calluses on his hands." Lobbying against bills that would have restricted Mexicano immigration in the late 1920s, the Los Angeles Chamber of Commerce argued that "much of California's agricultural labor requirements consist of those tasks to which the oriental and Mexican due to their crouching and bending habits are fully adapted, while the white is physically unable to adapt himself to them." A Whittier citrus grower characterized a white picking crew as "crabbing, grumbling, ill-natured, complaining of conditions." Growers repeated "whites can't and won't work" as a mantra: they were "ill-natured" and would complain about conditions, while Mexicans were naturally suited to them and "uncomplaining."[17]

Still, some growers and newspapers worried about the investment in a racialized workforce. Many white Californians felt that the importation of Chinese undermined their own freedom and prospects. Racist images of Chinese inflamed Denis Kearney's Workingman's Party in the 1870s, as well as Henry George's take on why poverty existed amidst abundance. E. J. Wickson had believed that the shift from vast wheat farming to intensive fruit growing would make the (white) family farm ideal become a reality in California. To realize Jeffersonian agrarianism meant creating a classless community, but most growers subscribed to a racial nationalism that excluded nonwhites from the body politic.

Turning the racialism of those who favored the employment of foreign labor inside out, this nativist agrarianism depicted the Chinese and other groups as menaces to the white race and democracy itself. In 1910, the *Fresno Morning Republican* asked its readers to judge California agriculture according to dreams of whiteness rather than wealth. "Suppose the citrus fruit of Southern California can not be picked without Oriental labor," the *Republican* asked. "Does it follow that we must get oriental labor? Or may we consider the other alternative, that possibly the citrus fruit industry . . . might fail if necessary, to preserve something more important?" What needed protecting was the white republic, for the menace of intermarriage would pollute the racial stock. But even if measures were taken to prevent this, the newspaper argued, democracy would still be destroyed as a consequence of enforcing strict racial apartheid. The newspaper concluded that "to raise oranges is important, but to raise men is more important."[18]

The *Republican* believed that California agriculture should grow only men—white men, that is (nonwhites were in this discourse perpetually boys or less than men). Maintaining that they needed wage earners, some growers tried recruiting white workers as a way of preserving at least the semblance of their agrarian dream. A traveling lecturer was sent back east. He showed stereopticon views of the country's natural attractions and helped distribute a mountain of literature enticing would-be workers with the promise of eventual farm ownership. White growers found it possible to imagine white farmworkers going on to stake their own claims in the soil. But they wouldn't dream of Chinese, Japanese, Mexicano, or Filipino workers doing the same.[19]

By 1910, most growers had given up on the dream of a classless white republic of farmers. "California growers did not abandon the fantasy of a white man's California," Steven Stoll explains, "they simply redefined it to mean the dominance of white growers over a labor system that used poor people to harvest specialized crops." Growers produced scientistic ethnographies that portrayed their workers as naturally suited to the labor, content with their position, and unlikely to remain. Mexicano workers were depicted as "homing pigeons" who would seasonally fly south across the border. Immigrants would be allowed to cross the border as workers, as *bodies,* but not as full human beings who might eventually make civic claims on American soil.[20]

IMMIGRANT AGRARIAN DREAMS

While growers themselves had given up on a large part of the agrarian dream, many workers tried to take the promise of California agrarianism into their own hands. If, as Kevin Starr puts it, these workers bore the idyllic "myths on their backs," we should recognize that many of them bore them in their hearts as well. The literature on California farmworkers has long neglected the agrarian dreams of workers. Placing too much emphasis on overriding economic structures, mandates of agricultural ecology, or immovable racial hierarchies may have reinforced the image of the docile laborer. Even in sympathetic accounts, California's immigrant farmworkers often seem akin to the Energizer bunny—going and going but never able to plot their own course.[21]

Recent scholarship has paid more attention to the creative agency of immigrant farmworkers that has been there all the time. In making a life for themselves in California, farmworkers were also coming to terms with new racial and national identities. Identities were always in the making. As George Sánchez shows, immigrants from various parts of Mexico only came to see themselves as Mexican (rather than identifying with a town or region) after they had left the country. Similarly, a Filipino labor organizer expressed how difficult it was to convince his fellow immigrant workers that "[we] are brothers rather than . . . Visayans or Ilocanos or Tagalog[s] or Pangasainan[s] . . . that we are one Filipino race." Growers found it useful to group immigrant workers in single racial categories, but workers also found uses for adopting overarching cultural identities.[22]

As they struggled to become American, these immigrants often found that America's racial nationalism blocked their path. Under the Naturalization Act of 1790, Asian and other nonwhite immigrants could not become citizens. Mexicanos, though technically eligible for naturalization, encountered a perceptual barricade. Nonetheless, many farmworkers, challenging the nation's race-based quarantine on citizenship, acted on their own agrarian dreams and put down roots in American soil. They would become Mexican American growers, Japanese American floriculturists, or Filipino American farmers.

Contrary to common belief, in the nineteenth century hundreds of Chinese operated their own farms and truck gardens, worked as tenant fruit farmers, and even pioneered fruit growing in some regions. Working under ten-year leases, Chinese planted trees, intercropping them with vegetables until they matured. They played a crucial role as tenant farmers, not just as laborers, in the transformation of the wheat landscape into a fruit landscape. Though the land they had made fruitful had to be turned over to the landlord after ten years, they had secured a larger portion of the agrarian dream than harvest workers. Moreover, many Chinese owned their own farms, often capitalizing on their ability to envision different possibilities in the landscape than immigrants from the Eastern United States. Sandy Lydon points out that "with their wide experience of more intensive farming in a crowded land, the Chinese brought a wider vision to California than did Yankee farmers." Willows were a sign of marginal land to whites but a "symbol of life and regeneration" to Chinese, who reclaimed the whites' leftover land for agriculture. The wild mustard of Monterey County, first brought by the Spanish, was seen as a weed by most white farmers, but an immigrant turned the "weeds" into "Chinese gold." Capitalizing on their different knowledge of nature and its possibilities, some Chinese were able to make good on their own agrarian dreams.[23]

Abiko Kyutaro made America's story of agrarian uplift his own, using his newspaper *Nicheibei* ("Japan-America") to urge Japanese immigrants to "go into farming, own land, be productive, put down roots in America." Kyutaro organized a land colony of Issei (first-generation Japanese Americans), purchasing thirty-two hundred acres of land near Livingston and dividing it into forty-acre plots. Hundreds of acres of grapevines and fruit trees were planted and irrigated with the waters of the Merced River. At the river's headwaters in Yosemite, Kyutaro had had a profound nature experience, seeing the wilderness not as a refuge from culture (as had another fruit grower, John Muir), but as inspiration for his agricultural colony. "When I saw the magnificent scenery of Yosemite I felt as though I had been given a sign," he wrote. Perhaps he had: ten years later, the San Francisco *Chronicle* reported that "fruit shipments from Livingston have increased from nothing in 1906 to 260 carloads in 1917." Unfortunately, nature was not the only source of signs. Others made sure that the Issei farmers' experience would not translate easily into a sense of belonging to the land. One farmer expressed his sense of alienation in a poem:

A wasted grassland
Turned to fertile fields by sweat
Of cultivation:
But I, made dry and fallow
By tolerating insults.[24]

The sense that the agrarian dream was for whites only was deepened when growers, jealous of the many successes hardworking Issei accomplished in agriculture, agitated for the passage of the Alien Land Act of 1913. The law forbade "aliens ineligible for citizenship" (all nonwhites) from owning land. For Japanese who were becoming American, it must have seemed that the promise of fruit growing was a cruel sham. Despite this and other restrictions placed on Japanese, many found ways to become successful growers in California. Wataru Tomosaburo Donashi, an Issei who had immigrated from Japan in 1907, bought twenty acres on the corner of Casa Loma and Citrus in Yorba Linda with the help of his former employer. Donashi "put it all in citrus trees," but he planted tomatoes, peas, and other crops between the rows as he waited for the trees to mature. In the meantime, the whole family harvested and packed vegetables and drove them to Los Angeles to sell them. As his daughter recalls, "That's how he got his first start, got his foot on the ground."[25]

Because land prices had jumped considerably by the time Filipino and Mexicano immigrants arrived in large numbers, their opportunities for owning or leasing land were even more restricted than they had been for Japanese and Chinese immigrants. By 1930, 16.2 percent of Japanese in agriculture owned or leased land, as did 13.9 percent of Chinese, but only 2.6 percent of Mexicanos and 0.8 percent of Filipinos did. Though they were not often realized, Filipinos still held agrarian dreams. In the San Fernando Valley, a Filipino man told Carlos Bulosan,

> When I first came to this camp . . . these lemon trees were only a foot high. The land to the west of my camp was still a desert. I went to the town and recruited Mexican laborers. Afterward I went to Los Angeles and carted off Filipinos who had just arrived from the sugar plantations of Hawaii and from the peasant country of the Philippines. I have made this valley fruitful and famous.

Like white farmers, he could claim to have transformed a desert into a garden and to have grown close to the soil. But he could not claim ownership of the land or its fruits. "Some ten years ago I wanted to go into farming myself, so close I was to the soil, so familiar with the touch of clay and loam," he explained. "But I found that I couldn't buy land in California." As Bulosan observed, the original desire to "possess a plot of earth and draw nourishment from it . . . after long years of flight and disease and want, had become an encompassing desire to *belong* to the land."[26]

Turner's Cumberland Gap procession was not the only party to carry with it romantic dreams of life on the land in the West. Patricia Limerick points out that "the Chinese agrarian dream and the Japanese agrarian dream joined up with the American version in bringing an ideal of order and productivity to bear on the 'wild' American landscape. But . . . federal legislation gave official support to the American agrarian dream, while the Chinese and Japanese versions had to persist in spite of racial harassment [and] official obstacles to land ownership."[27] Exclusion was codified in the law, making sure that whenever Chinese, Japanese, or Filipinos wanted to climb the ladder of agricultural progress, they would find it pressed flat against the ground.

The relationship between growers and racialized workers was expressed in the landscape itself. "Throughout the citrus belt," Carey McWilliams observed, "the workers are Spanish-speaking, Catholic, and dark-skinned, the owners are white, Protestant, and English-speaking. The owners occupy the heights, the Mexicans the lowlands." This system of "social apartness" created spatial as well as social and psychological borders. "As more and more barriers were erected, the walls began to grow higher, to thicken, and finally to coalesce on all sides," McWilliams suggested. "While the walls may have the appearance of being natural growths, they are really man-made." With unequaled sharpness, McWilliams exposed the naturalization through which manmade social relations appear to be "made-in-nature."[28]

"Nature's workforce" was created and maintained through a set of stories turning human beings into fieldworkers and a spatial segregation that excluded them from the center of white communities. Through white growers' self-serving ethnographies, workers were at once racialized and pictured as products *of* nature. When it came to working in it, they were seen as exceptionally able-bodied. But when it came to claiming equal access to the agrarian dream, they were made out to be pest-ridden fruits that needed to be quarantined from the body politic and driven from the land. "The rats are in the granary," a California senator proclaimed. "If this is not checked now, it means the end of the white race in California."[29]

SCIENTIFIC MANAGEMENT OF THE BLUE MOLD MENACE

Growers had actual biological menaces to contend with, and how they dealt with them would shape how workers experienced nature in the groves. At the turn of the century, a certain blue mold was ruining large percentages of oranges shipped East. Growers were losing up to $1.5 million a year. Some assumed that the railroads were to blame. Perhaps the refrigeration systems were run improperly. Perhaps, during backups, the blue mold set in as oranges baked on the tracks. Others surmised that too-rich soil produced "fat" oranges susceptible to the malady. Still others, in an explanation echoing contemporary fears of racial enervation, attributed the declension to a degeneracy taking hold of older trees. (When Teddy Roosevelt helped replant one of the original Washington navel trees in Riverside, he joked that he was glad "this tree shows no sign of race suicide.") Some blamed the machines used in the packing houses, complaining that proper care of oranges was lost amidst "the natural hurrah" of the busy plants. To sort this all out, growers appealed to Washington. In 1904, help arrived in the person of G. Harold Powell, the USDA pomologist who might rightly be called the Frederick Winslow Taylor of the citrus industry.[30]

As Powell began investigating, he became increasingly concerned with the function of workers' bodies in the labor process. As Taylor had done in an industrial setting, Powell and his team closely studied the work laborers did in the groves, the layout of the packing plant floors, the practices of human graders and packers—all the while measuring and counting. But unlike Taylor, Powell was not searching for ways to shave time off of various tasks. To him, efficiency meant something other than speeding up the work. While the Taylorized assembly line capitalized on ever greater efficiencies to put dead material together into the nearly living form of consumer goods, mass production in the citrus industry was possible only by preserving and protecting the living qualities of the orange. "The orange is a living organism," Powell pointed out, "and it must be treated as such."[31]

The USDA scientist soon found that growers had lofty expectations, looking to him for "a prescription that in one magic moment will drive away all the troubles and make lemon growing as good as a gold mine. When they reach that stage of evolution that their lemons are grown on a bed of roses, the fruit picked by fairy angels and shipped by a Marconi message, they may realize their dream."[32] But if Powell here is puncturing the growers' fantasy, he did in fact try to realize their dream. Of course, the physical transportation of the fruit could not be accomplished through the Marconi wireless telegraph, but the next best thing would be to create a full state of suspended animation for oranges as they were transported in refrigerated rail cars. And while earthbound workers needed ladders to reach the fruit, he promoted a number of changes so that the oranges they picked would seem to have passed only through the hands of angels.

Having built his early reputation working on apples, Powell was confident that he could find a comparable solution for oranges. He investigated all of the blue mold hypotheses, but he soon gathered enough evidence to confirm his original suspicions: the mold destroyed only oranges whose skins had been damaged. It was the *mis*handling of fruit, in both groves and packing plants, that turned the gold of oranges into a mold of ashy blue. He found great variety among workers he studied: some left no scars on the fruit they handled, while others damaged up to 50 percent of the harvest. To his credit, he made no attempt to correlate these rates with the race of the workers. All workers could do the job well, he insisted, if a system of incentives was put in place and care was given to the "instruction and supervision of labor" to ensure "careful handling."[33]

Nevertheless, the changing makeup of the citrus workforce may have played some role in the growth of the blue mold problem. The first generation of orange growers had gotten more than they bargained for when they hired Chinese laborers: many of them had experience and expertise in the growing and harvesting of fruit. Citrus was an important crop in Guangdong, the home of most Chinese immigrants in the nineteenth century. Back home, some of the them may have been fruit brokers—people who would mark the fruit on the landowners' tree and then pick, pack, and sell it in distant markets. In an article from the *Pacific Rural Press,* Chinese were described as "expert pickers and packers of fruit." They could efficiently arrange oranges of different sizes to create the "Chinese pack," a crate of oranges so tight and stable that it could make it to Eastern markets in good condition.[34]

But when Powell arrived on the scene, Chinese had largely disappeared from the groves, and Japanese workers were taking their place. While Japanese immigrants often had farming experience (either in Japan or Hawai'i), few would have had any experience in fruit growing. Until the late nineteenth century, fruits were not a very large part of the Japanese diet and so were not grown extensively. Many of the mandarin oranges, grapes, and pears that were grown were offered up at shrines and temples, not consumed in large quantities. The increase in the rate of spoilage, then, may have had something to do with the loss of expertise in fruit picking and packing that accompanied the gradual disappearance of Chinese from the groves after the Exclusion Act of 1882.[35]

Still, Powell was correct to emphasize that it was mainly a combination of economic and technological elements that created the blue mold problem. Putting a premium on quantity rather than quality, growers, packers, and pickers "were actually causing . . . much injury to the fruit." The problems "result from ignorance, carelessness, or improper supervision of the labor." At every stage between the tree and the railroad car, oranges were scraped, bludgeoned, or punctured. "It is not unusual," he reported, "to see the professional picker, with a hoop fastened in the top of the picking sack to hold the mouth open, with a deft movement of the clippers cut the oranges and shoot them directly into the bag." Pickers rested their weight on their picking sacks, pressing on the oranges within. Clippers used to cut oranges from the stem often inadvertently nicked the skin. Stems cut too long would puncture other oranges in the sacks or picking boxes. Gravel, dirt, and twigs in the bags or boxes could bruise the oranges. Powell's investigators looked under the fingernails of pickers and packers and discovered orange skin. Rough handling in the transportation from grove to packing house was also a problem, and at the end of the journey fruit was often haphazardly dumped into the receiving hopper.[36]

At the packing houses, investigators found loose screws and protruding nails, workers shoving oranges through machines with paddles, and oranges barreling down gravity chutes and making footlong falls. Powell portrayed these seemingly modern factories, jammed with pieces of machinery that did not work well individually or together, as veritable junkyards. Machines that brushed the oranges, often out of adjustment or poorly designed, routinely damaged the skin. Washing was also a culprit, and should "be avoided." "There were many places along the line of the grading and sizing machines," one observer reported, "that in one way or another took a piece of orange hide." The packing house subjected oranges to the "thousand natural shocks that flesh is heir to." What's more, the mounds of "rotting oranges in the bins, on the floor, and on the ground around the house" increased the density of the menacing molds in the air. Powell felt that "this lack of attention to the cleanliness of a packing house has a bad effect on labor, and is invariably accompanied by rough handling and slovenly work in general."[37]

Long before Powell came onto the scene, some growers had fulminated against slovenly conditions and preached the doctrine of careful handling. Oranges should be handled like eggs, they said. But this view lacked the legitimacy of science, and the market seemed to favor the acceleration of processing, whatever the impact on the oranges. In the face of the apparent economic incentive to get more oranges into the boxes faster, careful handling was dropped. Oranges were pushed through machines at twice their capacity. Workers, paid piece rates, tried to keep up with the machines and produce enough to get by. Such speedups, Powell forcefully argued, were a "false economy."[38]

Powell compiled statistics on the degree of fruit rot attributable to bad handling. To drive his point home, Powell, like other scientists and efficiency experts, told stories. Scientific management spread into work environments through stories that were "*told to* employers who wanted more productivity at less cost for the sake of greater profits." Similarly, the "Powell Method" gained its power through narratives: scientific treatises complete with graphs and photographs, grower testimony delivered at conventions, and experiments conducted as spectacles. With his assistants, Powell went into the groves and staged publicity stunts disguised as experimentation. They would pack up crates as if they were going to ship them, and then store them for weeks on end in the packing house. Returning to the scene, they would unpack the crates in front of growers and reporters. Together, they would discover what Powell already knew: in carefully handled packs, the oranges had done fine, while in those packed haphazardly, many of the golden globes had turned blue. He also told a good farmer/bad farmer parable: the good farmer and the bad farmer were neighbors, so their soils and fruits were essentially the same. One said he did not want to change his handling practices, that it would be impossible. The other had a more progressive spirit and began to mouth words that could have been Powell's own (and probably were): "It is poor business policy to invest a large amount of money in groves . . . unless the fruit is picked and packed with at least enough care to preserve its natural keeping quality." The farmer who believed in the gospel of careful handling was rewarded with the pride of "work well done" *and* with higher prices for his oranges. Growers found the stories persuasive and soon began making changes.[39]

In the end, Powell offered no technological fix for the blue mold menace. He apparently did not even consider disinfecting the oranges as a solution. His explanation reveals his prejudices: "If it were possible to kill the blue mold in the washing tank, it would place a premium on the shiftless management of the groves and on the rough, careless handling of the fruit." There were a number of small things that could be done: wearing gloves, cleaning out boxes, changing wash water more often, eliminating brushing, using clippers with blunted ends, and others. At bottom, though, Powell's solution was *managerial.* To effect all of the little changes that would collectively conquer blue mold, Powell ushered in a "conceptual revolution" in citrus production.[40]

Powell argued that managers and foremen were key to rationalizing production and assuring a uniform standard in oranges. The problems of damaged oranges "are the most serious where each grower in an association picks and handles his own fruit. It is least where they are organized so that careful handling methods can be universally applied as a part of the fruit-handling system." Powell recommended that Sunkist and other cooperatives take charge of inspection, educate growers, and train and supervise workers to grade and harvest the fruit. The local association should be put in charge of dispatching and closely supervising crews to pick members' trees. Unlike many of its cousins in industrial settings, Powell's managerial revolution was not aimed at "deskilling workers." Since there were no unions in citrus and most of its workers were already

designated as unskilled (fumigators and graders may have been exceptions), there was no need for managers to appropriate the knowledge and
skills of workers. Powell thought that through cooperatively arranged
labor, "Only skillful workmen need be employed and very efficient work
is secured when the labor is directed by a competent foreman." Since the
decay problem could arise anywhere on the line of production, the doctrine of careful handling became the lever that lifted a new managerial
régime to power.[41]

For growers, the most difficult part of Powell's message was that they
should step out of the labor process. But the promise of a greater return on
their investment convinced them to make the change. Thus did the farmer
increasingly estrange himself from the soil; the grower now would become
part of a much larger machine that would—in the one best way—grow,
handle, and market the fruit. He would pursue pure and simple capitalism. In turn, growers vigorously recruited Powell to be the general manager of Sunkist. He took the helm in 1911. The natural scientist G. Harold
Powell's apotheosis in the organization is revealing: in Sunkist's workshop,
knowing business meant knowing nature, and vice versa.

Powell's knowledge of nature gave growers the power to create more
marketable fruit. Powell focused attention on the *flow* of oranges from
grove to market, arguing that at every juncture growers needed to ask,
How will this affect the appearance and eating quality of these oranges
when they are put up for sale in New York? "Undisciplined labor" could
do much to destroy the "natural keeping quality of oranges" on their way
to market.[42] A complicated technological and labor process separated the
grove from the consumer. Powell worked hard to have the oranges that
made it to market preserve the illusion that they were unmediated—pure,
fresh, natural. By standardizing operations, Powell cleared the path for
oranges to be advertised as "uniformly good." No disturbing encounters
with blemishes or dehydrated fruit would destroy consumers' Edenic
expectations. The Powell Method reformed the bodies of workers, so that
their motions in the groves and in the packing houses would more efficiently preserve the perfect bodies of oranges.

HANDLING FRUIT IN THE GROVES

For workers, the Powell revolution meant more supervision. Before the
doctrine of careful handling took hold, orange pickers had been regulated by low wages paid at a piece rate: to survive was to pick faster.

Powell championed hourly wages, arguing that a slow picker who picked perfectly was worth more to the grower than one who picked fast but whose fruit decayed fast. Many growers did establish an hourly wage (which amounted to about $4 a day until the 1930s, when it dropped to $3 or less). By the 1920s, most associations appear to have preferred a "quality-quantity bonus system" designed to reward faster pickers while still ensuring quality work. Workers were paid a basic rate until a quota was filled, and a bonus for each additional box. But not more than one or two oranges in a hundred could show any sign of injury.[43]

While the bulk of the labor in the groves consisted of picking, other operations had to be performed to bring a grove to maturity and keep it productive. Land needed to be cleared, trees plotted and planted, cover crops grown and harvested, soils cultivated, furrows formed, branches pruned. Sunkist often supplied growers with crews to perform these and other operations, including fumigation. Discovering that much of the intensive washing done in packing houses was done to remove a honeydew exuded by a black scale, Powell recommended that the scale be controlled in the groves through fumigation.[44] The Powell Method included the chemical control of organisms that might damage the appearance of the fruit.

Fumigation outfits were typically owned and operated by white workers, who would contract their services out to Sunkist or to growers directly. As Dean Millon explained, "The fumigating crews worked at night and those crews were mostly all Caucasians, I guess. It was dangerous work, and they were a little more skilled at what they were doing." Fumigating was constituted as requiring the kind of skill and knowledge Mexicano workers were thought to lack (though they were employed in the four- to six-member crews). Position within the race hierarchy did not always determine who would be exposed to the most hazardous work environment. The higher wages of white fumigators came at the price of greater exposure to toxins.[45]

Tent fumigation began in 1886.[46] Using poles, an octagonal sheet of canvas was pulled over the trees, transforming the citrus landscape into a Christo artwork. Using numbers written on the canvas and a tape measuring the circumference of the tree, a "pinker" would measure the volume of air inside. This would be used to determine how much of the active ingredient— usually cyanide—should be added to the mixture of water and sulfuric acid in the generating machine and then "shot into the tent." In the 1920s, liquid hydrocyanic acid (HCN), which did not have to be mixed in the field, came into wide use. Interrelationships among the environment, the fumigation technology, and the gases themselves determined the effectiveness of HCN fumigation, as well as the risk to workers. HCN is a highly volatile substance, reaching its boiling point at 80 degrees. The drums had to be covered in drenched canvas or packed with ice. But since navel orange trees were fumigated in July, when temperatures soared, handling this material, even at night, was extremely risky. When sulfur dusting was used in hot weather, it "would burn the foliage and damage some of the fruit." As relative humidity rose, it became increasingly inadvisable to fumigate, though sometimes fumigators continued until the canvas became "wet and too heavy to handle." Wet tents would pick up sand and grit, which would abrade the fruit. Despite this drawback, it was tempting to continue work, since damp canvas shrinks to create a tighter seal and more complete fumigation. This was good for killing scales, but since the gas did not dissipate, workers who unfurled the canvas were exposed to higher concentrations. If applied in too much sunlight, the HCN could damage trees. Fumigators also had to take into account the life cycle of the trees and its fruit (injury was likely if applied to a tree too young or oranges too small), the life cycle of the insect scale (too mature and it might be resistant), and the weather (too windy and the gas would escape). Optimum conditions for the safety of the worker, the safety of the tree and its fruit, and the vulnerability of the insect scale rarely coincided.[47]

Environmental, social, and technological conditions also determined when the time was ripe for picking. Under the Powell Method, picking was orchestrated by the local association. Usually each association operated a packing house located on a Santa Fe or Southern Pacific rail line. The house was the epicenter of the association, from which the groves of its ten to one hundred members fanned out. The central exchange contacted the local association with an order for a certain number of boxes of a certain grade. A foreman then assembled a crew of twenty-five to thirty workers, either at the packing house or in a local *colonia* or village. The truck was loaded with field boxes, and the workers were charged some twenty cents (at least a half-hour's wages) to be transported to the workplace. The foreman distributed boxes and workers, each of whom was assigned a section of four trees. One manager explained that it was "a very systematized way of handling so that the picker didn't have to carry any great weight on his shoulders beyond two rows."[48]

Workers could not pick just any round object off the tree: it had to be the right size and color to fill the order. Orange trees do not produce homogenous fruit, all ripening at the same time. The ripening process is affected by a number of factors, including something similar to what geographers call the slope effect: on the south-facing side of the tree, which receives more sunlight, fruit matures earlier. If unripe fruit was picked and packed, a state inspector might slap a red flag on the box to indicate that its fruits had less than the eight parts of sugar to one of acid allowed under the Fruit Standardization Act. Workers had to know some of nature's rhythms and put this knowledge to use, calibrating their picking to the growth cycle of the fruit.[49]

Because consumers do not want to eat oranges all at once, the fact that nature ripened fruit on trees at different rates was good for growers. But it was also good for citrus workers. Growers could use nature's variability to "store" their product on the trees and be able to supply the market with a steady flow of oranges. For workers, it made picking a skilled operation which, to some extent, bolstered their negotiating power. Because each tree was picked at least a few times in a season, citrus afforded more work for a longer duration than other crops. These two facts allowed citrus workers to avoid some of the worst aspects of California's migratory labor system. Still, work was seasonal and far from steady. Many regions only grew one variety of orange (Valencia or Navel), in which case the entire season might be over in fourteen weeks. But where both varieties were grown or where lemons predominated, packing houses might stay open nearly all year (though this might include only 180 actual work days).[50]

But workers also had to contend with environmental conditions that might cut into the work day. After paying twenty cents for transportation, a worker might arrive in a grove that could not be picked. Oranges had to be free from dew before picking could begin; rain stopped the picking altogether, for moisture on the oranges spurred decay. Rain days could be a real burden, especially for the navel harvest, which occurred in California's relatively wet winter months. Wind and fog also halted picking. Workers were not paid a dime for weather-related delays. Nature in Southern California was not always picture-postcard perfect, and the labor system was designed to make workers bear much of the cost of the bad days in Eden.[51]

Worker equipment consisted of ladders, field boxes, cotton gloves (leather ones were used in lemon picking, to help protect the picker from the abundant thorns), clippers, and canvas picking sacks. Picking sacks at first had a wire hoop that held the mouth open, but this facilitated the

Figure 15. At work, orange pickers could not help getting in touch with nature. Men usually worked in the groves, while women packed the oranges into crates in the packing houses. Photo by Russell Lee, near Welasco, Texas, February 1939. (322942 LC-USF33-011996-M5. Courtesy of Library of Congress.)

"shooting" of oranges into the sack. They were redesigned to prevent workers from dropping the oranges in. Pickers had traditionally used the sack as a cushion between themselves and the ladder while they were reaching for oranges to clip, but the Powell Method required them to keep the sack on their outer hip. Powell also thought this position would prevent leaves and twigs from falling into the sack. But knocking off leaves and twigs, and sometimes hitting thorns, seems inevitable in picking oranges. Photographs show pickers half disappearing into an embrace of tree and foliage as they reach for an orange (see figure 15). In some areas, pickers had to watch out for rattlesnakes, which enjoyed hanging out in the trees of Eden.

Since workers were also instructed to place their ladders as nearly perpendicular to the ground as possible to minimize the force on the tree limbs, gravity pulling on the hip sacks also tended to pull the picker off the ladder. Energy was needed to counter this force. A sack positioned between the worker and the ladder, by contrast, gave him (or occasionally her) greater stability. With a sack in front of you, it had been possible to cut and catch the orange in one action. Under the Powell Method, orange picking became a two-handed operation. Oranges could not be pulled off their stems, since this would risk tearing or breaking the skin. A clipper was handled in one hand while the orange was caught in the other. And since it was difficult to maneuver the clipper into a position in which the stem could be safely cut near the button, a double-clip was often required (some foremen insisted on it). All this had to be done wearing gloves, which no doubt made it more difficult to hold the orange and make a precise cut, the naked hand being a much more sensitive tool than a gloved one (many pickers cut the fingers off their gloves). Over the course of a day, some twenty thousand clips might be made. The clippers needed to be kept in good repair and in proper adjustment, and workers often had to pay for them (and a back-up) out of their own pockets.[52]

Descending the ladder with a full fifty-pound sack, the picker could not bump it against the ladder. Sacks had a flap on the bottom: pickers placed their sack in the field box, and then lifted the flap to let the oranges gently tumble into the box. If the foreman heard you doing this, you had done it wrong: noiselessness was the standard. But a slow and quiet unloading of the sack could work in the worker's favor, as some pickers discovered. "You'd *ease* 'em out of that bag, *ease* 'em out until you had a full box," one picker explained. "You shake that box and it wouldn't be full. But you let it *ease* real *easy*, there's a lot of holes in there. I'd probably gain six, eight boxes a day that way." Periodically, the foreman inspected the oranges in the field box, looking for cuts and abrasions. Rubbing the orange over his cheek, he used his own skin to determine if the stem as cut could catch the skin of other oranges in the box. If over 2 percent of the oranges in the box were prickly, the picker did not get any credit for the box; he might even be fired. This gave foremen tremendous power over workers, who had no formal means for seeking redress. Indeed, when pickers went out on strike, foremen's abusive practices were usually a main complaint. The imperative to pick oranges that bore no sign of labor turned Eden into a highly disciplined space.[53]

Two "loaders" lifted the field box, weighing fifty to seventy pounds, up to the truck or wagon, and two loaders on board carefully received the box and set it down. Skilled workmen turned this into a dance of kinetic energy: workers below put energy behind the box, no more than necessary, to thrust it up to workers above, who grabbed the box almost in flight, using but curbing its downward drive to put it gently in place. Stacked six high, the boxes were unloaded at the packing house using a handtruck with a twelve-inch nose.

The oranges arriving at the packing house had been pulled out of nature by a worker whose identity was inscribed on them—literally. Each box was chalked with the worker's number. For the inspectors at the packing house, then, the oranges became crystal balls through which they could see what had transpired earlier in distant groves. They could even go to the groves and find which trees the picker had picked, as the worker's number also hung on the tree. Powell's acute managerial sense led him to a paradoxical insight: only by maintaining the particular identity of oranges through parts of their journey to market could the consumer get a "uniform orange." In turn, the oranges that had passed through the picker's hands had left their mark on him—figuratively. As Gilbert González explains, "An easy identifying mark, a drooping shoulder and a strap tattoo, distinguished the picker from workers in other fields."[54] From the picker's point of view, the Powell Method changed the tree and its oranges, which changed his way of knowing and working in nature.

HANDLING FRUIT IN THE PACKING HOUSES

"The handling of the fruit in the house is just a matter of constant care and close supervision," declared Placentia Mutual Orange Association manager H. O. Easton. In a well-designed plant, the orange traveled some three hundred feet over belts, through washing, drying, waxing, and polishing machines, across sorting tables, and through a sizing apparatus before it arrived in the packer's bin, ready to be wrapped in a tissue and placed carefully in a box for shipment. The crude mechanisms in place when Powell made his initial survey were replaced, machines were improved, and by the mid-1920s, a form of Fordism was in operation in the packing plants. But even in the most modern houses, skilled laborers were still essential to creating a Sunkist orange. While machines could do an adequate job of sorting fruit by size, qualitative judgments could be done only by humans. An eye for aesthetic value that would match the advertising could not be manufactured (at least not yet). Packing an attractive and tight box of oranges was also a complicated procedure; good packers were "artists," as one house manager enthused. The Powell Method called for careful handling, something machines could not accomplish for every function needed to get an orange out of the grove and into a box. Machines, then, remained adjuncts of human beings, not the other way around.[55]

While Japanese American men had worked as graders and packers in the houses until around 1910, women almost exclusively filled these positions after that date. Men worked in the houses in other capacities. By 1913, half of laborers in the packing houses were women, and that ratio grew to 65 percent by 1939. Growers initially turned to women because of their availability. But the jobs that they performed—principally grading and packing—soon became sex-typed. Women began to be seen as naturally adapted to these positions, and men were not hired to fill them. During this period, positions that could be identified with the essentialized characteristics of womanhood—jobs needing a "personal touch" and anything having to do with emotional support or food—became female jobs. In the industrial sector, jobs that did not require great strength but did require "manual dexterity, attention to detail, ability to tolerate monotony" were often sex-typed as female. These two ways of sex-typing jobs made fruit packing and grading women's work, for these tasks required attention to detail and dexterity. The actuality of women quickly and precisely packing oranges could be combined with an image of women (or "womanhood") giving the oranges a nurturing touch. While the advertising seldom portrayed actual women workers, orange crate labels, as we have seen, often pictured idealized women holding up oranges in their nurturing, alabaster hands. Some packing and canning house managers preferred that white women handle the fruit in its final stages of preparation for the market, concerned that a perception of Mexicanas handling the fruit might spoil the image.[56]

Entering a packing house, any observer could see that women performed much vital work, including the all-important grading of oranges.[57] As one manager explained, "The grades were very closely looked at by Sunkist inspectors so every packing house had to conform to a set of rules that made a very uniform grade in all packing houses. That kept Sunkist pretty well in front of all others, because they had standardized the quality. . . . Buyer confidence was important."[58] After the oranges had been weighed, washed, dried, and waxed (to replace the orange's natural wax, which had been washed away), they were conveyed to the grading table. Here, the grader separated the oranges into "Extra Fancy," "Fancy," or "Choice" grades. The grader had to be able to notice small differences in color and texture and act quickly to keep up the flow of oranges. For each grade, a separate conveyer took the oranges away to a sizing machine.

The role was considered so important that an expert on light, color, and vision was hired to reengineer the grader's workplace so that it would be "fatigue-free and efficient." The first order of business was to sort out the *people* who did the job. The expert designed a test to identify sorters who would "have fast coordination between hand and eye . . . accurate color perception [and] visual systems of proper make-up to withstand long periods of light saturation." These tests would "eliminate the expense of attempting to train individuals not adapted to sorting operations." In addition to expressing the idea that evolution had adapted some women to this job, the test helps us see that sorting, albeit fast-paced, was no rote operation. After attending to the human element, the grading operation could be redesigned. Since natural lighting often produced glare, which interfered with "the seeing act" and "represents a positive waste of energy," artificial lights should be installed. Sorting should be done on yellow tables in order to calm the worker's "nervous system." These reforms were aimed at improving workers' efficiency and enhancing the aesthetics of the packed oranges. By defining "seeing" as an "act" that required energy, the packing house managers had begun to realize the degree to which workers put the energy of their bodies into the job.[59]

This was a lesson that Frederick C. Mills, having just graduated Phi Beta Kappa from the University of California at Berkeley, learned the hard way. In May 1914, his economics professor, Carleton Parker, hired him for a covert operation. Parker had just become the executive secretary of Governor Hiram Johnson's newly formed Commission of Immigration and Housing. Like the protagonist in Jack London's story "South of the Slot," Mills went undercover to discover how the other half lived and worked. In his costume of "worn blue over-alls," Mills set off for Tulare County. Becoming a "rustler" (one of the roles sex-typed for males in the houses) was tough for a tenderfoot. Mills waited for a packer to yell "Box," and then he would haul off the seventy-pound crate she had filled. He carted off seven hundred in a day. Mills's body, unaccustomed to such manual labor, registered in the soreness of its muscle groups the energy he had put into the job. "By the time I finished," he wrote in his diary, "my feet were blistered, my hands were torn, my arms almost numb, my back aching, and each of my thighs with a red hot sear across it where the edges of the box rubbed."[60]

Mills was both working and observing work. He noted that women talked among themselves as they worked, and that the managerial style at the house was rather blunt. When a box did not pass inspection, the boss instructed him to take it back to the packer, "and if she doesn't like it tell her to go to hell." He was soon promoted, becoming the rustler for a second set of packers—a more efficient, "gum-chewing" lot from Los Angeles. Mills complained,

> Constantly, unremittingly, the cry of "box," enunciated shrilly, harshly, irritably, mandatorily, pleadingly, angrily, nasally, and in various combinations of these tones, would ring out in twenty different sharps and flats. . . . Every time I thought I had a moment to rest, to relax the tortured tendons and muscles in my arms and back the shrill cry "box" would come from three or four different sections. How I cursed that sound before the day closed. "The damned," me thought, "use that word in Hell."[61]

The word that created hellish sensations in Mills most certainly was an expression of joy for the women. Each box they packed meant more money for them, while for Mills it increased the amount of energy he had to expend to earn his hourly wage. One citrus worker noted, "Their hands moved so fast . . . you couldn't see their hands." Photographs of packers capture this speed as well, showing a blur where the hands would be.[62]

In his official report, Mills turned the speed of these women's work into a moral story about the dehumanizing, and de-sexing, aspects of industry. "Hour after hour their flying hands repeat a monotonously mechanical movement," he wrote. "By closing time the girls are pale and worn looking, almost wilting before one's eyes as the days drag along, leaning forward on their boxes for an occasional rest." He concluded that the "rigorous nature of their work, while it lasts, cannot but render them unfit to serve the race by mothering the generation of the future." To Mills, the energy flowing out of these women and into the oranges came at a cost to their fertility—it was production *or* reproduction. He also suggested that women packers might seek to "augment their earnings by the same clandestine means to which many of the shop girls and factory workers of the cities are forced." With this veiled reference to the perils of prostitution, Progressive reformers thus layered a new set of concerns over the agrarian critique of agribusiness, charging the seasonal pattern of unstable employment in mechanized workplaces with eroding the sexual and psychological fortitude of female workers. Just a few years earlier, Louis Brandeis had expressed these concerns in the famous brief in the Supreme Court case *Muller v. Oregon* (1908), which argued that the "overwork of future mothers . . . directly attacks the welfare of the nation." The brief cited an 1887 report from the California Bureau of Labor Statistics: "Directly does Nature punish the disobedience of her laws." The conservation of sexual or reproductive energy was a central concern of people who sought to reform California's work environments. Katherine Phillips Edson, director of the Industrial Welfare Commission, which investigated conditions in factories and food processing plants, argued that "women were made long before industry, so we have got to make industry to suit women."[63]

Women packers did stress the demanding nature of this job of standing up all day wrapping and packing oranges. Julia Aguilar said simply, "I mean, we were exhausted." Many former packers felt that their rheumatoid arthritis was attributable to their work. But women also showed considerable pride in their workmanship. Despite injunctions against talking, female packers formed a community on the job, establishing social networks with their coworkers. Mexicana packers "had a strong respect for their occupation. Those who performed their job well, especially those who could pack one hundred boxes, the *cieneras,* or *compionas,* received considerable respect, which translated into a camaraderie enjoyed exclusively by women."[64]

But to pack any box at a rate that would bring in decent wages was a challenge. Because each size of orange was packed differently, at least ten different patterns had to be mastered. Wearing gloves, packers had to wrap each orange in tissue paper bearing the name of Sunkist and an image: "They were to twist the wrapper around the orange tightly making a very neat formation of paper over the printed part [of the tissue] and place them in the box so the prints were all lined up and the cracks in the wooden boxes showed the prints." Supervisors looked on to make sure that the packers did no "flagging" (incomplete wrapping jobs). Special care went into an Extra Fancy box: these were the best-quality oranges and they garnered the highest prices. To pack an Extra Fancy box was an art that was performed while the clock ticked. Managers took pride in these boxes and came to respect the skill that went into making a perfect box. Easton noted that "it was a case of having the finesse of putting out a first-class product." To pack an Extra Fancy box perfectly and then see on the house bulletin board that your crate had brought a premium price on the auction block in New York must have been rewarding. Easton reported, "All our employees feel it their duty to do all they can to keep our brands at the top of the list, and it is a source of satisfaction to see just how successful they are." Yet when the packer subtracted what she was paid for packing that fruit from the price at which it sold, she might not have felt so rewarded. In 1923, a packer would have received less than thirty cents for packing a crate that might have sold for more than seven dollars.[65]

Wrapping the oranges in Sunkist tissues was a way of giving them a new identity. The advertising promised uniform oranges. From a commercial standpoint, the tissues helped assure that retailers would not be able to pass off just any oranges as those featured in the advertising. By 1926, printing machines were beginning to be used to directly print the name on the oranges. But wrapping did not cease with the new printing machine, because the tissue that served aesthetic and commercial ends also served biological ones. If one orange was attacked by blue mold, the tissue would shield others in the pack. When the packer placed the branded and wrapped product into a crate, the oranges that nature had made in an infinite range of forms had been laboriously reduced to homogeneity and perfection.

CONTROLLING ENTROPY AND DIFFERENCE

The orange, having passed through human hands and an elaborate mechanical sequence, had been buffeted and buffed, washed and rewaxed, graded and stamped, wrapped and packed. Finally the lid was pressed on, and the crate was chilled and then loaded onto a refrigerated freight train heading east. The experience of workers both paralleled and was shaped by that of oranges. Nature and humans were both laboring—in other words, bearing fruit.[66] The energy of human muscle, and of the oil and steam that powered the motors, had been poured into these oranges. That energy was used to counter two ever-present aspects of nature: entropy and difference.

Entropy is the rule that things fall apart. The Powell Method had been designed to arrest this decomposition. In the late 1920s, the influx to Southern California of a new element from the Owens Valley—not water, but borax—provided a chemical fix. Borax could kill the blue mold, and so it was readily adopted as part of the process of preparing oranges. Later, the Food Machinery Corporation introduced Hypo-clor, a chlorine-based treatment designed to kill molds and sterilize the fruit. After going through the lethal bath, the orange was coated with a product called FlavorSeal, designed to allow the fruit to breathe while minimizing loss of moisture and maximizing shine and "eye-appeal." Its logo, a white woman wrapped in cellophane, reflects the drive to turn nature into a thing of beauty preserved under glass. These new treatments partly obviated the careful handling imperative and so began to erode the Powell Method. But whether employing borax or careful handling, the packing house was designed for the conservation of nature's energy—the solar power synthesized by the trees and accumulated within the skin of the oranges.[67]

Difference was controlled through another strategy. However much growers and pomologists had attempted to change the fact, nature was not a controlled environment. It was true that all of the Washington navel trees grown in California, some seven million by 1929, were genetically identical, the products of a mass production of fruit-bearing machines. Yet each grew apart, under the environmental influence of its particular landscape. Amidst the order of the carefully plotted and maintained citrus landscape, nature's disorder reasserted itself in small ways. The energy of workers and the skilled, coordinated action of human eyes and hands had gone into making identity out of nature's difference—oranges that were "uniformly good." In attaining uniformity, the oranges lost their identification with the grower, except as a slip of paper (the "pack out") redeemable for cash when other fruit analogous to the actual ones that were delivered from his grove were sold. As a house manager explained, "The packed fruit is loaded into cars. It loses its grower identity as it arrives at the loading area, because the grower has had his fruit tabulated according to the size and grade and the quantity of boxes. From there on it loses its identity into the car, just all put together to fit the orders of sizes and grades the way a buyer wants it." While the grower's connection to his or her fruit became abstract, the physical connection workers had had with these objects of nature was erased. In the marketplace, consumers would know the fruit by Sunkist's advertising: it would appear as a spontaneous production of Eden, bearing no traces of workmanship.[68]

Between the packing house and the grocery store, the magical transformation of nature into commodity had been laboriously accomplished. Workers put their bodies on the line to make the oranges' journey of out of nature as smooth as possible, to become like the fairy angel pickers in the growers' fantasy. In doing so, they helped make oranges that would match consumers' fantasy, which saw the fruit as having been kissed only by the sun. The oranges that were advertised as condensations of nature's purity were in fact constructions finished in a space abuzz with human activity appropriately called "nature's workshop."[69]

But was it forced labor? If our muralist, who had sought to depict citrus work as a sunny occupation, had returned to Fullerton three years later, he might have been moved to brush in the most curious pickers of all— German prisoners of war. Though locals said the prisoners were happy to work outside (and growers prepared instructional pamphlets in German to assure careful handling), Julian might have had to change the tone of his painting to accommodate them. We might wonder: Did the presence of the actual prisoners reveal that workers had been captive all along? Citrus workers' freedom was in fact limited and defined by the conditions of the work environment, which were, in turn, shaped by patterns of racialization that naturalized their subordinate position. But this did not amount to a prison. Workers negotiated within this system, and they did receive wages for their work that were, as the growers pointed out, significantly higher than those of their counterparts in Texas or Florida. They were free to leave. But when citrus workers united behind a union in Orange County in 1936 and were faced with pick handles, shotguns, tear gas, and handcuffs; when they were held in a stockade jail without bail; when they were denied jury trials; and when authorities told strikers they had to go to the groves or turn themselves in to the court, the citrus landscape began to look like a prison state in which workers had no control over their own bodies.[70]

The intensity with which the growers fought the strike infuriated workers, but the strike also disillusioned growers. To growers, who believed their own story that those who worked in citrus were answering an evolutionary call, the strike seemed like bucking the sun, an effort to go against the very laws of nature. Moreover, Sunkist's enlightened housing policy had been designed to make workers feel at home. The strike was a rude awakening, for growers had believed their workers were perfectly content with their lot.

FIVE

"The Finished Products of Their Environment"

THE MEMBERS OF A FAMILY of Mexicano agricultural workers in San Bernardino did their best to accommodate a woman from the government when she visited their home. Though the husband knew some English from his work in the groves, most of what this woman said was beyond him. He gathered that she was interested in children. She inspected their kitchen, looked closely at their food and at their bedding, and seemed disturbed that their small house had only a dirt floor. She pulled out a cigar box with Popsicle-stick legs attached, and pointed to his wife and to him. He understood that she wanted him to make such a box, and that she would expect to see it on her next visit. With his wife pregnant and his days in the groves already long, it seemed a bit crazy to spend his time this way, but he obliged nonetheless. When he produced his handiwork at her next visit, she began to shake her head, smiling at the couple with a mixture of warmth and condescension. Something was not right about the box. She was saying you were not supposed to use a cigar box but something bigger, like an orange crate. The man thought the government lady really crazy now—first she wanted him to make a box for *cigarros* to stand up in the air, and now she wanted him to put a box for *naranjas* up there as well.

In an official pamphlet published in 1938, the California Bureau of Child Hygiene turned this incident into evidence of the "literal mindedness" it thought typical of "the Mexican." The cigar box was a model from which the couple was expected to fashion a cradle. "They are incapable of complex reasoning or of deduction," the report concluded. The social worker felt it essential to make a space exclusively for the newborn on the way, so that it would not have to share a bed with older siblings. The image of a newborn baby, born of Mexicano citrus workers, being put in an orange-crate cradle—perhaps the brand with a picture of a white child playing with building blocks on its side—is, of course, ironic. But it is also telling.

Building its own legitimacy on stories of Mexican cultural and mental inferiority, the bureau saw its work as a matter of life and death. But much more was going on here than a laudable campaign to decrease infant mortality, for the mission of saving lives was tied to the project of changing a way of life. Through its report, the bureau produced an image of Mexicans as true primitives: they were ignorant and superstitious; illogical, as reflected in the way they dressed their children; and profoundly ignorant about nutrition, giving young children tortillas, beans, and, worst of all, chilies. Given this perspective, it is no wonder that the bureau felt justified in intervening whenever a Mexicana bore what it called her "inevitable baby." In its desire to manage the upbringing of Mexicanas' American-born children from the point of conception, the bureau was one state institution exercising what Michel Foucault has aptly called "bio-power." The term refers to how modern states aim to organize life in its most intimate quarters, how they construct and discipline bodies as a means of managing large populations.[1]

In the United States, bio-power was a vital dimension of that elusive entity called Progressivism. Though Progressivism sometimes seems like a grab bag of contradictions, a common belief of many Progressive reformers was that the key to improving society in general was to clean up life in the home. To a degree seldom seen since the heyday of the closed corporate communities of Puritan New England, progressivism made the private public. Progressives tended to believe that if all life came before the inspecting eyes of scientific experts, the body politic could be strengthened immeasurably. Improvement started at home.[2]

When the state or Progressive clubwomen showed up in the homes of Mexicano workers, the stakes involved more than the life of individual children. Children's health was the foot in door. Progressives were very concerned about the health and welfare of the poor; they wanted to help them for their own sake, as well as the sake of society at large. The Progressives, who tended to be white, middle-class professionals, tried their best to humanely incorporate the "other" while protecting the "self." In an era of rapid and tumultuous immigration and economic change, that self, understood either as the white middle class or American democracy, seemed to need protection from all manner of diseases—biological, social, real, and, most of all, imaginary. Without the clean and efficient living spaces being promoted by home economists and advertisers, Progressives believed that the home would become a breeding ground. The abnormal and the deformed would flourish, giving rise to the disorder in which radicalism could grow and the body politic would be infected.

Leading agricultural employers, including representatives of the citrus industry, lobbied to keep the border with Mexico porous in order to keep up the supply of workers whom they could employ on a no-risk basis (noncitizen worker advocates could be deported). But Sunkist also tried to create a stable, skilled, and thus reliable workforce by incorporating Mexicanos into American society to a degree. Convinced that environmental influence was critical to the creation of contentment and efficiency, Sunkist and the state's Progressive social agencies—foremost among them the California Commission of Immigration and Housing—agreed that the Mexicano worker had to be made at home.

THE HARVEST AT WHEATLAND, 1913

As much as anything, it was the lemonade that got to workers that blazing summer at Durst Ranch near Wheatland in 1913. Water was a mile away from the fields in which they gathered hops in 105-degree weather. The ranch owner's cousin operated lemonade concessions, charging five cents a cup for his artificially precious liquid. To compound matters, it was not even the real stuff: it was made of citric acid, something that could be had from Sunkist's Lemon By-Products Company. As one worker testified, the so-called lemonade "almost cut the insides out of us."[3]

The lemonade was not the only thing eating away at the workers' bodies and wages. Their pay had been kept low by the rancher's policy of advertising in three states to secure an oversupply of workers for the harvest, dissolving the power individuals might have had to negotiate a higher wage.[4] Picking sacks were in short supply, vines carried only a thin crop that year, and workers were often required to re-sort the bags they did manage to fill. Indeed, when it came to his hops, the owner insisted on "an unusual standard of cleanliness." Standards of cleanliness were also "unusual" in the camp. There were long lines for the roily well water, and garbage piled up in the surrounding puddles, creating a sludge that seeped back into the well. Workers had to wait in line for one of the few and "revoltingly filthy" latrines.[5] No provisions were made to take away the garbage. Under these conditions, a host of microorganisms flourished and colonized the bodies of workers, causing dysentery, diarrhea, a malarial fever, and typhoid.

By August 2, the workers had had enough. They drew up a list of demands and went on strike. Two thousand gathered for a rally the next day, listening to a speech by a Wobbly, a member of the Industrial Workers of the World (IWW), Richard "Blackie" Ford. Holding in his arms a sick child, he exclaimed, "It's for the life of the kids that we are doing this."[6] Here was a call for "child hygiene" from workers rather than government bureaucrats. When the sheriff arrived, a shot was fired, touching off a riot in which four people, including the district attorney, were killed. The state's response was twofold. First, Governor Hiram Johnson sent in the state militia and authorized a manhunt for Ford. Johnson also dispatched a former Berkeley economist to the scene, armed only with a pen. This man, Carleton Parker, was on more than a fact-finding mission: he was searching for an overarching theory that would explain labor unrest and identify a solution.

Wheatland presented a novel opportunity to approach the labor problem from a Progressive angle. In part because the riot involved the IWW and followed on the heels of its much-publicized free-speech campaigns, Wheatland received extensive exposure in the state's press. Bringing attention to an apparent breach of norms, Wheatland presented an occasion for rethinking labor relations in California agriculture. To find a solution to this crisis, the redressive machinery of the state was brought in. Conveniently, a special body had just been created to handle such matters—the California Commission of Immigration and Housing, for which Parker served as first administrative chief. Parker rightly observed that the riot "has grown from a casual, though bloody, event in California labor history into such a focus of discussion and analysis of the state's great migratory labor problem that the incident can well be said to begin, for the commonwealth, a new and momentous labor epoch." As such, it became an inaugurating event in what anthropologist Victor Turner has called "the social drama" (a drama that would be reprised in the 1930s).[7]

To Parker, the Wheatland riot was a symbol of a "sick social order."[8] While the Wobblies would have agreed that the social order was sick, they would not have appreciated being made out as the canker that led to the diagnosis. Parker saw labor radicals as the misshapen and damaged products of a sick environment. The solution to labor unrest was to have the state literally clean up the camps. By applying the best scientific knowledge about hygiene and housing, the ailing body of California agribusiness would be cured and its discontents, like bacteria growing on a pile of refuse, would be cleared away as well.

"Nature" appeared in several forms in the commission's analysis of the riot. First, it shaped the structure of California agriculture, creating varied microclimates in which certain fruits and vegetables grew best in particular localities and ripened at different times. "This nature-ordained agricultural specialization" Parker argued, "is the basic cause of the existence of the California migratory worker." Second, the commission proposed that certain conditions make people revert to an animal state. In the midst of the Wheatland riot, the rioting worker became "a wild and lawless animal." Finally, on a more basic level, Parker viewed human beings as biological creatures adapting themselves to their environment. He was influenced by his readings of Sigmund Freud's work and other literature on "abnormal and behaviouristic psychology." Inspired by those who saw human nature as a collection of instincts formed in relation to its surroundings, Parker proposed that the best way to prevent another Wheatland was to eradicate those environmental conditions in which "abnormality" grew. Workers were simply the "finished products of their environment."[9]

Like other Progressives, Parker saw human beings as "plastic lumps of human dough." Exposure to the frustrating conditions of migratory work life would create psychological and even physiological deformities, as their interior landscape would be shaped by the one they encountered outside. Finding a solution to the labor problem, then, required investigation and reform of the work environment. Responsibility for riots, in this logic, rested as much or more on the growers as it did on the radicals, for they had created the "unsanitary conditions." The radicals themselves were viewed as "the involuntary transmitting agents of an uncontrollable force set in motion by those who created the unlivable conditions." But however much they were rhetorically divested of agency, the Wobblies were nonetheless seen as carriers of a social disease who had to be quarantined from other farmworkers. As Don Mitchell argues, the IWW was turned into a public health problem, and was treated as such.[10]

But the commission was ultimately more interested in getting at the root cause than in locking up radicals. Confident in its diagnosis, Parker said that "the improvement of living conditions in the labor camps will have the immediate effect of making the recurrence of impassioned, violent strikes and riots not only improbable, but impossible." Sunkist took this claim seriously as well. Citrus growers had been frightened by the Wobblies' purported threat to drive copper nails into the limbs of orange trees. Growers wanted them out of California's groves, and they wanted to create a stable workforce impervious to the spread of radical ideas. The commission's idyllic portrait of the future of labor relations resonated with Sunkist's dreams. Through scientific management, the environment could be made over into one that fostered the growth of "human organic welfare" instead of debilitating social diseases. To transform California into this organic commonwealth, the commission and Sunkist alike soon focused their landscaping efforts on a vital place: the worker's home.[11]

THE PROGRESSIVE'S PLACE IS IN THE HOME

It was not always clear that homemaking would be a central concern of the new California Commission of Immigration and Housing. Its original raison d'être was the impending completion of the Panama Canal and the flood of new immigrants it was expected to bring. In 1912, Governor Johnson had appointed an ad-hoc immigration committee. The idea for it had come from his longtime friend Simon J. Lubin, a leading light of California's Progressive movement. Improving housing was something they took seriously. In the first draft proposal, the agency was to be called the Commission of Industries, Immigration and Housing. The second draft made it simply the Commission of Immigration, but the final draft restored *housing* to the title. To see why housing was ultimately elevated, it is important to understand something of Lubin's intellectual odyssey, his views on immigration, and the influence of female Progressives.[12]

Lubin, born in Sacramento in 1876, inherited an interest in agriculture and reform from his father, David, and his uncle, Harris Weinstock. Having become rich making their dry-goods store in Sacramento into the largest operation of its kind on the Pacific Coast, Lubin and Weinstock became "crusaders for industrial and agrarian reform." Having grown up in this reform milieu, Simon went off to Harvard and pursued what would become a lifelong interest: immigration. He spent vacations working in a settlement house in New York, and after graduating spent two years at the

South End House in Boston. Like Jane Addams (whose plank on immigration had inspired Lubin at the Progressive national convention of 1912), Lubin believed that immigrants carried gifts in their culture. Eschewing the "100 percent Americanism" of Teddy Roosevelt and others, these Progressives sought ways to incorporate immigrants into American society while respecting some of their cultural differences. A penetrating critic of California's waves of red-baiting and xenophobic hysteria, Lubin once said, "There may be Communists among us. Perhaps there are also vegetarians and Baptists. We need fear nothing on that account." Pluralism was at the core of Lubin's social philosophy, and his ideal of welcoming rather than demonizing immigrants shaped Johnson's administration.[13]

"The right kind of assimilation," Lubin told the San Francisco YMCA in 1913, is "not a one-sided affair, we only impart and the other only receives; but a mutual give-and-take." Challenging the assumption that immigrants should strive to become exactly like native-born Americans, Lubin asked, "Is the environment in most American towns so nearly perfect that we may well be satisfied if the new-comer merely fits in?" Citing statistics on literacy, crime, housing conditions, and economic welfare, Lubin said immigrants should learn to emulate "not so much these actual American practices and customs, but rather the American ideal." On pragmatic as well as psychological grounds, Lubin objected to forcing the immigrants to sever ties to their home culture. If you "get him to make fun of his national customs and ideals, you make him a very bitter, disconnected and reckless person and by no means a desirable citizen . . . to tear out of him at one stroke the ideals he brings [is to] take away the things that make a man, his very life itself."[14]

But if it was dangerous to try to take the country out of the child, it was inevitable that the immigrant's life would be transformed. In fact, Lubin thought their very bodies would be altered. He drew on a seminal study by anthropologist Franz Boas that had struck a powerful blow against scientific racism. Boas used the tools of physiometry to show that the physical characteristics of immigrants, especially their children, changed in the new world. "Race" did not singularly determine phenotype; environment had a shaping hand. More important, these somatic changes were believed to be the outward sign of more subtle but more profound internal changes. Lubin explained, "When we come to study the traits of the mind, the ways of thinking and acting, we find that these continue to develop long after the body stops growing; and [Boas] emphasizes the fact that changes in mind and heart are very much more marked than modifications in bodily form." The policy implications of these findings were twofold: the immigrant should be exposed to good living conditions (to grow the body) and to "American ideals" (to grow the heart and mind). Simply making the immigrant like the native was "a poor scheme for toning up the alien." Imagining the work of naturalizing the foreigner as a kind of body building, Lubin's toned-up alien would, in turn, contribute to "nation building."[15]

Historians have variously called immigrants "the uprooted" (to emphasize the cultural disruption of immigration) or the "transplanted" (to emphasize the resilience of immigrant cultural traditions in a new land). Lubin would have generally approved of this class of metaphor, for he tended to see immigration in environmental terms. He probably would have preferred a different organic metaphor: "the hybridized," or better, "the burbanked." But he was very much unlike the eugenicists whose idea of improvement was purifying the white race. Lubin would attempt to create a kind of greenhouse in which the old stock and the new scions would take to each other, fostering "a mutual give-and-take, where each gives and takes only the best in each."[16]

Lubin grounded his theory of environmental influence—of "nurture over nature"—in the home. From his experience in settlement house work, Lubin had become familiar with the idea that a proper home would uplift its residents. The home had long been viewed as a haven of cultural values and a nursery for citizenship. Gayle Gullet observes that "from the beginning of the nineteenth century women reformers believed that 'home defense,' or building a family environment that was supportive of the social order, was women's distinctive political responsibility." By the beginning of the Progressive era, the gap between private and public spheres had been bridged with the metaphor of "municipal housekeeping." Suffragist Carrie Chapman Catt argued, "It is sometimes thought that politics deals with matters difficult to understand, and quite apart from affairs of the home; that while politics touches business, which is man's sphere in all directions, it nowhere touches the home, woman's sphere." After showing all the ways that the home is regulated by government, Catt argued that women were enduring a kind of taxation without representation. Her solution: "Seat the 'Queen of the Home' upon the throne of government beside the 'King of Business,' and let them rule together." The powerful discourse of the "Christian home" used by rescue home workers and their religious supporters would meld into a discourse of the "American home" used by professional social workers and their political allies. Politics, in short, had been domesticated.[17]

But Lubin at first did not push housing as a central concern of the new commission. That task fell to Katherine Felton. Though some objected to combining immigration with housing, Felton argued that the "home is the basis of civilization in all lands. The house is the concrete aspect of the home. The house, generally overcrowded and in the slums, is the first point of contact between the immigrant and his new environment. And no culture can be fostered in a miserable hovel, but ignorance, vice and crime thrive therein."[18] She convinced the commission to put *housing* in its name and to take on the private sphere as part of its public charge. Lubin soon began to investigate the relationship of housing to immigration in great detail, writing to Hull House and his old residence in Boston for advice and collecting various pamphlets on the subject. The commission then put forward a thesis about the significance of housing in American history.

It turned the story of the log cabin into a parable legitimizing state involvement in domestic arrangements. There was once a golden age, the commission wrote, when workers lived not in tenements but in simple housing "built of enduring and honest materials." Ordinary Americans lived in such wholesome dwellings "during the formative period of the nation's growth," and so the nation experienced universal "progress and development." But in the early twentieth century, more and more Americans were forced into tenements. Such conditions threatened the foundations of the nation and gave rise to an anxiety about housing not unlike that experienced over the closing frontier. If the dark and debilitating dwellings continued to house Americans, the "very flower of our citizenry" would wilt. The commission concluded ominously: "Unless housing conditions of our people of moderate income are improved there will be no improvement in our civilization. Nothing so closely touches the individual or the race as its type of shelter—nothing has so forceful an influence on the individual as his immediate surroundings." Just as Turner had made the wilderness the protean force shaping American character, the commission saw the home as the most basic influence shaping American life. A sweet home was the garden in which American culture had grown, and would, if properly managed, continue to grow.[19]

To the commission, making sure that immigrants lived in and made for themselves an "American" home was key to their naturalization. But even natives, subjected to un-American conditions at work and at home, could become dangerously alienated. By making worker housing into a positive force of "Americanization," the protest of labor could quite literally be accommodated. To this end, the commission would attempt to shape both the physical construction of workers' housing and the cultural construction of their homes.

The commission's cultural construction of homes would follow a blueprint called Americanization. Historians have defined Americanization in various ways, some seeing it as the formal programs implemented by state or private organizations in the Progressive era, some seeing it as both these formal programs and more general forces like mass culture and work experience, and some emphasizing the institutional and informal ways through which working-class immigrant communities Americanized themselves from the bottom up. Several historians have presented especially illuminating examinations of the Americanization process as negotiated by Mexicanos in the Southwest. What emerges from this new interrogation of Americanization is not a simple top-down program that was either accepted or rejected by those who would be Americanized, but a multifaceted and constantly evolving struggle over the meaning of immigration, identity, and citizenship. Americanization was a contested concept, which is not surprising: after all, the term raised core issues about who and what counted as American.[20]

During World War I, some Americanization programs emphasized "100 percent Americanism" as an imperative of national security. A battle was waged between those groups that saw the American as an essentially homogeneous entity and those that saw the American as a product of a combination of traditions. The metaphor of the melting pot could work for both sides: all elements combining to make something new and multifarious or all differences melted down and boiled off so that a new person could be stamped out who would live according to the American way. At the Ford Motor plant, immigrant workers went through an Americanization program that promised to turn them into pure and patriotic products of America. Graduation was marked with a ritual: workers would walk into a six-foot-tall "melting pot" dressed in the peculiar clothes of their nation of origin, and walk out dressed like a department store mannequin and waving American flags. In contrast, the commission believed that "Americanization was not flag raising and 'patriotic' howling; that it was not suppression of speech and honest opinion; that it was more than teaching English to foreigners." Instead of using Americanization as a shibboleth to attack any traces of foreign values, the commission respected cultural difference and fostered "the attainment of decent standards [and] the development of national ideals." While conservatives stressed the importance of making the immigrant conform, the commission argued that an immigrant's origins should be respected and that it was American society that should be reformed.[21]

"Instead of approaching this delicate task of human adjustment with humility and studying the material with which we are to work," Commissioner Mary Gibson complained, "we . . . presume to make plans without reference to the needs or aspirations of foreigners of any sort, and then proceed like Procrustes of legend, to fit each individual to it by the old methods of stretching and sawing."[22] The commission favored a more gradual process through which immigrant culture would be given a chance to take root in American soil. It wanted its experts to act like ethnographers, first finding out where the group was coming from. Firmly grounded in his or her understanding of cultural difference, the Americanizer could then pull the immigrant into the mainstream.

As much as the commission celebrated mutual cultural respect in theory, in the field Mexicanos were most often viewed as people who had to adapt to the "American way of life." That American way of life, we should also note, was more of a fiction than a description of the way native-born Americans lived. In almost any rural county in America, social workers could find white families using the kind of child-rearing practices (e.g., having several children sleep in the same bed) deemed dangerously un-American when practiced by Mexicano immigrants. The American way of life did not exist; rather, it was being invented at the time by various apostles of modernity—social workers, academics, and advertisers. Americanization, then, was happening simultaneously to the native-born and to immigrants alike. Some were pulled into this way of life most powerfully by advertising. The state grabbed on to immigrants. Rather than seeing Americanization as an attempt to make the new immigrants conform to an already established mainstream or dominant culture, we should see the culture of immigrants as among the first frontiers into which this modern pattern of living, backed by the authority of the state and the images of advertising, intruded.

The commissioner who did the most to define and implement the actual program of Americanization was Mary Gibson. She linked the state programs of Americanization to the private efforts of women's organizations. The California Federation of Women's Clubs was particularly helpful, publishing Americanization pamphlets and supporting the commission's work. By 1915, Gibson had managed to generate considerable support for her California Home Teacher Act, which would create a cadre of instructors who would teach Americanization classes and also visit immigrant families in their homes. The state should not rely on educating only the immigrant children and offering night classes for their parents, Gibson argued. Americanizing the children without Americanizing their parents would lead to the loss of maternal authority and ultimately the breakdown of the family. Since adult women often found it impossible to attend classes at night, they had to be reached in their homes.[23] With the support of the Federation of Women's Clubs, the Home Teacher Act became law in 1915. The home teacher was "to work in the homes of the pupils, instructing children and adults in matters relating to school attendance and preparation therefor; also in sanitation, in the English language, in household duties such as purchase, preparation and use of food and of clothing and in the fundamental principles of the American system of government and the rights and duties of citizenship." The home teacher would be teaching *in* the home but also *about* the home.[24]

The home teacher often acted as an apostle for the religion of cleanliness, proselytizing with its prime icon: the bar of soap. As Amanda Chase reported, "Occasionally I linger for manual demonstration or to direct some deed of cleanliness but more often I leave soap and return later to behold results." Cleanliness was next to patriotism. She told prospective home teachers that lessons on "sanitation, including personal hygiene, and patriotic teaching" went hand in glove. In learning English by role-playing a trip to the store, the first thing the student was taught to say was "I would like to buy a bar of soap." The result would be not only a cleaner family, but what Chase considered a more respectable and American one. She felt particularly challenged in her efforts to get Mexicanos to conform to her standards, arguing that "they need education of a peculiar sort—education that shall be a disciplinary tonic—that shall give them standards—that amounts to evolution." Soap was an agent of Darwinian selection. And those who attended the classes underwent the "most striking evolution." Chase was thrilled with their growing intelligence and improved appearance, explaining how "one class of Mexican women, a timid, sloppy, baby-submerged lot to begin with, now take an honorable place on general school programs with songs and recitations in English." Photographs of such groups of women, "holding copies of the Commission's Home Teacher Manual," regularly appeared in commission publications to confirm its evolutionary tale.[25]

Home teachers had much to say about interior decorating as well. They taught their students how to use pictures—a few pictures—to liven up their surroundings. Don't clutter up the room with an array of images, the teachers advised. While these tips might seem innocuous enough, they ran roughshod over the aesthetic sensibility of the borderlands. A Protestant modernism, with its anti-iconographic prejudices, did battle with a vernacular Catholicism and its iconographic flourishes. However much respect was paid to immigrant cultures in the abstract, home teachers often attempted to install a wall-to-wall Americanism.[26]

The home teacher and the larger Americanization program were powerful forces in the lives of California immigrants, especially in communities of citrus workers. But we should not be led to believe that every Mexicana mother accepted the advice of the home teachers. "As far as the Americanization campaign itself," Gayle Gullet argues, "immigrants voted with their feet overwhelmingly against it." Like advertising agents, the home teachers and other Americanization experts functioned as "apostles of modernity." Step by step, they attempted to reengineer the culture of the immigrants. Progressive reformers, like their counterparts in advertising, had a keen understanding of what modern anthropologists have shown: that a people's standards of cleanliness both reflect and help make up the culture to which they belong. However, the home teacher typically had no sense of the relativity of such standards: cleanliness was not in the eye of the beholder. What the home teacher saw as an unquestionable liberation from dirt or bad taste, immigrant working women must often have seen as a new set of burdens and an overbearing critique of their own values.[27]

Taste itself was also up for grabs. As George Sánchez has pointed out, "Food and diet management became yet another tool in a system of social control intended to produce a well-behaved, productive citizenry." In her widely read primer "Americanization through Homemaking," home teacher Pearl Ellis posited that "Mexican families are mal-nourished, not so much from a lack of food as from not having the right varieties of foods containing constituents favorable to growth and development." The Mexican family needed less salsa and tortillas and more "body regulators and builders." Passing on the dietary knowledge then being disseminated by Sunkist, Ellis suggested twice that "orange juice is valuable food for young children" and a good source of vitamin C. Language instruction drove the lessons home. In one of the commission's pamphlets on English, immigrants learned to answer the question "Do you like fruit?" in the affirmative: "Yes, I like fruit. Fruit is good for us. It helps us to keep well. I will buy fruit to eat. I will give it to my children." Such scripted dialogues were really prescriptive monologues about proper food choice. The stakes were high, as Ellis's frightening parable about the Mexican child who goes to school without a proper lunch makes clear: "The child becomes lazy. His hunger unappeased, he watches for an opportunity to take food from the lunch boxes of more fortunate children. Thus the initial step in a life of thieving is taken." But this slippery slope from an inadequate lunch to a life of crime could be avoided. Her book included a picture of a child sent to school with a "good lunch" who was, consequently, a good and happy student. And just as the child needed to be sent to school with a proper lunch, so too did the worker. A proper lunch for a Mexican laborer consisted of a glass of milk, a minced meat or egg sandwich, a lettuce sandwich, a piece of sponge cake, a cookie, and a peach or an orange.[28]

Americanization advocates sold their programs to business with the promise that a better diet would lead to greater productivity. If Frederick Winslow Taylor's analyses could conserve worker energy on the shop floor, nutritionists would use the kitchen to increase workers' energy capital. Scientific management consultants often paid close attention to the diet of workers. When investigating the food eaten by workers at a twine factory, Gertrude Beeks "saw strange Lithuanian sausages, slabs of dark Slovak bread, and uncouth Polack pickles emerging every noon from lunch-baskets." After installing a lunch room to serve the workers a "wholesome lunch," the managers of the plant came to agree that *efficiency was being increased.*" In California, reformers saw salsa as being every bit as uncouth as the pickles of Polish extraction. Couth sauces came in two forms: a "hard sauce" of sugar, butter, and egg, and a "white sauce" of milk, flour, fat, and seasoning (to which a puree of vegetable pulp could be added).[29]

These efforts to change the dietary habits of immigrants were widespread and backed by science. Under the doctrines of the "newer nutrition," good health was not just a matter of abstaining from bad food, but the result of taking in the right vitamins and minerals (thus the increasing importance fruits and vegetables achieved in nutritional science after 1915).[30] Obviously, this was good news to California's fruit, vegetable, and canning industries. They worked closely with home economists and the state to create an ideal dietary template reformers could use to change the palates of Americans of all stripes. White middle-class Americans would be reached through the pages of the *Ladies' Home Journal* or *Saturday Evening Post* with stories of the increased "vim" they would have at the workplace, and the home teacher and other reformers would bring an analogous message into the homes of the Mexicano working class. Their work in the groves and in the packing plants required tremendous energy: the nutritional reformers promised that carefully chosen foods could reproduce that labor power in abundance, creating a more productive worker who would be less drained by his or her work.

But the effects ran even deeper. Faithful adherents of the new science of nutrition, the home economists believed in a powerful transubstantiation: workers would be naturalized, would become Americans, by eating the right foods prepared in the right ways. Theirs was, of course, an old belief: you are what you eat. Right eating would contribute to body building as well as Lubin's nation building: employers would be happy with the increased productivity of their workers and workers themselves would be earning more and feeling better at the job. Employers, Ellis stated,

> maintain that a man with a home and family is more dependable and less revolutionary in his tendencies. Thus the influence of the home extends to labor problems and to many other problems in the social regime. The homekeeper creates the atmosphere, whether it be one of harmony and cooperation or of dissatisfaction and revolt. It is to be remembered that the dispositions, once angelic, become very much marred with incorrect diet and resultant digestive disturbances.[31]

The formula for quelling the revolutionary impulses of a people living on tortillas and beans was quite simple: let them eat fruit.

THE OTHER HOME FRONT: CAMP SANITATION

If proper diet would reform workers from the inside out, improved housing would improve them from the outside in. While the Home Teacher Act allowed the commission to get into the homes of immigrants, the Labor Camp Sanitation Act, also passed in 1915, allowed it to move on a second home front. Under the sanitation act, the commission was given the power to establish and enforce standards for labor camps in agriculture, mining, and lumber. After eight years, the commission claimed that "the standards thus established by law in California have considerably lessened the just grievances of workers and have guarded against one of the most persistent causes of labor unrest and labor trouble, namely, bad housing and unsanitary living accommodations."[32]

The commission admitted that selling its vision to growers was not easy, but it made several pitches for model housing that it thought would appeal to them. It tried to "educate" growers that "'anything' was not 'good enough' for the men who came to seek employment, and that loyalty and efficiency could not be expected from men who were fed in dust-filled, fly-infested tents, and given a hundred acres for a bed." Using its environmental theory of the origin and spread of worker radicalism, the commission portrayed good housing as a prophylactic against strikes. Housing reformers connected the spatial dimensions of worker experience to their output on the job. A well-housed worker was a more efficient worker, they claimed. The commission warned, "A man has little opportunity of preserving his self-respect, which makes for efficiency, and respect for his employer, which makes for loyalty, if he lives in a filthy, over-crowded, foul-aired bunkhouse and sleeps in a vermin-infested bunk."[33]

Apparently, the loss in productivity due to improper housing and sanitation could be strictly quantified. The commission reported that "the efficiency of workers may be increased about ninety per cent by the screening of dwelling houses in localities where mosquitoes are present." The gains were attributed to a better night's sleep. Growers were informed of a novel technology that permitted them to use the same force that grew their crops to make a healthier work force: solar showers. Just as good housing and hygiene would aid in the reproduction of the labor force, growers were advised that they needed to provide for its recreation as well. Even the "best of men will grow dull and apathetic and dissatisfied if, after working hours, they have no choice but to lie back on their beds and listen to the coarse talk of chance companions." Providing books and magazines, billiards, and even movies could stave off a descent into bad morale, disease, or unionism. Being able to enjoy the products of mass culture would keep workers, no less than the children of growers, down on the farm. Moreover, it would prevent workers from turning to the radical literature of the IWW. Ultimately, the commission believed that the key to creating harmonious labor relations lay in managing the bodies and spatial experiences of workers. A worker who was clean of body would also be clean of mind and unsusceptible to infections of all sorts—biological *or* ideological.[34]

The commission provided growers with easy-to-follow guidelines for constructing such therapeutic environments. It provided blueprints for a cheap and efficient latrine and showed growers how to take advantage of sunlight as a "natural disinfectant." It calculated how much air space each worker needed for a fully restful sleep, arguing against the use of bunk beds and including floor plans of bed arrangements that would make for healthy living. The commission also put up a model camp at the Sacramento State Fair, showing growers who had come to display the products of their soil the kind of housing they could erect on it. Though it had the power to enforce camp regulations, the commission preferred to model good worker housing rather than punish growers who forced their workers to live in substandard conditions. It told parables to try to get more growers to comply. In fact, Durst Ranch was turned into a story of redemption. The place where workers had once been transformed into animals by poor conditions was now a bright spot on the California map, as the photographs of new housing featured in a commission publication confirmed. A satisfied grower reported, "Since the following out of the plan of camp sanitation as outlined by your inspector, we have been able to keep on our ranch a better class of men than we formerly employed."[35]

Ultimately, the commission hoped to lead California away from its reliance on the migratory labor of single men and toward a system that would allow families to thrive among the agricultural working class. A more efficient worker would emerge every morning from a well-kept and well-designed camp, the commission argued. But there were additional benefits to be had from a worker who could walk out of a *real* home, having been fed and nurtured there by a supportive family. It argued that "operators who once complained about the quality of labor which came to them, now plan to make their camps so attractive that they will draw and keep the better class of labor. The goal of this policy is to attract men with families, for the coming of families means a permanent labor supply, means a cleaner camp, means a camp of higher standards of morality."[36] In this way, the seedbeds of American strength—the family and the home— could be reproduced in the labor camp. Though farmworkers toiled for others in the land of agribusiness, the commission wanted to create an impression, however faint, of the Jeffersonian dream.

The California Commission of Immigration and Housing presented farmers with a radically new way of looking at the labor problem. Instead of thinking of workers as selling them unit powers of work per hour— instead of simply exchanging labor for wages—growers were asked to be involved in the more basic generation and reproduction of labor power. In essence, they were asked to think about labor *ecologically:* it was hitched to everything else, including social and political stability, and it was something that would grow in certain kinds of environments and grow dangerous in others. But carefully attending to home ecology, the commission insisted, would give growers better and more fulfilled workers.

SUNKIST'S HOME ECOLOGY

Though many agricultural employers ignored the advice of the commission, the citrus industry listened to the message of home ecology with open ears. The commission created one of its first camps for berry pickers in El Monte, and it was used as a model "to interest the citrus communities in constructing similar 'towns' for workers—mostly Mexican—who were living in shacks made of brush, weeds and tin cans reinforced by an occasional piece of discarded lumber." By 1923, the commission reported accurately that many model citrus camps had been established throughout Southern California. Sunkist became one of the commission's closest working partners, and Lubin singled out the orange industry for praise. A commission pamphlet featured before-and-after photographs of citrus camps, showing the transformation from ramshackle quarters to modern-looking homes. "The joy that these workers take in their new homes," the commission claimed, "is a revelation to the skeptics who have held that 'anything is good enough for Mexicans.'" These were images of growers and the state working together to accommodate labor unrest.[37]

What kind of houses did Sunkist build? For themselves, citrus growers built symbols of wealth and status—sprawling mansions, mission-style haciendas, estates befitting a landed gentry. As Anthea Hartig observes, "The ruling class of southern California borrowed, adapted, and twisted the factual, climactic, and spatial characteristics of other lands in formulating appropriate regional imagery, especially in architecture." Their homes and gardens became signs of their success and power, and concrete invocations of the kinds of pastoral life they romanticized. In the early 1900s, some growers turned away from architectural statements of lavish wealth and status, longing for a simple life, wishing to make their dwellings reflect the ideals of craftsmanship and embody the gifts of nature. The Arts and Crafts movement answered this desire, providing an architecture expressing, and taking advantage of, California's idyllic environment. With its celebration of the materials of their construction and with such motifs as that of the tree of life running throughout, these "poems of wood and light" were conceived as dwellings in harmony with nature. The brothers Charles and Henry Greene designed expensively simple bungalows, honoring in every visible joint and carved frieze both work and nature.[38]

Their clients included the likes of soap mogul David Gamble. But Greene and Greene also had a hand in the creation of worker housing on Sunkist president Charles Collins Teague's Limoneira ranch. Citrus growers believed that living in good, simple housing in the midst of California's resplendent environment could effectively "naturalize" workers. The housing would root them to the soil, building within them a loyalty to the place and their employer and creating the perfect conditions under which their labor power would be reproduced year after year.[39]

From 1918 through the early 1920s, a spate of articles on the proper housing of citrus workers appeared in *The California Citrograph*. George Hodgkin, head of Sunkist's industrial relations department, wrote that citrus growers fully recognized "the economy of durable construction and the efficacy of comfort and modern sanitation." Plant pathologist A. D. Shamel penned several of the *Citrograph* articles and argued that "by providing decent homes and surroundings and treating the Mexicans like human beings, the labor problem on citrus ranches in Southern California can largely be solved." Inspecting both housing and trees, Shamel was quick to draw a connection between the "physical condition" of the trees and the buoyant morale of workers who were provided good housing and humane treatment. Echoing the commission, Shamel explained how model citrus camps "take care of the physical and mental welfare of the workers in the orchard and packing house."[40]

Sunkist believed that labor supply and housing conditions were fundamentally linked. When some immigrant workers had been lured back to Mexico with better pay, Hodgkin said, "The only argument we have against these higher wages is permanent work and in order to make that argument attractive we must furnish permanent homes." "The day is gone," Limoneira's camp manager stated, "when a farmer could 'get by' while building relatively better accommodations for his horses and cows . . . than for his family and his hired help." Appealing to economics rather than humanitarianism, Hodgkin reasoned that "to make a citrus camp pay—to make it produce the desired workers—it is necessary to create an atmosphere that will attract and hold such workers."[41]

Initially, growers built adobe houses, for Mexicanos were thought to prefer buildings of this type. Some argued that adobe was the appropriate building material for Southern California. But soon small wooden structures, not unlike the most inexpensive ready-made houses on the market at the time, predominated. At a cost of about $300, growers could make these modern units, outfitted with plumbing and electricity, available to their workers. Plans could be obtained for free from Sunkist's industrial relations department.[42]

Sunkist believed that Americanization work would add to the positive impact of such housing. There is a "relationship between picking costs" and singing "songs in English about opening the windows, washing the baby and learning English." Combined with good housing, Americanization would help "make the labor camp pay" by retaining good workers and increasing "the physical and mental abilities of workers for doing more work." Local associations made sure to construct a house for a home teacher in the midst of their worker communities. Growers often selected the teachers and sometimes paid part of their salaries as well. These teachers, in turn, often reported to growers about what they saw going on in the Americanization classes. Thus, surveillance and uplift cohabitated. Furthermore, these workers' homes did not enjoy sanctity, as police would sometimes raid them without warrants.[43]

But growers generally put more energy into building homes than breaking into them. Sunkist, not unlike the commission, wanted to see real families occupy them. Orange picking and processing required the skilled labor of both men and women (and children worked as well). Since oranges and lemons could be picked almost year-round, the citrus industry was in an excellent position to replace migratory workers with rooted ones who would have opportunities for year-round employment. When they created homes in order to attract "the family unit as a source of labor," growers thought they would get two good things for the price of one: able-bodied workers who were more concerned with family life than radical politics. On some ranches, workers could only rent homes, but on others they could purchase them. Growers pointed out that workers who decided to buy these homes would be more attached to their employers. If the male worker's "family is well and happy, if his house is neat and clean, and his meals good—and above all if his yard is full of vegetables and flowers which he has planted—he will be pretty certain to think twice before uprooting himself." Such a worker would reject offers to work elsewhere, saying, as one camp manager reported, "'I have my home with my family and my garden, or my pig or my cow, and steady work.'" While camp operators emphasized that workers who were discharged would be given the home equity that was due them, workers who walked off the job also walked away from the investment they had made. To make it all work from the growers' perspective, Mexicanos who had their own place also had to be taught their place in the social landscape.[44]

While citrus camps were places where workers were instructed in Americanization, they were also places where growers received lessons in paternalism. The paternal vision rested on the recognition of the worker's basic humanity. Apparently, this truth was not self-evident, for Shamel felt the need to justify it with empirical evidence: "The writer has come to the conclusion that the Mexican laborers are human beings and that they respond to decent treatment as any other humans do." Having made the leap of recognition, growers were advised that the Mexican's "loyalty to his employer's interest may be secured to a far greater extent by a friendly expression of interest than any pecuniary advantage." "There is more than money in this world," state senator R. F. Del Valle of Los Angeles and member of the Latin American League told an audience of growers. "The Mexican will appreciate a friendly good morning and an inquiry into his family and home conditions." Growers imagined that they could re-create the happy hacienda days of lore. By showing a little goodwill and recognizing their employees as human beings, growers apparently thought that Mexicanos would accept the growers' ultimate control over the landscape, as if it had been mandated by God or nature.[45]

California's resplendent environment, growers believed, would captivate and energize workers. Hodgkin waxed eloquent about the "incomparable setting" of the Azusa Foothill Citrus Company's housing. "No more beautiful place could have been chosen for the very finest of residences—surrounded on the one side by eucalyptus trees and on the other by citrus groves, the houses face the splendor of the mountains," he said. "They are not arranged in straight rows but their line is curved to conform to the course of a concrete waterway. In short, the beauties of Southern California have been taken advantage of." Shamel gave his readers a picture of a rural idyll, where the "children of the employees have ample room for play and grow up amongst beautiful surroundings." Progressive housing placed carefully in the therapeutic California landscape would work wonders. "Amidst such surroundings, is it any wonder that peace and contentment reigns?" Shamel asked. In such surroundings, Mexicans would be happy to work away their lives with little thought of money or advancement. With a daily dose of sunshine, they and their children would grow up strong and content. Seeing the world through this sunny lens, it was possible for growers to forget that these worker houses, like the waterways, had been forced to conform to a channel laid over with concrete.[46]

Still, even in the model company camps, citrus workers lived their lives in these houses in ways that departed from the master blueprint. They negotiated these spaces and tried as much as possible to truly make them their own. Many Mexicano workers did not live in the camps at all, but in *colonias* (or villages). *Colonias* emerged on marginal land in citrus towns, places left to nonwhites under racially restrictive zoning laws. Marginal to the white community, *colonias* grew into "spiritual and cultural centers of Mexican immigrant life." Churches went up; stores and other businesses provided basic services; schools designed to teach appreciation, not derision, of Mexican culture were established; playgrounds were created, baseball teams formed; networks of community exchange and ties of kinship wove together the fabric of life. In the *colonias,* Mexicanos, as historian Matt Garcia makes plain, "insisted upon shaping the social, cultural, and physical space of their homes independent of grower control." Still, even as the *colonias* emerged as vibrant communities whose residents were making their own forms of citizenship, they were also socially and environmentally vulnerable places. The Ku Klux Klan, active in Southern California in the 1920s, used intimidation and "white supremacy" parades to keep Mexicanos from moving out of the *colonias.* Residents could be attacked by vigilantes. Basic city services did not reach them. And, since *colonias* were often located in floodplains, they could be washed away in storms (as happened with La Jolla village in Orange County).[47]

Nonetheless, citrus growers, who could not fully fathom what was going on in the *colonias* or in the camps, remained convinced that they had solved their labor problem. They had workers, they worked for low wages, and they were content with their lot. Indeed, the growers' domestic arrangements seemed vindicated in the midst of the Great Depression, when labor seemed less restless in the citrus industry than elsewhere. This, at least, was the conclusion of a major article on the citrus industry appearing in the July 1936 issue of *Fortune.* Prepared for America's business élite, the article lauded Sunkist for its cooperative marketing practices and its progressive handling of its workers. Even while agricultural workers were striking in Salinas, the Imperial Valley, and Sacramento, in Southern California, the article suggested, "Labor is contented." Photographs showed neat rows of well-made cottages with yards and trees; a smiling mother and child; two older boys, neatly dressed; and male workers coming "home after the day's work." The pictures told a story of healthy, agrarian living. Watercolor portraits of the citrus landscape evoked a sunny idyll, suggesting that Sunkist had found a way to reinvent the trouble-free hacienda of the mission myth for modern production. But if growers thought they had cultivated a perfectly content workforce by providing it with model homes and subjecting it to Americanization programs, they were in for a surprise: at the moment the *Fortune* article was going to press, citrus workers went on strike in Orange County, shattering the domestic arrangements growers had so self-satisfyingly constructed.[48]

Rather than being the "finished products of their environment," as Parker had it, workers both engaged in self-fashioning and tried to reverse the causal direction of "environmental determinism." They would use the strike to change their working environment. While growers thought they were making a naturalized workforce (in the sense of being out of sight, content, unquestioning of basic social relations), they were at the same time making possible a second kind of naturalization: their workers were coming to see themselves as Americans, and as such, entitled to full rights as members of the republic. All over the state and in every kind of agriculture, workers in the 1930s unionized and used the strike to try to improve the conditions in which they labored.

In all sectors of agriculture, those conditions deteriorated during the Depression. When Republican governor Friend Richardson gutted the commission in the 1920s, Lubin resigned in protest. Labor camps fell into disorder, and by the early 1930s the Wheatland conditions had again cropped up throughout the state. Lubin continued to insist that housing was a key factor in labor relations. On Thanksgiving Day 1934, he said that "the experience of eating and eating full, of building good houses and dwelling therein, to every fourth person is but a faded memory." He continued to maintain that improving housing was key to making California's system of agriculture into a moral economy, saying that "we need a socio-economic house-cleaning."[49]

In the citrus industry, adherence to many of the ideals of the commission nonetheless continued through the 1920s and into the early 1930s. But when labor unrest manifested itself in the groves, the citrus industry turned out not to be the beacon of social responsibility that Lubin hoped it would be. When its workers demanded more say in determining the conditions of labor, the humane planks of Sunkist's housing policy gave way. In Orange Country, workers were either evicted from camps or block-aded therein and bombarded with tear gas. At that most model of model camps, Teague's Limoneira, striking workers were also promptly thrown out of their houses. As we shall see, the citrus industry played a critical role in the funding and formation of the Associated Farmers and its constitutionally dubious battles against unionization in the Depression.

The turn to violence was all the more surprising considering the great promise of Sunkist. To be sure, its housing policy was at bottom a form of social control designed to enhance profits. What is remarkable, though, is the degree to which it forced the growers, however reluctantly, to recognize Mexicano workers as permanent members of their own community, not floating aliens or homing pigeons. But in the 1930s, the citrus industry helped transform the California landscape into a place where farmworkers could find no haven in a heartless world. In order to see how violent repression could grow out of Sunkist's progressive home ecology, we must turn our attention to the battle over another kind of home in California: the governor's mansion.

PART THREE

Reclaiming Eden

INTRODUCTION

BY THE 1920S, the Orange Empire had powerfully reshaped California. It had worked wonders with nature, re-creating the landscape and reinventing its fruits. It had pulled to it a vast reservoir of human labor and found a way to replenish that reservoir year by year. It had reached into streets and homes across America to create an enormous demand for its products. Along the way, it had secured the help of the state. By 1929, the Orange Empire exercised considerable control over social, political, and environmental matters across California and the nation. Its hegemony was made possible by a way of seeing.

Sometimes, not seeing is believing. That, at any rate, is what a number of observers of ideology say. Ideology filters out the things that might challenge its legitimacy, its accepted validity as a way of seeing the world. The Orange Empire's version of reality looked like this: The natural splendor of California had been harmoniously but spectacularly augmented through the application of science and business organization. What had once been a beautiful yet economically stagnant region had been transformed into a land even more beautiful and now productive almost beyond belief. Nature's abundance became economic growth, economic growth was cultural growth, and all of this together amounted to progress. What the empire's ideology covered up was this: the poorly paid workers who harvested the crops and whose bodies were taxed deeply for this growth; the workers who were rendered "other," naturalized as outgrowths of the crops rather than members of a democracy; the fact that many growers had little or no contact with the soil; the fact that land was falling into fewer hands and being controlled by larger interests; the plunder of aquifers and the alienation from nature that accompanied the ever intensifying commodification of the land.

Then the stock market crashed, and the control of the growth machine was weakened. But that was not an automatic effect. The facts surrounding the reversal of economic growth had to be made into a story or stories. Otherwise, the Depression was one person losing a job in Detroit, a factory owner closing his doors in Portland, a family forced to hit the road in Oklahoma. But when these fragments of experience were placed in a larger narrative, the Depression came into light. To be seen, it had to be represented.

In California, where the land still looked abundant but the people had become desperate, stories began to take shape implicating the growth machine in all of the suffering. Upton Sinclair, running for governor in 1934, pointed to the natural abundance and human misery and promised to "End Poverty in California" (EPIC). It was a powerful and politically charged vow, and the Orange Empire took notice. The president of Sunkist was instrumental in organizing the anti-Sinclair campaign, and Sunkist's former advertising manager created much of the publicity. And in 1933 and 1934, just as Sinclair was making his political challenge, workers were rising up to challenge the power of the growth machine in the fields and on the waterfront. A Senate committee concluded that "the unprecedented series of agricultural strikes in 1933 . . . riveted public attention upon the labor problem in California's industrialized agriculture."[1] To deal with these uprisings, the same individuals who had assembled the anti-Sinclair campaign resolved to strengthen the Associated Farmers. With money and leadership provided by Sunkist and other companies, the Associated Farmers had been designed to maintain the growth machine's control, fighting agricultural unionization on the ground, in the courts, and in the press. One hand massaged public opinion while the other strong-armed labor.

But out of the rubble of EPIC's defeat and the actions of the Associated Farmers rose a committed group of artists and intellectuals I call the agrarian partisans. The core of this group consisted of Dorothea Lange, a photographer with a remarkable ability to capture on film both human suffering and human worth and to connect each to the condition of the land; her husband, Paul S. Taylor, a labor economist at the University of California at Berkeley who believed passionately in the ideal of the family farm; Carey McWilliams, a young lawyer who was passionate about creating a society in California that would extend equal protection and equal opportunities to all of its people, regardless of race; and John Steinbeck, who wrote about people as if they were organisms in an ecosystem but still made his readers care deeply about the people he portrayed and the larger predicament their condition dramatized: the relationship between modern Americans and the natural world after the closing of the frontier and the ascent of corporate capitalism.

The agrarian partisans saw themselves as helping workers gain a more powerful voice so that they could make California more democratic and more just. I call them "partisan" because they took a side. I call them "agrarian" because the side they took was for the agrarian dream *and* for the people who worked in agriculture, including farmworkers and small-scale farmers. They were deeply committed to both. I am guided in this choice of terms by Steinbeck's reaction to an invitation by the San Francisco *News* to take part in a forum on California farm labor and agriculture. The forum was advertised as being "non-partisan." Steinbeck responded:

> I am afraid of the word non-partisan. . . . The Associated Farmers are non-partisan. In fact, the word non-partisan describes one of two kinds of people: 1.—Those who through lack of understanding or interest have not taken a side, and, 2, those who use the term to conceal malevolent partisanship. I am completely partisan. Every effort I can bring to bear is and has been at the call of the common working people to the end that they may eat what they raise, wear what they weave, use what they produce, and in every way and in completeness share in the works of their hands and their heads. And the reverse is also true. I am actively opposed to any man or group who, through financial or political control of means of production and distribution, is able to control and dominate the lives of workers. I hope this statement is complete enough so that my position is not equivocal. And please let me repeat—I shall not want my name used unless [militant] organized labor is strongly represented in the governing body of your group. I am writing this once for all to put to an end any supposition that I am non-partisan.[2]

Using documentary forms, the agrarian partisans brought to light what had once been invisible, cloaked by the ideology of the growth machine. The facts they mobilized were political, opening up a new way of seeing things so that an alternative reality could be created. Like most political documentary, their work was intended "to point out 'problems' within the social fabric of the nation with an aim to changing them . . . [constructing] not only a vision of truth and identity but an appropriate way of seeing that reality."[3] Their reports, histories, novels, and photographs were not neutral documents of reality, for they were the sparks of blade touching grindstone.

The agrarian partisans had a case to make. They represented farmworkers in a double sense: creating images of them and arguing on their behalf. The social drama in the fields came to have the look and feel of a trial. The Orange Empire was framed in a crime—a crime against nature and humanity. Calls for redress and the reclamation of Eden gathered force.

SIX

A Jungle of Representation

The EPIC Campaign versus Sunkist

CAMPAIGN FICTIONS

ON THE FIRST DAY of September 1933, Upton Sinclair—muckraking novelist, Pasadena transplant, physical culture enthusiast, and indefatigable dietary experimenter—changed his party registration from Socialist to Democrat. He ran for the gubernatorial nomination, won, and declared that his campaign marked a "new birth of Democracy."[1] Never one for modesty, Sinclair made a pretty big campaign promise—to "End Poverty in California" (EPIC). In his hands, California's economy would be driven by the principle of "production for use," not profit. The threat was not lost on the leaders of agribusiness, including Sunkist's president Charles Collins Teague. It is no wonder that Teague played a crucial role in orchestrating opposition to EPIC. With powerful campaign fictions created by both camps, the 1934 race for governor marked a turning point in the relationship of Californians to nature and the fruits of Eden.

Though Sinclair told himself, "You have written enough. What the world needs is a deed," his campaign began with a story, *I, Governor of California, and How I Ended Poverty: A True Story of the Future*. Sinclair's "anticipatory report," as Albert Einstein called it, was a utopian projection set in the future, like Edward Bellamy's *Looking Backward*. "I had hit upon the lively idea of putting my program into the form of a story, imagining myself elected Governor and doing the job," Sinclair explained.[2]

Like most good California stories, Sinclair's begins in a garden, from which he is about to be expelled. He loves "go into my garden with a high wall around it." Taking in the fragrance and colors of the flowers, he sits writing in the sunshine. But a snake intrudes: "Now it is proposed that I shall drop this routine of life, and go out as a political organizer and campaigner! Travel around making speeches, and saying the same things over and over! Set up a mimeograph machine! . . . Have the telephone ringing all day!" Not only would his quiet life be turned upside down by the media, his very body would be imperiled. "I should have to face all kinds of slander and misrepresentation, perhaps betrayal, perhaps destruction by the cruel and wicked forces which rule our world today."[3]

In *They Call Me Carpenter* (1922), Sinclair had Jesus turning up in a Western city of the twentieth century. Now he suggested that his own campaign might recapitulate the stages of the cross. Jesus, as Michael Rogin argues, had "sacrificed his body mortal and gave birth to his mystical body, the regenerate community." Similarly, Sinclair pledged to sacrifice himself in order to rehabilitate a California that "is going the way of the slave empires of history; decaying with luxury at the top, and destroying . . . democracy by ruthless repression." "If I am Governor," Sinclair promised, "every man, woman and child will have opportunities for self-development, not merely physical but intellectual, moral, aesthetic." To reclaim the garden and restore community, Sinclair was willing to put his body on the line.[4]

Switching from a biblical to a Jeffersonian idiom, Sinclair wrote, "If I were to put my hands to this red-hot plow it would mean goodbye to peace, rest, health, happiness—possibly forever!" Plows burned bright in the public imagination in the Depression, symbolizing a return to the land and a restoration of the American dream. Sinclair must lay his hands on "the red-hot plow" in order to recreate the paradise lost outside the walls of his private garden.[5] In a campaign play called "Depression Island," Sinclair told the story of how a landscape of abundance had been turned into one of scarcity. He set his allegory of California on a tropical island, with coconuts representing nature's bounty. Performed to a packed house at the Shrine Auditorium in Los Angeles, the play has three men—Abie, Bing, and Crunk—stranded on the island. At first, they live gleefully in a state of nature, surviving on coconuts. But then Crunk, who is a realtor, gains control of the island (finding a way to turn place into profit). Soon Abie and Bing are bringing him coconuts; when a surplus is accumulated, they are fired. Despite Crunk's attempts to naturalize the island's inequality and repress dissent, rebellion breaks out. As the crowd in the auditorium chanted, "Author! Author!" Sinclair stepped onto the stage—presumably walking across water—and delivered his campaign speech. If the tropical island had become a dangerous jungle, Sinclair told a story of how abundance could be restored in real-life California. Everyone would enjoy usufruct—the right to harvest the fruits of the earth.[6]

While Sunkist identified mental depression with "acidosis" and suggested that the cure for this malady was oranges, Sinclair told a parable about economic depression being the result of the "profit system" and offered "production for use" as its cure. In fact, the stories told by both Sunkist and Sinclair bore similarities to biblical parables. "Like the parables of Jesus," Roland Marchand says of modern advertising, "these advertising stories employed stark contrasts and exaggeration to dramatize a central message." Furthermore, Sinclair and advertisers even depart from biblical parables in the same way, for while these parables are "encounters with our sense of the limitations of reality, the parables of advertising promised readers no insurmountable limitations."[7] For these reasons, EPIC's messages sounded a lot like those of an advertising campaign. From Sinclair's utopian point of view, scarcity was an artificial creation; abundance could, should, and would be enjoyed by all.

EPIC went on the road with this message. There were EPIC rodeos, parades, and flea markets. Sinclair went on the radio, seeking to extend his presence, to multiply himself throughout the state and write himself into the stories his audiences were living. "I have to make this my own story," he said, "and you have to decide whether you wish it to be yours."[8] Advertisers and Sinclair were both itinerant storytellers, spreading narratives in which crisis was dramatized, its causes identified, and its solution shown to be near at hand. The people simply had to reach for it, by buying or by voting. But EPIC was not equivalent to an advertising campaign, for Sinclair's political vision struck at the heart of the individualistic, consumerist, and profit-oriented world advertisers cultivated with every story they told. He envisioned creating a cornucopia from which fruits would flow freely.

To face down the Sinclair threat, the growth machine put its own storytelling operations into high gear. In a lot of the stories it spread, the kettle was called black. William Randolph Hearst, one of the leading forces in the anti-EPIC campaign, characterized the Democratic candidate as an "unbalanced reformer whose remedies, like his writings, are pure fiction." His words were loaded with unintentional irony. Hearst's own brand of journalism was anything but objective. Recalling his days as a cub reporter

Figure 16. In this piece of anti-Sinclair literature, a man returns to Orange County after EPIC has taken control, only to find that "Sunny California! Golden California!" has become a paradise lost. (Originally appeared in Upton Sinclair, *I, Candidate for Governor: And How I Got Licked* [1935; reprint Berkeley: University of California Press, 1994], 119.)

for a Hearst paper, John Steinbeck said, "I learned that external reality had no jurisdiction in the Hearst press and that what happened must in no way interfere with what WR wanted to happen." Hearst, after all, is the one who is said to have told his reporter in Spanish Cuba in 1898, "You furnish the pictures, I'll furnish the war." The border between fiction and reality was crossed and recrossed many times during the campaign, creating an entangling jungle of representation.[9]

Parodying Sinclair's vision of the future in *I, Governor*, the opposition painted its own fictionalized version of a Sinclair régime in a pamphlet called "Thunder over California" (the title alluded to Sinclair's involvement in Sergei Eisenstein's great unfinished epic *Thunder over Mexico*). It tells the story of a man who had grown up in Orange County and moved away, and who returns after Sinclair has become governor. The "California Secret Police" put the man under surveillance. The moment he runs out of money, the state closes in to conscript him for service (but the pamphleteers fail to note that the penniless in Orange County, whether Indian or Mexican, had long been pressed into service). "Thunder" describes "Sunny California! Golden California!" as a paradise lost (see figure 16). Such battles about the meaning of the Sinclair candidacy, waged on the terrain of the future using the techniques of fiction, would dominate the campaign.[10]

One observer has argued that the EPIC campaign marked the "birth of media politics," noting that the powerful force of advertising was mobilized as never before in the political realm. Indeed, a former advertising manager for Sunkist was put in charge of much of the anti-EPIC publicity. Advertising worked its narrative magic, this time on a political product: Sinclair was reinvented, much like the orange. But instead of becoming irresistible, he was to become a product unfit for consumption. We might say that the growth machine processed Sinclair much like the workers in *The Jungle* who entered the factory as human beings and left as "Durham's Pure Leaf Lard . . . and peerless fertilizer."[11]

SINCLAIR'S GARDEN

Body-Building Politics

Sinclair had a life-long fascination with the care of the body that informed his vision for the body politic. The promise of corporeal rehabilitation melded with a larger recovery narrative, a plan to reclaim the garden lost in California's abundant yet debilitating landscape. Like several American presidents, Sinclair confused his mortal body with "the mystic body, America."[12] But while Abraham Lincoln, Woodrow Wilson, Richard Nixon, and Ronald Reagan sought transcendence from their physical bodies by identifying with the body of the nation, Sinclair felt that his own experience with his "mortal body" fitted him for leadership. He linked his personal constitution to the health of the nation and drew conclusions about governance from his experiments with the management and care of his own body.

About his most famous book, *The Jungle* (1906), Sinclair said that he "aimed for the public's heart, and by accident hit it in the stomach." The novel shone a light on how the meat-packing industry in Chicago beat down the bodies of workers and sold unsanitary food to consumers. Workers would be "ground up": their bodies, which had originally been "fresh and strong," fast became "second-hand . . . the worn out parts of the great merciless packing machine." Capitalism operated as a kind of blue mold; it was everywhere in the air, and ready at any moment to enter into workers' bodies and destroy their strength.[13] As consumers, workers would slowly starve on sausage whose "colour was made by chemicals." The packing plant was a jungle, but so was the marketplace. It was saturated with the artificial, a place where workers confronted "the evils of denatured foods" and "those forces of modern civilization that were destroying the body."[14]

The Jungle originally appeared in a Socialist weekly, and the conditions depicted in it were investigated by a Doubleday lawyer before Doubleday published the book. The facts checked out. Later, Theodore Roosevelt sent his own investigators, backed by the authority of the state, to Chicago. Roosevelt then turned *The Jungle* into a sermon delivered from his bully pulpit; it spurred the passage of the Pure Food and Drug Act (1906). *The Jungle* was answered with a law that ignored the plight of workers and instead protected the consumer. But Sinclair had hoped to do something more with his exposé of the environmental hazards of the capitalist workplace—inspire a Socialist revolution.[15] Still, it would be wrong to think that to hit the public in the stomach was to miss the political target. Enforcing purity in food processing was a political response to several interrelated crises involving health, authenticity, nature, and national identity—all of them in the end political issues.

Consumers had become worried about not only packaged meats but also the fruit supply. Growers in California and other Western states often sent apples and pears to market with a cloudy film on them. The film was arsenic, a residue of spraying. Fruits for sale sometimes harbored botulism and toxic residues, agents that could break down the body of the consumer in quick order. Others worried about a more gradual debilitation caused by processed foods of all varieties. Were modern Americans deepening their alienation from nature by consuming things that were too refined or artificial? Did this make them weak? Harvey Wiley, the leading chemist in the Department of Agriculture, told Congress, "Of everything made by man, almost nothing has the hygienic value of that made by nature."[16]

At a gathering of "pure food" advocates, Eugene Hilgard, a University of California soil scientist, argued that nothing should be present in food that "is not naturally an ingredient of the food itself or of the human body." Stanford's David Starr Jordan said flatly that food adulteration was a criminal act. The anxiety over adulteration expressed the growing distrust of the emerging national food market and the anxiety that post-frontier Americans were losing their direct connections to nature. Chicago's meat packing industry had perfected techniques through which the live and unique animal—each with a "hearts desire," as Sinclair put it—was put through a disassembly line that turned it into just so many packaged cuts. The industrial production of food led to a pervasive yet subtle "separation—the word 'alienation' is not too strong—from the act of killing and from nature itself."[17]

Liberty Hyde Bailey, who served as chairman of Roosevelt's Country Life Commission, was deeply troubled by the ways that crops and meats could be dressed up for the market. He warned that "danger may lie in any untruthfulness with which we use the raw materials of life." The adulteration of foods amounted to "a staggering infidelity in the use of the good raw materials." But two-timing nature would not go unpunished, for adulterated foods threatened "vigor and good morals." There were "so many disguises and so much fabrication" in the modern canning industry, Bailey complained, that "the fruit is lost in the process. . . . I wonder whether in time the perfection of fabrication will not reach a point that some fruits will be known to the great public only by the picture on the package or on the bottle."[18]

Bailey's outlook on nature dovetailed with that of Walt Whitman and other contemporary intellectuals who were striving "to restore an authentic connection with real things." Direct involvement with nature was essential to the healthy growth of children, Bailey felt. He quoted a Whitman poem: "a child went forth every day, / And the first object he look'd upon, that object he became . . . / The early lilacs became part of this child." Contact with an authentic nature, either in the wilderness or at the dining table, was considered essential to staving off degeneracy. Those values that grew from contact with and struggle against nature—values that Turner had identified and Roosevelt worried were being lost—might be replaced by the vast sham of the commercial world. Roosevelt and Sinclair had both visited the Battle Creek Sanitarium, whose director, Dr. J. H. Kellogg, propounded a theory connecting the fiber and integrity of food to the moral fiber of the body politic. Kellogg believed that "the decline of a nation commences when gourmandizing begins." The danger, as Roosevelt put it, was "the unhealthy softening and relaxation of fiber that tends to accompany civilization."[19]

In *The Jungle*, Sinclair had presented a picture of food production under industrial capitalism beating down bodies at every stage, in the processing plant and in Chicago's rural hinterland, where people lived in what he considered a condition of ignorant drudgery. And all of this came together at the dinner table. Thus was the nation's table set, filled, as Sinclair saw it, with the most unwholesome fare. Sinclair's voice contributed to "the swelling chorus of progressive reformers demanding a wholesale purification of the body politic." Part of the purification drive was aimed at cleaning up food. Part of it was aimed at patent medicine dealers, who took advantage of people's desires for magical transformation by selling false cures. Providing for purity in what went into Americans' stomachs was thus much more than a simple health measure. The Pure Food and Drug Act was a legal response to a more general complex of anxieties about authenticity, nature, and national character in post-frontier America.[20]

If Sinclair had been aiming for the public's heart when writing *The Jungle*, his own stomach was constantly on his mind. When discussing the novel in his autobiography, Sinclair mentions his own "poor stomach" twice, and speaks of being undernourished and "white faced." "Externally," he writes, "the story had to do with a family of stockyard workers, but internally it was the story of my own family."[21] After the strain of writing *The Jungle*, Sinclair needed rest and recuperation. He made a pilgrimage to the health capital of America—Battle Creek, Michigan. In search of the "secrets of natural living," he wound up at Bernarr MacFadden's Physical Culture City. MacFadden published the popular magazine *Physical Culture*, which had once featured Theodore Roosevelt's ideas for leading a "strenuous life."[22] Sinclair became a regular contributor to *Physical Culture* and soon established himself as a leading authority on diet and health. His interest in natural living took him to the Golden State in 1915.

Like countless other immigrants before him, Sinclair was attracted by the promise of restoration though climate and sunshine.

Six years later he published *The Book of Life,* his first true California work and a kind of nonfictional sequel to *The Jungle. The Book of Life* linked management and improvement of the body to a plan to reform the political economy of the nation. Rather than passively enduring natural selection, people could and should take control of nature and growth. Citing Pyotr Alekseyevick Kropotkin's *Fields, Factories and Workshops,* Sinclair argued that "the modern intensive gardener, by use of glass and chemical test-tube, has developed an entirely new science of plant raising. He is independent of climate, he makes his own climate."[23] Though Sinclair admitted that "man is a part of nature and a product of nature," he felt that "modern civilized man" had "revised and even supplanted the processes of nature." People could make their own laws, direct their own growth, even create a society to match their dreams. To Sinclair, "nature" was "our ancient mother," a nurturer who cared for and preserved the "species." But modern human beings, having weaned themselves from Mother Nature with technology, had to consciously re-create a nurturing and invigorating environment. Like Roosevelt, Sinclair felt that modern human beings had to "devise imitations of the chase and battle" to keep the "physical body up to the best standard of nature." And when it came to food, Sinclair felt that modern technology did not hold all the answers. Modern man, he warned, "will not eat nature's fruits, he prefers the kind he himself has brought into being." It was fine to improve vision with glasses, but modified foods could be dangerous. When it came to diet, it was best to "go back to nature," for "denatured," "artificial" and "refined" foods were dangerous to the body. One must get plenty of "mineral elements," which were absolutely vital to good health. Sinclair cited an experiment done on two chickens. One was fed only denatured foods. Deprived of nature's goodness, it came down with the chicken equivalent of "headaches, colds, sore throats, decaying teeth and boils." Sinclair's text could have been lifted from Sunkist ads.[24]

But Sunkist would object to Sinclair's attempts to connect the personal politics of eating and growth to political prescriptions for the growth of the people as a whole. Sinclair insisted that "the problem of disease is not merely a problem of the body, but is . . . a problem of politics." Modern civilization had become a frightening chimera, "part healthy and progressive" and part "as foul and deadly as a gigantic cancer." The root cause of the cancerous growth "must be diagnosed," and Sinclair was ready to offer his diagnosis: "There is one disease which is the deadliest of all, and the source of all others, and that disease is poverty." Poverty was responsible for breaking down bodies and the body politic. So when Sinclair proposed to end poverty in California, it was just what the doctor had ordered thirteen years earlier, when he wrote *The Book of Life*.[25]

The Co-Op Story and Technocracy

The prognosis was good, Sinclair confidently proclaimed in 1934. Poverty was simply an artificial creation, the result of dividing up nature's bounty into the private property out of which economic empires are created. To make nature pay, it was processed, repackaged, advertised, and adulterated. All of this impoverished people: it alienated them from nature's vitality and weakened their bodies. As Sinclair saw it, the key to rehabilitating the body and thus the nation was to assure open access to nature's bounty.

The message was carried into every corner of the state. In 1939, Carey McWilliams, then serving as commissioner of immigration and housing, saw "the slogans of the Epic campaign painted on rocks in the desert, carved on trees in the forests, and scrawled on the walls of labor camps in the San Joaquin Valley." The inscriptions on trees and rocks and labor camp walls declared that EPIC would restore "the people's" claim to nature. EPIC's supporters, Rueben Borough explained, "were after security which they thought they could get and were trying to get by reconnecting with the resources of the earth."[26]

Borough, who served as editor of the *EPIC News*, emphasized the link between physical rejuvenation and getting back to nature. Borough's column "What Price Health?" discussed "right living habits" and called "attention to the value of simple, healthful food, and of proper exercise and wholesome thinking."[27] This editorial attention to the body was reinforced by the advertising. In one issue, more than half of the ads were directed at readers' concerns about the body. An advertisement for the Nu-Jo-Wa Institute argued, "If you are run down, nervous . . . try NU-JO-WA, the WATER OF LIFE, a POSITIVE NEUTRALIZER of STOMACH ACIDS and POISONS, and learn what it means to REALLY LIVE AGAIN." A muscular Indian complete with feathered headdress assures readers that Nu-Jo-Wa is a back-to-nature remedy.[28]

While the advertising tried to channel the reader's feelings of being "desperate and despondent" into the purchase of a product, the *EPIC News* sought to connect symptoms of physical malaise to economic paralysis. Remedies could not be contained in a bottle, for they had to address the social and economic condition of the state. One cartoon, aimed at Sinclair's Republican opponent Frank Merriam, linked the failure of the political system to bodily ailments. California was portrayed as a bedridden patient. A malignant growth is on his face, and his legs and arms are in casts labeled "unemployment" and "poverty." Presiding over the invalid is a smugly grinning "Dr. Merriam, Reactionopath," administering the "Dole Sedative" and other "special privilege drugs." Earlier, Sinclair had portrayed Herbert Hoover as a quack doctor who dopes his patient and refuses to prescribe a cure. Rather than safely channeling illness into consumption, the *EPIC News* encouraged readers to see their own problems as symptomatic of an illness that had spread throughout the political body.[29]

Sinclair proposed to get Californians off of the gurney by getting them back onto the land. Regaining their mobility, Californians would travel "not into new physical territory, but into a new social order that is to be erected in the midst of collapsed industries and ruined agriculture."[30] According to Sinclair and the *EPIC News,* this new territory had been pioneered by a couple of out-of-work veterans. One day, they asked a Southern California farmer if they could exchange work for some of his surplus crop. They started to reclaim the wealth of nature by launching the cooperative movement of the unemployed. The movement soon took off. In 1932, 181,000 tons of peaches, 178,000 tons of pears, and 696,000 lugs of tomatoes went unharvested. But that same year, many small truck farmers and growers in Los Angeles County agreed to take part. Members of cooperatives fixed fences, painted barns, and did any number of other odd jobs in exchange for the right to harvest excess crops. Their labor transformed the private lands of orchards into a temporary commons to which they claimed usufruct rights. One group based in Santa Monica worked out an exchange with the University of California: they maintained its ten-acre experimental citrus plot for the right to harvest some of its oranges. The self-help cooperatives, by exchanging labor for the right to harvest such surplus fruit, were a social adaptation to California's paradoxical condition: it had ripening fruit when the market had withered.[31]

By February 1933, over 90,000 people were participating in self-help cooperatives scattered across Los Angeles County. The cooperatives apparently functioned as machines for making Democrats; members who were originally Republican often switched parties. In one survey, Sinclair enjoyed tremendous support from cooperative members, who saw him as a "great champion, a deliverer." A majority of cooperative members had been born in the Midwest, and many had originally been attracted to

California by booster literature and Sunkist advertising that equated health and wealth with California's nature. Sinclair promised to make good on the picture-postcard expectations of these disillusioned immigrants.[32]

The *EPIC News* saw these cooperatives as "the most powerful argument in favor of the EPIC movement." The cooperative movement demonstrated that Sinclair's plan was not disconnected from reality, the imaginative tract of a dreamer.[33] In answer to the charge that Sinclair was utopian (the literal meaning of the Greek *ou* and *topos* is "no place"), he could point to the cooperatives already in place in California. He had seen with his own eyes one such group, canning peaches and tomatoes that otherwise would have rotted on the ground. The cooperatives exuded self-reliance, a quality that Sinclair played up. He argued that "if the unemployed were to raise their own wheat," they would be able to get off relief and thus lower the burden on working taxpayers. In addition, since Sinclair thought that relief itself was a racket benefiting agribusiness, he argued that having the unemployed grow their own food "would reduce the profits of the great feudal wheat ranches of our State." The dole fattened private interests and made the people weak, but self-help work on farms would transform the downtrodden into proud, productive, and robust Americans.[34]

At the Democratic convention in Sacramento, Sheridan Downey, Sinclair's running mate, pledged "to put the resources of the State behind these groups and enable them to function and grow." But just what would the groups grow into? Sinclair's soft-sell of EPIC encouraged more moderate voters to think about his proposed cooperatives as simply efficient ways of dealing with the problem of unemployment while reducing taxes. But many growers and manufacturers feared that such a plan would create producers who would compete with them and drain consumers from the marketplace. And when Sinclair tried to appeal to more radical voters, he said that "the present system is like a row of tin soldiers: when you permit the first to fall, he knocks down the second, which in turn knocks down the third. That is the terror which confronts Big Business today." While many Socialists and most Communists looked at EPIC as a pathetically incomplete plan, Sinclair portrayed EPIC as the seed of a powerful plant: the cooperatives would grow and eventually choke out capitalism.[35]

But Sinclair, like other observers, also saw the cooperatives in their present form as limited. His admiration for them was combined with condescension, as when he described the "infinitely touching" efforts at self-help by people working with "primitive equipment." Though validating the spirit of the cooperatives, Sinclair saw them as insufficiently modern. But if the state could provide them with access to land and better equipment, Sinclair concluded that their possibilities were "unlimited." Sinclair wanted to restore people's access to the land. He also wanted to give them the power of modern technology.[36]

In short, the co-ops might benefit from a dose of technocracy. Though William Smyth coined the term, Thorstein Veblen, the former Berkeley economist, was one of the intellectual wellsprings for the movement that would become popular in the 1930s. As Veblen saw it, modern industry held the promise of producing a world of abundance. But the captains of industry, operating under the narrow logic of corporate profit, worked to "sabotage" this utopian potential. They delayed production or destroyed surpluses in order to restrict supply and increase prices. Further waste came from "advertising and maneuvers of salesmanlike . . . prevarication." Veblen proposed putting engineers in charge of production and replacing the price system with the principle of production for use—one of Sinclair's central ideas.[37]

On the eve of Sinclair's campaign, a flurry of articles on technocracy appeared in newspapers and national magazines. A widely circulated cartoon portrayed "financial considerations" keeping "Mother nature" from distributing her overflowing cornucopia. The extraordinary popularity of technocracy in Southern California can be traced to a series of front-page articles published in Manchester Boddy's *Los Angeles Daily News* in 1932. Crowds assembled to get each installment hot off the press. Study groups were formed. More than twenty books were published on the subject between 1932 and 1934, and countless pamphlets. Will Rogers wryly commented, "This Technocracy thing, we don't know if it is a disease or a theory."[38]

A pamphlet published in Los Angeles in 1933, "Towards Humanocracy," was read alongside EPIC campaign literature by at least one person. In B. Bloomfield's copy of the pamphlet, several clippings describing *I, Governor of California* were pasted onto the front pages. Bloomfield would have found many parallels between "Towards Humanocracy" and the EPIC campaign. Both portrayed capitalism as parasitic, politicians as corrupt, the press as an organ of misrepresentation, advertising as a form of hypnotism, industrialism as wasteful, and the price system as an engine of social degeneration. Both used the dumping of fruits as a symbol of what was wrong with capitalism. And both compared the individual's body to that of the body politic. "A government should epitomize . . . the perfected individual," the pamphlet proclaimed. The ideal governmental body would be "of symmetrical proportion with an unimpeded circulatory system, and a governing vehicle, capable, not only of maintaining through knowledge and judgment, the material needs of that body, but also capable of contracting and extending, through responsive instrumentalities, the moral and spiritual essentials of cultural advancement." The body politic would only be as efficient and strong as its body parts, so "Towards Humanocracy" advocated "intelligent Burbanking in the field of human potentialities."[39] In his *Book of Life,* Sinclair also supported eugenics. The author of the pamphlet and Sinclair both believed that science could stimulate the evolutionary potentialities of people and nature.

Which Way Back to the Land?

EPIC News editor Borough felt that "the EPIC movement was in one aspect a movement back-to-the-land."[40] But Sinclair proposed a kind of technocratic return to nature. For him, going back to the land would not be going back to the farming conditions of the pioneer. He may have played on Jeffersonian and Turnerian themes linking the farmer to democracy, but he was a trenchant critic of the individual homestead. In *The Jungle,* Dr. Schliemann argues that "independent small farming [produces] a stunted, haggard, ignorant man, mated with a yellow, lean, and sad-eyed drudge." From his autobiography it is clear that Schliemann was expressing Sinclair's own views. He claimed that the farm families living on small homesteads he had known in New Jersey all "contained drunkards, degenerates, mental and physical defectives, semi-idiots." Their close contact with nature did not keep them, in Sinclair's eyes, from biological and cultural degeneration.[41]

Sinclair did have faith in the power of nature and country life to restore health. His protagonist in *The Jungle,* whose wife and child have died on the streets of Chicago, wanders into a therapeutic countryside. Having escaped from a factory that produces fertilizer, his own body is caked with the stuff. Still a young man, Jurgis has grown old and decrepit in short order in Chicago, as if the vitality of his body had been sucked into the fertilizer. He takes a baptismal bath in a country stream, and then the sun, water, trees, and open sky work their magic. His "youthful vigor" returns, "as if his dead childhood had come back to him."[42] Still, if he had to make his living there as a homesteader on a few acres, his prospects might not be much better than they had been in the city. It would be a régime of toil, a primitive struggle for existence, that would eventually suck his vitality away again.

In Sinclair's ideal world, urban people would come to the countryside as tourists and benefit from the therapy of nature, and there would be no poor farmers living a life of drudgery. In *The Jungle,* Sinclair presented his utopian picture of agriculture under scientific management: "apples and oranges picked by machinery, cows milked by electricity [creating] an unlimited food supply." Almost thirty years later, many elements of this technocratic agrarianism made their way into Sinclair's EPIC plan.[43] If elected governor, Sinclair promised to create a California Authority of Land (CAL) that would establish "land colonies" across the state. The state would acquire lands on which taxes were owed. People would be needed to run the farms, but they would not live like the pioneers of old. These land colonies would not be individual homesteads that would condemn farmers to a life of "poverty and drudgery." Returning "the unemployed to the land," Sinclair insisted, "does not mean dump them out on the desert without tools or training." He eulogized the family farm often, without remorse or nostalgia.[44]

Sinclair envisioned agriculture as a form of mass production in which vast tracts of land, advanced machinery, and expert direction would all be required. But he was critical of agribusiness, "in which great land corporations work Chinese, Japanese, Hindus, Filipinos, Mexicans, and other kinds of foreigners, under what amounts to peonage." Under Sinclair's proposal, farm work would become attractive to Americans with middle-class sensibilities. CAL would channel the benefits of mass production into the growth of cultural institutions in the countryside, for "'man does not live by bread alone.'" Farmworkers would "live in what will amount to new villages: kitchens and cafeterias operated by the community, a social hall with opportunities for recreation, a church, a school-house, a store, a library, a motion picture theatre." His vision was not that different from that of the California Commission of Immigration and Housing. But while the commission relied on the enlightened self-interest of growers, CAL's version of Hull Houses in the countryside would be financed "by the saving of all waste involved in the competitive and speculative handling of foods." "If the goods are canned, or packed," Sinclair pointed out, "the State will not have to send salesmen around looking for purchasers, nor will it have to spend tens of millions of dollars advertising its various brands."[45] To reclaim the garden, the land would first be loosened from the tentacles of a production-for-profit-based agribusiness. Through the methods of cooperative production, the proceeds of nature working as an efficient factory would go to enriching the cultural life of workers on the land.[46]

Sinclair was not clear about what would happen to the "foreigners" who had been working in "peonage," but one might infer that these so-called foreigners would be moved out and "Americans" moved in. This substitution of white workers for workers of color was implicitly suggested in one of Sinclair's favorite campaign parables, the story of the four men and the plow in Alhambra. He began the story by noting that some critics thought that "our people would not be interested in 'land colonies,' . . . saying that they leave such humiliating work to Mexicans, Japanese, Hindus, etc." Sinclair then referred to a picture printed in the *Los Angeles Times* showing "where the cooperatives had got the use of a vacant tract of land, and having no horse, four men were hitched to the plow." Sinclair promised that "the EPIC Plan will give them the best modern machinery and tell them to work like civilized men." Sinclair's intent here was to challenge the system that "takes it for granted that the workers have to live in squalid surroundings and be ignorant and dirty."[47] In doing so, though, he leaves intact the image of racialized workers as "ignorant and dirty," closer to nature. Sinclair makes no space for them in his technocratic cornucopia. His white colonists are the ones who would benefit from the promise of the machine age—working "like civilized men."[48]

Sinclair was very adamant about not romanticizing the state of nature. When Raymond Moley, a Franklin Delano Roosevelt "Brain Truster," charged that "Sinclair sounded to the people of California the call for a blessed retreat—back beyond industrial civilization . . . back to barter, back to nature," Sinclair was indignant.[49] He shot back in an editorial under the emphatic title "EPIC 'Not Back to Nature,'" "I am at the opposite pole from Rousseau and all his 'back to nature' ideas." Sinclair insisted, "I believe in modern machinery as the instrument of saving mankind from slavery . . . the aim of the EPIC system is to give the people access to the best land and the best machinery, and to enable them to start mass production by the best modern methods and with the best technical advice available." Instead of going back to nature, Sinclair would colonize it: the fruits of mass production and city life would be available to the people, who would live and work in the mechanical garden.[50]

But within EPIC, another version of a return to the land took shape—one that emphasized the aesthetic and spiritual windfalls to be gained by reconnecting with the soil. That is what Borough had in mind when he spoke of the co-ops' effort to find security in "reconnecting with the resources of the earth."[51] Borough's vision of "organic homesteads" was very different from Sinclair's land colonies. Long before he threw himself into EPIC, Borough had been working out a plan to restore the garden. In 1932, he published a back-to-the-land manifesto, "I Secede: An Argument for a New Frontier." He escaped "the Market and the Mass Production Machine" by finding an undeveloped canyon near Los Angeles. Breathing the intoxicating "clear air," seeing "the sunlight molten upon hills and valley," and sensing "the furtive wild life," Borough was overcome by a profound nature experience. He finds himself in "silence, vast, all-embracing, in which no note of civilization obtrudes." In the struggle to transform "wild land" into a garden using his own hands, he returned to "an almost forgotten integrity of body and soul, to the glowing vigor and health that flow from lusty victories in our daily lives." Those who rejected the urban jungle and instead lighted out for the territory would "re-create the old American community."[52]

Borough insisted that his land do more than provide spiritual and physical regeneration. He wanted it to feed him as well. "I'm talking about getting food and clothing out of the earth," he explained. Battling poison oak and "winged devils" (hornets), Borough worked to transform his landscape of chaparral into one of "fruit trees, vines, vegetable plots, chicken coops, rabbit hutches, goat sheds." For inspiration, he searched out surviving models of the "old 'home economy'" in the environs of Los Angeles. At first, he was disappointed as he "passed scores of miles of orange, lemon and walnut groves, spic-and-span, with their spic-and-span 'city' lawns in front of their spic-and-span 'city' residences." Such ordered, modern, and seemingly abundant farms did not impress him, for they grew "Oranges, lemons and walnuts only . . . specialized products for The Market." But he did find what he was looking for among " 'backward' members of the older generations or among a newly appearing class of rebel 'nature nuts.'" The "backward" people lived in "cheap little shacks" and had "messy gardens"—but these gardens were fat. One "nature-nut" in the San Fernando Valley told him that she was able to grow three-quarters of the food her household needed on a one-acre plot. She raised goats, chickens, pigeons, rabbits, eggplant, lima beans, cucumbers, squash, carrots, spinach, cabbage, onions, beets, figs, peaches, apricots, plums, grapes, and oranges. This was Borough's kind of cornucopia.[53]

Borough had also been inspired by Ralph Borsodi's experiments, begun in the 1920s, to create an "organic homestead."[54] In his writings, Borsodi attacked the waste, cultural impoverishment, and pollution that attended centralized mass production. Like Sinclair, he singled out advertising, production for profit, the squalor that workers endured in capitalist factory production, and the dangers of processed food. Like Sinclair, he envisioned a return to the land and production for use as a "way out." And Borsodi shared at least some of Sinclair's enthusiasm for the liberatory potential of machines. But unlike Sinclair and the technocrats, Borsodi was a staunch decentralist who saw mass production, whether operating under capitalism or socialism, as the root cause of the modern alienation from nature.

Borsodi felt that factory production threatened to make "mankind . . . into appendages to machines." He was particularly concerned with industrial capitalism's effect on the family. "By destroying the economic foundations of the family," Borsodi charged, "it has robbed men, women and children of their contact with the soil; their intimacy with the growing of animals, birds, vegetables, trees and flowers."[55] Borsodi and his wife, Myrtle, advocated small-scale household production, arguing that electricity and efficient small appliances promised to remake the home into a viable site of production.[56] By growing and preparing food themselves, these new homesteaders would be saved from all of the dangers of mass-produced foods; a can opener would not be among the small-scale appliances put to use on the organic homestead, for eating "factory packed foodstuffs" would inexorably link them to "city life" and destroy their health. When they had lived in the city, Ralph reported, "we lacked the zest of living which comes from real health . . . our lives were barren of real beauty—the beauty which comes from the growth of the soil, from flowers and fruits."[57] The Borsodis' solution was to create "true *organic homesteads*—organic in that they are consciously and with the maximum of intelligence organized to function not only biologically and socially but also economically."[58]

Aldous Huxley, who was member of the Authors' League for Sinclair, made the tension between Sinclair's technocratic cornucopia and Borsodi's organic homesteads clear in *After Many a Summer Dies the Swan,* his 1939 novel set amidst the orange groves of Southern California. Huxley had visited Borsodi's School for Rational Living, and he used him as the model for a character in the novel who says, "Socialism seems to be fatally committed to centralization and standardized urban mass production." He wants to create decentralized organic homesteads that would cultivate "moral craftsmanship," Jeffersonian democracy, and make the "human world safe for animals and spirits." In the eyes of Borough, the Borsodis, and Huxley, small-scale producer cooperatives would enable a rebirth of

American democracy, foster a deeper sense of place, and lead to a more ethical relationship with nature.[59]

But in 1934, the decentralists and the more centralist Sinclair found common ground in the belief that the state could play a beneficial role in supporting homesteads that would demonstrate the value of production for use. Despite his skepticism of the state, Borsodi even ended up advising the National Recovery Administration's Subsistence Homestead Division efforts in Ohio "to put into effect a workable back-to-the-land movement." Though Sinclair was disappointed that Roosevelt failed to endorse production for use in a fireside chat, he could argue that the New Deal's Subsistence Homesteads embodied the spirit of EPIC.[60] One *EPIC News* cartoon portrayed the New Deal and EPIC as two mules hitched together on the same team. Sinclair, wearing a farmer's hat, is driving the plow. From a "dole" bucket, Republican Frank Merriam is watering grapevines labeled "poverty"—producing grapes of wrath avante la lettre. The caption is "We'll Plow under a Row." In this variation on the plow parable, EPIC's body politics were linked to agricultural reform. As they reclaimed the garden, the people would be revitalized by working in the soil.[61]

Orange Inferno

Though the plowing cartoon emphasized the connection between EPIC and the New Deal, it also highlighted an area of major disagreement. The New Deal's Agricultural Adjustment Act paid growers to plow under a portion of their crops in order to reduce supply and thereby raise prices. Even Secretary of Agriculture Henry Wallace acknowledged that destroying "a growing crop" amidst the want of the Depression was "a shocking commentary on our civilization." By taking land out of production and by favoring large farmers over small, the act had multiple impacts on the agricultural landscape of California. It contributed to the flow of migrants to California by uprooting tenant and small-scale farmers in the South and the Dust Bowl region; it increased the power of large growers in cotton and other crops; and it subsidized the formation of the anti-labor Associated Farmers. Even though such consequences may have been unforeseen, Sinclair and his supporters thought the act was a monstrosity on its face, a state-sanctioned form of sabotage.[62]

Sinclair did not let the issue lie fallow. The best of California's produce had been gleaned to feed the national market and satisfy the "Wall Street parasites," he charged. Then, a sizable portion "rots on the ground, or is gathered and dumped into washes—with quick-lime poured over it to make sure that it does not help any unemployed person to keep away from the grocery store." Tons of fruits and vegetables are "dumped into San Francisco bay every year, to keep up the price." To top it all off, "the Federal Government subsidizes farmers to perform such acts of vandalism."[63] In Sinclair's story, the "parasites" and the "vandalism" combined to alienate Californians from their own nature.

But EPIC would change all that, for among its twelve principles were the self-evident truths that "God created the natural wealth of the earth for the use of all men, not a few" and "the destruction of food or other wealth, or the limitation of production, is economic insanity." To the self-help cooperatives in California, agricultural surpluses had come to be seen as common property. In trying to control the market during the Depression by destroying surplus fruits, growers had given EPIC a powerful weapon. Boosters and Sunkist had done so much to identify California's vaunted landscape with oranges that they became an obvious, and loaded, symbol for the lost garden.

Nature's oranges were hybridized with culture once again, this time becoming a political spectacle.[64] The *EPIC News* featured a photograph of "a mile-long pile of oranges left to rot . . . because their owners could not make a profit by selling them." Under the headline "As Thousands Starve," a series of five photographs showed oranges being "Dumped!" "Oiled!" and "Fired!" "While hundreds of thousands go without the stored-up sunshine of the golden fruit," the *News* charged, "mile-long piles of it are being burned." These images asserted the people's right to usufruct. Having promised for so long that the orange was a key to health and a distillation of nature's restorative powers, the Orange Empire found itself under attack for withholding surplus oranges from the people, as if it were cutting off a public utility.

In *The Day of the Locust,* Nathanael West satirized Midwesterners who had come to California for its sunshine but then "get tired of oranges" and secretly long to see Los Angeles go up in a "holocaust of flame." But well before the literature and films of Los Angeles began to turn dark, the EPIC campaign made the destruction of the oranges a *noir* narrative: to send oranges up in flames was to consume the California dream itself. As political symbol, the orange dump served as an indictment of California agribusiness, and, more broadly, the human relationship to nature under the price system. EPIC envisioned creating another way of life and a more just social ecology, one in which people could "tie into the resources of the earth directly, that is the land itself." Restoring usufruct would rehabilitate ailing Americans and save the body politic, EPIC promised. Against a backdrop of an orange inferno, EPIC proposed a return to a garden in which no fruit would be forbidden.[65]

C. C. Teague Assembles the Growth Machine

On September 11, 1934, Charles Collins Teague made front-page news, or what passed for it during the *Los Angeles Times*' campaign to defeat Sinclair. Sinclair was a "wild, visionary dreamer with a ridiculously impractical platform," Teague said. He would "destroy the prosperity and industry of this fair State of ours." In speeches after the election, Teague explained why he had felt the need to fight Sinclair. In periods of severe economic depression, Teague said, "Our people whose intelligence is above the average of the people of the United States cannot be depended upon to come to sound conclusions, but will follow unsound leadership that promises Utopian relief. . . . The people are being led to believe, by demagogues of the Long, Coughlin, Sinclair type, that the men who have accumulated enough capital to be large employers are a menace to society." Teague accurately observed that many voters "just can't understand why, in this great country with its evidence of wealth and abounding production, they cannot find employment." Economic depression predisposed the masses to "listen to the siren song of the theorist or demagogue preaching 'production for use.'" "Had the election been held six weeks earlier, without doubt Sinclair would have been elected governor," Teague shuddered. "Even after the most thorough educational campaign that has ever been put on in the State some 850,000 of our citizenry voted for Upton Sinclair."[66]

The front-page article on Teague played only a small part in this "educational campaign." It was but a drop in the bucket of anti-EPIC material carried by the *Times,* the San Francisco *Chronicle,* and most other leading dailies in the state.[67] But the Sunkist president's contribution was not confined to this prepackaged news item, for he was instrumental in orchestrating that "most thorough educational campaign." To break the spell of the "siren call," Teague called on the talents and money of the growth machine. In fact, the Sinclair challenge forced the growth machine—an alignment of forces that usually operated in concert but not through active, face-to-face planning—to actually caucus. The day before the *Times* article appeared, Teague had met with its publisher Harry Chandler and leading financiers, industrialists, and Hollywood leaders at the élite California Club. Teague's proposal was to "raise thousands, even millions, of dollars (illegally if necessary), direct it to a nonpartisan front group in Los Angeles, retain a crackerjack advertising firm to churn out propaganda, and go to work, ignoring Merriam's reactionary tendencies and basing the entire campaign on saving the state from Upton Sinclair." In a week the well-connected Teague, who was president not only of Sunkist but also of the California Walnut Growers Exchange and the California State Chamber of Commerce, was back in Los Angeles raising half a million dollars from corporations. The campaign strategy would be developed in close association with Chandler and Joseph Knowland of the *Oakland Tribune*. Teague had assembled the motive forces of the growth machine: publishers, entertainment moguls, industrial and agribusiness leaders, and a candidate willing to be its standard bearer.[68]

The *Times* was conscious and proud of its role as the dynamo at the heart of Southern California's growth machine. On October 17, 1934, just a few weeks before the election, it ran a feature called "City's Growth Paralleled by That of Times." Architectural wonders, including the new *Times* building, were paraded across the pages of a special section. Two days earlier, the *Times* had printed photographs of the "crumbling walls" of Llano del Rio, a utopian cooperative community founded in 1914. These ruins were "What's Left of Most Recent Trial of Theorist's Dream in California." The *Times* hoped that Californians would go forward "in proven paths; their progress undistracted by the fantastic lures of economic dreamers, false prophets or political demagogues." Only the growth machine could create the wonders of the modern world, the *Times* argued. Its opponents would bring dystopian ruin.[69]

The feature said that the growth of the city and that of the newspaper had paralleled one another; in fact, they ran on the same tracks. The *Times* (as well as its publishers) benefited from having its booster visions realized. Population growth meant circulation growth, and development drove the exchange value of the *Times*' extensive land holdings ever upward.[70] In analyzing growth machines, sociologists say that they work to maximize exchange, not use, values. It is no coincidence that their model so easily maps onto the EPIC campaign. Sinclair's principle of production for use challenged the growth machine's investment in exchange value. Backed up by the spectacle of poverty amidst abundance, EPIC confronted the growth machine's equation of gross exchange value with the well-being of the body politic. EPIC told voters a simple and powerful story: the growth machine had failed, but EPIC could make the natural abundance of California into a garden for all.

To unravel EPIC's storyline, Teague realized that the growth machine would have to "build up a great group of crusaders against Upton Sinclair between now and election time—and what our campaign is lacking is crusaders." Materials could be mailed to potential crusaders in the American Legion and other conservative civic groups. But to send them effective messages—narratives designed to transform electoral bystanders into obstacles to Sinclair's drive to Sacramento—a different sort of crusader would be needed: paid professional publicists and advertisers. In Northern California, that job would go to longtime Republican Party strategist Chester Rowell and the new kid on the block, Clem Whitaker. Whitaker was owner and inventor of Campaigns, Inc., perhaps the first political consulting firm in the country. In the south, Teague established a group called United for California, hiring Don Francisco to create and direct the anti-EPIC campaign. After serving as Sunkist's advertising manager, Francisco had become the West Coast director of Lord & Thomas, the advertising agency that handled the Sunkist account. He had once said that "the chief use of advertising lies entirely beyond its competitive value. It creates new markets, new demands, new products, new ways of doing things, a better national life." Now, advertising would be used to re-create the Sinclair product and thereby protect that "better national life" Francisco and the growth machine believed they had manufactured. Lord & Thomas would team up with Sunkist once more, but this time to plant the kiss of death on Sinclair.[71]

Framing Sinclair

American politics was no stranger to fiction. Generations of presidential candidates had told log-cabin origin stories. On a more basic level, campaign promises are fictions, portraits of a reality that has yet to materialize. Long before the birth of media politics, the Greeks developed a name for such political narratives, *prohairesis*. As Aristotle explained, prohairesis was used to persuade the citizenry to take a particular course of action. The leader tells a story about what will happen in the future if something is done. It is, then, a projection, an imaginative configuration of a chain of events necessarily put in the form of a narrative. To convince voters to vote for them, candidates place themselves into such projections, arguing that their election will allow a new and better future to unfurl. Sinclair's fundamental campaign story was a utopian projection. The fundamental story for the Merriam campaign was dystopian: it sought to make a steady course look attractive by projecting a victory by EPIC as catastrophic.[72]

Sinclair reportedly spoke with great authority, claiming expertise and often persuading even skeptics. To shatter his story of the future, the first step was to break down Sinclair's integrity. The anti-EPIC campaign would deconstruct the political body Sinclair was building and substitute for it an array of impostors. The *EPIC News* complained about this strategy in a cartoon that depicted the "Old Guard" as a graphic artist searching through a dictionary for new labels to affix to Sinclair, already having painted him as a "Bolshevik," "Red," "Nazi," "Dreamer," and so on. In *I, Governor*, Sinclair accurately forecast that this tactic would be used. Referring to treatment of Robert M. La Follette in the 1924 presidential campaign, Sinclair described the effect of media representations in strikingly corporeal terms: "I watched the thing with the feeling of a man bound hand and foot and witnessing a murder."[73]

Noting the demands of the gubernatorial race, Sinclair said, "I ought to have been able to grow by fission, like the amoebae; first there would have been two of me, and then four, then eight, sixteen, thirty-two—and so on until there were a thousand."[74] He should have been careful what he wished for: his body was in fact multiplied in the campaign, but instead of having clones to command, he found himself confronted with an array of troubling doppelgangers. From fragments of Sinclair's large corpus, his opponents composed bodies that they would substitute for the real candidate. As the *Sacramento Bee* put it, "Sinclair's Works Rise to Confront Him in Governorship Drive."[75] Words of Sinclair's characters were spliced out of his novels, recombined, and then put in the mouth of Sinclair himself.

Given that Sinclair was figuratively put on trial during the campaign, he would have found it useful if his writings had been covered by the Fifth Amendment, for anything he had written could be used against him, and much of it was. His muckraking corpus would provide the clay for several Sinclair bodies. From one book alone, *The Profits of Religion* (1918), a heretic tailor-made for every sect could be cut. In his effort to be ecumenical in his exposé of corruption in churches, Sinclair had provided ample verbal fodder for Francisco to create specific pamphlets to convince everyone from Mormons to Catholics that electing Sinclair would spell religious ruin. With quotes that were for the most part accurate, as even an

EPIC worker admitted, such "narrow-cast" pamphlets could present a powerfully persuasive picture. Special pamphlets were also prepared for every group from UCLA alumni to doctors and the Boy Scouts, all quoting inflammatory things Sinclair had written about them (or things that could be made to appear inflammatory). With the growth machine providing mailing lists, expert writing, and unlimited copies, six million pamphlets with a score of carefully constructed Sinclairs went into circulation.[76]

Radio listeners were treated to the drama of the Bennetts, a typical middle-class family imperiled by Sinclair's supposed home-wrecking tendencies. The father is worried about losing his job at the factory, the daughter wants to go off to choir practice before Sinclair shuts down the churches, and the boy is eager to take in what might be the last picture show. The tone is ominous as the Bennetts say grace over their dinner, for in this narrative food would become scarce under a Sinclair régime.[77] While Sinclair's campaign narrative opened with a vision of poverty, the radio drama began with a vision of middle-class abundance. The radio shows were like dramatizations of Norman Rockwell portraits of Franklin Roosevelt's Four Freedoms, culminating with the family feast on Thanksgiving. But unlike FDR, the message went, Sinclair would destroy freedom of speech and religion, spread fear, and create an era of want.

Sunkist had already discovered the magic of radio combined with celebrity. Now Francisco hired first-rate radio talent to create compelling dramas of EPIC's impending dystopia. For Francisco, this was all second nature—with a twist. Here was a product that would not make you healthy, that would not give you vim, that experts agreed would be disastrous to your personal well-being, that would make you earn less, that would break up your family, that would make you look ridiculous to your neighbors in conspicuous ways, that would impede growth and a higher standard of living, that was not what it appeared to be, that was 100 percent less wholesome than the competing product, that was not a gift from nature.

To complete the disintegration of Sinclair, the candidate was portrayed as a scattered personality trying to go in all directions at once. A *Times* cartoon split Sinclair into six figures, all tugging on a different limb of the person representing the "public" to bring him out of "the economic woods." In "The Epic Tea Party," Alice is the voter, Sinclair's running mate Sheridan Downey is the March Hare, and Sinclair is the schizophrenic Mad Hatter, pontificating ad nauseum: "This is a permanent crisis. . . . It is caused by overproduction of things that do not wear out. Only I know the solution of it, I have been working on it for thirty years. . . . I am an economic scientist." Did he study economics in college? Alice asks. Sinclair-as-Mad-Hatter replies, "I studied music, vegetarianism, fasting, single tax, the Abrams Reactions, the Appeal to Reason, the all-meat diet, Communism, the League of Nations, the conscription of wealth, Fletcherism . . . mental telepathy, the Little Theater movement, vers libre, sex hygiene," and so on and so on. Aside from the fact that it was not at college that Sinclair studied these subjects, the list is fairly accurate. But of course, it was the way these facts were configured that helped attack Sinclair's authority and fix him with an unstable, or, better, a multiple personality. On this particular editorial page, the framing of Sinclair was completed by an anti-EPIC letter to the editor saying, "I hope that those of you who have the power will also have the intestinal fortitude to rise to the occasion and save your commonwealth from the ridiculous." The editorial cartoon, actual quotes from Sinclair and Downey, light-hearted satire, and the letter from the reader all conspire, to make Sinclair look ridiculous.[78]

To speak of a conspiracy to frame Sinclair may not be inappropriate, for journalists and other symbol handlers routinely "organize discourse, whether verbal or visual" into "media frames."[79] A frame is a structure of parts fitted together, or an arrangement of words. It is also one's body. To frame is to fabricate or invent something, as well shape or "discipline" the action, faculties, or inclinations of someone or something. And one can be framed in a crime. All of these senses apply to the growth machine's representations of Sinclair. It designed and assembled the narratives within which it would frame Sinclair. It used Sinclair's words, usually out of context, to frame him in past and future crimes against the state. Finally, the media frames were intended to discipline voters, that is, give them the "intestinal fortitude" to reject Sinclair.

Patent Medicine Man

In anti-EPIC cartoons, Sinclair was turned into all manner of strange creatures. He appeared as a tiger, a porcupine, a prickly pear, a leopard, and a Pied Piper. Amidst this menagerie, one figure, uniquely embodying danger, transgression, and duplicity, appeared again and again in Sinclair's place: the patent medicine peddler.

One mock EPIC pamphlet has Sinclair promoting "the EPICAC Plan." After eliminating poverty, this patent medicine peddler as politician says,

"I should have ample time during my four years as governor to eliminate bad morals, infantile paralysis, halitosis, athlete's foot and the other evils which have been forced upon us by big business." As professional advertisers, the authors of this pamphlet certainly knew that "halitosis"—a creation of the Lambert Pharmaceutical Company, manufacturers of Listerine—had been "forced upon us by big business." The scientific sounding term "halitosis" (unpleasant breath) was followed by other creations such as "bromodisis" (sweaty foot odors), as well as Sunkist's own "acidosis." If infantile paralysis was not an invention of advertising, parables of children with stunted growth were certainly part of Sunkist's campaigns. In caricaturing Sinclair as a quack selling false remedies for seemingly intractable maladies of the body, the advertisers were, like the unmarried woman in a Listerine advertisement who was tragically unaware of her own halitosis, looking in a mirror.[80]

Until the early twentieth century, advertising was part and parcel of the patent medicine business, which "promoted the persistent dream of bodily revitalization." Itinerant peddlers and Wild West showmen, often pitching patent nostrums, sold dreams of magical transformation. But in the early twentieth century, reformers made the patent medicine peddler the prime symbol of a hucksterism imperiling the republic.[81] The advertising profession worked hard to shake off the scent of the snake-oil salesman, hoping to identify its advertised products "with rationality and progress, and to cleanse advertising of its associations with peddlers." In the process, advertisers like Francisco recast themselves not as seducers of vulnerable people but as educators helping consumers adapt to the modern world and live better. Their work paid off. In 1926, no less a figure than Calvin Coolidge proclaimed that advertisers were "part of the great work of the regeneration and redemption of mankind." Advertising had become a key part of corporate America, selling its goods and spreading the faith that the nation had entered an era of unlimited economic and personal growth. It was only natural that advertisers would see EPIC—making similar promises but attacking the growth machine for destroying what it said it was delivering—as a dangerous interloper. After all, as a 1925 article in *Printers' Ink* proclaimed, advertising was the "arch enemy of poverty and disease." Advertisers now attacked Sinclair as the *real* patent medicine huckster, seeking to undermine EPIC's claim of being the slayer of poverty.[82]

Still, Sinclair's work had made him a receptive screen on which to project the image of the patent medicine peddler. In his search for alternative medicines, he had been particularly intrigued by the experiments of a

Dr. Albert Abrams on "the diagnosis and cure of disease by means of radio-active vibrations." Like the scientists at the citrus experiment station, Abrams thought that radioactivity might be fashioned into a magic wand. Sinclair championed Abrams's methods, but they were subsequently discredited. During the 1934 campaign, the *Times* re-broke that story. It interviewed Robert Millikan, the Nobel laureate who had destroyed Abrams's reputation with a report published in *Scientific American* in 1924. The "eminent physicist" said, "Sinclair's program for 'ending poverty in California' is just as desirable and effective as the program for eliminating disease . . . based on the Abrams theory of 'electronic reactions.' That was a stupendous medical fake which the public fell for to its detriment." Using the legitimacy of a Nobel laureate to flay Sinclair was a masterful stroke. Never mind that the *Times* had given favorable notice nine days earlier about the use of radioactivity in medical therapy. Never mind that *Times* publisher Harry Chandler himself, having arrived in California in 1883 suffering from pneumonia, had been cured by a therapy Sinclair would have approved of—work on a fruit ranch, going shirtless to absorb more of the rejuvenating powers of the sun.[83]

From October 1 to October 20, 1934, the *Times* gave over twelve column inches of the front page to a comic strip called "Wynndebagge, the Ipecac Candidate." Worried about the state of the union, Wyndebagge-Sinclair works himself into a state of delirium. Seeking relief, he goes to a pharmacist, who gives him a bottle of Ipecac. He storms off to tell the world that his personal cure should be consumed by the body politic. Before a crowd, Wynndebagge assumes the particular form of peddler-charlatan perfectly adapted for Southern California: the rainmaker. "IPECAC can control the winds, the seas, the temperature," Wynndebagge enthuses; his "high fog commission" will make it rain. In substituting this rainmaker for Sinclair, the *Times* could draw on people's memory of the rainmakers who had flourished in Southern California around the turn of the century. In 1905, one rainmaker promised to deliver Los Angeles eighteen inches of rain. Denounced by some as a charlatan, his mysterious "chemical affinity high-ball" nevertheless seemed to do the trick. But soon the engineering of William Mulholland would make the streams of the eastern Sierra flow into Los Angeles, and the rainmakers became obsolete. Just a week before printing the Wynndebagge strip, the *Times* celebrated the Owens River aqueduct as a fount of growth, though it did not mention that *Times* owner Harrison Gray Otis made a fortune using inside information to purchase land cheap in the San Fernando Valley, land that would become prime citrus growing land once the water came through. In another case of the pot calling the kettle black, the *Times* strip went on to attribute grandiose schemes of reengineering nature to Wynndebagge. Like all good satire, this strip caught something essentially true about its target, for Sinclair did entertain a technocratic dream of reinventing nature. So did the *Times*. They just differed about how it should be done and into whose cup the water should flow.[84]

Depicted as disorganized, irrational, undisciplined, and equipped with nothing more proven than an elixir that produced nausea, EPIC was made to look foolhardy and its leader crazed. With Sinclair made out to be the patent medicine peddler, the politics of EPIC would appear to be utopianism stuffed in a bottle—a sham whatever the mix.

Foreign Bodies

The IPECAC Plan, as one leaflet put it, came straight "Out of the Moscow Medicine Chest." "Underneath the sheep's clothing of pleasing euphemisms is the . . . red wolf of radicalism and destructive doctrines," warned the *Times* in a front-page editorial.[85]

Los Angeles's premier religious showwoman, Aimee Semple McPherson, gave the parable of foreign bodies its most dramatic expression, performing an operatic sermon against EPIC (which in her rendition stood for "Enemy Power is Invading Christianity"). On stage appeared a kind of melting pot, flanked by Uncle Sam and Columbia. Then a "colorful array of immigrants filed past, tossing different kinds of 'fruit' into the melting pot." But after several immigrants had made their contributions, an ill-clad man stalked on stage and tossed in a red flag. "I tell you there is death in the pot!" Aimee cried out. "Someone has cast in the poisonous herb and if we eat thereof we shall all perish." Here was an answer to the political spectacle of the orange dump: EPIC as a toxic plant that would contaminate America's diverse cultural "fruits" and poison the body politic.[86]

McPherson's title for another anti-EPIC performance said it all: "America! Awake! The Enemy Is at Your Gate!" The *Times* had already prepared her audience for this martial metaphor, saying that EPIC was like a "hostile fleet off our shore." The dominant anti-EPIC imagery, though, pictured an invasion not by sea, but by land. In cartoons, an army of unemployed surges over the Sierra Nevada and swarms down on Eden. Sinclair, often dressed as a Pied Piper, leads the way. Describing one of these cartoons, an editor wrote, "You see the beautiful mountains of California, the sun setting in the West and Upton Sinclair's 'EPIC' blazing in the light of the setting sun . . . you see the unfortunate unemployed of other States, pouring into California to dwell forever happy in the land that has 'ended poverty.' . . . If only poverty could be ended and an Eldorado-Utopia . . . could be created," the editor sighed, "how the angels in Heaven would rejoice." Sinclair's portrayal of California as "Eldorado-Utopia"—an image the Orange Empire had been circulating for decades—would now do damage to the Golden State.[87]

Sinclair accidentally aided and abetted the creation of the specter of California overrun by the unworthy poor. After a meeting with Federal Relief Administrator Harry Hopkins, Sinclair told reporters that he had jokingly told Hopkins that "if I am elected, half of the unemployed of the United States will come to California, and he will have to make plans for them." This would become *the* quote of the campaign, endlessly reprinted in leaflets, newspapers, and, probably most effectively, on some two thousand billboards across the state. The billboards also pictured a stream of these unemployed, a bindle stiff leading the way, and a scripted Upton Sinclair "signature." Some voters apparently read the message as if it were an EPIC campaign promise. Sinclair's words had been once again conscripted to fight against him.[88]

The narrative of overrun California was bolstered by the state registrar of motor vehicles (a Merriam appointee), who reported that 218,000 people had come to California since EPIC had received national attention. Notes from border officials appeared in the press, describing immigrants such as "A. C. Tow, Oklahoma—Car very poor shape. . . . Expects lots of work after election of Sinclair." The California Department of Agriculture released figures showing a near record influx of immigrants in the summer of 1934—416,000 in July alone. But most of these people were simply *returning* to California. Many others were arriving for seasonal agricultural work. At the border inspection stations, set up to protect California's agroecosystem from natural enemies, these workers would have their baggage searched for potential pests. Inspectors questioned them about their opinion of Sinclair and supplied reports to newspapers. These border crossers were entering not just the state of California but an intense social drama. Under normal circumstances, to be poor and looking for work was to be welcomed by California agribusiness. In the context of the campaign, such a person became part of a "great horde," "a swarm of indigent newcomers," "an invading army of unemployed"—able bodies in the campaign against Sinclair.[89]

Pictures of the "Invading Army of Unemployed Charging California State Line" made the front page of the *Times* on October 24. The article described a family of eight from Texas pulling into an agricultural inspection station in a "dilapidated truck." The photograph's caption read, "The 1934 version of the covered wagon is shown here, only this year the moving households do not represent pioneers striking out for a new and undeveloped land but only emigrants lured westward by the prospect of being supported in idleness by taxpayers of a highly developed community—that is, if Sinclair is elected." The reporter gets everyone to whom he talks—and he talks only to the least well off—to tell him about their great expectations if Sinclair is elected. At the border, the swarming indigents always ask, "How does the Utopia thing work out?" or "Where do we register to become members of the EPIC people?" In contrast to the aversion to charity usually expressed by Southwestern migrants to California during the Depression, the reporter found opportunists who readily admitted they were attracted by the dole. Invariably, these newcomers had large families, poor clothing, and almost no money. Here were grassroots politics in reverse: ascribing to EPIC the support of common people, all too common.[90]

"Multiply these scenes by almost every hour in the day, each day in the week," the reporter instructed, "and one gets a picture of the great migration of 'end poverty.'" The scenes were indeed multiplied, in newspapers across the state. The Los Angeles *Herald-Express* even published a still from the movie *Wild Boys on the Road* to verify the migration. Still, the selected images of people coming into California looking for a better life were in fact part of a great migration. In the 1920s, 250,000 to 300,000 Southwesterners had moved to California. The 1930s saw perhaps as many as 400,000 enter the state.[91] But while the earlier wave was absorbed without notice during a period of phenomenal growth, the latter migrants were made part of a public social drama. They had roles to play, and so found themselves on center stage.

There was much truth to Sinclair's charge that if people were flocking to California, it was at least as much as a result of the chamber of commerce pictures of beautiful orange groves that had been sent out to the nation as it was because of his plan. Throughout the 1930s, the imagery exported by the Orange Empire would be carried back home by migrants. One Okie song, for example, spoke of the "shining of your sun / the beauty of your orange groves."[92] But these migrants had been pushed as well as pulled to California. The 1933 Agricultural Adjustment Act provided incentives for farmers to take land out of production, and this resulted in many tenant farmers being turned off the land. The act also encouraged modernization, resulting in tenant farmers being, as they put it, "tractored out." Drought further exacerbated conditions, leading to the famous dust storms. Although the first major dust storm had occurred in May 1934, no mention of any possible connection between that event and the new migrants was ventured in the newspaper coverage. Indeed, the *Times* denied that these migrants were forced out by catastrophes caused by nature ("flood or pestilence") or culture ("an invading army"). Instead, the migrants themselves were the invading army, the flood, the pestilence.[93]

Four decades after Turner proclaimed the closing of the frontier, the growth machine would try to finally put to rest the idea that the westward movement of the worthy poor meant national improvement. Instead, the frontier should be closed, the Sinclair menace quarantined. One cartoon showed Sinclair standing on the far side of a fence under an overflowing orange tree, "The Fruits of Victory." The fence is labeled "Quarantine. California EPIC Rash."[94]

The Reel Campaign

On October 19, moviegoers across the state saw a film short called *California Election News*. This newsreel, the first in a series of three, featured interviews by an "Inquiring Cameraman" who purported to travel "the highways and the by-ways . . . all for the purpose of digging out voters of California to express their views for your edification." "I'm impartial," he added. As images of people from all walks of life flashed across the screen, the Inquiring Cameraman said, "Remember they're not actors, they're *nervous*." In fact, some of them may have been actors, or at least aspiring ones. The newsreel had been produced by Irving Thalberg of MGM, and it was anything but impartial. As Thalberg maintained, "Nothing is unfair in politics."[95]

In the third installment of *California Election News*, the Inquiring Cameraman travels the highways and byways to the California-Arizona border. We hear from a Southern Pacific switchman that there are wanted criminals among the flood of migrants. The migrants think "they're going to get something for nothing." At last, the reporter ventures into the lurid world of these dangerous others. "When they're not living in trains most of them live in jungles," he says. "And now we're going to give you a real inside view, an actual interview in a genuine hobo jungle. Look at them. Listen to them, and *think*."[96]

Sinclair had wanted to use film for his own campaign, but his plans never panned out. But there was a film made in 1934 that could have served as EPIC's answer to the Inquiring Cameraman: King Vidor's *Our Daily Bread*. Vidor had been inspired by a *Reader's Digest* article about ending the Depression by bringing *"unemployed men and unemployed acres"* together. "Inspired by the facts of the day," *Our Daily Bread* would interpret them in a realistic mode. *Our Daily Bread* was clearly a work of fiction, but it was meant to be taken as a documentary, while *California Election News* was covertly a work of fiction meant to be seen as transparent to reality.[97]

The movie opens with a city couple reduced to trading one of their last possessions, a ukulele, for a scrawny chicken. An uncle (Sam?) is willing to let them live on a country property of his. After unsuccessfully trying to till the soil, the tenderfoot John decides to start a cooperative, inviting refugees passing by to join in. In a town meeting, John gives an inspirational speech about how the pilgrims didn't sit around complaining about the "unemployment situation" but set to work to "build their own houses and grow their own food." At first, everyone pulls together, making their cars into tractors or hitching themselves to the plow (as in Sinclair's plow parable). They soon transform the run-down property into a working farm. When the corn plants first come out of the soil, John, teary-eyed, says, "There's nothing for people to worry about, not when they've got the earth . . . it's like a mother." As most of the members of the cooperative gather for a prayer in the fields ("God has made the earth fruitful, that our labor be productive"), we learn that a woman has given birth. That night, the community celebrates in a down-home American fashion—dancing to an impromptu folk ensemble, with the proud father passing out IOUs for the cigars he will give out once the crop is harvested. In *Our Daily Bread*, as nature blooms, so does culture.

But the co-op faces a series of trials: threatened foreclosure, dwindling food supplies, John's seduction by a jazz-loving bombshell, and drought. The communal homestead nearly disintegrates into so much dust, its crop withered and its members left to drift along the roads once again. At the last moment, John hits on the idea of digging an irrigation ditch. They only have two days, and there is a lot of ground to cover from stream to field. As the route is surveyed, the men line up and begin delivering synchronized strikes of their picks. Muscles strain against boulders, trees are pulled out to make way, and as the dust settles we see the phalanx of men coming through. As the water rushes into the ditch, a break opens up and a man throws his body into the breach to keep the water in the channel. When the water reaches the field, it is, in Vidor's words, "welcomed with rejoicing and unrestrained demonstration. Prayers and pratfalls in the wet earth were indulged in." The finale becomes an almost erotic merging and release: humans, their machines, and nature all celebrating together, enjoying an organic redemption.[98]

The *EPIC News* tried to make the film work for its cause, saying that it would show "millions how they, too, may help themselves." But in fact, it showed almost no one—at least during the campaign. In California, it was kept out of movie theaters. Sinclair lost the all-important battle of narratives.[99]

In the process, he also lost control of his body. In a radio broadcast the night before the election, Sinclair made one last attempt to reclaim his image. "Your minds have been poisoned with a lie barrage," he said, "and tonight, as you listen to me, you must be wondering whether I am a human being or some monster sent up to this earth by the devil in order to betray and wreck the institutions of our state and nation." Sinclair compared the effect to that of fun-house mirrors he had seen as a child in New York's Eden Musee—"One made you tall and lean, and the other made you short and dumpy, and yet another twisted your figure and your features into all kinds of grotesque shapes."[100] How fitting—in California, itself a museum of Eden writ large, Sinclair became the serpent. Californians heard that story again and again, and when they went to the polls more of them saw Sinclair as a threat to the garden than as its savior.

The Associated Farmers and the Orange Strike

Meanwhile, back at the Limoneira ranch, Teague was at work assembling another arm of the growth machine: the Associated Farmers, Inc. Spawned by the California State Chamber of Commerce, the AF, organized to fight labor unionization in agriculture, was first conceived in Los Angeles exactly one year before election day. It would lobby for anti-picketing ordinances, push a "No Work, No Eat" policy designed to keep striking workers from receiving relief, prosecute labor leaders under the state's Criminal Syndicalism Law, and use strong-arm tactics to intimidate strikers. But by November 1934, the funds originally raised for the AF had been used up.[101]

Teague wanted to turn over the remains of the anti-EPIC war chest to the AF. He had been the "prime instigator" of its accumulation, and he saw Sinclairism and the unionization of farmworkers as kindred menaces.

Though he "put up a hard fight," the funds were not actually turned over. Undaunted, Teague joined a fund-raising committee with the *Times'* Harry Chandler. He opened up Sunkist's headquarters for AF meetings. He got Sunkist packing houses to tax themselves to raise money. He even gave them $500 out of his own pocket. As Robert La Follette's Senate committee, which came to California in 1939 to investigate labor conditions and agribusiness in the Golden State, concluded, "The major success in raising funds for the Associated Farmers in the Los Angeles area came through the efforts of C. C. Teague . . . and Harry Chandler." Compared to the $83 million the Orange Empire would harvest that year in sales, bankrolling the AF seemed like a small price to pay to prevent unionization of its workers. Income had dropped off by some $25 million since 1929, and Sunkist sought to keep its costs down.[102]

The Sinclair campaign was actually a windfall for the AF. By convincing Teague and others that the threat to their control was real, it galvanized their support. In addition, the anti-EPIC campaign bequeathed to the AF narratives it could use. During the campaign, the agricultural press had made Sinclair the embodiment of farmers' worst nightmares. For the *California Citrograph,* Francisco prepared an advertisement warning his former employers that Sinclair would turn "California into one huge Russianized farm." Ads with headlines like "Plundering the Farmer," warning of the "'Epic' scheme to Russianize California agriculture and destroy independent farming," appeared in the *Pacific Rural Press* (whose editor was a big supporter of the AF). After creating the specter of Sinclairism, advertisements for Merriam ran with his "Pledge to all California farmers." He would stop the "hordes of penniless immigrants" at the border (as well as beef up the plant quarantine work there). He promised "to assure every California farmer a chance to harvest his crops without rioting and intimidation of workers by radicals."[103]

The AF made the same pledge. But just who were the Associated Farmers? By 1938, everyone seemed to be asking that question. A pamphlet published by the Simon J. Lubin Society posed it, as did an article in *Survey Graphic.* Even the Associated Farmers' own publications listed "By Whom Organized" as one of the questions most frequently asked about it. It answered emphatically: "By farmers; run by farmers, with a farmer directorate, and financed (except for emergency expenditures) by farmers—in spite of all the propaganda to the contrary." In one radio address, AF president Colonel William Garrison insisted, "Our organization was formed by farmers. . . . During the four years the Associated Farmers has made a remarkable growth, and always that growth has been made possible by the cooperation of real farmers . . . men of the soil."[104]

Yet these farmers were not so real after all. In a private letter, the Riverside chapter of the AF suggested "that real farmers be acquired as members of the organization"—thus revealing the gap between the image and reality. Even the name Associated Farmers was a calculated choice, picked because "the publicity factor will be an important one." The name allowed the growth machine to wear the symbolic clothes of the American farmer, "the man who grows the nation's food supply." "Cartoonists," Richard Neuberger wrote in a 1939 exposé, "portray him as a perspiring toiler with a rugged countenance." As we have seen, Sunkist's growers had for many years tried to disassociate themselves from the humble toiler, seeing themselves as members of the managerial class. But during the Depression, with distrust of big business on the rise, growers found it useful to trade in wingtips and business suits for boots and denim.[105]

Though Sunkist played a leading role, all components of California's growth machine contributed to the birth of the AF. The early organizational meetings included representatives of the Santa Fe and Southern Pacific railroads, Standard Oil, and the Bank of America, as well as the California Packing Company and San Francisco's anti-union Industrial Association. As the La Follette committee concluded, "The Associated Farmers constituted an attempt by powerful antiunion industrial interests to assure the retention in California's industrialized agriculture of their favored labor policies by the highly organized techniques they had used in industry." The industrial and agricultural sectors of capital, as well as the state chamber of commerce, cooperated closely in forming the AF because they wanted to preserve "complete control of employer-employee relationships by the employers, free from . . . collective bargaining." But the AF went to great lengths to conceal the sources of its funding so that it could "parade before the public as a 'farmers' organization."[106]

If they weren't tilling the soil, just what did AF members do? Executive secretary Guernsey Frazer explained that it was "the only organization in California that has systematically attempted to identify the leading Communists through the collecting of a rogues' gallery." The AF established a photographic unit to take pictures at demonstrations and identify "agitators." In a letter to Sunkist, the AF offered that its "rogues' gallery" included "600 photographs of known Communists . . . together with their descriptions, fingerprints, aliases, records, etc." In addition, "We have pounded continuously on the Press, supplied them with data, and I believe, have been responsible in a large measure for publicity which has been highly detrimental to the Communist group." The AF distributed tens of thousands of pamphlets with titles like "The Red Network" and "California's Embattled Farmers." The AF also fought battles directly on the ground. "We have gone into the fields where agitations were in process and battled on the firing line," it reported, "and have succeeded up to date in licking them without exception." Conducting martial as well as public relations campaigns, the AF waged a battle of representation both in the fields and in the media.[107]

In Orange County in the summer of 1936, the AF got a chance to put all of its power into action. Uniting behind the Confederación de Uniones Obreros Mexicanos (CUCOM), Mexicano citrus workers had gone on strike. They wanted higher wages, an end to foreman abuses, and, most important, union recognition. For several months, Stuart Strathman and Holmes Bishop, leaders of Orange County's AF chapter, had been quietly administering doses of propaganda to the local press, law enforcement agencies, and civic groups. When the strike came, they helped the media portray it as the work of outside agitators—Reds, EPICs, and assorted other malcontents.[108]

Working with local growers and packing houses, the AF composed a blacklist. It had distributed a set of instructions to citrus growers, advising them to stock up on "no trespassing" signs. It had made ties with the local immigration official, assuring that any worker arrested for trespassing would be subjected to an immigration test. Striking workers were evicted from Sunkist housing. The state highway patrol and the local sheriff (also an orange grower) attempted to control every inch of space in the county. Tickets were issued to strikers for improperly inflated tires, for failure to carry registration materials in billfolds, for parking a few feet into growers' property, and for crossing white lines that existed only in the imagination of the officers. The sheriff even issued shoot-to-kill orders, explaining, "This is no fight between orchardists and pickers. . . . It is a fight between the entire population of Orange County and a bunch of Communists." Vigilantes, most likely with the support of the sheriff and the AF, threw tear-gas bombs into a building where strikers were meeting. A group of 116 workers was arrested for rioting and put in an improvised bullpen to await trial. Many were denied food for days. In the courthouse, guards carried machine guns.[109] These legal and extralegal terror tactics undermined the strike, and the workers eventually lost their battle. Many workers were permanently blacklisted.

One citrus grower was critical of the way the AF and its Sunkist supporters had taken control of the citrus landscape during the strike. Frank Stokes had been a member of Sunkist for twenty years, and he was generally pleased with all that the association had done for him. In a dissenting article published in *The Nation,* he noted that the Fruit Growers Supply Company provided him many things at cost. He was grateful that Sunkist arranged to have his fruit picked and packed; that it lent him money; and that "I can sleep through winter nights or until a voice on the telephone tells me that my thermometers have dropped to a danger point." He repeated the origin story that fills Sunkist literature—there was a time when citrus growers were being "exploited and robbed by brokers and shippers," and then they had banded together "to obtain a better return for their sweat and labor." But now, he charged, "they are determined that others shall not be permitted to organize for the same purpose."[110]

Stokes was ashamed that citrus growers had "taken over . . . the whole vicious machinery of vigilantes, strike-breakers, night riders, tear gas, and prejudiced newspapers." During the strike, he traveled the county only to see "scab pickers, often high-school boys, 'glomming' the 'golden fruit' in the beautiful California sunshine, while mocking birds sang on the housetops, snow-covered Mount Baldy glistened in the distance—and armed guards patrolled the groves behind long rows of 'no trespassing' signs." The picturesque landscape had become militarized, now better represented by the "no trespassing" signs than the idyllic crate labels.[111] Carey McWilliams was also on hand to witness the violence. After seeing the firearms on display in the groves and in the county courthouse, he gave Sunkist's product a new brand name—Gunkist Oranges. His article on the strike was illustrated with a stark woodcut of a body lying lifeless beneath an orange tree (see figure 17).[112]

A few months after Orange County's conflagration, in a coastal valley in Northern California, a young novelist watched a similar veil of repression envelop his town. Lettuce workers went on strike and the AF moved in to quash the strike. Privately referring to the AF as "ass farmers," he was moved to write on behalf of farmworkers and express his dreams for a more socially and ecologically sound agriculture. In a piece called "Starvation under the Orange Trees," John Steinbeck wrote that "the spring is rich and green in California this year . . . the orange trees are loaded." But the "men who harvested the crops of California, the women and girls who

Figure 17. After the violent repression of the 1936 citrus strike, Carey
McWilliams wrote an article charging that oranges had become "Gunkist."
Reversing the message that orange growing and eating make a body strong,
this illustration portrays a lifeless body beneath an orange tree. (From Carey
McWilliams, "Gunkist Oranges," *Pacific Weekly,* 20 July 1936, 38–39.
Courtesy of the Bancroft Library, University of California, Berkeley; UCB
Bancroft, F850.P232.)

stood all day and half the night in canneries, are starving." The article
could have been illustrated with the picture of the orange dump that had
appeared in the *EPIC News* or the *Pacific Weekly* woodcut. When the
Simon J. Lubin Society reprinted this juxtaposition of perfect oranges and
broken-down bodies, it would be accompanied by the penetrating photographs of Dorothea Lange.[113]

In 1934, Sinclair became entangled in a jungle of representation. The growth machine had employed the techniques of social documentary to represent the "jungles" of migratory workers and defeat Sinclair, beating the muckraker at his own game. It had used Sunkist's advertising expertise to take control of the public sphere in California, setting loose patent medicine men and Pied Pipers to push EPIC off a political cliff. But a new set of storytellers soon came on the scene, and they would hold their ground.

SEVEN

A Record of Eden's Erosion

THE BORDER OF EDEN

HAROLD BISSONETTE, the grocer played by W. C. Fields in *It's a Gift* (1934), journeys to California in a beat-up jalopy with suitcases tied to the running boards. Dreaming of life as an orange grower, Harold has plunked down an inheritance on a plot of land near the fertile groves he sees pictured in a promotional brochure. Just after crossing the state line, Harold and his motley crew drive into an opulently landscaped estate and disembark for a picnic, mistaking it for a typical public park in America's Eden. After being run off the property, Harold drives on to the orange ranch he has purchased sight unseen. Of course, it turns out to be a desecrated landscape more characteristic of a drought-stricken Oklahoma than the irrigated cornucopia of California. No matter: a developer wants the land for a race track, and Harold is able to swap his weed lot for the orange grove pictured in the brochure. While *It's a Gift* emplots the migration to California as a farce, in the years afterward this history would be repeated as tragedy.

If Harold had made his journey in the spring of 1936, he might have been turned away at the border. "For a month at least," Kevin Starr notes, "the entrepôts of California, north, south, and central, seemed more like the border checkpoints of fascist Europe than those of an American state." Woody Guthrie—"the Dustiest of the Dust Bowlers," as his business card boasted—made a sketch titled "The Garden of Eden" that showed a policeman with his billy club chasing the guitar-toting bard at the California-Arizona state line. The Los Angeles Police Department, which had clearly overreached its jurisdiction in this attempt to keep unwanted migrants out of the state, soon left the borders. But throughout the decade travelers crossing into the Golden State continued to go through a mandatory rite of passage at the state line. As one Oklahoman recalled, "When we came into the State of California we were stopped. . . . They went through our car, through our grips and everything we had . . . looking for insects, fruits, or anything like that." The fruit inspector worked for the California State Department of Agriculture, maintaining its border quarantine. In response to the lobbying of Sunkist and other agricultural groups, a system of eleven permanent inspection stations had been established by state law in the 1910s. "Maintenance of the state border quarantine inspection stations," the *California Citrograph* and the California State Chamber of Commerce agreed, "is imperative for the protection of the two and a quarter billion dollar agricultural industry, as well as to the prosperity of the state as a whole."[1]

Ironically, this particular migrant was not trying to smuggle fruits into California. They were hard to come by in his home state of Oklahoma. "You go out to buy fruit, oranges and stuff, and you give 40 to 50 cents a dozen for common oranges like you get here for 5 cents," he explained. "Maybe on Christmas [my children] will get an orange, you know." One Okie folk song spoke of Santa Claus and oranges in the same breath, wondering if they were real:

California, California,
Here I come too.
With a coffee pot and skillet,
And I'm coming to you.
Nothing's left in Oklahoma,
For us to eat or do.
And if apples, nuts, and oranges,
And Santy Claus is real,
Come on to California,
Eat and eat till your full.

Where they had come from, oranges and Santa Claus both seemed like short-blooming annuals, symbols of a life of abundance more illusory than actual. Many California migrants during the Depression (not unlike their predecessors in the 1920s) associated the state with the paradise of abundance Sunkist and other boosters had created. In one 1935 survey, almost a quarter of the migrants noted California's therapeutic climate as their reason for coming. One explained the lure in verse, noting the "shining of your sun / The beauty of your orange groves." John Steinbeck gave fictional voice to these real sentiments. "Jus' let me get out to California where I can pick me an orange when I want it," says Grandpa Joad in *The Grapes of Wrath*. Ma chimes in with her vision of a life that would match the fruit crate labels: "I like to think how nice it's gonna be, maybe, in California. Never cold. An' fruit ever'place, an' people just bein' in the nicest places, little white houses in among the orange trees."[2]

Borders have a way of defining things. They separate one space from another. In moving across them, migrants (or tourists) enter new jurisdictions. Often, the border crossers are seen in new ways in the new land, and are slapped with new labels. The anti-Sinclair campaign had created a frame through which the migrants were seen as an invading horde. Hoping to open another door of perception, others represented the migrants in the iconic form of pioneers lighting out for the territory. Paul Taylor, a labor economist at the University of California at Berkeley, and photographer Dorothea Lange were among those casting a narrative lifeline to the migrants, pulling them from the waters of demonology. Working for the California Division of Rural Rehabilitation in the spring of 1935, Taylor and Lange drove past the border inspection station at Fort Yuma to witness migrants streaming across the bridge over the Colorado River. Large trucks and tourists' cars zoomed into the state, but at intervals "appear slow-moving and conspicuous cars loaded with refugees." He connected these travelers to the dust storms that had been raging in the southern plains. "Wind erosion" had left "land and life impoverished. . . . After the drifting dust clouds drift the people . . . [a] shifting of human sands." Through this frame, the migrants could be seen as people blown out of place by economic and ecological storms. Sponge off the rhetoric of deadbeat opportunism in which they had been encased, look again, and, Taylor implored, realize that "we are witnessing the process of social erosion."[3]

Some 350,000 more would come that way by decade's end. And though only a fraction of the total came from the Dust Bowl region itself, they became known as exodusters, or Dust Bowl migrants. Taylor and Lange would bear witness to the migrants' experience in California and help turn the migration into a compelling social drama. Along with John Steinbeck and Carey McWilliams, they would be instrumental in defining who the newcomers were and what their arrival meant to California and the nation. Like the dye used by a physician to make visible the complex pathways of arteries and capillaries, the agrarian partisans would use the Okies, recast as worthy pioneers, to manifest California's repressive agricultural labor relations. While previously racialized others had moved through this system generally unnoticed, now white Americans flooded the ranks of California's agricultural workforce. Inequities were brought to light by a compelling set of images and the sheen of the Okies' whiteness.

For years, Taylor had tried to get the public to take notice of what he called the "shifting reservoir of human distress known as migratory labor." An early article on the migrants featured two full-page photographs by Lange. One was of a gaunt Mexicano in the Imperial Valley saying, "I have worked all my life and all I have now is my old body." That image would fade from collective memory, but the other one, showing a white mother with an infant and two children, was burned into national consciousness. It came to be called "Migrant mother." The contrast in the way the two images were received and circulated reveals much about how race, migration, and borders figured into America's consciousness. The way for the new migrants had been partly cleared by an exodus at California's other border: some 170,000 Mexicanos had been coerced to get on trains and were "repatriated" to Mexico. Mexicanos moving north and south across the border were either ignored or seen as a menace, while westering whites moving into this hierarchical labor system could compel attention, spur reflection, and even drive reform.

But they could do so only if they could avoid being perceived as just the latest wave of people consigned by nature to harvest labor—"fruit tramps" who happened to be white. If they could be seen as latter-day pioneers entitled to a stake in the agrarian dream, they could become the protagonists in a story of environmental failure, calling out for a reshaping of human relations to the land from the ground up. As Taylor told the story in a nationwide radio broadcast, the migrants were signs of "the human havoc wrought when man leaves the earth unprotected." This large-scale social erosion called on the nation to contemplate deep changes: "We must take stock, revise both our methods of land utilization and the relation of large numbers of citizens to the land, and we must resettle them in a manner to enable them to obtain from our natural resources an American standard of living." Lange and Taylor framed their overall narrative in biblical and ecological terms, titling their book devoted to the migrants' story *An American Exodus: A Record of Human Erosion.*[4]

This narrative did not arise out of thin air. The agrarian partisans all went into the fields to listen to what the migrants had to say. They relayed their stories, allowing them to testify in the media—before what some have called the "jury of the nation." But the agrarian partisans also had their own story to tell, a case they wanted to make against California's agricultural system. They all believed in the California dream of Eden but felt that the growth machine had usurped the garden, expelled its denizens, and then invited the exiles back in only under conditions of servitude. Black-and-white photographs of the migrants and a degraded landscape functioned as depositions for a social drama of human erosion. Though the social drama was about the general relationship between people and the land, the agrarians focused special attention on the citrus landscape—for there, the land's promise was greatest, and there, its breaking seemed all the more criminal. The Orange Empire was effectively put on trial, charged with the wanton destruction of the fruits of Eden.

THE SOCIAL DRAMA AND TALKING PICTURES

To McWilliams, what he saw happening in California's fields was "a social drama so intense, that I felt I had to find out what was going on." While McWilliams used the phrase casually, Victor Turner's theory of the social drama may help us better understand what was being acted out in those fields. A social drama is inaugurated by some "breach of a norm, the infraction of a rule of morality, law, custom or etiquette in some public arena." Some person or group transgresses the norms of everyday life, sometimes deliberately (as in the Boston Tea Party). This breach calls the order of things into question, and may escalate into a full public crisis. At this stage, the social drama "takes up its menacing stance in the forum itself, and, as it were, dares the representatives of order to grapple with it." In a forum of some kind, redressive procedures are set in motion. The redressive stage of the social drama "has its liminal features, for it is 'betwixt and between,' and, as such, furnishes a distanced replication and critique of the events leading up to and composing the 'crisis.'" Witnesses are called and stories told, all competing to establish a particular version of events as well as a path to redress and reconciliation. Witnesses help publish the story of the social drama and confer legitimacy on the process. In the end, some kind of decision will be handed down. The transgressors will be reincorporated—or ostracized—and the social norms and practices of the community may themselves be reformed.[5]

There were radically different ways of emplotting the social drama going on in the fields and groves in Depression-era California. To the Associated Farmers, workers who went on strike were the transgressors, turning to violence, threatening the rights of other workers, and usurping the right of property. They were portrayed as outside agitators, Communists, or their unwitting dupes. The agrarian partisans saw agribusiness itself as the transgressor—the machine in the garden. To them, the inequitable treatment of farmworkers showed that a fundamental American ideal was being broken. They accused the growth machine of betraying the promise of Eden, and each migrant worker living in poor conditions stood as a witness to the tragic hemorrhaging—Lange and Taylor's "human erosion." By 1939, hundreds of thousands of people in California and across the nation would have their attention drawn to California's social drama. Seeing it through the eyes of the agrarian partisans, most observers would agree that events in California—the strikes, the vigilante actions, the influx of the Dust Bowlers—had all the elements of a tragedy.

The agrarian partisans testified themselves in various forums—reports, newspaper, and magazine articles, on the radio, and at formal hearings. But more important, their *representations* of the victims of the transgression also bore witness. Steinbeck's Joads were taken as real, made all the more so because the photography of Lange and others seemed to verify the Joads' experience (if not their strict existence). The camera was understood as a device that allowed victims of transgression to tell their own stories. In *An American Exodus,* Lange and Taylor put it this way: "Our work has produced the book, but in the situations we describe are living participants who can speak. Many whom we met in the field vaguely regarded conversation with us as an opportunity to tell what they are up against to their government and to their countrymen at large. So far as possible we have let them speak to you face to face."[6]

Getting pictures to talk had been one of the main goals of the Historical Section of the Resettlement Administration (later the Farm Security Administration, FSA) when it came under the direction of Roy Emerson Stryker in July 1935. Stryker's unit was essentially in charge of public relations for the New Deal agency. He later claimed that "we introduced America to Americans," and many agreed. In reviewing a collection of FSA photographs, William Carlos Williams wrote, "The pictures talk to us. And they say plenty." Edward Steichen defined *documentary* as pictures that "tell a story," instructing readers of a magazine featuring FSA photographs to "have a look into the faces of the men and women of these pages.

Listen to the story they tell and they will leave you with a feeling of a living experience you won't forget." Just how did photographs function as talking pictures?[7]

In order to understand the "voice" of the photographs we will have to look at how realism and photography were associated in the 1930s. The camera, as a mechanical instrument, had long been privileged as an instrument that could objectively record reality. Lange tacked the words of Francis Bacon to the door of her darkroom:

The contemplation of things as they are
Without substitution or imposture
Without error or confusion
Is itself a nobler thing
Than a whole harvest of invention.

But she did not take this to mean that recording "things as they are" was an end in itself. Instead, like many of her contemporaries, she saw the camera as an instrument of social change. She would harvest the truth as a way to change the harvest. Lange and her cohort saw the camera as a means of truth-telling that went far beyond the recording of mere fact. Many observers attributed a kind of metaphysics to the recording of facts, so that the camera could become an "instrument of revelation." Paradoxically, the notion that the camera could only record what was really there helped photography transcend a mere cataloguing function.[8]

The photographer had to approach his or her subject from "an angle" in order to make the representation reveal some larger truth. As Stryker explained, the "documentary photographer feels obliged to bring home more than a cold record. Somehow he has to incorporate into that rectangle which he has cut out from the surrounding therefore formless reality, what the real thing sounded like, what it smelled like—and most important, what it felt like." The photograph was supposed to have a phenomenological effect on the viewer—Steichen's "living experience"—by evoking the larger physical and social world of the people being photographed. The photographer is thus both factual recorder and interpreter, as the particular object, fact, or person is supposed to reveal something about the life-world within which it is situated.[9]

Stryker had this kind of social revelation in mind when he recruited Lange. He thought that her photographs captured "the social forces present in a scene," serving especially well to expose what Henri Lefebvre calls the social production of space. Lange's "record of human erosion" brought the cultural and ecological crises of Depression America into the same frame. FSA photographs often featured "the end of rural America and its displacement by a commercial, urban culture with its marketplace relationships . . . a profound breach in the relation of American society to its 'nature' and to the production of sustenance from the land." But the pictures were not meant to present a *fait accompli* fatalism: the social drama of human erosion opened a space in which the relationship between people and nature was put up for revision.[10]

Like phrenology, documentary photography was also thought to have the power to unveil inner states: pictures of faces, bodies, or even shoes could reveal the interior landscape. But while the pair of boots that Walker Evans photographed for *Let Us Now Praise Famous Men* might tell us a lot, they could also limit understanding. Rexford Tugwell, Stryker's boss at the Resettlement Administration, said, "Roy, a man may have holes in his shoes, and you may see the holes when you take the picture. But maybe your sense of the human being will teach you there's a lot more to that man than the holes in his shoes, and you ought to try to get that idea across." In fact, the photographers saw their job as convincing people that the subjects they photographed, however destitute, were worthy citizens who deserved a helping hand. Shoes could be revealing, but getting the face on film could work wonders. As Stryker put it, "The faces to me were the most significant part of the file." Steichen said, "Look into the faces . . . listen to the story they tell."[11]

Only the face could create what might be called the witness effect. Just as the conventions of photography created a reality effect by appearing to be transparent to reality, the photographed people were meant to be regarded not as inert objects but as living people with a story to tell. Because they are at once degraded and noble, they bear witness to a transgression—the abrogation of the American dream and its agrarian promise. Such photography transported bodies out of the real world and placed them into the reflexive, performative, and political realm of the social drama. Though taken out of context in this way, the photographs encouraged investigation of their place of origin, leading attention back to the material and ecological conditions of the people being represented. The surface of the body, its interior state, and a larger social, cultural, and ecological landscape all were exposed by this instrument of revelation.[12]

While some have argued that the photographs were simply self-serving constructions—inventions designed to bolster the authority of the photographers and the New Deal—they should not be written off this way. Though some of the photographers did become famous, it is ultimately more significant that attention that was drawn to the people and the landscape through their works. The photographs and narratives created ameliorative action for the migratory workers, and they gathered support for Senator Robert La Follette's committee to come to California to investigate their plight. When La Follette's committee was attempting to resolve the social drama, its investigators wanted to put together "a photographic exhibit on living conditions of ag workers to be used at the hearings." They asked Lange to supply them with some twelve images that would be "enlarged to huge affairs." These photographs would stand at the hearings, silent but not mute. They were the agrarian partisans' exhibit A, depositions submitted in black and white.[13]

"AGAIN THE COVERED WAGON": IMAGES OF THE LOST FRONTIER

The images of the Dust Bowl migrants commanded the nation's attention in part because they were linked to an American epic: the story of the frontier. Recognizing this, Taylor and Lange published a photo-essay in *Survey Graphic* called "Again the Covered Wagon." Though Taylor noted that there were "a few Mexicans" crossing into California, his story focused on the "white Americans of old stock. . . . Oklahomans with small heads, blue eyes, an Abe Lincoln cut to the thighs." Taylor wondered if the grandchildren of the migrants of 1935 would take the same kind pride of pride in their ancestral crossing as do the descendents of Forty-niners.[14]

Configured this way, Lange's pictures of the new covered wagons "straggling west" could become part of a drama of national identity. If Americans were exceptional because of the westering experience—more democratic, independent, self-sufficient, practical, more a part of nature and because of that better able to transform it, as Frederick Jackson Turner had it—then the experience of these new migrants was of vital concern to the body politic. If they were beaten down, it meant not only that the frontier had closed but that the American dream had withered on the vine. Archibald MacLeish gave voice to this frontier anxiety in his book *Land of the Free* (1938), illustrated with FSA photographs: "We wonder whether the great American dream / Was the singing of locusts out of the grass to the west and the / West is behind us now." To MacLeish, American freedom and history were bound up with the soil, and the soil was now exhausted.[15]

Taylor was one of the first observers to connect the migrants to the dust storms. As he came to recognize, though, it was not dust alone that had set the refugees on the road west. Only about 5 percent of the so-called Dust Bowl migrants came from the Dust Bowl region proper.[16] Yet Taylor and Lange felt that the Dust Bowl symbolized the larger story about human erosion they wished to tell. To them, the Dust Bowl was not an act of nature but the result of a relationship between people and the land that had become unsustainable and unjust.

Elements of this view had been visualized in the documentary that Pare Lorentz made for the Resettlement Administration, an ecological tragedy called *The Plow That Broke the Plains* (1936). The narrator begins, "This is a record of land . . . of soil, rather than people." The film seems to emplot the Dust Bowl as an act of nature, concluding that "the sun and winds wrote the most tragic chapter in American agriculture." Lorentz explains, "Our heroine is the grass, our villain the sun and the wind, our players the actual farmers living in the plains country. It is a melodrama of nature, the tragedy of turning grass into dust."[17] Yet this "melodrama of nature" turned out to be a social drama as well. On one level *The Plow* is a story of greed, of mining the land for wheat. While the narrator repeats the "wheat will win the war" slogans of World War I, footage of tractors on the plains is intercut with tanks in Europe. Steel disks churn through domestic soil as bombs explode soil "over there." Though the surface message is that the power of the soil assures an Allied victory, the film also suggests a link between the agricultural machinery and the war machine. A stock ticker is shown wildly spitting out tape as a jazz number plays. When the piece reaches its frenetic crescendo, the ticker crashes to the floor. We then are exposed to a silent vision of the eroded landscape: a plow half buried in the sand, a child playing listlessly in the dune. *The Plow* ends with images of refugees: "On to the West! Once again they headed West out of the Great Plains and hit the highways for the Pacific Coast, the last border. Blown out—baked out—and broke." Lorentz had borrowed that last line from the testimony on one of Lange's photographs (and Lange had helped line up some migrants in their jalopies to pull into a government camp for Lorentz's camera). *The Plow*'s narrative questioned progress itself, reversing Turner's plot: wilderness is found and made fruitful for a while, but ultimately that wilderness is re-created and made doubly forbidding, breaking down the bodies of Americans rather than building them up. The frontier experience had despoiled land and people alike; erosion follows the plow. Lorentz may have said that grass was his heroine,

Figure 18. For Dorothea Lange, the tractor became a symbol of the mechanization of nature and the dehumanization of the landscape. Childress County, Texas, June 1938. (From Dorothea Lange and Paul Taylor, *An American Exodus: A Record of Human Erosion* [New York: Reynal and Hitchcock, 1939], 72–73. Copyright the Dorothea Lange Collection, Oakland Museum of California, City of Oakland. Gift of Paul S. Taylor.)

but the film's real hero is the state—the agent that might put this broken landscape and these broken people back together again.

As in *The Plow*, Lange and Taylor show tractors dehumanizing the landscape. "Tractors replace not only mules, but people," reads the caption to one of Lange's pictures. "They cultivate to the very door of the houses of those whom they replace" (see figure 18). Testimonials of tenant farmers about being "tractored out" accompany the images. The agrarian partisans used the images of tractors, erosion, and mobile families in jalopies to challenge what Donald Worster, in his environmental history of the Dust Bowl, called "an economic culture that now dominated the rural landscape [that] never recognized any limits or restrained the appetite for gain."[18]

Lange's images circulated widely in such popular magazines as *Life, Look* (under the headline "Caravans of Hunger"), and *Collier's* ("California, Here We Come"). The Dust Bowl migrants also appeared in many government publications, such as a WPA report on rural families featuring Lange's photograph of a "California fruit tramp and his family."[19] Of course, Lange could not wholly control how her photographs would be seen. Each publication laid them out in its own way and wrote its own captions. Readers did much of the work of interpretation. Yet the images of the Okies on the road received so much attention partly because they were fitted within a larger story—what the *New York Times* called the "lost frontier." This narrative frame constrained possible interpretations. Much of the newsworthiness of the stories on Okie migration derived not from the fact that there were desperately poor people in America (the poor are always with us), but because the living experience of these people seemed to jeopardize something vital in American mythology—that its genesis and strength came from the soil and expansion westward. Even though Lange and Taylor took pains to show that Mexicanos and other nonwhites were part of the story of human erosion, the mythology of the frontier served as casting agent. These other faces were not called back to play parts in the revamped covered wagon epic. Jalopies on the road were turned into icons of white settlers' epic journey westward into the promised land. But Taylor and Lange pointed out that this journey had a destination but no end: once in California, the families would "serve the crops of California [and] live literally on wheels" (see figure 19).[20]

Spokesmen for the growth machine had pictured the migrants' life on the road in a positive light. The *Pacific Rural Press* suggested that Mexicano migrant workers were more like lower-class tourists than an exploited class. They financed their vacation by working along the way, "buzz[ing] around in [their] own battered flivver, going from crop to crop, seeing Beautiful California, breathing its air, eating its food." In 1935, the National Association of Manufacturers put forward an image of middle-class life on the road to bolster Americanism and fight radicalism and the New Deal. The pictures it pasted on billboards showed a family in the car, with a smiling father in charge behind the wheel. The headline announces, "There's No Way Like the American Way." The American public was not to worry, for the country, as always, was headed in the right direction ("stay the course," the billboard seems to say). Lange made photographs of the association's billboards, as if to ask her viewers to compare these idealized road trips to her other pictures of the "covered wagon" jalopies with the grizzled faces of migrants at the wheel.[21]

Lange took several photographs of windshields (see figure 20), and they force the viewer into a reflective position. We can see in them Henry

TO SERVE THE CROPS OF CALIFORNIA TENS OF THOUSANDS OF FAMILIES
LIVE LITERALLY ON WHEELS

Breakfast beside US 99. February 1938

Figure 19. Refugees, by Dorothea Lange. U.S. Highway 99, California, February 1938. (From Lange and Taylor, *American Exodus,* 124. Copyright the Dorothea Lange Collection, Oakland Museum of California, City of Oakland. Gift of Paul S. Taylor.)

Adams's old question "whether the American people knew where they were driving." Lange's caption reads, "Car of migrant agricultural worker on strike for wage increase in cotton." The worker was engaged in a struggle with cotton growers backed by the Associated Farmers in the fall of 1938 in the San Joaquin Valley. (While Lange snapped her photo of the windshield, the Associated Farmers' photographer may very well have taken a snapshot of its license plates.) Whites, Mexicanos, Filipinos, and

Figure 20. Windshield, by Dorothea Lange. Bakersfield, November 1938. (LC-USF34-018384-E. Courtesy of Library of Congress.)

blacks all walked off the job. The John Steinbeck Committee to Aid Agricultural Organization, with Carey McWilliams as president, came to Kern County to help the cotton pickers win union recognition. Organizers hoped that their cause would be helped by the upcoming gubernatorial election of 1938. The sticker on the windshield in Lange's photo bore the names of the Democratic candidates, including Culbert Olson for governor, who had been elected to the state Senate in 1934 as an EPIC candidate.[22]

The windshield image can also be seen as Lange's reflection on her role in representing workers. With the help of the caption, we have to imagine the car's owner and other workers organizing and striking in order to represent themselves. Lange took the picture right after she photographed desperate conditions in an "auto camp which rents tent space where migrant citrus workers live."[23] At first it appears that no one is in the car. This apparent absence helps break the naturalizing spell of many of the "covered wagon" photos, in which the migrants seem symbiotically attached to and trapped in their vehicles—in short, disempowered. Look closer, though, and a man in the driver's seat emerges from the shadows. Lange's picture of the battered flivver with its political sticker carries a critical, if subtle, message: workers, even Dust Bowl refugees, are not determined by forces beyond their control (as in Parker's "finished products of their environment") but can take hold of the social wheel. In fact, they helped elect Olson, who in turn appointed Carey McWilliams to head the Commission of Immigration and Housing.

MIGRANT MOTHERS AND FATHERS

The complex relationships of representation were very much at play in the taking and circulation of Lange's most potent photograph of human erosion. On a fateful day in March 1936, Lange was driving home on the Pacific Coast Highway after a long field trip. She passed a pea pickers' camp in Nipomo but drove on, telling herself that she had "plenty of negatives . . . on this subject." But a few miles up the road, she suddenly turned around and headed back to the camp. A thirty-two-year-old woman with four of her seven children saw Lange drive up. "Pay her no mind," the mother thought to herself, "she thinks I'm quaint, and wants to take my picture." Lange approached the family, explaining that she worked for the government and she was taking pictures to spread the story of the migrant workers' plight. "O.K., if you think it will help," the woman remembered saying, though she also thought that Lange told her that the pictures would never be published. According to Lange, the woman "seemed to know that my pictures might help her, and so she helped me. There was a sort of equality about it." In ten minutes the shoot was over. Six photographs had been taken; the final one—picturing the woman with two of her children facing away from the camera, an infant on her lap, and her hand on her chin—would make the woman's face famous (see figure 21). Lange did not ask the woman her name or history. She took no photos of the other migrants in the camp, for "it was not necessary. . . . I had recorded the essence of my assignment."[24]

Figure 21. Migrant mother, by Dorothea Lange. Nipomo, March 1936.
(LC-USF34-009058-C. Courtesy of Library of Congress.)

Most everyone would agree. In Styker's estimation, the photo was "*the picture of the Farm Security*."[25] Lange rushed home, and, on March 10, two other photographs from the shoot were published in the *San Francisco News* under the caption "Ragged, Hungry, Harvest Workers Live in Squalor." Thanks to "a chance visit by a Government photographer," the

News reported, relief was now on its way. The next day, the *News* published the famous image for the first time. The headline asked, "What Does the 'New Deal' Mean to the Mother and Her Children?" "Here, in the strong face of this mother," the *News* editorialized, "is the tragedy of lives lived in squalor and fear, on terms that mock the American dream." *Midweek Pictorial* published the photograph in October, asking viewers to "Look in her eyes! . . . You can see in her eyes the horror of what is happening [to America], for she is not looking at it with the objectivity of the statistician or professor . . . but is feeling its lashings." After presenting some statistics, the article concluded, "An enlightened nation looks to its government . . . to salvage the land and those on it so that by the time these frightened children in this photograph reach maturity the American farmer will once again stand on his feet and call the plot of ground he works his home."[26]

The absent father is crucial to the political power of the photograph. The woman's condition—exposed to the elements, without a proper home, having even been forced to sell "their tent to get food"—begged questions about the family farm. For her family's sake, the farmer must be rehabilitated, made able-bodied enough to "stand on *his* feet." The viewer is left to wonder: Is this or is this not a broken family? According to Lange's captions, there was a father and he was a "native Californian." But Lange, apparently, had been told only part of the story, for this mother, Florence Thomson, was a widow when the picture was taken. After swimming in the Feather River to wash off the peach residue that clung to his body after a day of picking, her husband had suddenly fallen ill and died. With no man pictured, the photograph seems to hail the return of a strong father— or a paternal state devoted to the mother's welfare.[27]

At the beginning of the school year, high-schoolers across the country encountered such a message in *Scholastic: The American High School Weekly.* "Migrant mother" appeared, its subject identified as a former Okie farmer who was "now an itinerant hand in the large farms of California." On her behalf, people were asked to lend their support to an enlightened government that would reform nature and control social erosion. In narratives such as this, the New Deal assumed almost divine power. One of the visual clichés of FSA photography was the farmer, hand over brow to protect his eyes from the sun's relentless glare, "looking for rain." In the *Scholastic* spread featuring such a supplicant farmer, the government took on the role of savior from the sky: "The answer to the farmer's prayer is Conservation." Conservation would make the beaten farmer productive again and allow him to regain his self-worth. A New Deal agency was devoted to this "rural rehabilitation." Life in the countryside would be restored, as the "bodies" of the land and the farmer would be healed symbiotically. Another Lange photo perfectly expressed this goal. With a broad straw hat shading out the sun, the "rehabilitation client" wears a wide grin, cradling in his arms a rooster and a lamb. Erosion has been left behind: with government help, he has quite lovingly reconnected with the land. A message of potential redemption is also carried in Lange's photograph of a neatly dressed man with a determined and slightly hopeful gaze, sitting on the bumper of his car with his son in a camp and waiting for the orange picking season to begin (see figure 22). Match either one of these good husbandmen up with the migrant mother and the American dream is rehabilitated.[28]

Migrant Mother quickly become an icon, *the* mother, the Madonna miraculously appearing in California's fields. She became a body of evidence. She was reproduced literally millions of times in newspapers, magazines, and pamphlets. The mother with children was a potent symbol, one that the New Deal used time and again to drive home its points. Whenever a social worker had a job to do, Migrant Mother was there. Whenever a New Deal agency had a program to introduce, Migrant Mother was there. Though no one knew at the time if Migrant Mother was from Oklahoma, she became the archetypal Okie. (In fact, Florence Thomson had come from Oklahoma, but she had arrived in 1922.)[29] Migrant Mother, embodying the connection between soil erosion and human erosion, bore witness to the dehumanizing and denaturalizing force of corporate agriculture.

When the San Francisco *News* ran John Steinbeck's series of articles on farm labor in California in 1936, one of the Migrant Mother shots was used to lend urgency and authenticity to the novelist's words. Steinbeck began his exposé by pointing out the central moral paradox of "the present system of agricultural economics. . . . The migrants are needed, and they are hated." Constructed as racial others—"ostracized and segregated and herded about"—they are "never allowed to feel at home in the communities that demand their service." If they "committed the one crime that will not be permitted by the large growers . . . [attempting] to organize for their own protection," they could be deported or jailed. America's racial nationalism, Steinbeck made plain, rendered these workers vulnerable. And since no one with power became their advocates, "they were never able to get a hearing for their problems." The agrarian partisans would at

Figure 22. Father and son in citrus camp, "awaiting the opening of the orange picking season," by Dorothea Lange. Porterville, November 1936. (LC-USF34-016070-C. Courtesy of Library of Congress.)

last take up their cause; they would have more success in getting a hearing for Okies than Mexicanos, Filipinos, or other racialized others.[30]

Steinbeck and the *News* called for the formation of "a militant and watchful organization of middle-class people, workers, teachers, craftsmen and liberals" to meet this advocacy need. In honor of the recently deceased man who had been a tireless advocate for farmworkers since the 1910s, the Simon J. Lubin Society was formed in October 1936. One of its first official acts was to thank Steinbeck for his articles.[31] Soon thereafter, Helen Hosmer, the driving force of the Lubin Society, decided to republish Steinbeck's articles (including his earlier piece "Starvation under the Orange Trees") in a pamphlet. Issued in April 1938, the booklet carried on its cover another Lange portrait of a migrant mother. In this photograph, both the nursing child and the mother confront the viewer. The title the Lubin Society gave the pamphlet assured that the social drama would be seen as a race drama: "Their Blood Is Strong."

In recasting the migrants as latter-day pioneers in his articles, Steinbeck had reached for the vocabulary of whiteness. "They have weathered the thing," he says, "and they can weather much more for their blood is strong." He wrote that "They are descendants of men who crossed into the middle west who won their lands by fighting. . . . It should be understood that with this new race the old methods of repression, of starvation wages, of jailing, beating and intimidation are not going to work: these are American people. Consequently, we must meet them with understanding and attempt to work out the problem to their benefit as well as ours." However strongly Steinbeck had criticized the pattern of farmworker ostracism, the oppositional story he wrote reproduced exclusion. After paying homage to Mexicano and Filipino unionization efforts, Steinbeck, citing the repatriation and deportation of Mexicans and Filipinos, pictured these groups as "receding waves." He chose instead to focus on "the river of dust bowl refugees [which] increases all the time . . . the future workers are to be white and American."[32] To be sure, Steinbeck had been asked by the editor of the *News* to write about the Dust Bowlers. In his "Harvest Gypsies" stories, Mexicanos and Filipinos flee from the page to make room for the great mythology of westering. Though the growth machine had broken the promise of the West, Steinbeck insisted that the new migrants, owing in large part to their pioneer heritage, would reclaim it.

With its references to the migrants being of the "best American stock," Steinbeck's Dust Bowl series may seem to be a dubious example of "racial populism," as Michael Denning has charged. But it is important to recognize that Steinbeck's effort to build up the Americanness of the Dust Bowlers was not intended to come at the expense of Mexicanos and others considered nonwhite. He wanted to counter the xenophobic and racist representations of the Okies that had been gaining momentum. In *The Grapes of Wrath*, he used the conversation of a couple of gas station attendants on the California border to expose how the Okies had been racialized. As the Joads leave the station, one attendant says, "Jesus, I'd hate to start out [over the desert] in a jalopy like that." The other replies, "Well, you and me got sense. Them goddamn Okies got no sense and no feeling. They ain't human. A human being wouldn't live like that. . . . They ain't a hell of a lot better than gorillas." The first time they are slapped with the name *Okie,* the Joads wonder what it means. Someone in the know tells them, "Okie use' ta mean you was from Oklahoma. Now it means you're a dirty son-of-a-bitch. Okie means you're scum."[33]

The Okies had in fact been smeared and stained. The California Citizens Association, with support from the California State Chamber of Commerce, the Bank of America, the American Legion, and large agricultural corporations such as Miller and Lux and DiGiorgio Farms, as well as the Associated Farmers, confronted the "migrant problem" with a campaign aimed at denigrating the newcomers. Like Steinbeck, they thought that the new migrants were "not tractable labor." But for them, this was something to fear—and change. Adapting an image from the anti-EPIC campaign, the California Citizens Association portrayed the migrants as "freeloaders" who would bring economic chaos to the state. It charged that the migrants were carriers of disease and depravation. A certain Dr. Stone wrote that the migrants were immoral, lazy, and "incapable of being absorbed into our civilization." One college student proposed that they be put "on reservations." *California,* the publication of the state chamber of commerce, wrote that "there is so much unmorality among them—not immorality. They just don't know any better. There was a father who was arrested for outraging his daughter. His whole family appeared in court to defend him, and when he was sent to jail his wife said, 'They outn't to send paw to jail for that. She's his own property and he can do what he pleases with her.'" While the agrarian partisans connected the Dust Bowl migrants to the mythology of the pioneer, the growth machine used grotesque stories to link them to the mythology of "white trash." The California Citizens Association regarded their blood as something other than strong.[34]

But if Migrant Mother helped combat the stereotypes of migrant workers—and she most certainly did—that achievement came at a price. Instead of the white Madonna, imagine putting the Mexicana mother and child used in the Bureau of Child Hygiene pamphlet on the cover of Steinbeck's pamphlet. Or imagine Lange's photograph of a Mexicana mother and child (see figure 23) appearing under the title "Their Blood Is Strong," and give Migrant Mother the caption "Okie Woman with Her Inevitable Child."

Figure 23. Mexicana mother, by Dorothea Lange. California, June 1935. (LC-USF34-000825-ZC. Courtesy of Library of Congress.)

Such iconographic sleights of hand help reveal how much racial nationalism was imbedded in even the reformers' perspectives. By universalizing the face of Migrant Mother, patterns of exclusion were repeated. To see her as *the* representative of migratory labor, as the emblematic witness, is to foster the invisibility of Mexicano, Filipino, Japanese, Indian, and other workers. Indeed, Mexicana Mother was unseen; her testimony—"Sometimes I tell my children that I would like to go to Mexico, but they tell me 'We don't want to go; we belong here'"—was unheard.[35] Clearly, Lange had hoped to get her image and story out, but there were apparently no takers, and the photograph languished in the archives. Such testimony would have added race to the discussion of farm laborers, rights, and citizenship. (Among the agrarian partisans, it was McWilliams who took up this agenda in earnest.) Still, Migrant Mother reached audiences in ways that other images could not (and it was as much the audience's desires as those of the image-maker that led to only white bodies being placed on the pedestal of national concern). She compelled many middle-class white Americans to see migrant workers as worthy and human and led them to question California's system of agricultural labor relations.

Furthermore, any changes in that system designed to ameliorate her plight might also benefit Mexicano migrants. Lange had taken pictures of Mexicano families in a pea pickers' camp in Nipomo in 1936. Though they would not receive the wide circulation that Migrant Mother enjoyed, the pictures of Mexicano children appeared alongside those of Migrant Mother in the Council of Women for Home Missions' pamphlet "They Starve That We May Eat." If those children were still in Nipomo on March 11, they probably received some of the food and supplies that Florence Thomson's white face brought to the scene. Okies and other farmworkers were ultimately caught up in the same system (though Okies' chances of extracting themselves from it proved to be far better).[36]

Steinbeck attributed the desperation of Migrant Mother to California's pattern of specialized crops stretching up and down the state and its enormous but punctuated need for labor. To supply the need, the migrant laborer was called into service, a floating army that traced with their bodies the geography and seasonality of vegetables and fruit across the state. But "if the migrant is a little late the places may all be filled." "The crop may be late," Steinbeck explained, "or there may occur one of those situations like that at Nipomo last year when twelve hundred workers arrived to pick the pea crop only to find it spoiled by the rain. All resources having been used to get to the field, the migrants could not move on."[37] To growers, the desperation at Nipomo in 1936 was caused by a natural disaster, pure and simple. The growers' financial losses were great, but they would not lose anything on labor. With no claim on the growers' resources, these migrants were literally left out in the cold. The agrarian partisans exposed the inequity that made the most vulnerable bear the brunt of nature's unpredictability.

But the plight of Migrant Mother and the other Okie and Mexicano pea pickers was not just a sad chapter written by sun and rain, for the development of California's system of intensive agriculture was not simply ordained by nature. In fact, it had been burbanked. As we saw in chapter 2, Burbank had created a plant with small peas that ripened all at once.[38] Nipomo's *petite pois,* which in normal years called for an enormous labor supply for a short period of time, had been made to order. Nature had been adapted to the growth machine. As a witness, Migrant Mother testified that it had not been adapted to the needs of its human workers.

ORANGE PICKERS' CAMP

Lange's photographs of migrants in citrus camps are not as intimate as the one of the migrant mother. The camps are usually seen from a distance and the backs of the workers are often turned to the camera, their bodies stooped. Nonetheless, they have the same power. Against the background of California as Eden, these images reveal a paradise in shambles.

This landscape was a long time in the making. Most of Lange's photographs of the citrus landscape were taken in Tulare County in the Central Valley, not in the heart of the Orange Empire in Southern California. In 1872, Charles Nordhoff saw this area as a cultural wasteland given over to vast wheat ranches. "When one compares the possibilities of this region with what he finds actually accomplished," he wrote, "he is always disappointed." Though oranges could be grown in the region, there were only six orange-bearing trees in the vicinity, Nordhoff complained. "The truth is, that much of this great valley is so fit for a garden that it is wasteful to use it for a cattle or sheep range, or for field crops." He felt that California's wheat ranches had not produced a proper cultural pattern on the land. Instead, farming was "sloppy and slipshod" and the Central Valley was a barren landscape—no proper homes, no vegetable gardens, no trees.[39]

But when Nordhoff returned ten years later, he was pleased to see that irrigation was turning the Central Valley "into a vast garden." Compared to wheat ranchers, a writer in the *Pacific Rural Press* argued, fruit growers "tend to give added charm to the home, and to make it, with its garden and orchard and flowers, the most attractive place in the world." The Southern Pacific—a large landholder in the Central Valley—had used booster literature to drive the succession from a wheat to a citrus landscape. A 1906 *Sunset* article noted that 400,000 orange trees were being planted in the region. A visual story across the top of the article celebrated the change from wheat to the "orange groves [that] are fast covering these foothill wheat fields." Before the reader's eyes, the pictures presented the manifestation of the garden.[40]

Yet, as Frederick Mills discovered in 1914, this garden did not transform the landscape into an inviting place. That year, Mills (whom we met in chapter 4) went undercover for the Commission of Immigration and Housing to find out what life was like for citrus workers in Tulare County. He was so well disguised as a fruit tramp that boarding houses in Lindsay refused him lodging. Searching aimlessly for a place to sleep—a haystack in some forgotten corner of a barn, perhaps—he finally settled for the hard ground beneath an orange tree. A second night was spent in a boxcar, and he got a good night's sleep only when he was allowed to make his bed in a packing house on a bundle of the Sunkist tissues used to wrap oranges. Finally, Mills made his way to the camps of citrus workers. "This camp is unsanitary and unsatisfactory in every way," he reported. "It is impossible that full working efficiency could be kept up living in such a place."[41] Mills, as we saw in chapter 4, believed that the "efficiency" of women workers was particularly in peril in such camps. "The rigorous nature of their work," he reported, "cannot but render them unfit to serve the race by mothering the generation of the future." What was worse, he speculated that the seasonal nature of the work might force women into prostitution to supplement their unsteady income. Privately, he wondered if "modern industry demand[s] the development of a class of female workers who are worn out, ready for the scrap heap at thirty?"[42]

In 1938, Lange, representing the FSA, went back to Lindsay to investigate the conditions in which men, women, and children lived in the camps. Lange's images also revealed a crisis of motherhood. Photographs of an orange pickers' camp in Tulare County show women stooped over barrels and buckets, struggling to cook, clean, take care of children, and keep their lodgings—ramshackle canvas tents—in some kind of order. One photograph shows a toddler, alone, silhouetted by the black triangle of the tent's open flap. Unlike Migrant Mother—who confronts the viewer with her forward gaze—the woman in Lange's photograph from an orange pickers' camp disrupts the image of Edenic California with her posture and placement (see figure 24). With one hand at her side, showing signs of a child on its way, she looks down toward the stew of trash and logs between the staked tents. The Orange Empire had pictured maidens offering up nature's golden fruit, glowing in the sun-splashed groves; Lange showed women in the orange pickers' camp with nothing to give, just sticks in

Figure 24. Woman in citrus camp, by Dorothea Lange. Tulare County, November 1938. (324942-LC-USF34-18425. Courtesy of Library of Congress.)

their hands, stirring the soil from which they have derived neither strength nor solace.

Only part of Nordhoff's dream had come to pass: much of the land looked like a garden, and there were some very nice homes in the towns of Visalia, Tulare, and Hanford. By focusing her lens on the labor camps with their marginalized workers, Lange rehearsed Nordhoff's critique of the social landscape: though the agriculture was rich, the human culture had not grown to match it. Indeed, the culture of the valley was riven by race and class. To meet their harvest labor needs, growers relied on a transient flow of workers who were constructed as "other": Japanese, Mexicans, (East) Indians, Filipinos, and white "fruit tramps." In 1926, the San

Joaquin Labor Bureau was formed to oversee the importation of temporary workers and keep wages uniformly low. Each group lived in separate camps. Of the Mexicano camp, Mills reported that "a small section is sown in Indian corn, in order, it is said, that they may not be ejected." The workers' right to rent land was so tenuous that they had to prove they were improving it. No room was ever made in the county's established towns for Tulare's fruit workers, even as labor needs increased. The Dust Bowl migrants had to create separate "Little Oklahomas," establishing a virtual racial fault line as the Dust Bowl migrants were treated "like an alien social group." Citing a boy's testimony that "when they need us they call us migrants, and when we've picked their crop, we're bums and we got to get out," Steinbeck concluded that migrant farmworkers "are never received into a community nor into the life of a community." Democracy itself, which was supposed to be enhanced by the work of farmers, was here being fatally undermined.[43]

Lange took careful photographs of the camps and houses of Anglo as well as Mexicano citrus workers.[44] She and Taylor linked the existence of these camps with their debilitating conditions to the logic of "modern industry" as it had taken hold in California's fields and groves. Framed by the barren, uninhabited foreground, with a line of boxcars bifurcating the countryside, her photograph of an orange packing shed in Strathmore emphasized how orange growing had created not a modern idyll but what McWilliams called "factories in the field" (see figure 25). In all of her work as a government photographer, Lange took no pictures of the idyllic citrus landscape. There are no views of valleys covered with orange trees and surrounded by snowcapped mountains, no views of California that confirm the images sent out to the rest of the nation on orange crate labels and in tourist brochures. But such images are evoked in her photographs. Looking at the margins, the scattered camps and houses in which the victims of human erosion dwell, reorients one's perspective on the groves themselves.

The U.S. Bureau of Reclamation had a use for direct photographs of the idyllic citrus landscape. It dispatched a photographer to take a picture of a grove near Lindsay (in which the people in Lange's orange pickers' camp probably worked.) These trees were "benefiting from the Friant-Kern canal . . . a part of the Central Valley reclamation project." Urged on by California agricultural interests, the federal and state governments had been building support for many years to complete this massive project to redirect the flow of water in the state. By the mid-1930s, many growers were having

Figure 25. Factory in the field—an orange packing house in the Central Valley, by Dorothea Lange. Strathmore, February 1939. (LC-USF34-018826-E. Courtesy of Library of Congress.)

trouble irrigating their orchards. Pumping water out of the aquifer, they had lowered the water table precipitously—over one hundred feet under the citrus worker camps Lange photographed. In a book celebrating the "California spirit," with its drive to overcome the "impossible" and make "rivers flow uphill," schoolchildren were exposed to pictures of an orange grove that had shriveled and died due to lack of water. These pictures of eroding nature could be used to build support for the government project.[45]

Paul Taylor initially supported the water project, believing that it would provide the means to turn drought refugees into family farmers. But he was outraged that its benefits ultimately went to large growers. Taylor would come to criticize the Central Valley project on ecological grounds as well. In reflecting on the West's "hydraulic society" at the very canal that flowed past the Bureau of Reclamation's idyllic grove, historian Donald Worster argued that "Friant-Kern offers a study in ecological and social regimentation . . . [of a] culture and society built on, and absolutely dependent on, a sharply alienating, intensely managerial relationship with nature." Speaking at the dedication of the Friant Dam in 1939, Secretary of the Interior Harold Ickes said, "America is building a Maginot Line"—an unwittingly portentous metaphor.[46]

Though Taylor and Lange supported water development, they insisted that the true reclamation of the citrus landscape would come from improving the living conditions of workers. In this light, we can see Lange's photographs of FSA camps for migrant workers as her version of the idyllic citrus landscape. In her original collaboration with Taylor, she had worked on a project to construct a system of state-operated labor camps across California. The plan was later adopted by the FSA, and by the end of the decade twelve camps had gone up. Archways marked the camps' threshold and separated them from the landscape at large. The space within became federal sanctuaries for migrant workers. As John Steinbeck saw them, these camps were places that "restore the dignity and decency that has been kicked out of the migrants by their intolerable mode of life."[47] Lange's photograph of the Farmersville camp shows an ordered space designed to foster a microcosm of democracy: well-built prefabricated homes, a communal laundry in the center, and a commons for baseball and other recreation. Established in May 1939, this camp was meant to redress the conditions Lange had exposed in the nearby orange pickers' camp the year before. Designed to physically and mentally rehabilitate the victims of human erosion, in the eyes of the agrarian partisans these FSA camps were outposts of a reclaimed Eden.

THE EMPIRE OF SIGNS

Sunkist shot back with images of its own, defending the landscape it had created. An issue of *Sunkist Advertising News* showed workers living in neat, well-equipped houses, playing baseball, and playfully swimming in a pool (ingeniously, part of the irrigation system). In an inspired image of stability, one picture showed workers picking up mail. "Several hundred 'dust bowl' families have found work and homes like these in Ventura County this past spring. Great correspondents, they write the folks back home that all the jobs [and houses] are filled," the caption reads. In answer to Lange's portraits of frightened youngsters, Sunkist presents a clean young boy eating an orange in the sunlight: "This transplanted Oklahoma lad likes California sunshine and Sunkist oranges better than he does photographers." In this brilliant layout, the citrus industry stressed its social responsibility, telling a story of how the Okies were being given a stake in the California dream. It did not mention that many of these Okies had helped break a strike led by Mexicanos, who had been promptly evicted from their company housing when they walked off the job.[48]

Though Sunkist exaggerated in making the living conditions of citrus workers seem nearly idyllic, it would be a mistake to conclude that the camps Lange photographed were typical. She focused on Tulare County, a part of the Orange Empire that had never adopted the Progressive approach to worker housing. In the Central Valley, the picking season was shorter than in Southern California, and packing houses relied on migratory labor to do their picking and packing. While not typical of the citrus industry as a whole, the camps Lange photographed were typical of much of California agribusiness. Even though the citrus industry generally provided better conditions for workers, it felt threatened by the exposure of poor living conditions. It joined forces with other agricultural sectors and the growth machine as a whole to contest the burgeoning movement to reclaim the California landscape.

One form that contestation took was a national billboard campaign launched by the National Association of Manufacturers. We have seen that Sunkist used billboards to take control of urban space and sell its fruits (as well as defeat Sinclair). NAM's campaign would try to sell not a particular product but an ideological package called the "American Way." Judging by the slogans of the campaign, the American Way was one that did not recognize the right of workers to negotiate for higher wages (they were already the highest), better working conditions (they were already the best), a higher standard of living (it was already paramount). One billboard pictured a perfect fantasy of middle-class family life: father arriving home from work, holding ecstatic daughter in his arms as apron-clad wife stands lovingly in the doorway (see figure 26).

For Lange, this sign was an easy target: looking up at it from a debris-strewn ditch evoking Dust Bowl erosion, her photograph brought the fantasy down to earth. The skeptical pictures that Lange and other FSA photographers took of the billboards led the La Follette committee to investigate NAM. The Lubin Society's *Rural Observer* reported that the committee looked "into nation-wide propaganda campaigns, exposing the role of big business in controlling the public mind through expensive advertising and coordination with other organizations."[49]

Figure 26. "American Way" billboard, by Dorothea Lange. U.S. Highway 99 in California, March 1937. (LC-USF34-016213-C. Courtesy of Library of Congress.)

The *Rural Observer* also used its pages to dismantle the signs that the growth machine had planted in California's countryside. It reprinted a Lange photograph of migrant families camping behind the billboards advertising "California Lands" with a picture of the perfect family farm. The *Observer* used it bluntly, charging that small farmers across the state were "caught in the octopus clutches of Bank of America's 'California Lands, Inc.'" The *Observer* used it again for a photo essay on the destruction of the agrarian dream. The first photograph pictures a man driving a mule team. "This is a real farmer," the caption explains, distinguishing him from the faux farmers of the Associated Farmers the *Observer* had photographed in their business suits. Then comes the billboard and the migrant family: "This is what happens to the working farmer—foreclosure." Finally, a Lange photograph of an "Oklahoma Child with a cotton sack ready to go into fields with parents at 7 A.M." showed "what happens to the working farmer's child." In the *Observer's* narrative, both farmers and farmworkers were imperiled by corporate farming and by banks that were not building up California (as a Bank of America billboard advertised), but gobbling it up like Norris's Octopus.[50]

In one of her most widely circulated photographs, Lange captured two bindle stiffs walking toward Los Angeles beneath a Southern Pacific billboard saying "Relax—Next Time Take the Train." With her photographs, Lange attempted to wrest control of the public sphere away from the growth machine by exposing the gap between the American promise and vagrant experience. Her citrus camps, with their cars indicating their inhabitants' link to life on the road but not to a community, are located on lonely and eroded landscapes. Billboards loom in the distance (see figure 27). Moving closer in, she shot a billboard featuring the face of a distressed infant. It summons the baby as a witness for the Orange Empire: "What hurts business hurts me," the baby says (see figure 28). We might want to call Lange's photograph of the scene an example of ironic juxtaposition. But this picture is a vessel for a feeling that overwhelms irony: it is a deposition of outrage.

We do move from indictment to something closer to irony with Lange's photograph of a billboard advertising the film version of *The Grapes of Wrath*. Under the sign's protection, a group of Dust Bowl migrants had gathered (see figure 29). This photograph addresses the interplay between actual bodies and their representation. Has the billboard, with its advertisement for a movie based on a novel, supplanted and effaced the actual people it is supposed to represent? Has Lange captured an early example of the postmodern eclipse of the real, where the sign does not refer to the Okies but instead floats freely above them, performing an unbounded dance in which Twentieth Century Fox will make a profit and the "people" become a simulacrum?[51]

Lange's intentions were probably less abstract. The photograph serves in part as an act of verification, showing that the novel does speak of real people and real situations. As an act of verification, the photograph is part of a large body of work designed to authenticate the novel. Twentieth Century Fox had sent a photographer into the fields to investigate before making the film; the FSA assembled a display with quotes from the novel and photographs placed side by side; *Life* magazine did much the same thing in its June 5, 1939, issue, and then published more photographs when the film was released. *Life* got it right when it said, "Never before

Figure 27. Citrus camp with billboards, by Dorothea Lange. Near Lindsay, February 1939. (LC-USF34-018876-E. Courtesy of Library of Congress.)

had the facts behind a great work of fiction been so carefully researched by the newscamera."[52] Linking the novel to images was not difficult, as Steinbeck had been influenced by the FSA's representations of the Dust Bowl. Readers recognized the connection: as one person wrote to Roy Stryker, "I am reading Steinbeck's great book, and it is great. When you read it, notice how like the pictures of D. Lange it is."[53] That was because their ways of representing the Dust Bowl migrants had developed in tandem.

Figure 28. "What Hurts Business Hurts Me," by Dorothea Lange. Near Porter-ville, February 1938. (LC-USF34-018307-E. Courtesy of Library of Congress.)

Lange's picture of the migrant mother was published with Steinbeck's first journalistic pieces on the Dust Bowl migrants. When Steinbeck's article "Starvation under the Orange Trees" was published in the *St. Louis Post Dispatch,* Lange's photographs backed it up.[54]

The photograph of the billboard is not a sign of the "Hollywoodization" of the Okies, their seamless incorporation into the very corporate and con-sumer world the agrarian partisans wanted to confront. Instead, it is an emblem of their partial triumph: even in the Central Valley, the film, with its sympathetic portrait of the Dust Bowl migrants, would be seen.

Figure 29. *Grapes of Wrath* billboard with Okie encampment, by Dorothea Lange. Central Valley, 1939. (Copyright the Dorothea Lange Collection, Oakland Museum of California, City of Oakland. Gift of Paul S. Taylor.)

Though some theater owners would bill it as the story of the "Bull-simple" Joads who say "Let's get on relief," it would be hard to sustain that dehumanizing vision of the Okies in the face of Ma Joad's resounding closing words, "We're the people." For the agrarian partisans, Lange's photograph was at once a visual trophy and a reminder that their representations still had redressive work to do.[55]

We might wonder how well the photographs and the novel represented the interests and desires of migrant workers. What did the migrant fruit pickers want? Did the man—still strong, composed, and hopeful, sitting with his son and waiting for the orange picking season to begin in Porterville—hold agrarian dreams? Lange's photograph of another picker, Jack Neill, holds the glimmer of an answer. The description tells us that he was "a migrant fruit tramp . . . he owns a one-acre subsistence farm near

Figure 30. Okie orange tree. (From Visalia Migratory Labor Camp newsletter, "The Hub," 22 December 1939. Copy in collection 1243, box 23, Carey McWilliams Papers, UCLA. Courtesy of Department of Special Collections, Charles E. Young Research Library, UCLA.)

Porterville, represented migratory laborer as a speaker at the Commonwealth Club in San Francisco." Neill was a man who could represent himself as well as benefit from the state's helping hand. With his one-acre plot near the citrus region in Tulare, he was a participant in California's subsistence farm program. In an orange pickers' camp, Lange interviewed another self-described "fruit tramp" who wanted to anchor her migratory life with a small garden plot of her own. "We want a place more than anything to help out on the living," she explained, "with chickens, a little garden patch, a goat, maybe we could get two-thirds of our living that way even on an acre." Creating a record of human and environmental erosion was Lange's attempt to reclaim the garden and restore its fruits to the people—a goal very much in line with the desires of many of the people she represented.[56]

Residents of the FSA's Visalia camp, situated on the edge of Tulare's orange belt, published their own newsletter, "The Hub." For the cover of the Christmas 1939 issue, a migrant artist portrayed an agricultural worker picking fruit. With the question "Idealism . . . ?" looming in the background, "The Hub"'s tree is a meditation on the issue of whether oranges and "Santy Claus" are real (see figure 30). It shows what the migrants hoped California's orange trees would bear: the fruits of respect, honesty, tolerance, understanding, neighborliness, and peace.[57] These were the very fruits the agrarian partisans wished to reclaim as well, as they pressed their case for environmental justice.

EIGHT

"A Profit Cannot Be Taken from an Orange"

Steinbeck's Case for Environmental Justice

THE CROP OF 1939

IN 1939, California's cornucopia yielded 462,000 tons of prunes, 2 million tons of grapes, 10 million bushels of pears, and 75 million boxes of oranges. The oranges brought in over $100 million, and the $383 million paid for all of California's crops made it the richest agricultural state in the union. But half a million American consumers also bought a book that cast a pall over these fruits and their place of origin. For Americans who had been fed a steady diet of romantic images of the Golden State, *The Grapes of Wrath* was a gut-wrenching, myth-breaking novel. It pulverized those images, revealing a hemorrhaging landscape. The American dream was gushing out of the land of promise, Steinbeck insisted, and justice was drying up under the sun. In *An American Exodus: A Record of Human Erosion*, Paul Taylor, with sociological insight, and Dorothea Lange, with her human landscapes of exile, showed Americans a land and a people being blasted away. Seeking answers, many turned to Carey McWilliams' hard-hitting historical exposé *Factories in the Field*, making it a best seller as well. At the end of the year, growers could not simply close off the season by balancing their books. A nation aroused by the agrarian partisans' documentary wrath demanded a deeper reckoning.[1]

John Steinbeck's fictional family, the Joads, left an indelible mark on the California landscape. The uprooted Oklahomans embodied America's agrarian dreams. As they moved into the verdant valleys of the Golden State, the repression and alienation of corporate agriculture was written on their bodies, clear for everyone to read. They became the witnesses of the larger forces that moved through them, driving home the case that the growth machine had severed a farm family's—and thus an agrarian nation's—ties to the land. Before their very eyes, it had destroyed the fruits of Eden.

Bolstered by the amicus briefs submitted by McWilliams and Taylor and Lange, Steinbeck presented a compelling case. The charge was taken seriously, bringing the nation's media and the Senate's Civil Liberties Committee to California to look into matters. Growers, including leaders of the Associated Farmers and Sunkist, were subpoenaed to appear before the committee. McWilliams and Taylor also testified, Lange's photographs were present as silent yet eloquent witnesses, and Steinbeck's novel loomed in the background, shaping what was asked, and said, and seen. Convinced that growers were acting in ways that were essentially criminal, the agrarian partisans pressed the nation to provide redress and devise a remedy to the ills suffered by the land and the people. They were seeking what would today be called environmental justice.

"Living into It": Representing the Joads

The "real" American family has always been a work of fiction. Anthropologists may tell us of a group's marriage rites, if it is matrilineal and patrifocal or vice versa; sociologists can tell us how many children the average family has and give us a figure for its gross domestic income. But in searching for the real American family we often find ourselves staring at its representation or idealization. By this measure, the Joad family—noble, embattled, and earthy—is as real as it gets for Depression America. The Joads, of course, were a fiction, a family whose existence Steinbeck's literature conjured whole. But after the novel galloped across the nation's horizon in 1939, the Joads began to be taken as real. Newspapers, politicians, and reformers all talked about the plight of the Joads and debated "What should America do for the Joads?"[2]

But we might wonder how real Okies regarded their fictional counterparts. Did they see themselves beneath the sign that Steinbeck created, or were they estranged from the billboard under which some of them had camped? Some scholars have argued that Steinbeck's relationship to the people he portrayed was one of betrayal, that his methods of research were secretive, exploitative, even voyeuristic, and that he was more interested in winning accolades and pushing his own agenda than in listening to the needs and desires of those he claimed to represent. The charge is serious and goes to the heart of the problem of representing those who, in Marx's words, "cannot represent themselves." Many Okies did in fact resent the novel, while many others saw it as a gift. Considering his acts of representation as a whole, though, it is fair to say that Steinbeck showed a legitimate measure of aesthetic and moral fidelity to the real Okies.[3]

One Dust Bowl migrant said *The Grapes of Wrath* made Oklahomans "look like a bunch of ignorant people who had never seen a pencil or a piece of paper." Indeed, the novel helped solidify a sympathetic though still condescending image of the Okies. "Steinbeck kept his characters close to nature, close to the soil, so as to realize his critique of the machine and its civilization," one historian concludes. By using the Joads as a vehicle of antimodern sentiment, Steinbeck fueled the stereotype of the Okies as backward. But many other Okies did relate to Steinbeck's representations, and some were deeply moved by them. One couple from Sallisaw, Oklahoma (the Joads' hometown), went to the movie theater in Delano in 1940 to see the film. As Dan Morgan reports, the "movie made Ophelia very sad. She related to the scenes of the journey, especially to the one where the Joads have to bury Grandpa by the side of Highway 66. Her people had left a grandma behind. . . . Watching the movie, Ophelia understood for the first time how poor and uneducated they'd been. Vernon thought those times even 'worse than Steinbeck made them out to be.'" This testimony both confirms and questions the charge that Steinbeck's portrayals were inappropriate. Ophelia Tatham clearly thought *The Grapes of Wrath* expressed parts of her own experience. But the film helped her reconstruct her own past, persuading her that she had once been "poor and uneducated" by making the journey into California seem like a passage from the nineteenth into the twentieth century.[4]

Dust Bowl migrants had been watching Steinbeck's representations of themselves for years, stretching back to October 1936, when the "Harvest Gypsies" series first appeared in the *San Francisco News*. One migrant stated vehemently that "none of our folks—neither side—never lived like gypsies, and we sure never set out to." For many of the migrants the title of Steinbeck's collection was a slap in the face, an affront to their whiteness. Steinbeck wrote a letter to the editor explaining that he had used the term *gypsy* ironically and that he "had no intention of insulting a people who are already insulted beyond endurance." After hearing the articles read out loud at Weedpatch, the Farm Security Administration camp where Steinbeck had done much of his research with Tom Collins, the Camp Central Committee wrote back to Steinbeck:

> We all understand just Why you found it important to use that word. . . . we also Know that their are more people that dont Know how farm workers live, and never would know if it weren't for your trying to exPlain and Show them. We think you did a fine job for us and we thankyou. this is a big battle which cannot be won by ourselfs. we kneed friends like you.[5]

The growth machine actually did much to spread the idea of deep Okie resentment over Steinbeck's portrayals. In 1939, a *Los Angeles Times* reporter interviewed Steinbeck at his ranch in Los Gatos. The reporter stated that Steinbeck had "padlocked himself against the world [because he] has himself stamped out a bitter vintage of wrath—the enmity of the bewildered refugees from poverty and hunger whose cause he pleaded." He asked Steinbeck if he had received threats from the Okies themselves, which is a bit like asking a husband if he's stopped beating his wife. Did he have any proof that the Okies appreciated his work? Only the Oklahoma City Chamber of Commerce people were upset with his book, Steinbeck insisted. He refused to show the reporter any supportive letters, but said, "I've got them—lots of them!" But the author did bring out a "stuffed dog, made of vari-colored little squares of cloth, [which] bore around its neck a tag reading, 'Migrant John.'" This rag-tag dog symbolically verified his acceptance into the community of migrants. "That ought to convince you the Okies aren't after me," Steinbeck said triumphantly.[6]

Steinbeck and the Okies alike had to contend with intense public attention. Steinbeck explained to the *Times*, "There's getting to be a fictitious so-and-so . . . out there in the public eye. He's a straw man, and he bears my name. I don't like him—that straw man. He's not me—he's the Steinbeck the public has created out of its own imagination and thinks ought to be me." Likewise with the Okies. A central thesis in the "Harvest Gypsies" articles was that the way Californians saw and received the Okies would determine who they would become (good and productive citizens or a people filled with wrath). Steinbeck had studied Heisenberg's uncertainty principle and believed that perception changed reality. By giving them a human face (albeit the mythic one of the American pioneer), Steinbeck did much to break down malicious stereotypes. To represent the Okies, Steinbeck created the Joads; but, as he must have recognized, in representing the Joads, he re-created the Okies. In the process, he may have created his own straw men, Oz-like scarecrows of the imagination.[7]

We have to make an excursion into Steinbeck's philosophy to better understand his acts of representation. He believed that the observation and representation of anything—whether individuals, groups, or animals—always changed both the thing observed and the observer. "All observers viewing external reality through eyes set in a conditional thinking pattern," he wrote in the preface to an unpublished book on marine invertebrates, "will of necessity bring some residue of that pattern to reality. Such a process however it may distort the object is never the less *a creative association between observer and object.*" In a book based on his trip to the Gulf of Mexico with Ed Ricketts (the model for Doc in *Cannery Row*), he advised the reader to give up the "myth of permanent objective reality. . . . Let us go . . . into the Sea of Cortez, realizing that we become forever a part of it; that our rubber boots slogging through a flat of eelgrass, that the rocks we turn over in a tide pool, make us truly and permanently a factor in the ecology of the region." Just as the environment is constructed interactively, so too with people, for "personalities are not fixed and stable, but subject to and influenced by the interpretations of the observer." These ideas were part of the larger philosophy he and Ricketts called "non-teleological thinking." Such thinking challenged the scientific distinction between subject and object, insisting instead on the greater organic unity of the world. "The method extends beyond thinking even to living itself," Steinbeck explained; "it postulates 'living into.' . . . Anything less than the whole forms part of the picture only, and the infinite whole is unknowable except by *being* it, by living into it."[8]

Steinbeck sought to "live into" the Joads' life and world. Like an anthropologist, he was living his way "into an alien expressive universe."[9] He did fieldwork in a double sense. He picked crops. Visited squatters' camps. Slept in ditches. Like Frederick Mills of the California Commission of Immigration and Housing, he went undercover, but he was better prepared for it than Mills. Growing up, he had worked from time to time as an agricultural laborer in and around Salinas. "I was a bindle-stiff myself for quite a spell," he once said. And while Mills acted like a spy (turning in reports on the Wobblies' organizing strategies, for example), Steinbeck was a fellow traveler. When told that Ruth Comfort Mitchell was going to write a novel to refute his own, he shot back, "I know what I was talking about. I lived, off and on, with those Okies for the last three years." This claim was only a bit of an exaggeration: Steinbeck had spent considerable time among the Okies in the FSA camps, in squatters' camps, and in the fields in 1937 and 1938.[10]

His research was indirectly sponsored by the federal government. In Washington, Steinbeck went to the FSA, explaining that he "needed the experience of a migrant worker, if it was to be a realistic story of how they actually lived." The FSA decided to help, in part because the AF was threatening the FSA's camp program. Collins was given a leave with pay from his post as camp manager, so that he and Steinbeck could become "a two-man team, both working in the Imperial and San Joaquin valleys as migrant workers." With Dorothea Lange officially on its payroll and Steinbeck being aided by Collins, the FSA had assembled a crack team in California to build legitimacy for the camp programs. After driving through Oklahoma and taking Route 66 back to the Golden State, Steinbeck met up with Collins at an FSA camp in Northern California. The two spent some days working on a nearby ranch and staying in a squatters' camp. Steinbeck had purchased an old pie delivery truck, and the two spent a few weeks traveling around the state and out to the California-Arizona border. All the while, Steinbeck was making observations, doing a little farm work, and training his ear to the speech of the people. He returned to Los Gatos in early November and began writing the first draft of his "big novel."[11]

That winter was exceptionally wet. In Orange County, one of the citrus worker villages, located in a floodplain, was washed away when the Santa Ana River flooded, killing twenty people. The storms created a crisis across much of rural California, as the tents of thousands of migrant families flooded. Hunger and disease ran rampant. In February, Steinbeck left for Tulare County to help the migrant families living in and around the orange pickers' camps that Lange had photographed a few months earlier. In these floods Steinbeck took "living into it" to another level. The FSA asked him to write some newspaper stories. "I'm going to try to break the story so hard that food and drugs can start moving," he wrote in a letter to his agent. "Shame and a hatred of publicity will do the job to the local bankers. . . . If I can sell the articles I'll use the proceeds for serum and such."[12]

Though he thought his pen would do the most good for the most numbers, he ended up putting his entire body into the effort. He joined up with Collins, who described how "for forty eight hours, and without food or sleep, we worked among the sick and half starved people, dragging some from under trees to a different shelter." At 2:00 A.M., they both collapsed in a muddy field. In the morning, Steinbeck "was a mass of mud and slime." They soon found another tent, and with the mother inside despondent and starving, Steinbeck set out for the nearest store to get food. They worked hard for another nine days "in that vast wilderness of mud and deep water."[13]

Steinbeck arranged to return to Visalia with a photographer to do a story for *Life,* hoping that the images would "pin a badge of shame on the greedy sons of a bitches who are causing this condition and it is definitely caused, make no mistake about that." To Steinbeck, the flooding was not simply an "act of God": it was ultimately the creation of California's agricultural system, a calamity waiting to happen. "I know that name calling won't do anything," he acknowledged, "but they are touchy about the tourist who might not come to California to spend his money because he might see such suffering."[14]

Life never published the article he wrote (though it did print the photographs after the novel became a hit), but a version did appear as "Starvation under the Orange Trees." "The spring is rich and green in California this year," the article began. But despite the fact that "the orange trees are loaded," "thousands of families are starving." Steinbeck inveighed against the "Associated Farmers, which presumes to speak for the farms of California and which is made up of such earth stained toilers as chain banks, public utilities, railroad companies and huge corporations called land companies, this financial organization in the face of the crisis is holding Americanism meetings and bawling about red flags and foreign agitators." Steinbeck then presented testimony from the fields: "I talked to a man last week who lost two children. . . . I talked to a girl with a baby . . . she hadn't eaten for two days. . . . I heard a man whimpering that the baby was sucking, but nothing came out of the breast." California's cornucopia was in fact empty, because "our agriculture for all its great produce is a failure." Steinbeck wanted the article, which was published first in the *Monterey Trader,* to receive wide circulation. Despite the help of Lorentz at the FSA and the fact that Steinbeck would accept no money for it (inviting readers to give money to relief efforts instead), only a few publications agreed to print it. But Steinbeck would recycle it, turning it into a key chapter in *The Grapes of Wrath,* where it would be read by millions.[15]

His experience "living into it" in the rain and mud was also molded into the final chapter of *The Grapes of Wrath,* where he shoots back at the press for not publicizing the story. In that chapter, we are in the middle of the rain storm, and the river is rising. The men are trying to build a dike against the torrent. In a nearby boxcar, Rose of Sharon is in labor. The Joads have been starving for days. When Pa comes in to ask about the baby, Rose of Sharon's midwife "picked up a lantern and held it over an apple box in the corner. On a newspaper lay a blue shriveled little mummy."[16] Migrant farmworkers relied on newspapers, soup cans, and fruit crates to build their homes on the road. In this respect, the fact that the lifeless baby is placed in an apple box on a newspaper is certainly incidental, a circumstantial framing. But it can also be read as an indictment of the fruit industry and the complicity of newspapers. Steinbeck had mixed feelings about newspapers, calling them "the mother of literature and the perpetrator of crap." Earlier in the novel, William Randolph Hearst is made into a symbol of California's lost garden as well as an embodiment of journalism as a purveyor of fecal matter: "They's a grove of yella oranges—an' a guy with a gun that got the right to kill you if you touch one. They's a fella, newspaper fella near the coast, got a million acres. . . . Got guards ever'place to keep folks out. . . . I seen pitchers of him. Fat, sof' fella with little mean eyes an' a mouth like a ass-hole" (265). In a short story called "The Lonesome Vigilante" (1934), Steinbeck exposed the harm that can come of newspaper stories. A mob gathers, pulls an innocent black man out of jail, and lynches him. They know he is a "fiend" because they have read it in the newspapers. After the hanging, they burn the "bluish gray" corpse using a "twisted paper."[17]

In *The Grapes of Wrath*, Uncle John carries the apple crate to the rising river and sets it in the current to carry the news downstream. He shouts, "Go down an' tell 'em. Go down in the street an' rot an' tell 'em that way. That's the way you can talk." Here was Steinbeck's witness: "Go on down now, an' lay in the street. Maybe they'll know then" (571–72). Look carefully into the crate, this writer rages, and you will know them by their fruit.

"No Relation": Representing the Land

Steinbeck begins *The Grapes of Wrath* with a picture of the land in drought: "The sun flared down. . . . The surface of the earth crusted. . . . In the water-cut gullies the earth dusted down in dry little streams. . . . Little by little the sky was darkened by the mixing dust, and the wind fell over the earth, loosened the dust, and carried it away" (1–2). The writing is cinematic: long shots of the landscape and close-ups, reproducing in fiction the techniques used by Lorentz in *The Plow That Broke the Plains*. He then turns from land to people. How did they react? Would their faces register defeat? Would the families remain whole? In *The Grapes of Wrath*, the relationship between land and people is elemental.

Someone once quipped that Ansel Adams photographed rocks as if they were people, and vice versa. Steinbeck's descriptions of the landscape were also human portraits, and vice versa. He treated people as biological beings, integral parts of nature. Describing one of his earlier novels, Steinbeck wrote, "Each figure is a population, and the stones, the trees, the muscled mountains are the world—but not the world apart from man—the world *and* man—the one inseparable unit man plus his environment."[18] This does not mean that his people became one-dimensional, environmentally determined monoliths. Because he loved both land and people, and because he had closely observed both and learned something of their complexity, Steinbeck's "naturalism" was deeply humanistic. While naturalist writers had typically sought to separate themselves from their subjects to view them objectively, Steinbeck was deeply involved with his people and the land; they were always revealed as dynamic and multifaceted. The author closely identified with the natural world, even believing that the boundaries between self and the larger living world were illusory.

Steinbeck's trees often represented the interconnection between people and the land. In his own life, he strongly identified with a pine tree he had planted and watched grow. When the time came to cut off the lower limbs because they were threatening his house, he felt "a powerful reluctance to do it, such a reluctance as I would have toward cutting live flesh. Furthermore if the tree should die, I am pretty sure I should be ill."[19] A similarly totemic tree is cut down in *To a God Unknown*, and the man connected to it falls ill, as does the land generally. In *The Grapes of Wrath*, the symbiosis of people and place is brought to the surface when the Okies depart. A voice hopes, "Maybe we can start again, in a rich new land—in California, where the fruit grows." Another answers,

> Only a baby can start again. . . . This land, this red land, is us; and the flood years and the dust years and the drought years are us. . . . How'll it be not to know what land's outside the door? How if you wake up at night and know—and *know* the willow tree's not there? Can you live without the willow tree? Well, no, you can't. The willow tree is you. (113, 114–15)

For Steinbeck, capitalism is a wedge alienating people from the land and thus from themselves. Tractors—"great crawlers moving like insects, having the great strength of insects"—represent the larger economic forces on the ground. The tractor driver is a cyborg: "The man sitting in the iron seat did not look like a man; gloved, goggled, rubber dust mask over nose and mouth, he was part of the monster, a robot in the seat." From this metal perch "he could not see the land as it was, he could not smell the land as it smelled; his feet did not stamp the clods or feel the warmth and power of the earth." The tanklike tractors "did not run on the ground, but on their own roadbeds." He drives in straight lines, right up to the tenant houses (as in Lange's photograph), for "the monster that built the tractor . . . had somehow gotten into the driver's hands, into his brain and muscle, had goggled him and muzzled him." The land is rationalized into straight furrows, ignoring its character and contours, ignoring dwellings of all kinds. While hungry children look on, the cyborg driver eats a lunch appropriate for a cyborg—Spam and "a piece of pie branded like an engine part." Someone recognizes him as "Joe Davis's boy" and demands, "What you doing this kind of work for—against your own people?" "Three dollars a day," he replies. He has to think about his own family. Besides, "Times are changing, mister," he says. "You don't kick up a howl because you can't make Fords. . . . Well, crops are like that now" (47–48).

Eros has been chased out of this agricultural landscape, for "no man had touched the seed, or lusted for the growth. Men ate what they had not raised, had no connection with the bread. The land bore under iron, and under iron gradually died; for it was not loved or hated, it had no prayers or curses." Steinbeck conveys the loss of Eros with an image of cold sexual conquest, in which "the long seeders" of the tractors become "twelve curved iron penes erected in the foundry, orgasms set by gears, raping methodically, raping without passion" (45–47). When there is a visceral connection between farmer and land, the earth becomes a living and growing being that is part of the community. But under conditions of mechanical reproduction, the land becomes a thing, its soil dead pan.

Lange and Taylor cited farm papers that celebrated the convenience and efficiency of tractors that could run day and night. Steinbeck's novel admits that working the land with machines "is easy and efficient." But it is

so easy that the wonder goes out of work, so efficient that the wonder goes out of land and the working of it, and with the wonder the deep understanding and the relation. And in the tractor man there grows the contempt that comes not only to a stranger who has no understanding and no relation. For nitrates are not the land, nor phosphates. . . . Carbon is not a man, nor salt nor water nor calcium. He is all of these, but he is much more, much more; and the land is so much more than its analysis. (148–49)

Mechanization can lead to a violent reductionism, alienating men and women from the land and from their community. "The man who is more than his chemistry, walking on the earth, turning his plow point for a stone, dropping his handles to slide over an outcropping, kneeling in the earth to eat his lunch" does not become estranged from nature and humanity, for he knows "that land that is more than its analysis." Steinbeck shares the view of other romantic defenders of agrarianism, who, as Richard White observes, maintain that "work on the land creates a connection to place that will protect nature itself."[20] Instead of riding the plow close to the earth behind a team of living horses, "the machine man [drives] a dead tractor on land he does not know or love . . . and he is contemptuous of the land and of himself" (149).

Yet Steinbeck, who was a great admirer of gadgets of all kinds, makes clear later in the novel that it was not simply machines that were responsible for the destruction of the garden. "Is a tractor bad?" a voice asks. "If this tractor were ours it would be good. . . . We could love that tractor then as we have loved this land when it was ours." Technology, then, is not an autonomous force driving humanity inexorably away from nature. Ultimately, the tractor is being driven, not by the man in the seat, but by an entity seated far way. The dispossessed farmers want to know who to shoot. A voice explains that shooting the owners of the land would not solve their problem, for the owners are only parts of a larger being that demands their land. The land owners say that "the Bank—or the Company—needs—wants—insists—must have—as though the Bank or Company were a monster." The voice explains the reorganization of the land. Tenant farmers have to make way for tractor farming and its greater efficiencies. Cotton will be grown until the "land dies" and then the denuded landscape will be turned into country homes for "families in the East." The land must produce ever more profits, for "when the monster stops growing, it dies. It can't stay one size" (193, 41–42).

In this way, *The Grapes of Wrath* dramatizes the growth machine's conversion of place into profit. Through the Joads, the human toll of economic growth was registered, and the tractors become both instrument and symbol of this process. They cut through the land, they wreck homes, they split individuals from their community, they expel people, they metabolize all they can and then move on—and then "the monster" sells the denuded debris to Easterners, reincarnated through advertising as a rural idyll. Steinbeck *denaturalizes* these changes, refusing to accept them as the inevitable fruits of progress or evolution. His farmers insist it is "not like lightning or earthquakes. We've got a bad thing made by men, and by God that's something we can change" (50).

"From 'I' to 'We'": The "Anlage" of Social Ecology

The social, political, and ecological stance of *The Grapes of Wrath* stems from Steinbeck's theory of the group. Drawing on a range of fields, from biology, ecology, and physics to history, anthropology, and Jungian psychology (as explored with his neighbor Joseph Campbell), Steinbeck believed that human beings are drawn to and shaped by a level of organization beyond the individual. Just as the human body is made up of cells—each with its own needs, drives, and character—human beings are part of a larger body. Borrowing the Greek term for Alexander's fighting machine, he called this super-organismal unit the *phalanx*. Art, he thought, enables "a feeling of oneness with one's phalanx." In an earlier story, Steinbeck presented his thesis on the significance of the phalanx in American history. An old pioneer says, "It wasn't Indians that were important, nor adventure, nor even getting out here. It was a whole bunch of people made into one big crawling beast. . . . It was westering and westering. Every man wanted something for himself, but the big beast that was all of them wanted only westering." In the Joads' exodus westward, they are drawn up into a larger phalanx as they recapitulate the frontier experience.[21]

But unlike Turner, Steinbeck refused to equate continental conquest with progress. Indeed, the frontier phalanx was not necessarily just. "Once California belonged to Mexico and its lands to Mexicans," he wrote, "and a horde of tattered feverish Americans poured in. And such was their hunger for land that they took the land—stole Sutter's land, Guerrero's land, took the grants and broke them up and growled and quarreled over them." It was not this original sin of theft that destroyed the garden, but the land's commodification. The once land-hungry farmers lose their salt-of-the-earth identity and become "little shopkeepers of crops . . . [who] farmed on paper." "No matter . . . how loving a man might be with the earth and the growing things," Steinbeck states, "he could not survive if he were not a good shopkeeper." With Eros driven out of the landscape, growers imported Chinese, Japanese, Mexicans, and Filipinos to grow the crops at their beckoning. "They wouldn't know what to do with good wages," Steinbeck has the shopkeeper farmers say. "Why, look at how they live. . . . And if they get funny—deport them" (297).

Steinbeck saw the Dust Bowl migrants as another wave of land-hungry migrants, a phalanx that might take the land away from those who had grown weak and alienated living within the walls of ownership. As the new immigrants arrive, the West's "great owners" grow "nervous as horses before a thunder storm." They attack the federally sponsored camps and unionization, not realizing that "these things are results, not causes." The deeper cause is "hunger in a stomach . . . hunger in a single soul . . . muscles and mind aching to grow, to work, to create, multiplied a million times." As the dispossessed migrants head west, they camp together along the road, exchanging stories, working in the same conditions, and forming relationships. At first, each family is focused on its own story of loss. But as they share their experiences, the individuals become conscious of a larger pattern. "Here is the node, you who hate change and fear revolution," Steinbeck's narrator insists. "Here is the anlage of the thing you fear. . . . For here 'I lost my land' is changed; a cell is split apart and from its splitting grows the thing you hate—'We lost *our* land.' . . . This is the beginning—from 'I' to 'we'" (192, 194).

Jim Casy, the earthy minister who has given up the cloth, embodies the phalanx's social solidarity and its orientation toward nature. Casy gave up the ministry after he had a numinous experience in nature. "There was the hills, an' there was me, an' we wasn't separate no more," he tells Tom. "We was one thing. An' that one thing was holy." But he does not use this experience to create a cult of wilderness. Instead, he connects his nature experience back to people, saying that "when they're all workin' together, not one fella for another fella, but one fella kind of harnessed to the whole shebang— that's right, that's holy" (105). He almost sounds like John Muir saying, "When we try to pick out anything by itself, we find it hitched to everything else in the universe."[22] In Casy's (and Steinbeck's) view, this ecological position includes humans: individuals are ultimately harnessed to nature as well as all of humanity.

In California, Casy, having lost contact with the Joads, becomes a labor organizer and leads a strike on a peach ranch. The Joads later arrive at the ranch and inadvertently sign on as scabs. Their first day picking fruit is a trial. Encountering a version of the Powell Method, they receive no credit for picking several boxes of slightly bruised peaches. Still, they have meat to eat that night. Tom asks Casy, "Think Pa's gonna give up his meat on account a other fellas?" After Casy is martyred by Associated Farmer–like vigilantes, Tom takes up his mantle, becoming the arm of the phalanx that avenges Casy's death. Becoming a fugitive wanted for murder, Tom tells Ma that he is free to seek justice for "our folks." Maybe Casy is right, he says, and "a fella ain't got a soul of his own, but on'y a piece of a big one—an' then . . ." Ma interjects, "What then?" How will she keep in touch? "I'll be everywhere—wherever you look," he says. "Wherever they's a fight so hungry people can eat, I'll be there. Wherever there's a cop beatin' up a guy, I'll be there. . . . An' when our folks eat the stuff they raise an' live in the houses they build—why, I'll be there" (465, 493, 537). With his mystical sensibility and unwavering sense of justice, Tom can at once lose himself in the group and still be on hand to fight with his body. He is the kind of hero Steinbeck strove to be as the author of *The Grapes of Wrath:* a ubiquitous witness and partisan fighter packing a good punch.

Steinbeck was trying to bear witness to the abrogation of the land's promise and fight for its reclamation. To do so, he melded a holistic view of society with a holistic view of nature, coming up with a perspective similar to the land ethic Aldo Leopold articulated at the same time. Steinbeck saw individualism as an illusion that had real, and debilitating, effects. It divided people from each other, establishing class divisions and patterns of ownership that in turn separated people from nature. His heroes, realizing they were indeed "harnessed to the whole shebang," did not lose sight of the divisions within society. Because Steinbeck's analysis of the domination of nature was stitched to his analysis of domination within society, his work was directed toward achieving environmental justice. His belief in social ecology was reflected in the way he went about writing his novel. He sought to establish a fluid relationship with those he would represent by "living into" their world—a world that he saw as ecologically connected to his own. On both social and ecological grounds, Steinbeck argued that the "present system of agricultural economics" was simply unsustainable.[23]

"The Golden Mountains"

Descending out of the Tehachapi Mountains, the awestruck Joads behold the "morning sun, golden on the valley. . . . The peach trees and the walnut groves and the dark green patches of oranges." The children say simply, "It's California. . . . There's fruit" (292–93). This was the crate label vision, one that Steinbeck will spend the rest of the novel destroying. His most vivid exposure of California's mythic abundance comes in what he called "the general chapter of the rotting fruit, and of the destroyed fruits and vegetables."[24]

Though it was one of the key chapters of the novel, it was also among Steinbeck's least original. Its central trope—the destruction of fruit while people were starving—had already been turned into a political spectacle in the EPIC campaign. The Simon J. Lubin Society was using photographs of oranges being destroyed in its *Rural Observer,* and the preamble to the Lubin Society's constitution reads like a condensed version of the chapter. It made reference to "straight trees . . . order and growth . . . testifying to human knowledge." It contrasted this vision of improved nature with the want of workers and the "fear-suppressed rage" that was growing among their ranks.[25] Steinbeck takes up these images and elaborates on them in the chapter. Perhaps it was a fair trade, for Steinbeck had given the group his "Harvest Gypsies" series to publish. Steinbeck, who once referred to himself as a magpie who collected shiny things wherever he found them, also borrowed from his own article "Starvation under the Orange Trees."

The result was brilliantly cinematic: a color-saturated tour through California's groves and fields; close-ups of the fruit blossoming and growing, of men grafting rootstocks to scions; pictures of each kind of fruit swelling, ripening into new colors; and then visions of that fruit turning color once more, filling the air with the smell of rot, being stacked up and set afire deliberately; and the faces of people looking on in disbelief and anger. We see splendor and the hope of progress; hear rancor and disbelief; witness putrescence and starvation. It would have made a fine scene in a movie (if John Ford had chosen to make it in color). And it would have been a riveting statement to hear in a courtroom.

"The spring is beautiful in California," the chapter begins. After providing a view of how "all California quickens with produce, and the fruit grows heavy," Steinbeck points out, "Behind the fruitfulness are men of understanding and knowledge and skill, men who experiment with seed, endlessly developing the techniques for greater crops of plant." He includes the border inspectors, the spray applicators, and the grafters of the vineyards with their "surgeon's hands." "The men who work in the experimental farms," he reports, "have made new fruits, nectarines and forty kinds of plums. . . . And always they work, selecting, grafting, changing, driving themselves, driving the earth to produce" (447). Here was a vision of an artifactual garden, a nature made all the more colorful and abundant by those agricultural scientists like Burbank who had "transformed the world with their knowledge." If they had had Steinbeck's poetic genius, the chapter up until that point would have fit nicely into any of the publications of the Citrus Experiment Station, the Los Angeles Chamber of Commerce, or Sunkist.

But then the idyllic landscape collapses. Voices complain about the price of crops: they can't be harvested. Blame is laid on the large corporations that own the canneries, which push the price for fresh fruit so low that they drive smaller growers out of business. Now the sweet smell of rot "is a great sorrow on the land. . . . Men who have created new fruits in the world cannot create a system whereby their fruits may be eaten." At the end of the chapter, Steinbeck presents his most damning charge:

> Men with hoses squirt kerosene on the oranges. . . . A million people hungry, needing the fruit—and kerosene is sprayed over the golden mountains. . . . There is a crime here that goes beyond denuncia-tion. . . . The fertile earth, the straight tree rows, the sturdy trunks, and the ripe fruit. And children dying of pellagra because a profit cannot be taken from an orange. . . . The people . . . come in rattling cars to get the dumped oranges, but the kerosene is sprayed. And they stand still and watch . . . the mountains of oranges slop down to a putrefying ooze. (449)

Turn the page and we confront Ma looking over her young boy Winnefield, who for several days has only had fried dough to eat: "He's a-jerkin' an' a-twistin' in his sleep. Lookut his color" (450). In Steinbeck's portrait of human erosion, the discoloration of rotting fruit is mirrored by that of human bodies. This was an inflamed retort to Sunkist's advertising. Even as the company held out the promise that its products were vital to the healthy growth of children, it helped put those oranges out of reach of the needy. Here was a fabricated Eden that also fabricated want because "a profit cannot be taken from an orange." Steinbeck had hoped to make the reader "participate in the actuality."[26] And so when he concludes the indictment, he makes them into witnesses of the putrefication of Eden's fruits: "and in the eyes of the people there is the failure; and in the eyes of the hungry there is a growing wrath. In the souls of the people the grapes of wrath are filling and growing heavy, growing heavy for the vintage" (449).

This was powerful imagery for a mass audience in the 1930s. As Carey McWilliams observed, Americans' "rudimentary common sense tells them that the destruction of surpluses when people are starving represents the original, biblical conception of wickedness itself."[27] The sight got under McWilliams's skin as well: "When you have seen, as I have, tons and tons of citrus fruit being dumped in huge sumps, sprayed with tar to make them inedible, then guarded by high barbed wire fences to make sure that some errant Mexican youngster is not tempted to steal an orange, it does begin to occur to you that something just might be wrong with the way the economy functions."[28] Though Sunkist occasionally seemed to realize that crop destruction was seen by some as "morally wrong," it was a staunch supporter of this method of stabilizing markets. Indeed, it had been destroying surplus oranges on its own, and in the 1930s the state lent its regulatory power to the plan. Working with the citrus industry, in 1937 the Agricultural Adjustment Administration developed a citrus marketing agreement or "prorate plan."[29] The prorate plan authorized and subsidized the destruction of a portion of the total volume of the total citrus crop ($600,000 in federal money was spent destroying citrus in 1938 and 1939).[30] To Sunkist, this plan was justifiable on economic grounds, for it could cure the "market gluts and famines" that were "disastrous to growers returns."[31] Sunkist's general manager reasoned that "no one would presume to insist that a shoe factory be operated at a loss or that houses be built without a profit in order that people be adequately clothed and sheltered."[32]

But Steinbeck's biblical imagery trumped such economic logic. To the growers' assumption that "a profit cannot be taken from an orange," Steinbeck shot back that hungry people were morally entitled to the surplus oranges. If the oranges were really Eden's fruits, they were priceless. Steinbeck's narrative framed the Orange Empire in a crime—the original one, in fact. By so vividly envisioning the transgression, Steinbeck gave shape to the social drama and helped gather the force behind the call for Eden's reclamation.

THE HEARING

Contested Stories

Thinking about Truman Capote's *In Cold Blood*, the political philosopher Jürgen Habermas concludes that "what grounds the primacy and the structuring force of the poetic function is not the deviation of a fictional representation from the documentary report of an incident, but the exemplary elaboration that takes the case out of its context and makes it the occasion for an innovative, world-disclosive, and eye-opening representation in which the rhetorical means of representation depart from communicative routines and take on a life of their own."[33] This take on the relationship of fiction to historical events is useful in understanding *The Grapes of Wrath*. The authority of the novel largely rested on its claim that it was based on the facts. Steinbeck made this claim, but he had a lot of help: from *Life* magazine, Lange's photographs, the testimony of Eleanor Roosevelt, and, especially, McWilliams's *Factories in the Field*. Yet, as we have seen, the novel did something more than report on existing conditions. Its "poetic function" was to configure those events into a larger narrative, one that was for readers a "world-disclosive and eye-opening representation." Steinbeck sought at once to portray that world and structure the way it would be seen by readers far removed from the actual scenes, so that disclosure might lead to discussion and, ultimately, dramatic change.

The Grapes of Wrath took on a life of its own because it was a contested narrative, a version of real events that various interests felt compelled to challenge or support. The publication of the landmark study *Factories in Field* did much to bolster the credibility of Steinbeck's fiction. A lawyer and writer who became increasingly involved in farmworker civil rights over the course of the decade, McWilliams wrote an indictment published in the form of a history. He sought to unveil the "hidden history" of California's "fabled land," exposing its "violent history of racial exploitation." Beneath "the dramatic conflict between man and nature," McWilliams maintained, are "social conflicts no less dramatic and no less impressive." California agriculture had become "large-scale, intensive, diversified, mechanized." These factories in the field were "charged with social dynamite." Based on his experience in Orange County during the citrus strike of 1936, he charged the growers' exchange with manufacturing "Gunkist oranges."[34]

The book was charged with dynamite as well, exploding myths and causing alarm, especially among growers and their spokespersons. They became concerned largely because the book was received as a factual confirmation of *The Grapes of Wrath*. "M'Williams Verifies the Steinbeck Story" was a typical newspaper headline outside of California. "Disaster in a Veritable Garden of Eden," announced the *New York Herald Tribune;* "The Merciless Facts Which Give Economic Significance to 'Grapes of Wrath.'"[35] One disgruntled reader of *The Grapes of Wrath* "bustled" into a bookstore demanding "an answer to that book." The bookseller replied,

"Yes, Madam, we have it right here for you," and sold her *Factories in the Field.*[36] For many readers who had already adopted Steinbeck's frame of reference, McWilliams's book was taken as the novel's historical and factual verification.

But for those who objected to Steinbeck's version, some alternative reality needed to be composed. Speaking before the AF annual meeting nine months after *The Grapes of Wrath* appeared, the public relations chief of the organization lamented that we "have allowed ourselves to be jockeyed into a position of explaining and defending ourselves." *The Grapes of Wrath* was "making a fortune for the author and stirring national and international comment because of damming sensationalism written so cleverly as to appear to be based on fact." "Isolated instances" were blown out of proportion to smear California "as an uncivilized area of brutality and ruthlessness" and "build an indictment of the farmers." To escape this criminal charge, he recommended that the AF "advance to the frontier of the threat . . . and establish our Maginot line in San Francisco and the other danger points, and from there tell the people about major problems which are essentially theirs in the last analysis."[37]

After an unsuccessful attempt to have *The Grapes of Wrath* banned statewide (the effort backfired), the AF commissioned and distributed a barrage of counternarratives. Philip Bancroft, vice president of the AF and in 1938 a candidate for the Senate, wrote a tract answering the question "Does the 'Grapes of Wrath' Present a Fair Picture of California?" Of course not, he argued. California farmers paid the highest wages in the United States, and large farms did not dominate agriculture. Much of the literature audaciously charged Steinbeck himself with creating dehumanizing stereotypes of the Okies. In "The Grapes of Gladness," the Citizens Association of Bakersfield accused Steinbeck of portraying the migrants as "moral and mental degenerates." One pamphlet concluded that "the migratory families are of good pioneer stock, asking nothing more than a chance to work, a chance to get back on a piece of land of their own."[38] The pamphleteer was apparently plagiarizing Steinbeck in order to discredit him.

Of Human Kindness, a novel by Ruth Comfort Mitchell, was the most polished literary response. In August 1939, Mitchell had discussed the negative publicity growers were receiving with the AF at a Pro-America meeting, where *The Grapes of Wrath* was labeled "smear literature." With whitewash, she would go to work on the smear. Mitchell's California farmers are the perfect yeomen who treat their hired help with the utmost care and respect. They farm for the love of the land, because it is a noble way of life. Like *The Grapes of Wrath,* Mitchell's novel features a rain storm flooding the fields. In Steinbeck's book, the flood pushes Rose of Sharon, having just delivered her stillborn child, into a realization of the unity of all of humankind. In the novel's most controversial scene—intended as a redemptive image of the communion of all life—she offers her breast to a man on the edge of starvation, smiling "mysteriously." Mitchell's analog to this scene is revealing: a farmer mounted on a tractor drives in to save the flood victims. The tractor—in Steinbeck's book an instrument of alienation—becomes a vehicle of kindness. In her novel, the good-hearted but politically naïve farmers are told by a visitor that the "Associated Farmers are popularly believed to wear horns and carry red-hot pitch forks." In the battle of public relations, "The other side beat you to the jump, and now you're definitely cast in the public mind as the villain of the piece."[39]

Though they envisioned the farmer carrying a pick handle rather than a pitchfork, this was in fact the image that many people had of the AF by the time *Of Human Kindness* was published. The AF threw a vast amount of literature at the problem, distributed through many of the same channels that the anti-Sinclair campaign had used. But Steinbeck's novel proved to be more difficult to blunt and disarm than Sinclair's EPIC had. In the end, the AF's literary campaign proved to be an "utter failure."[40] Mitchell's book never became anything close to a best seller, and it certainly could not check the power of Steinbeck's. In a review, McWilliams captured how this literature contributed to the social drama: "Now that the briefs have been filed, so to speak, for both sides, the public should be able to render a verdict. But *Of Human Kindness* and *The Grapes of Wrath* should not be read alone. There is still another document that should be studied, the transcript of the La Follette Committee Hearings in California. . . . They give the facts without the fiction, and the facts support Mr. Steinbeck."[41]

A Verdict: The Orange Grower Is a Manufacturer

The La Follette committee hearings were the formal culmination of the social drama. In effect, California's growth machine, with the orange industry as its most prominent representative, was put on trial. The hearings and the report the committee issued were inspired by the work of the agrarian partisans.[42] Paul Taylor had been urging Robert La Follette, an old friend from college and the Marines, to come to California. Lange's photographs had focused the committee's attention on California's chaotic rural landscape, and *The Grapes of Wrath* and *Factories in the Field* generated enough public support to bring the committee to California over the opposition of the Bank of America, the AF, and Sunkist. And Sheridan Downey, Sinclair's running mate in 1934, who went on to win a Senate seat over AF vice president Bancroft in 1938, introduced the appropriations bill that made the hearings possible.[43]

Officially charged with investigating violations of labor law and civil liberties, as set forth in section 7(a) of the National Industrial Recovery Act of 1934 and the National Labor Relations Act of 1935 (also known as the Wagner Act), members of the committee came to California looking for "factories in the field." They came looking for them because Taylor had told La Follette about the "industrial pattern" of California agriculture. They came looking for them because all that they had heard about the AF made the group sound like something out of the automobile or steel industry. And they came looking for them because California's farmworkers had to be seen as *industrial* workers or the committee had no business being there. They were working to enforce the Wagner Act, but that legislation had explicitly excluded agricultural workers from its definition of *employee*.[44]

They found them. At the hearings, growers fought a rear-guard battle by attacking McWilliams's thesis, calling it a "mastery of misstatement." Complaining of his efforts to help farmworkers negotiate contracts, a grower said "of all the pests with which the crops of California are infested, Mr. McWilliams is Agricultural Pest Number One." But these objections were not enough to overturn the narrative the hearings had created. The "factories in the fields" idea prevailed, and has shaped most historical investigations of agriculture in California down to the present.[45]

At the hearings, a story about the transformation of agrarian life into an industrial mode of production took shape. The vigilantism of the AF, the support that group received from industrial groups, the machines used in harvesting and packing California's fruits—all of these facts on which the committee focused were taken as the symptoms of this transformation. Out of the wide-ranging investigation and the hundreds of pages of testimony that were given, a succinct three-part storyline took shape: first, AF members were not farmers at all, but industrialists wearing farmers' clothes; second, their farms were factories rather than homesteads; and third, farmworkers worked under debilitating conditions and faced violent repression by the AF. The Orange Empire was taken as the best example of this new form of agriculture, and the citrus grower became the emblematic farmer who was not really a farmer.

Many witnesses were well prepared to testify to the fact that California's agriculture had become industrialized. On the first day of the hearings, which were held in San Francisco, Governor Culbert Olson told the committee about California's "large-scale industrialized corporate farms." McWilliams, appointed by Olson to head and revitalize Lubin's old immigration and housing agency, had drafted the governor's statement. He front-loaded the word *farms* with three adjectives designed to strip it of bucolic associations. McWilliams himself "spent a great deal of time with the [committee] staff, briefing them, lining up witnesses and cooperating in other ways." Even recalcitrant witnesses saw their testimony become part of the factories in the field narrative. The committee investigated and questioned "the role of large employers who are engaged in farming as a business rather than a 'way of life.'"[46] It probed into the character of the labor process in the citrus industry and its use of machinery in the packing houses. In the eyes of the committee, the Sunkist orange was little different from any other manufactured product.

In his testimony, Paul Taylor presented citrus growers as representatives of the industrial farmer. Growers were not "embattled farmers," for a farmer was "one who operates a 'family sized farm' for a living rather than for 'an actual or potential modern fortune.'" These "farm operators who are really 'agricultural employers'" have transformed agriculture into "an industrialized pattern." Ever since the EPIC campaign, growers had been trying to dislodge the image of vast factory fiefdoms by arguing that California agriculture was actually made up of small farmers. In 1934, Associated Farmer Frank Taylor published a series of articles titled "California's Embattled Farmer" in *Forum* and *Reader's Digest*. He vigorously disputed the idea that "most of California's farm lands are in great holdings," pointing out that almost 30 percent of California's farmland was in farms of less than a hundred acres. But Paul Taylor pointed out that 7 percent of the farms in the state controlled 42 percent of the farmland, thus revealing "the opposite of what the author intended to prove." Furthermore, he pointed out that acreage alone was not a good measure of large-scale farms, using the citrus industry as a case in point. In Orange County, the average farm size was just over forty acres. But these farms had more than the proverbial mule to go along with the land. They were highly capitalized. Using numbers provided by a representative of the citrus industry, Taylor found that the average farm in Orange County represented a $64,821 investment, while the average investment in farms nationwide was $4,823. Average gross income from Orange County farms was $59,000, making them large-scale farms according to the census definition.[47]

To describe the functions of agricultural employers, Taylor cited testimony in a National Labor Relations Board case involving the North Whittier Heights Citrus Association (a member of Sunkist). Citrus industry expert J. Coit had stated that "The term 'farm' in the old and commonly accepted sense . . . is long since obsolete in respect to the highly specialized agricultural occupation of growing such products as citrus fruits. In fact, there are some farmers who do no manual work on their farms." This became *the* quote of the hearings. It was cited over and over again because it so well typified the industrial transformation of agriculture.[48] As Taylor concluded, the farmer's toil had "been progressively assumed by associations, corporations, and labor contractors." In this view, citrus growers were made out to be oxymorons: farmers who did no work in the soil.[49] To call them farmers—or growers or ranchers or horticulturists—was incorrect. To Taylor, they were employers, pure and simple.

Yet Coit had argued that citrus growing was in fact an agricultural rather than an industrial enterprise. In the Whittier case, the citrus association maintained that the National Labor Relations Board had no jurisdiction over its labor relations. The facts in the case were fairly straightforward. The association had broken an American Federation of Labor–sponsored strike by firing one of its leaders and shutting down operations in August 1937. When it reopened, it did not rehire twenty-seven of the strikers. Under the Wagner Act, this was clearly illegal. The sticky issue was a matter of classification. How were these packing plant workers to be seen? Did they work on a farm or in a factory? The stakes were high: if the plant was a farm, then the board had no jurisdiction and could do nothing for the men and women who packed fruits for a living.

Coit advanced a "the more things change, the more they remain the same" thesis. In the early days of the industry, growers would do all of the work to bring a tree into bearing and then pack the fruit themselves under the trees. If we accept this as a farm, he suggested, then we should accept the packing plant as merely an extension of the farm. The machine had not intruded on the garden; the packing house was merely the mechanical manifestation of that garden. Sunkist had long celebrated the technological and business revolutions of its organization, and likened the grower to the engineer or the industrialist. The Wagner Act had encouraged the growers to make a change of identity and rewrite their history. Now it argued that beneath all of the machinery, all of the technical expertise, and the million-dollar advertising budget lay the same rural idyll pictured on the crate labels.

The court did not buy it. Ironically, it could have been quoting from any number of celebratory articles in the *California Citrograph* when it concluded that "the growers have, through standardization of their products, advertising, and better distribution, brought about a tremendous increase in consumption and a constantly expanding market. The organization of individual orchards into cooperative marketing associations has led to highly efficient and mechanical methods of packaging the crop. In the light of such changes in packing methods it is idle to argue that no change . . . can have taken place." It added that "the growers themselves have separated from the farms." The committee questioned growers about the "processes through which oranges pass" as they were prepared for market, and concluded that the "packing of oranges is . . . a machine operation." It saw the packing plants, with their conveyer belts, washers, box-making machines, and X-ray scanners, as little different from an assembly line in Detroit. The workers are "auxiliary to the machines," for their work "consists chiefly in operating or feeding material to machines [and] is highly routinized, calling for the performance of fairly simple, usually repetitive operations . . . synchronized with the operations of machines."[50]

In the committee's narrative, the worker had become an automaton. The image conjured was not unlike the one of Charlie Chaplin in his 1934 film *Modern Times,* working on an assembly line, using wrenches to tighten bolts, over and over again, until his body becomes merely the twitch of the machine. There was indeed much routinization in the packing plants. But the committee made no reference to the skill of these packers, no acknowledgment that their expertise was as necessary to the industry as were the machines. To function, the machines were dependent not just on the mechanical motions of human adjuncts, but on the thousand complex choices and movements that went into every perfectly packed box. Ironically, recognition for the workers would be won not on the basis of their human worth, but on the degree to which the citrus industry had dehumanized them.

Sunkist and the AF, though insisting that they did not oppose unions, proved themselves to have what the committee called a "bitter antiunion attitude."[51] Much of the hearings was devoted to documenting the violations of farmworkers' civil rights by the AF, and to tracing the genesis of this organization back to its source (Sunkist as well as many other important components of the growth machine). However much they normally identified with captains of industry, under the scrutiny of the state, growers argued that they should be allowed more leeway in determining labor conditions than factory owners. When they spoke about labor issues, growers were quick to point out that nature had not been completely conquered. While workers often bore the brunt of nature's irregularities (witness the pea pickers at Nipomo or citrus workers stranded in groves without pay while the rain fell), growers used nature's unpredictability as an argument for limiting the voice of workers. Because crops "are highly perishable in nature," Frank Taylor argued that California's farmers were especially vulnerable.[52] *Pacific Rural Press* editor John Pickett argued, "Nature doesn't recognize eight-hour days and five-day weeks in the growing of food. . . . Crops insist on getting ripe after hours. Not even the Wagner Labor Board can make the sun stand still and the seasons halt."[53] Nature did not have an on-and-off switch, growers repeatedly noted. Relying on a nature that had not really been made into a factory, growers felt justified in demanding absolute power over labor.

According to growers, consumers also stood to lose if labor won more control of the groves. They would suffer from nutritional scarcity. "To deprive people of these foodstuffs means death and strikes at the very root of our national health," the Orange County chapter of the AF argued. Having advertised oranges as an essential ingredient to daily life, Sunkist could now argue that maintaining their flow to consumers was a national imperative. "Any delays in production or harvesting are not merely an economic loss to the farmer," Sunkist's president wrote, "they are a loss of essentials to the consuming public." Using the body of the consumer as a shield, growers tried to deflect the assaults of the agrarian partisans and labor leaders. While Steinbeck had argued that a profit could not be taken from an orange, the growers countered that workers' rights could not be allowed to obstruct the flow of oranges to their rightful consumers.[54]

But the committee assured that workers striving to break the romantic spell and assert their rights would get a fair hearing. Their bodies, physically beaten by AF vigilantes, took the stand as witnesses; they made a case for environmental justice. The committee rendered a clear verdict. In California, farms were factories. The AF were not farmers at all, and they used espionage, tear gas, pick handles, and official law enforcement agencies to prevent farmworkers from organizing. Orange growers had become manufacturers rather than farmers. In their relentless drive to commodify the fruits of Eden, they had abrogated the agrarian dream and threatened democracy itself.

According to Victor Turner, the redressive phase of a social drama "furnishes a distanced replication and critique of the events leading up to and composing the 'crisis.'" The hearings did just that, and the publications that the committee issued codified the agrarian partisans' version of those events and the transgressions of the growers. As Kevin Starr notes, the committee's reports "climaxed on a note of intellectual and moral triumph all efforts to document the Depression." Though the agrarian partisans may have won the moral victory, they won little else. The redressive phase of any social drama presents opportunities to both see and revise the basic order of the society. Social dramas are "our native way of manifesting ourselves to ourselves and, of declaring where power and meaning lie and how they are distributed." The final stage of the social drama also affords opportunities to change where power and meaning lie and how they are distributed. La Follette tried to do just that by introducing a bill that would prohibit many of the anti-union tactics used by the AF. Proponents said it would bring "industrial peace" to a riven landscape. But as the war heated up in Europe, the bill's opponents were able to make it out to be an instrument of a fifth column. Freighted down by riders turning it into a defense measure, the compromised bill passed the Senate but was never voted on in the House. Having reached a verdict, the committee was unable to devise a legal remedy.[55]

But the New Deal was ready to offer one concrete solution: millions of tons of it poured across the Columbia River. The great dams would create new "pastures of plenty," as Woody Guthrie would put it in a song. Instead of reclaiming California's Eden, reclamation would create yet another Eden in the Northwest. Franklin Delano Roosevelt said, "I would like to see the Columbia Basin devoted to the care of the 500,000 people represented in 'Grapes of Wrath.'"[56] The press picked up Roosevelt's message. *Life* magazine ran a photo-essay on "the Joads," using the photographs its photographer had taken with Steinbeck when "he lived in California's migratory labor camps" (though it did not mention that at the time, it had opted not to publish "Starvation under the Orange Trees"). Peering out from boxcars and ramshackle tents were the Joad prototypes, people who "are still in California, squatting in hideous poverty and squalor on the thin margins of the world's richest land."[57] Elsewhere in this issue, *Life* offered redemption in its story on the Columbia River Project. Headlines announced "America's Future: Pacific Northwest: The Story of a Vision and a Promised Land," "Irrigation Makes the Northwest Bloom," "American Frontier, 1939," "The Land Is Rich in Nature's Goods: Lumber,

Metals, Wheat and Fruit." The Joads should pack their bags and head out along the new Oregon Trail. That was also the message of the film *Three Faces West* (Republic, 1940). Released the same year as the film version of *The Grapes of Wrath,* it featured John Wayne as a Dust Bowl victim leading his townsfolk to the promised land. He chooses to head to Oregon instead of California, for the Duke knows that the land of sunshine and oranges is illusory. Literalizing the agrarian partisans' charge of farm fascism, the film's subplot has Nazis infiltrating the Golden State. They would in fact be there in a few years—as prisoners of war picking lemons. By 1940, war was on the horizon, transforming the way the California landscape would be perceived—and reformed. Grand visions of redress were abruptly shelved. Eden would not be reclaimed for the people.

The Empire may have suffered the embarrassment of having its officers called before the state's tribunal. And the emperor's clothes may have been taken away. But as Eden geared up for full production, he remained seated on his throne.

EPILOGUE

By Their Fruits Ye Shall Know Them

THE EMPEROR AND THE BRACEROS

BORN IN CARIBOU, Maine, in 1873, Charles Collins Teague seemed to have a commanding presence. Expecting to "find a tropical country," he made his way to California in 1893, the year that Sunkist was founded. Teague worked his way up through the ranks of citrus growers, inspiring the confidence of those around him. By 1908, he had become president of the Teague-McKevett Association, and by 1917, of the Limoneira Company. His apotheosis was complete in 1920, when he was made president of the California Fruit Growers Exchange (a position he would hold until his death in 1950). Whether serving on Hoover's Farm Bureau, as president of the California State Chamber of Commerce, or as a member of the Prorate Commission, Teague seemed to have a hand in all aspects of the agricultural politics of his era. From his palatial home in the Santa Paula heights, Teague's influence reached far and wide. If the Orange Empire had an emperor, he was it.[1]

Having fought off such statewide challenges as EPIC, Teague was more than a little surprised to be confronted by an insurrection close to home. But in January 1941, the predominantly Mexicano citrus workers of Ventura County—workers Teague had assumed were content—united behind the AFL's newly created Agricultural and Citrus Workers Union and went on strike. One day in May, some three hundred striking lemon pickers and packers headed for the gates of the Teague estate. The sheriff turned them away. "We weren't going to start any trouble," explained spokesperson Henry Garcia. "We just wanted to talk to Mr. Teague." There would be little face-to-face communication during the six-month strike. Teague refused to negotiate with AFL organizers, insisting that they did not represent his employees. Talks were never initiated. Teague preferred to issue statements to the press, including a letter to citrus workers explaining the position of the growers. Teague believed that outside agitators had "incited" his workers with false promises. The economic facts put growers in a bind: the market was not favorable, and growers were having to send as much as 35 percent of their crop to the by-products plant. "Under these conditions," Teague explained, "it is impossible to grant you any increase in wages. We cannot and we will not." Lemon picker Robert Miranda received the news incredulously. Why was Teague so set against their union? Hadn't he preached the value of cooperation? Wasn't he the "president of one of California's strongest and richest UNIONS—the California Fruit Growers Exchange?" Citrus grower Frank Stokes had made the same point in the aftermath of the Orange County strike of 1936. "But when the lowly and very much despised picker tries to organize into a union where he can get a word in edgewise about working conditions," Miranda charged, "you put your mighty thumb down and all your millions, power and prestige to crush the lowly worm who has at last started to open his eyes."[2]

"I am not opposed to organized labor," Teague explained in his memoirs, "but I am opposed to the exploitation of workers by irresponsible labor leaders." During the strike, Teague and other growers evicted Mexicano workers from company houses. With more than five hundred families looking for shelter, "Teaguevilles" were set up in Ventura's county parks. The Farm Security Administration sent in a mobile camp to house the refugees, earning the agency Teague's lasting ire. Growers recruited Dust Bowl migrants from the Central Valley to break the strike. Some Okies in Tulare County had become quite adept pickers and had little compunction about breaking a strike led by Mexican Americans; as one strikebreaker put it, he had come to California to work. In July, the National Labor Relations Board finally came to look into the strike. Ignoring the La Follette Committee conclusion that the citrus business was in fact industrial in character, the NLRB saw packers as agricultural workers and thus outside its purview. The Agricultural and Citrus Workers Union was flung away like the rattlesnakes that sometimes dangled from the branches of the trees in the Santa Paula garden.[3]

Like everyone else, the growers soon turned their attention to the gathering storm overseas. Reiterating the "food will win the war" theme heard in the previous great conflagration, Teague told the state chamber of commerce that "the production of food will be generally recognized as being of even more importance than the production of airplanes, ships, guns and tanks." To spread this conceit, Sunkist lobbied to place oranges on the list of essential foods, sent concentrated orange juice to the Allies as part of the Lend-Lease program, placed four thousand Sunkist electrical juice extractors in the armed forces, and advertised in the *Saturday Evening Post* about the "Job of Oranges and Lemons in the Serious Business of War." A Sunkist memo stated that this created "the strongest demand we have ever experienced."[4]

But the Okies would not be able to provide all the labor growers required. And though some growers gave the Okies high marks as pickers, Teague was not satisfied. As he wrote to Sunkist's general manager, "The labor from the Dust Bowl is very inefficient and they will not pick lemons if there is any other work of any kind to be obtained anywhere else." Thousands walked off the job anyway, lured to Los Angeles and the San Francisco Bay Area to work in the war industries. What Paul Taylor called the "shifting reservoir of human distress known as migratory labor" was soon forgotten or absorbed into "the vast reservoir of new job opportunities." Growers faced a labor shortage and upward pressure on wages. They turned to the YMCA, high schools, and other local sources for help harvesting the crops in 1942, and soon enlisted the government to secure a source of labor. Although the Associated Farmers floated the idea of importing a Chinese Land Army (if for no other reason than to have "something to hold over [the] heads of . . . social planners and organized labor"), the main source of labor would come from Mexico. Under a bilateral agreement with the Mexican government, workers would be hired under six-month renewable contracts to work in the Southwest as agricultural laborers. Under this bracero program, their transportation would be paid for, their housing provided, and they would be guaranteed work. The federal government allocated $26 million to the program in 1943, to which California taxpayers added $1.5 million for the welfare of their state's agribusiness.[5]

Though organized labor and many Mexican American organizations opposed the program, it initially won the support of the man growers had dubbed "Agricultural Pest Number One"—Carey McWilliams. Impressed with the contract's guarantees of equitable treatment and fair pay, he lauded the program, which was administered at first by the Farm Security Administration. He wrote, "The existence of an agency capable of handling mass labor importation on a planned, intelligent, and scientific basis was a major stroke of luck." McWilliams talked with a few braceros, including Jesús Díaz, who spoke excellent English, expressed how much he missed his family in Mexico, and had had generally favorable experiences working in the lemon groves of Southern California. His only complaint was the segregation practiced in movie theaters and a government official who "'belongs in Germany, Italy, or Japan' [since he] didn't regard Mexicans as human beings." McWilliams reported that the braceros for the Glendora Lemon Growers Association made their own camp rules and formed a governing body (just like the Dust Bowl migrants in the FSA camps). Even the manager of the Growers Association was apparently satisfied with these workers, who were quickly learning to pick lemons efficiently. "They have saved the day for us," he said.[6]

Teague was equally pleased with most of the braceros, but he did not approve of the FSA. He complained to the War Food Administration that some of his pickers were abandoning their contracts to seek higher-paying employment elsewhere. He was frustrated with FSA officials, who simply issued a warning. Teague wanted something to be done that would "put some discipline into these men." He had deportation in mind. At the state chamber of commerce meeting, Teague blasted the FSA for making "impractical and unworkable" contracts with the braceros. As an agricultural representative chosen by the new governor, Earl Warren, Teague told the Senate that it had "appointed the wrong agency."[7]

In response, the Senate turned over the program to the War Food Administration. A disillusioned McWilliams said that this was "tantamount to turning the whole program over to the farm associations." Growers gained much more control over the working conditions of the braceros, as well as over the working conditions in all of Western agriculture. Pointing to scattered unionization efforts among agricultural workers, Teague championed the bracero program and concluded, "In my opinion the greatest mistake that organized labor has made in its history is its announced intention to organize agricultural labor." With these arms conscripted for service, the growers found a way to once again reinvent those dimensions of the Spanish labor system on which they had come to rely: its abundant supply of laborers, its racially inscribed division between those who owned the land and those who worked it, and the absence of collective bargaining. The Emergency Farm Labor Program (as it was officially called) would continue to supply this form of indentured labor from Mexico for almost two decades after the war ended. The presence of the braceros, who could be deported at any time, weakened the potential of all citrus workers to strike, and thus refortified the dual labor structure in California agriculture—a structure that the social drama had revealed as dangerous to democracy. These workers, dehumanized as hands and arms without faces, could make few claims to citizenship and soil.

In 1947, a group of braceros being deported died in a plane wreck in Los Gatos (not far from Steinbeck's ranch). In the crash, Woody Guthrie, the bard of the Okies, saw the significance of the bracero program flash incandescently. He sang of the "skyeplane" turning into a "fireball of litening" while below there were "or'nges all pil'd in . . . [the] creosotey dump." Guthrie demanded to know, "Is this muy best way I c'n growe muy bigg orcharde? / Is this muy best way I c'n growe my good fruite?"[8]

EXILE

Under Executive Order 9066, President Roosevelt authorized the uprooting of over 100,000 Americans of Japanese ancestry (most of them citizens) from the West Coast. They were sent to government camps that looked very much like those of the FSA, except for the guard towers and barbed wire. It would be the largest forced migration in American history, the twentieth century's trail of tears. At the end of the Depression, the social drama of human erosion had put America on the verge of making its farm labor system more democratic. Now the government would push people out on the road but mask the "human erosion" it was creating. Instead, as the War Relocation Administration put it in its official history, this was all "a story of human conservation."[9] Dorothea Lange's powerful portrait of a father and daughter, which was included in the War Relocation Administration book, did not quite break the spell that had turned a group of Americans into natural resources stripped of constitutional rights. They were fugitives accused of imaginary crimes and refugees from a catastrophe that did not occur. Farm Security Administration photographs of the twin migrations are haunting: braceros moving north, Japanese Americans moving east, members of each group wearing identification tags, evoking for postwar viewers a simultaneous forced migration of a people across the Atlantic.

Of course, the braceros only faced discrimination and demeaning treatment, not outright destruction. And Japanese Americans incarcerated at

Manzanar in the eastern Sierra Nevada and in the other camps did their best to cope with the injustice. Many grew gardens to supplement the poor rations they were given. The WRA hoped to make the camps self-sufficient, marketing the internees' fruits and vegetables. But some growers worried that the Japanese Americans, many of whom had been farmers in their own right on their own land, would now compete unfairly with "American growers."[10] Instead, many of the dislocated Japanese Americans would be called on to harvest crops in the region of the camps, thus becoming native braceros. Russell Lee's photograph taken in July 1942 helps us see the moral irony in this practice: a group of Japanese Americans who have "saved the crops" are being taken into town for supervised recreation. Their transportation is a truck emblazoned "A Product of Western Farms."[11] From Thomas Jefferson onward, Americans believed that farms did something more than grow crops: they grew a democratic people. But in the West, farms grew divisions between people and created inequality. *Race* was a product of Western farms.

Unlike most white Americans, the agrarian partisans raised questions about the forced internment, writing articles and pamphlets (Paul Taylor), proposing an alternative system by which Japanese Americans would guarantee their loyalty (Steinbeck), taking humanizing photographs of the evacuees and exposing racist anti-Japanese billboards (Lange), inducing the Tolan Committee to hold hearings, participating in radio debates, and writing a book called *Prejudice* (McWilliams).[12] In 1942, at the Tanforan race track near San Francisco, a group of West Coast deportees awaiting shipment to one of the camps insisted on celebrating Independence Day. Their words underscore how race and citizenship were connected to the symbol of California fruit: "Let us turn our thoughts to the future, both of this country and of our place in it. It is our task to grow to a fuller faith in what democracy can and will mean to all men. To stop growing in this faith would be to abandon our most cogent claim to the right of sharing in the final fruits of a truly emancipated world."[13]

Upon the emancipation of Japanese Americans from the camps, the War Relocation Administration told stories about specific Japanese Americans returning to their farms, ostensibly proving its claim that it was in the business of human conservation. One WRA photograph featured Mr. Kiyoshi Robert Kanagawa on his eighty-five-acre citrus ranch "budding young trees." According to the caption, the Kanagawas said that "they had no trouble whatsoever in marketing their citrus fruit upon their return home." The violation of Japanese American civil rights became a georgic epic with a happy ending—uprooting, journey, return, rerooting. Mr. Kanagawa's budding the new trees was an act of faith in the future and his place on American soil. But he must have also feared that he might once again be separated from the fruits of his growing trees. Would other Californians be able to disgorge the steady diet of Japanese demonology they had consumed during the war? The novel *Invasion* (1943), for example, depicted an insectlike horde of Japanese paratroopers descending on Los Angeles after dropping incendiary bombs. As the American empire is reduced to ashes, the Japanese fiendishly gorge on oranges.[14]

THE COURSE OF EMPIRE

The Orange Empire would not fall to an invading force of Japanese. But in the ten years after World War II, it would step down from power. Citrus trees began to be attacked by a new virus, carried by wasps and aphids, that sent the trees into "quick decline." But it was a cultural rather than biological vector that was responsible for the empire's fall. Industrial development and population growth created incentives to sacrifice the citrus landscape on the altar of development. As two geographers put it, "Bulldozers uproot thousands of acres of citrus groves to make way for a population increase of *one every 55 seconds!*" In the decade after World War II, Southern California lost a quarter of its citrus landscape. By 1970, agricultural acres in Los Angeles County had dropped by over 96 percent. With population soaring, it became more profitable to grow houses than fruit. A new infrastructure was laid out to handle all of the people and their movements across the urbanizing landscape. As Mike Davis notes, "What generations of tourists and migrants had once admired as a real-life Garden of Eden was now buried under an estimated three billion tons of concrete (or 250 tons per inhabitant)."[15]

"The Orange Empire," Richard Lillard noted in his book *Eden in Jeopardy* (1966), "declines as the invaders subdivide and rule." It is easy to see the razing of citrus as a battle between industrial and agrarian America, with the bulldozers becoming the machines in the garden. But we should bear in mind that the Orange Empire was already fully part of the industrial world. Its fruit trees were not so much destroyed as metabolized by the growth machine, which found new ways to turn the landscape into growth and profits. Growers could transfer their capital, now made liquid, into other ventures, or they could colonize a new landscape. Many sold their land in Southern California for $10,000 an acre and purchased new land for $2,000 an acre in Tulare County, "a mecca of the citrus industry."[16]

Perhaps it was destiny. As early as 1906, *Sunset* magazine had been promoting Tulare as the rightful heir to the empire. J. Parker Whitney claimed that there were three epochs in orange growing: first was the mission era, in which the trees were of "inferior quality." Eliza Tibbets's planting of the Washington navel trees in 1873 inaugurated the second epoch: improved trees grown by an enterprising people. However, the climate south of the Tehachapis was not perfect for oranges, Whitney maintained. The final epoch would witness "the gravitation of the orange tree to its proper and superior locality." In the same issue of *Sunset,* another writer said that "oranges will be as much at home here [in Tulare County] as if . . . they had migrated here by a kind of instinct, or natural selection." The prophecy came true. In Tulare County, a citrus kingdom was created, but the sun was setting on the greater empire. Sunkist would continue to be a powerful force, but citrus and agriculture became lesser kingdoms as other industries rose to power.[17]

Meanwhile, Southern California continued to witness the razing of the citrus landscape. Long-familiar green groves were uprooted and piled into clumps around the exposed acreage, then burned. By 1995, just a thousand acres of oranges were left in Orange County. The packing plants had to go as well. Abandoned, these remnants of the Orange Empire became eyesores and safety hazards. Before the bulldozers started their demolition work on one house in Orange County, local citizens gathered to commemorate the passing of history. "It's hard to see it go," said Gordon McLelland, who grew up working in citrus and has since become an expert on crate labels. At the gathering, many others voiced their lament at the passing of the citrus landscape. "It's our history," said one resident of the city of Orange (see figure 31).[18]

Their sense of violation echoes that of every group that has lived through a succession of landscapes, from Indians and Californios to ranchers and growers. When the landscape is gone, people look beyond the land to other ways of remembering themselves and their past. Interest in orange crate labels has boomed in recent years, and many collectors seek out the colorful images as mementos of a vanished landscape, tokens of a way of life now gone. Those sun-splashed groves—so full of color and promise, yet so replete with violence and tragedy—have also been repacked and served up as nostalgia. But nostalgia, while pretending to reconnect us with the past, actually strips history of its flesh, bone, and marrow.

Figure 31. Local residents and former growers, pickers and packers of oranges turned out to witness and lament the demolition of this packing house in Placentia, shown here on the eve of its destruction on February 7, 1997. Many Californians see the loss of agricultural lands to urban and suburban development as a sign that Eden has been lost, but the garden that is gone was itself an expression of an earlier phase of development. (Photograph by the author.)

In 1997, the same year that the packing plant was demolished, Disney broke ground on its California Adventure theme park elsewhere in Orange County. Strolling through the Bountiful Valley of the park's Golden State attraction, visitors to Southern California can now get a glimpse of the vanished landscape. But Disney has really done nothing new. From its genesis, boosters conjured the citrus landscape with images. After the Orange Empire's manifest decline, it is somehow fitting that the Magic Kingdom preserves that landscape as simulacrum.

THE GOLDEN GATE OF EDEN

Like all the world's fairs, the San Francisco Golden Gate Exposition of 1940 celebrated growth and progress. It did so on grounds that had been invented. The four hundred acres of Treasure Island were manmade, "a

Genesis-like creation of the very Earth itself." The new land was seeded with splendid plants to create "the greatest California garden of them all." Inside the Palace of Foods, Beverages, and Agriculture, visitors would be treated to visions of the lush citrus landscape. Few "will leave the Exposition without having a glass or two of California's native, world-renowned drink: orange juice." A thirty-seven-foot-tall globe was the central feature of the agricultural exhibit, highlighting San Francisco's dream of becoming the capital of a new Pacific Empire. An eighty-foot-high Pacifica welcomed the visitors as if she were Statue of Liberty's sister on the West Coast. No foreboding cherub with a flaming sword, Pacifica welcomed people through this gate of Eden.[19]

Like some twenty million others, John Steinbeck couldn't stay away. Diego Rivera was there too, painting a mural, *Pan-American Unity*. Visitors flocked to his "Art in Action" exhibit, where they could watch as the California and Mexico landscapes unfolded under this energetic artist's hands. On one panel, Rivera represented the epic of the West: covered wagons, gold panning, tree clearing, hydraulic mining, a tractor turning the soil, and Shasta dam (then under construction). Amidst all of this "creative mechanical power," a child learns her letters. Rivera had not been in the United States for several years, and his mural bears no trace of the technological skepticism the agrarian partisans had articulated. There is no image of erosion, either of soil or of humans. Rivera hybridized the organicism of the South with the industrialism of the North for his central figure, creating "a colossal Goddess of Life, half Indian, half machine." Like the Golden Gate bridge itself, it was an optimistic work, an assertion that difference could be spanned and nature reinvented for the common good. If there is any threat to this landscape—and there is—it comes from beyond: bombs dropping, a gas-masked figure slumped over barbed wire, and multiple pictures of Hitler (one showing the "Great Dictator" as impersonated by Charlie Chaplin). Below his earth-machine goddess, Rivera painted two human figures joining hands to plant the "tree of love and life."[20]

The male figure was Diego Rivera; the woman was Paulette Goddard. Why had he painted himself holding hands with the American movie star? a reporter asked. "It means closer Pan-Americanism," Rivera quipped.[21] Goddard had played the waterfront gamin in *Modern Times* (1936), Chaplin's exploration of the modern fable of abundance versus the reality of deprivation and dehumanization. The alienation that the Little Tramp experiences in the world of scientific management is remembered by all—his body becoming a cog in the machine, twitching with the rhythm of the assembly line even while he is on break (like a boy McWilliams found picking plums in his sleep). Another key scene has the two wandering into the garden landscape of a typical Los Angeles suburb. Sitting on the curb, the Little Tramp fantasizes about life in such a home. He has only to open the front door, and a cow walks up to deliver fresh milk. Oranges grow right outside the living room window, ripe for plucking. But the couple's idyllic reverie is interrupted by a policeman, the gatekeeper in this dream of Eden. Determined to find a job so he can achieve the dream, the Little Tramp lands one as a night watchman in a department store. After a wonderful night in the Oz of consumption, the two are promptly expelled from this "land of desire."[22] After yet another failure, the two are expelled again, and they hit the road like the migrants pictured by Lange. Instead of riding westward into the sunset, the two tramp toward a rising sun in the east. *Modern Times* brilliantly captured the paradox of California: the simultaneous creation of and expulsion from Eden.

God, it is said, used the fruits of the garden to reveal something about human nature, and his son used parables of fruit to instruct his followers on how to return to the promised land beyond. "Enter ye in at the strait gate," he says, but "beware of false prophets, who come to you in sheep's clothing, but inwardly they are ravening wolves." How would they recognize the bestial imposters? "Ye shall know them by their fruits," he instructs. "Do men gather grapes of thorns, or figs of thistles? Even so every good tree bringeth forth good fruit; but a corrupt tree bringeth forth evil fruit" (Matthew 7:13–20). Luther Burbank was fond of quoting this passage, but what sense does it make when we think of his experimental trees on which grew a hundred different varieties of fruit? All our trees today seem to some degree "corrupt." But even when the words were supposedly spoken, a careful grower of orange trees would have known that on a tree that regularly bore fine fruit, occasionally a *bizzaria* might appear. Of course, the biblical parable speaks about human beings, not trees. But looking closely at the nature of creation complicates the moral of the story. Nature is multifaceted and surprising; it does not necessarily teach us that the manifest works of a person must correspond to that person's inner being.

In postmodern times—in a world in which nature has been intricately reconstructed—the quest for the absolute truth, the unmediated real, the unadulterated natural has become quixotic. In this brave new world, even our clichés about nature have become obsolete. Apples and oranges are not so different anymore, for we can easily imagine creating an "appleorange" and a cornucopia of "promising transgenic fruit."[23] With biotechnology promising to give us another Eden, we will continue to confront deep cultural and environmental issues as we transform nature—and, with it, ourselves and our country. The story of the Orange Empire can help orient us as we move into this new country, perhaps still searching for that garden with its golden fruits that has so often been imagined as growing somewhere in the American West. I have argued that such a garden has always been a fabrication. There is no Eden, only a landscape we have created through a combination of nature and culture. Still, just because nature has become artifactual does not mean that it is corrupt or somehow irredeemable. Its redemption is ours, for we plant the trees, we grow the garden, and we build the walls. However crossed our nature is today, the parable of fruit remains relevant: we need to cultivate those "trees of love and life" on which good fruit grows. "Wherefore," a man once said, "by their fruits ye shall know them."

NOTES

ABBREVIATIONS

BL   Bancroft Library, University of California, Berkeley
CC   *The California Citrograph*
CCIH   California Commission of Immigration and Housing
CFGE   California Fruit Growers Exchange
HEH   Henry E. Huntington Library
LAT   *The Los Angeles Times*
OHA–CSUF   Oral History Archives, California State University, Fullerton
PP–LC   Prints and Photographs Division, Library of Congress
UCLA   Department of Special Collections, Research Library of the
            University of California, Los Angeles

PROLOGUE. AN ALLEGORY OF CALIFORNIA

1. Diego Rivera, *Portrait of America* (New York: Covici, Friede, 1934), 15.

2. Diego Rivera, *My Art, My Life: An Autobiography* (New York: Dover Publications, 1960), 19; Laurance Hurlburt, *The Mexican Muralists in the United States* (Albuquerque: University of New Mexico Press, 1989), 100; *San Francisco*

Chronicle, 11 November 1930; telegram, Hoover to Daly, Department of Justice, New York City, 15 October 1927, file no. HQ100-155423, Federal Bureau of Investigation, Washington, DC, cited in Terry Smith, *Making the Modern: Industry, Art, and Design in America* (Chicago: University of Chicago Press, 1993), 206; United Press dispatch, 23 September 1930, cited in Bertram Wolfe, *The Fabulous Life of Diego Rivera* (New York: Stein & Day, 1963), 285; *San Francisco Chronicle*, 25 September 1930.

3. Anthony Lee, *Painting on the Left: Diego Rivera, Radical Politics, and San Francisco's Public Murals* (Berkeley: University of California Press, 1999), 64; Diego Rivera, "Scaffoldings," *Hesperian*, Spring 1931, n.p.; Wolfe, *Fabulous Life*, 189.

4. Emily Joseph, "Rivera Murals in San Francisco," *Creative Art*, May 1931, cited in Hurlburt, *Mexican Muralists*, 107; Rivera, *My Art*, 105; Rivera's statement on Moody in *San Francisco Examiner* (n.d.), cited in Hurlburt, *Mexican Muralists*, 102. On California as a second Greece, see Kevin Starr, *Inventing the Dream: California through the Progressive Era* (New York: Oxford University Press, 1985), 128–75.

5. Rivera, *Portrait*, 14; Walt Whitman, *Leaves of Grass* (New York: Library of America, 1992), 246.

6. Rivera, *Portrait*, 14.

7. Rivera, "Scaffoldings"; Frank Norris, *The Octopus: A Story of California* (1901; reprint New York: Penguin, 1986), 289.

8. Luther Burbank, "Evolution and Variation with the Fundamental Significance of Sex," in *Official Proceedings of the Second National Conference on Race Betterment* (Battle Creek, MI: Race Betterment Foundation, 1915), 45; Rivera, "Scaffoldings."

9. John Logan and Harvey Molotch, *Urban Fortunes: The Political Economy of Place* (Berkeley: University of California Press, 1987), 32, 53.

10. William McLung, *Landscapes of Desire: Anglo Mythologies of Los Angeles* (Berkeley: University of California Press, 2000), 78. Ronald Tobey and Charles Wetherell persuasively demonstrate that the citrus industry was the major engine of California's economic growth in "The Citrus Industry and the Revolution of Corporate Capitalism in Southern California, 1887–1944," *California History* 74 (Spring 1995): 6–21.

11. Clifford Zeirer, "The Citrus Fruit Industry of the Los Angeles Basin," *Economic Geography*, January 1934, 57. On the economic geography of the fruit industry, see Steven Stoll, *The Fruits of Natural Advantage: Making the Industrial Countryside in California* (Berkeley: University of California Press, 1998).

12. Rivera, *Portrait*, 15, and *My Art*, 107.

13. Ken Kraft and Pat Kraft, *Luther Burbank: The Wizard and the Man* (New York: Meredith Press, 1967), 74, 131.

14. From an interview with one of the children: Elise Stern Haas, "The Appreciation of Quality," interview by Harriet Nathan, 1972, transcript, Regional Oral History Office, BL. Cited in Patricia Junker, "Celebrating Possibilities and Confronting Limits: Painting of the 1930s and 1940s," in Steven A. Nash, ed., *Facing Eden: One Hundred Years of Landscape Art in the Bay Area* (Berkeley: University of California Press, 1995), 66.

15. Rivera, *Portrait,* 15.

16. Victor Turner, "Social Dramas and Stories about Them," in *From Ritual to Theatre* (New York: PAJ Publications, 1982).

17. Rivera, *My Art,* 82.

18. Hurlburt, *Mexican Muralists,* 108; Rivera, *My Art,* 82; Carolyn Merchant, *The Death of Nature: Women, Ecology, and the Scientific Revolution* (San Francisco: Harper and Row, 1980), xvi.

19. "U.S. Dust Bowl," *Life,* 21 June 1937, 60, cited in Lee Rosen DeLong, *Nature's Forms/Nature's Forces: The Art of Alexandre Hogue* (Norman: University of Oklahoma Press and Philbrook Art Center, 1984), 24.

20. Isabel Allende, *The Infinite Plan: A Novel,* trans. Margaret Peden (New York: HarperCollins, 1993), 21, 28; Jack Kerouac, *The Dharma Bums* (New York: Penguin, 1958), 145.

21. Carey McWilliams, *Southern California: An Island on the Land* (1946; reprint Layton, UT: Gibbs Smith, 1973), 295–96; Clifford Geertz, *The Interpretation of Cultures* (New York: Basic Books, 1973), 5; Karl Marx, *Capital, Volume 1* (1867), in *The Marx-Engels Reader,* ed. Robert Tucker (New York: Norton, 1978), 346. While environmental historians have generally concentrated on either economic or ideological engagement with nature, oranges invite an integration of material and ideological levels of analysis. See William Cronon, "Modes of Prophecy and Production: Placing Nature in History," *Journal of American History* 76 (March 1990): 1122–31.

PART ONE. INTRODUCTION

1. Carlos Fuentes, *The Orange Tree* (New York: Farrar Straus and Giroux, 1994), 37. The image of "Rev. Father N. Duran and Indian Child" appears in Eugène Duflot de Mofras, *Exploration du Territoire de l'Oregon, des Californies, et de la mer Vermeille* (Paris: A. Bertrand, 1844), 199; Leon Batchelor and Herbert Webber, eds., *The Citrus Industry,* vol. 1, *History, Botany and Breeding* (Berkeley: University of California Press, 1943), 19–22.

2. Esther H. Klotz, "Eliza Tibbets and Her Two Washington Navel Orange Trees," in Esther Klotz, Harry Lawton, and Joan Hall, eds., *A History of Citrus in the Riverside Area* (Riverside, CA: Riverside Museum Press, 1989), 16;

Geraldo Hasse, ed., *The Orange: A Brazilian Adventure, 1500–1987* (São Paulo: Duprat and Iboe, 1987), 42; Batchelor and Webber, *Citrus Industry,* vol. 1, 531.

ONE. MANIFESTING THE GARDEN

1. Horatio Rust, "Report on the Condition of Mission Indians," October 1892, manuscript, box 9, Horatio Rust Papers, HEH; letter from Rust to James McLaughlin, 20 November 1900, box 12, Rust Papers. See also Jane Apostol, "Horatio Nelson Rust: Abolitionist, Archeologist, Indian Agent," *California History* 58 (Winter 1979/80): 304–15, and David Wallace Adams, *Education for Extinction: American Indians and the Boarding School Experience, 1875–1928* (Lawrence: University Press of Kansas, 1995).

2. *CC,* December 1923, 42.

3. Leslie Marmon Silko, *Gardens in the Dunes* (New York: Simon and Schuster, 1999).

4. On fiction and environmental history, see William Cronon, "A Place for Stories: Nature, History, and Narrative," *Journal of American History* 78 (March 1992): 1347–76; on turning plants into gold, see Cronon, *Nature's Metropolis: Chicago and the Great West* (New York: Norton, 1991), esp. 97–147.

5. Harvey Rice, *Letters from the Pacific Slope; or, First Impressions* (New York: D. Appleton & Company, 1870), 95.

6. F. Llewellyn, "Pomona," *Out West,* June 1903, 412.

7. Charles Francis Saunders, *Finding the Worth While in California* (New York: Robert M. McBride & Co., 1916), 26; Bertha Smith, "The Making of Los Angeles," *Sunset,* July 1907, 236.

8. Mike Davis, *Ecology of Fear: Los Angeles and the Imagination of Disaster* (New York: Metropolitan Books, 1998).

9. John Knight, "Redlands," *Land of Sunshine,* February 1899; Kevin Starr, *Material Dreams: Southern California through the 1920s* (New York: Oxford University Press, 1990).

10. Simon Schama, *Landscape and Memory* (New York: Knopf, 1995), 538.

11. Allan Bogue, *Frederick Jackson Turner: Strange Roads Going Down* (Norman: University of Oklahoma Press, 1998), 412–13. Patricia Limerick wryly notes the missing scholarship on the "fruit frontier" in "The Adventures of the Frontier in the Twentieth Century," in James Grossman, ed., *The Frontier in American Culture* (Berkeley: University of California Press, 1994), 75; Frederick Jackson Turner, "The Significance of the Frontier in American History" (1893), reprinted in John Mack Faragher, ed., *Rereading Frederick Jackson Turner* (New York: Henry Holt, 1994).

12. Cronon, *Nature's Metropolis.*

13. See William Preston, "Serpent in the Garden: Environmental Change in Colonial California," and Kat Anderson, Michael Barbour, and Valerie Whitworth, "A World of Balance and Plenty: Land, Plants, Animals, and Humans in Pre-European California," in Ramón Gutiérrez and Richard Orsi, eds., *Contested Eden: California before the Gold Rush* (Berkeley: University of California Press, 1997).

14. Tómas Almaguer, *Racial Fault Lines: The Historical Origins of White Supremacy in California* (Berkeley: University of California Press, 1994), 33.

15. Frank Pixley, "Annual Address to the San Joaquin Valley Agricultural Association," *Transactions of the California State Agricultural Society, 1880*, 229.

16. Ezra Carr, "Art and Nature," *Southern California Horticulturalist*, November 1878.

17. E. J. Wickson, *The California Fruits and How to Grow Them*, 7th ed. (San Francisco: Pacific Rural Press, 1914), 351, 355; Richard Orsi, "Selling the Golden State: A Study of Boosterism in Nineteenth-Century California" (Ph.D. dissertation, University of Wisconsin, Madison, 1973), 306; Wickson, "The Orange in Northern and Central California" (San Francisco: California State Board of Trade, 1903), 5. William Mills, the Central Pacific's land agent, had played a large role in the 1887 founding of the State Board of Trade, which published this pamphlet by Wickson.

18. C. E. Ramsey, "Evolution of a Tourist" (1905), cited in H. Vincent Moses, *To Have a Hand in Creation: Citrus and the Rise of Southern California* (Riverside, CA: Riverside Museum Press, 1989), n.p.; California Fruit Growers' Convention, "Hand in Hand Go Horticulture and Civilization: A Short Narrative of Fruit Raising in the United States and Particularly in California" (Sacramento: Weinstock, Lubin & Co., 1917); Ian Tyrrell, *True Gardens of the Gods: Californian-Australian Environmental Reform, 1860–1930* (Berkeley: University of California Press, 1999), 9. See also Kevin Starr, *Inventing the Dream: California through the Progressive Era* (New York: Oxford University Press, 1985), 137–39.

19. Helen Hunt Jackson, *Glimpses of California and the Mission* (1883; reprint Boston: Little, Brown, and Company, 1902), 221–24.

20. On landscape as a realm rather than a picture, see J. B. Jackson, *Discovering the Vernacular Landscape* (New Haven: Yale University Press, 1984), 1–8; on deterritorialization, see Gilles Deleuze and Félix Guattari, *A Thousand Plateaus: Capitalism and Schizophrenia* (Minneapolis: University of Minnesota Press, 1993). The spatial dimension of conquest is addressed in Lisbeth Haas, *Conquests and Historical Identities in California, 1769–1936* (Berkeley: University of California Press, 1995), esp. 1–12.

21. See Carolyn Merchant, "Reinventing Eden: Western Culture as a Recovery Narrative," in William Cronon, ed., *Uncommon Ground: Toward Reinventing Nature* (New York: Norton, 1995), 132–59.

22. E. R. Dille, "Annual Address," *Transactions of the California State Agricultural Society during the Year 1887* (Sacramento: California State Printing Office, 1888), 555.

23. Walter Woehlke, "Los Angeles—Homeland," *Sunset,* January 1911, 3; A. C. Fish, "The Profits of Orange Culture in Southern California" (n.p.: Semi Tropic Land and Water Company, 1890), back cover, 25.

24. *Semi-Tropic California,* October 1881; Starr, *Inventing the Dream,* 45; Charles Dudley Warner, *Our Italy* (New York: Harper and Brothers, 1891), 15, 18; Davis, *Ecology,* 12.

25. Warner, *Our Italy,* 5; Allan Schoenherr, *A Natural History of California* (Berkeley: University of California Press, 1992), 313–26; Elna Bakker, *An Island Called California* (Berkeley: University of California Press, 1984), 345–54; John McPhee, *Assembling California* (New York: Farrar, Straus and Giroux, 1993), 264–66; Jeffrey Mount, *California Rivers and Streams: The Conflict between Fluvial Process and Land Use* (Berkeley: University of California Press, 1995).

26. Warner, *Our Italy,* 15, 18–19; Charles Nordhoff, *California: For Health, Pleasure, and Residence* (New York: Harper and Brothers, 1872), 170–73; Major Ben J. Truman, *Semi-Tropical California: Its Climate, Healthfulness, Productiveness, and Scenery* (San Francisco: A. L. Bancroft and Co., 1874), 70.

27. Thomas Garey, *Orange Culture in California* (San Francisco: Pacific Rural Press, 1882), 7–8.

28. A. J. Cook, *California Citrus Culture* (Sacramento: California State Printing Office, 1913), 8.

29. Norris Hundley, Jr., *The Great Thirst: Californians and Water, 1770s–1990s* (Berkeley: University of California Press, 1992), 59; Haas, *Conquests,* 26.

30. Harry Lawton, "A Brief History of Citrus in Southern California," in Esther Klotz, Harry Lawton, and Joan Hall, eds., *A History of Citrus in the Riverside Area* (Riverside, CA: Riverside Museum Press, 1989), 10.

31. Figures from U.S. Bureau of the Census, *The Fifteenth Census of the United States: 1930, Irrigation* (Washington, DC: U.S. Government Printing Office, 1932), 86–93.

32. Donald Worster, *Rivers of Empire: Water, Aridity, and the Growth of the American West* (1985; reprint New York: Oxford University Press, 1992), 214.

33. Advertisement for the Santa Fe Pipe and Supply Co., *CC,* October 1925, 427. On irrigation practices, see Leon Batchelor and Herbert Webber, eds., *The Citrus Industry,* vol. 2, *Production of the Crop* (Berkeley: University of California Press, 1948), 445–88; Worster, *Rivers of Empire,* 52.

34. Wickson, *California Fruits,* 364.

35. Mary Vail, *"Both Sides Told," or, Southern California as It Is* (Pasadena: West Coast Pub. Company, 1888), 16.

36. Los Angeles County Pomological Society, *Southern California Souvenir* (n.p., ca. 1888), 30, copy at HEH, Rare Books.

37. Alla Clarke, "In Orange Land—Riverside," *Sunset,* January 1902, 113–18; *Semi-Tropic California: Devoted to Agriculture, Horticulture, and the Development of Southern California,* October 1881, 168; T. J. Jackson Lears, *Fables of Abundance: A Cultural History of Advertising in America* (New York: Basic Books, 1994), 21.

38. Los Angeles Chamber of Commerce, *Exhibit and Work of the Los Angeles Chamber of Commerce* (Los Angeles: Los Angeles Chamber of Commerce, 1910), 4–5.

39. Norman Stanley, *No Little Plans: The Story of the Los Angeles Chamber of Commerce* (Los Angeles: Los Angeles Chamber of Commerce, 1956), 9; see also Tom Zimmerman, "Paradise Promoted: Boosterism and the Los Angeles Chamber of Commerce," *California History* 64 (Winter 1985): 22–33; Orsi, "Selling the Golden State," 294–95, 512. Turrill quoted in Southern Pacific Company, *Catalogue of the Products of California* (New Orleans: Press of W. B. Stansbury, 1886), 16.

40. See Orsi, "Selling the Golden State," 517–24; *Riverside Press and Horticulturist* (27 April 1886), copy in the J. E. Coit Scrapbook, Special Collections, University of California, Riverside; *Sacramento Bee,* 15 January 1886, copy in the Coit Scrapbook. The *Bee* was writing of the Citrus Fair of Northern California, an attempt to pull the Southern California citrus boom northward.

41. *Final Report of the California World's Fair Commission* (Sacramento: A. J. Johnston, Supt. State Printing, 1894), 49–50, 74.

42. Harry Brook, "The Land of Sunshine: Southern California" (Los Angeles: World's Fair Association and Bureau of Information, 1893), 23; *LAT,* 8 April 1886, quoted in Orsi, "Selling the Golden State," 524.

43. *Wasp* [San Francisco], 26 March 1881 and 29 January 1881, quoted in William Deverell, *Railroad Crossing: Californians and the Railroad, 1850–1910* (Berkeley: University of California Press, 1994), 58; "Address by the Settlers League of Tulare and Fresno Counties to the People of the United States," *Pacific Rural Press,* 26 June 1880, 424.

44. Frank Norris, *The Octopus: A Story of California* (1901; reprint New York: Penguin, 1986), 50, 288–99. Norris had collected railway commission maps in his research. Frank Norris Papers, BL.

45. Richard Orsi, "*The Octopus* Reconsidered: The Southern Pacific and Agricultural Modernization in California, 1865–1915," *California Historical Quarterly* 54 (Fall 1975): 198; Spencer Olin, *California's Prodigal Sons: Hiram Johnson and the Progressives, 1911–1917* (Berkeley: University of California Press, 1968), 2.

46. See Orsi, "*The Octopus* Reconsidered," 202–3.

47. Wheat prices dropped from $1.42 a bushel in 1880 to $0.87 in 1894.

48. W. W. Robinson, *Land in California* (Berkeley: University of California Press, 1948), 157; Glenn Dumke, *The Boom of the Eighties in Southern California* (San Marino, CA: Huntington Library, 1963).

49. Jerome Madden, *California: Its Attractions for the Invalid, Tourist, Capitalist and Homeseeker* (San Francisco: H. S. Crocker and Co., 1890), 13.

50. See Richard Orsi, "'Wilderness Saint' and 'Robber Baron': The Anomalous Partnership of John Muir and the Southern Pacific Company for the Preservation of Yosemite National Park," *Pacific Historian* 29 (Summer/Fall 1985): 136–56; Alfred Runte, *Yosemite: The Embattled Wilderness* (Lincoln: University of Nebraska Press, 1990), 54–55, 84–85, 105; Southern Pacific Company, "Eat California Fruit: By One of the Eaters" (San Francisco: Southern Pacific Company, 1908), 6–10.

51. J. Parker Whitney, "Educational Orange Growing," *Sunset,* August 1906, 161–70; Orsi, "*The Octopus* Reconsidered," 209–12, and "Selling the Golden State," 348–60.

52. Clarke, "In Orange Land—Riverside," *Sunset,* January 1902, 113.

53. John Bauer, *The Health Seekers of Southern California, 1870–1900* (San Marino, CA: Huntington Library, 1959), 4; Madden, *California. Its Attractions*; Wickson, *California Fruits,* 358; *The Pacific Rural Press,* 2 April 1881, 232; *CC,* 15 March 1890, cited in Bauer, *Health Seekers,* 120.

54. Southern Pacific Company, *California Industries: Personal Testimonies of Experienced Cultivators: How Energy Enterprise and Intelligence Are Rewarded in California* (San Francisco: Southern Pacific Company, 1902), 7; Southern Pacific Company, *Catalogue,* 11; T. S. Van Dyke, *Millionaires of a Day: An Inside History of the Great Southern California "Boom"* (New York, 1890), 45, cited in Robert Fogelson, *The Fragmented Metropolis: Los Angeles, 1850–1930* (Berkeley: University of California Press, 1993), 66–67.

55. Llewellyn, "Pomona," 400; Cook, *California Citrus,* 5.

56. See Ronald Tobey and Charles Wetherell, "The Citrus Industry and the Revolution of Corporate Capitalism in Southern California, 1887–1944," *California History* 74 (Spring 1995): 6–21.

57. I. N. Hoag, "Address by I. N. Hoag to the Farmer's Institute," *The Rural Californian,* January 1895, 22; *The Rural Californian,* October 1893, 510; Los Angeles Chamber of Commerce, *Los Angeles: The Center of an Agricultural Empire* (Los Angeles: n.p., 1928).

58. United States Bureau of the Census, *Thirteenth Census of the United States Taken in the Year 1910* (Washington, DC: U.S. Government Printing Office, 1913); Clifford Zeirer, "The Citrus Fruit Industry of the Los Angeles Basin," *Economic Geography* (January 1934): 53–73.

59. A. J. Wells, "An Orange Empire," *Sunset,* January 1910, 112; Anthea Hartig, "'In A World He Has Created': Class Collectivity and the Growers'

Landscape of the Southern California Citrus Industry, 1890–1940," *California History* 74 (Spring 1995).

60. Victoria Padilla, *Southern California Gardens* (Berkeley: University of California Press, 1961), 236.

61. Thorstein Veblen, *Theory of the Leisure Class* (1899; reprint New York: Penguin, 1994), 132.

62. Walter Woehlke, "The Land of Sunny Homes," *Sunset,* March 1915, 470; Padilla, *Southern California Gardens,* 109; Knight, "Redlands," *Land of Sunshine,* February 1899.

63. Padilla, *Southern California Gardens,* 13; David Streatfield, *California Gardens: Creating a New Eden* (New York: Abbeville Press, 1994), 63; Los Angeles County Pomological Society, *Southern California Souvenir,* 30.

64. Vera Norwood, *Made from This Earth: American Women and Nature* (Chapel Hill: University of North Carolina Press, 1993), 119; see also Tyrrell, *True Gardens*; Thomas Dunlap, *Nature and the English Diaspora: Environment and History in the United States, Canada, Australia, and New Zealand* (New York: Cambridge University Press, 1999); Vail, *"Both Sides Told,"* 9–12.

65. Gilbert González, *Labor and Community: Mexican Citrus Worker Villages in a Southern California County, 1900–1950* (Urbana: University of Illinois Press, 1994), 66; Dolores Hayden, *The Power of Place: Urban Landscapes as Public History* (Cambridge, MA: MIT Press, 1995), 112–22.

66. Jeanne Carr, "Paper Relating to the Wild Flowers of California," box 2, Jeanne Carr Papers, HEH; "Partial List of Ornamental Trees and Shrubs at Carmelita, 1883," box 2, Carr Papers; Charles Saunders, *The Story of Carmelita* (Pasadena: A. C. Vroman, 1928), 29; Padilla, *Southern California Gardens,* 214.

67. John Muir, "The Hetch-Hetchy Valley," *Sierra Club Bulletin,* January 1908, 212, 217, 219–20.

68. Albert Carr, "The Genesis and Development of 'Carmelita,' 1886–1892," manuscript, box 9, Carr Papers. On the Spanish Fantasy Past, see Carey McWilliams, *Southern California: An Island on the Land* (1946; reprint Layton, UT: Gibbs Smith, 1973); and William Deverell, "Privileging the Mission over the Mexican: The Rise of Regional Identity in Southern California," in Michael Steiner and David Wrobel, eds., *Many Wests: Place, Culture, and Regional Identity* (Lawrence: University Press of Kansas, 1997), 235–58. Helen Hunt Jackson, *Ramona* (1884; reprint New York: Signet, 1988), 16.

69. H. Jackson, *Ramona,* 239. Indian resistance to this violent dispossession is traced in Albert Hurtado, *Indian Survival on the California Frontier* (New Haven: Yale University Press, 1988).

70. Richard Henry Dana, *Two Years before the Mast* (1840; reprint New York: Modern Library, 1964), 163; H. Jackson, *Glimpses of California,* 257–58.

71. On Kinney, see Starr, *Inventing the Dream,* 78–80; and Tyrrell, *True Gardens,* 42–47. Helen Jackson and Abbott Kinney, *Report on the Conditions*

and Needs of the Mission Indians of California (Washington, DC: U.S. Government Printing Office, 1883), 6–7, cited in Michael Dorris, "Introduction" to H. Jackson, *Ramona*, x; James J. Rawls, *Indians of California: The Changing Image* (Norman: University of Oklahoma Press, 1984); David Starr Jordan, "Helping the Indians," *Sunset*, January 1909, 57–61.

72. David Rich Lewis, *Neither Wolf nor Dog: American Indians, Environment, and Agrarian Change* (New York: Oxford University Press, 1994); letter from Richard Henry Pratt to Horatio Rust, 11 July 1890, box 9, Rust Papers; Rust, "Notes on the Mission Indians," 1893, box 10, Rust Papers.

73. C. W. Barton, "Riverside's New Indian School," *Sunset*, October 1901, 153–156; Lawton, "Brief History of Citrus," 10. Thanks to Tanis Thorne for bringing a photograph of Indian pickers to my attention.

74. Clipping, box 11, Rust Papers; "Petition to the Mayor and Council of South Pasadena," 15 June 1906, box 15, Rust Papers; McWilliams, *Southern California*, 223.

TWO. A CORNUCOPIA OF INVENTION

1. Ovid, *Metamorphoses* (New York: Penguin, 1955), 205.

2. John Steinbeck, *The Grapes of Wrath* (1939; reprint New York: Penguin, 1976), 447; Donna Haraway, "The Promises of Monsters: A Regenerative Politics for Inappropriate/d Others," in Lawrence Grossberg, Cary Nelson, and Paula Treichler, eds., *Cultural Studies* (New York: Routledge, 1992), 296–98.

3. A. S. White, "Address of Welcome," *Synopsis of the proceedings of the eighth Fruit Growers' Convention of the state of California* (Sacramento: Supt. State Printing, 1888), 72.

4. Ellwood Cooper, "President's Address," *Synopsis of the proceedings*, 69; Abbot Kinney, "Our Forests," *Synopsis of the proceedings*, 126; Richard Sawyer, "To Make a Spotless Orange: Biological Control in California" (Ph.D. dissertation, University of Wisconsin, Madison, 1990), 16–32; *Synopsis of the proceedings*, 136.

5. E. J. Wickson, *The California Fruits and How to Grow Them,* 7th ed. (San Francisco: Pacific Rural Press, 1914); the book went through seven editions between 1889 and 1914, selling over 19,000 copies. Tómas Almaguer, *Racial Fault Lines: The Historical Origins of White Supremacy in California* (Berkeley: University of California Press, 1994), 33; Leonard Pitt, *The Decline of the Californios: A Social History of the Spanish-Speaking Californians, 1846–1890* (Berkeley: University of California Press, 1966).

6. See www.pbs.org/weta/thewest/wpages/wpgs100/w13_007.htm, accessed 25 January 1998.

7. *Synopsis of the proceedings*, 77.

8. Ibid., 155.

9. Quoted in Rosaura Sánchez, *Telling Identities: The Californio* Testimonios (St. Paul: University of Minnesota Press, 1995), 10.

10. Luther Burbank with Wilbur Hall, *The Harvest of the Years* (New York: Houghton Mifflin, 1927), 26, 14; John Whitson, Robert John, and Henry Smith Williams, eds., *Luther Burbank: His Methods and Discoveries and Their Practical Application*, vol. 3 (New York: Luther Burbank Press, 1914), 7; Burbank with Hall, *Harvest*, 39.

11. Burbank with Hall, *Harvest*, 14; Orsi, "*The Octopus* Reconsidered: The Southern Pacific and Agricultural Modernization in California, 1865–1915," *California Historical Quarterly* 54 (Fall 1975): 203; Governor Pardee, "A Tribute," in California State Board of Trade, "A Toast, an Introduction, a Few Words, a Tribute at the Banquet in Honor of Luther Burbank" (Chicago: Oscar E. Bitmer Co. and Luther Burbank Publishers, n.d.), 7–8; definition cited in Peter Dreyer, *A Gardener Touched with Genius: The Life of Luther Burbank* (Berkeley: University of California Press, 1985), 13.

12. Ken and Pat Kraft, *Luther Burbank: The Wizard and the Man* (New York: Meredith Press, 1967), 130, 131; Evelyn Fox Keller, *A Feeling for the Organism: The Life and Work of Barbara McLintock* (New York: Freeman, 1982); Luther Burbank, "How to Produce New Trees, Fruits, and Flowers," paper read at the American Pomological Society meeting in Sacramento, 18 January 1895 (copy in Edward J. Wickson Papers, Special Collections, University of California, Davis); David Channell, *The Vital Machine: A Study of Technology and Organic Life* (Oxford University Press, 1991); Carolyn Merchant, *The Death of Nature: Women, Ecology, and the Scientific Revolution* (San Francisco: Harper and Row, 1980); William Harwood, *New Creations in Plant Life: An Authoritative Account of the Life and Work of Luther Burbank* (New York: Macmillan Co., 1907), 351; Kraft, *Luther Burbank*, 131.

13. Richard Levins and Richard Lewontin, *The Dialectical Biologist* (Cambridge, MA: Harvard University Press, 1985), 169.

14. Whitson, John, and Williams, *Luther Burbank*, vol. 1, 16; Dreyer, *Gardener*, 259; Whitson, John, and Williams, *Luther Burbank*, vol. 1, 141.

15. Quoted in Dreyer, *Gardener*, 98.

16. *Pacific Rural Press*, 6 January 1900, 4–5; for the economic geography of fruit, see Steven Stoll, "Insects and Institutions: University Science and the Fruit Business in California," *Agricultural History* 69 (Spring 1995): 219–21, and *The Fruits of Natural Advantage: Making the Industrial Countryside in California* (Berkeley: University of California Press, 1998).

17. Dreyer, *Gardener*, 84–88; Harwood, *New Creations*, 113–14.

18. Burbank with Hall, *Harvest*, 111–14; Dreyer, *Gardener*, 225, 226; William Friedland, *Social Sleepwalkers: Scientific and Technological Research in California Agriculture*, University of California, Davis, Department of Applied Behavioral Sciences, Research Monograph No. 13, 1974; Langdon Winner,

The Whale and the Reactor: A Search for Limits in an Age of High Technology (Chicago: University of Chicago Press, 1986), 26–27; Whitson, John, and Williams, Luther Burbank, vol. 3, 13.

19. Edward J. Wickson, "Luther Burbank: The Man, His Methods and His Achievements," Sunset, December 1901, 57; Sunset, May 1923; Southern Pacific Company, "Eat California Fruit: By One of the Eaters" (San Francisco: Southern Pacific Company, 1908), 10, 27.

20. Quoted in Kraft, Luther Burbank, 10; "To Breed Perfect Men and Women," New York American, 24 September 1905, Burbank Scrapbook, Wickson Papers; Barbara A. Kimmelman, "The American Breeders' Association: Genetics and Eugenics in an Agricultural Context, 1903–1913," Social Studies of Science 13 (1983): 184–85; Luther Burbank, "The Training of the Human Plant," Century 72, no. 1 (1906): 127.

21. Frank Todd, The Story of the Exposition (New York: G. P. Putnam's Sons, 1921), vol. 1, 17; vol. 3, 18; vol. 4, 237; Gray Brechin, "Sailing to Byzantium: The Architecture of the Panama Pacific International Exposition," California History 62 (Summer 1983): 120. See also Robert Rydell, All the World's a Fair: Visions of Empire at American International Expositions, 1876–1916 (Chicago: University of Chicago Press, 1984), 208–33; On the Shores of the Pacific: Opening of the Panama Canal—1915 (San Francisco: n.p., 1915?), cited in Bill Brown, "Science Fiction, the World's Fair, and the Prosthetics of Empire, 1910–1915," in Amy Kaplan and Donald Pease, eds., Cultures of United States Imperialism (Durham: Duke University Press, 1993), 149.

22. Kraft, Luther Burbank, 191; Burbank, "Evolution and Variation with the Fundamental Significance of Sex," in Race Betterment Foundation, Official Proceedings of the Second National Conference on Race Betterment (Battle Creek, Michigan: n.p., 1915), 50, 45.

23. Quoted in Jack Doyle, Altered Harvest: Agriculture, Genetics and the Fate of the World's Food Supply (New York: Viking, 1985), 51; see also Glenn E. Bugos and Daniel Kevles, "Plants as Intellectual Property: American Practice, Law, and Policy in World Context," Osiris 7 (1992): 75–104; Burbank, "Protection for the Originator of New Plant Creation," statement delivered to the National Nurserymen, 1904, in Wickson Papers; Burbank, How to Judge Novelties (1911), quoted in Dreyer, Gardener, 184; Senate, 71st Congress, 2nd Session, Calendar No. 307, Report No. 315, "Plant Patents," 2 April 1930, 3, copy in Charles Collins Teague Papers, UCLA.

24. "Plant Patents," 6–7, 3.

25. Ibid., 1; Doyle, Altered Harvest, 50.

26. Doyle, Altered Harvest, 48–49.

27. Advertisement for Armstrong Nurseries, CC, February 1939, 104. A second variety being sold at the nursery had been originated by Howard Frost

of the Citrus Experiment Station. The Robertson was a found variety, not one that had resulted through artificial hybridization. The Plant Patent Act apparently could work retroactively, for the Robertson sport had been discovered in a Redlands grove in 1925. See Leon Batchelor and Herbert Webber, eds., *The Citrus Industry,* vol. 1, *History, Botany and Breeding* (Berkeley: University of California Press, 1943), 538; "The Orange: The Fairest of Fruits Is Entertainingly Discussed: A Talk with Luther Burbank," n.d., copy in Wickson Papers.

28. Kraft, *Luther Burbank,* 182.

29. Quoted in ibid., 199.

30. See Harry Lawton and Lewis Weathers, "The Origins of Citrus Research in California," in Walter Reuther, E. Clair Calavan, and Glenn E. Carmen, eds., *The Citrus Industry,* vol. 5 (Berkeley: University of California, Division of Agricultural Science, 1989): 281–335.

31. Harry Lawton, "John Henry Reed and the Founding of the Citrus Experiment Station," in Esther Klotz, Harry Lawton, and Joan Hall, eds., *A History of Citrus in the Riverside Area* (Riverside, CA: Riverside Museum Press, 1989), 47; William Cumberland, *Coöperative Marketing: Its Advances as Exemplified in the California Fruit Growers Exchange* (Princeton: Princeton University Press, 1917), 200.

32. More than fifty sites, ranging from Tulare County to San Diego, were submitted. Box 9, Citrus Experiment Station Papers, Department of Special Collections, University of California, Riverside; Riverside *Daily Press,* 23 December 1914; *CC,* March 1925, 151; *CC,* May 1915, 23.

33. Esther H. Klotz, "Eliza Tibbets and Her Two Washington Navel Orange Trees," in Esther Klotz, Harry Lawton, and Joan Hall, eds., *A History of Citrus in the Riverside Area* (Riverside, CA: Riverside Museum Press, 1989), 22; John Beattie, *Other Cultures: Aims, Methods, and Achievements in Social Anthropology* (New York: Free Press, 1964), 219–24.

34. Klotz, "Eliza Tibbets," 21; *CC,* June 1944, 213.

35. Leon Batchelor and Herbert Webber, eds., *Citrus Industry,* vol. 2, *Production of the Crop* (Berkeley: University of California Press, 1948), 47–48 (as of 2002, the tree was still alive and well).

36. *CC,* July 1923, 302.

37. Herman Vincent Moses, "The Flying Wedge of Cooperation: G. Harold Powell, California Orange Growers, and the Corporate Reconstruction of American Agriculture, 1904–1922" (Ph.D. dissertation, University of California, Riverside, 1994), 129–30; Deborah Fitzgerald, *The Business of Breeding: Hybrid Corn in Illinois, 1890–1940* (Ithaca: Cornell University Press, 1990), 3.

38. F. Q. Story, "Remarks Made in Opening the Agricultural Conference," *University of California Chronicle* 20 (October 1918): 508.

39. *CC,* May 1918, 154; Jean François Lyotard, *The Postmodern Condition: A Report on Knowledge* (Minneapolis: University of Minnesota Press, 1984), 32.

40. See Philip Pauly, *Biologists and the Promise of American Life* (Princeton: Princeton University Press, 2000), 214–38; D. T. MacDougal, "The Trend of Research in Evolution and the Utilization of Its Concepts," *University of California Chronicle* 20 (October 1918): 532; *CC,* July 1916, 13.

41. *CC,* May 1918, 154; MacDougal, "Research in Evolution," 539.

42. Batchelor and Webber, *Citrus Industry,* vol. 1, 817, 867, 887.

43. Ibid., 818–19.

44. Jules and James Moore, eds., *Advances in Fruit Breeding* (West Lafayette, IN: Purdue University Press, 1976), 509; see also Frederick Davies and Gene Albrigo, *Citrus* (Wollingford, UK: CAB International, 1994), 17.

45. Howard Frost, "Polyembryony, Heterozygosis and Chimeras in Citrus," *Hilgardia: A Journal of Agricultural Science* 1 (May 1926): 365, 398.

46. Batchelor and Webber, *Citrus Industry,* vol. 1, 915.

47. *CC,* July 1937, 389, and December 1936, 52; Doyle, *Altered Harvest,* 48–55.

48. *CC,* February 1937, 142; Evelyn Fox Keller, *Secrets of Life, Secrets of Death: Essays on Language, Gender and Science* (New York: Routledge, 1992), 102.

49. Quoted in Keller, *Secrets,* 99–100.

50. Upton Sinclair, *Depression Island* (Pasadena: by the author, 1936), 111, 91; Philip Pauly, *Controlling Life: Jacques Loeb and the Engineering Ideal in Biology* (New York: Oxford University Press, 1987), 108–11, 180; see also Daniel Kevles, *In the Name of Eugenics: Genetics and the Uses of Human Heredity* (New York: Knopf, 1985), 187–92.

51. *CC,* July 1948, 380.

52. Batchelor and Webber, *Citrus Industry,* vol. 1, 902–4.

53. Ibid., 591; Davies and Albrigo, *Citrus,* 45.

54. Batchelor and Webber, *Citrus Industry,* vol. 1, 891 (emphasis added).

55. Ibid., vol. 2, 847, 719; Davies and Albrigo, *Citrus,* 54. On the "biological control of insects" in the citrus industry, see Sawyer, "Spotless Orange."

56. Davies and Albrigo, *Citrus,* 22–23.

57. Stoll, *Fruits,* 95.

58. *CC,* January 1937, 126.

59. *CC,* January 1931, back cover, and July 1938, back cover; regarding the wariness consumers had of insecticide residues on fruits, see James Whorton, *Before Silent Spring: Pesticides and Public Health in Pre-DDT America* (Princeton: Princeton University Press, 1974), 187–93.

60. Stoll, *Fruits,* 94, 106; see also Sawyer, "Spotless Orange," and Tyrrell, *True Gardens of the Gods: Californian-Australian Environmental Reform, 1860–1930* (Berkeley: University of California Press, 1999).

61. Fruit Growers Supply Company, *Annual Report, 1939* (Los Angeles: California Fruit Growers Exchange, 1940) (copy in Teague Papers); H. J. Webber, "Some Achievements of the Citrus Station during the Last Two Decades," in "Addresses Delivered at the 197th Meeting of the Synapsis Club Commemorating the 20th Anniversary of the Establishment of the Citrus Experiment Station," 5 June 1933, 68–72, typescript, box 2, Citrus Experiment Station Papers. See also Stoll, *Fruits,* 94–123.

62. *CC,* February 1938, inside front cover; Gilbert González, *Labor and Community: Mexican Citrus Worker Villages in a Southern California County, 1900–1950* (Urbana: University of Illinois Press, 1994), 155; Edmund J. Russell III, "'Speaking of Annihilation': Mobilizing for War against Human and Insect Enemies, 1914–1945," *Journal of American History* 82 (March 1996): 1512; U.S. Congress, Senate, Subcommittee of the Committee on Education and Labor, *Hearings on Senate Resolution 266, Violations of Free Speech and Rights of Labor,* 74th Congress, 2nd session (Washington, DC: U.S. Government Printing Office, 1939), part 69, 25283–85, 24759.

63. On the Riverside-based Food Machinery Corporation, see H. Vincent Moses, "Machines in the Garden: A Citrus Monopoly in Riverside, 1900–1936," *California History* 61 (Spring 1982): 26–35; *CC,* May 1944, back cover; John Dower, *War without Mercy: Race and Power in the Pacific War* (New York: Pantheon, 1986).

64. David Goodman and Michael Redclift, *Refashioning Nature: Food, Ecology and Culture* (New York: Routledge, 1991), 150; Sawyer, "Spotless Orange"; Stoll, "Insects and Institutions," 216–39; Goodman and Redclift, *Refashioning Nature,* 192, 202; *CC,* October 1943, 344. By the 1950s, Sherwin-Williams had become a multinational corporation with manufacturing plants in six countries in North and South America; "The 'Cover-the-Earth' symbol," an official company history explained, "can be seen in practically every part of the globe." Sherwin-Williams Company, *The Story of Sherwin-Williams* (Chicago: Lakeside Press, n.d.).

65. Rachel Carson, *Silent Spring* (Boston: Houghton Mifflin, 1962), 8; Webber, "Some Achievements," 70.

66. Laura Pulido, *Environmentalism and Economic Justice: Two Chicano Struggles in the Southwest* (Tucson: University of Arizona Press, 1996).

67. Haraway, "Promises of Monsters," 298.

THREE. PULP FICTION

1. *Rand-McNally Guide to the World's Fair* (Chicago, 1894), n.p., quoted in T. J. Jackson Lears, *No Place of Grace: Antimodernism and the Transformation of American Culture, 1880–1920* (Chicago: University of Chicago Press, 1983), 116; *Final Report of the California World's Fair Commission* (Sacramento:

A. J. Johnston, Supt. State Printing, 1894), 75. Fine reproductions of this and other crate labels can be found in Gordon T. McClelland and Jay T. Last, *California Orange Box Labels: An Illustrated History* (Beverly Hills: Hillcrest Press, 1985).

2. *Chicago Daily Inter-Ocean,* 10 September 1893, quoted in *Final Report,* 75; Henry Adams, *The Education of Henry Adams,* ed. Ernest Samuels (1907; reprint Boston: Houghton Mifflin, 1973), 344.

3. *Kate Field's Washington,* quoted in *Final Report,* 75.

4. John Gunther, *Taken at the Flood: The Story of Alfred D. Lasker* (New York: Harper, 1960), 160.

5. Roland Marchand, *Advertising the American Dream: Making Way for Modernity, 1920–1940* (Berkeley: University of California Press, 1985), 1–24; Richard Ohmann, *Selling Culture: Magazines, Markets, and Class at the Turn of the Century* (New York: Verso, 1996), 85–94; Don Francisco, "New Features in Advertising California Agricultural Products," *Proceeding of the Sixty-ninth Convention of California Fruit Growers and Farmers* (Sacramento: California State Printing Office, 1937), 104; William Leach, *Land of Desire: Merchants, Power, and the Rise of a New American Culture* (New York: Pantheon, 1993), 3.

6. *Sunset,* July 1917, 43, 82, quoted in Earl Pomeroy, *In Search of the Golden West: The Tourist in Western America* (New York: Knopf, 1957), 147.

7. James Collins, "Recollections of Harold Powell," letter to Lawrence Clark Powell, 3 May 1942, box 9, Powell Family Papers, UCLA.

8. *Labels: Suggestions for the Shipper Who Is Seeking to Give His Pack a Worthy and Effective Mark of Identification* (n.p.: Advertising Department of the California Fruit Growers Exchange, 1918).

9. Don Francisco, letter to local exchanges, 5 September 1916, box 22, Pasadena Orange Growers' Association Papers, HEH.

10. The original organization was called the Southern California Fruit Growers Exchange, but it changed its name to the California Fruit Growers Exchange in 1905. It now is officially called Sunkist Growers, and I have used that designation to refer to the CFGE; *CC,* July 1929, 359. On the rise of agricultural cooperatives, see Victoria Saker Woeste, *The Farmer's Benevolent Trust: Law and Agricultural Cooperation in Industrial America, 1865–1945* (Chapel Hill: University of North Carolina Press, 1998), esp. 24–31.

11. Kevin Starr, *Inventing the Dream: California through the Progressive Era* (New York: Oxford University Press, 1985), 133; *CC,* October 1937, 555. Sunkist as a quasi-corporation is examined in H. Vincent Moses, "G. Harold Powell and the Corporate Consolidation of the Modern Citrus Enterprise, 1904–1922," *Business History Review* 69 (Summer 1995): 119–55; and Ronald Tobey and Charles Wetherell, "The Citrus Industry and the Revolution of Corporate Capitalism in Southern California, 1887–1944," *California History* 74 (Spring 1995): 6–21.

12. Fruit Growers Supply Company, *Annual Report, 1939* (Los Angeles: California Fruit Growers Exchange, 1940), 10 (copy in Charles Collins Teague Papers, UCLA); William Cumberland, *Coöperative Marketing: Its Advances as Exemplified in the California Fruit Growers Exchange* (Princeton: Princeton University Press, 1917), 202. The standardization law provided for the establishment of an office of "inspector of fresh fruit and vegetables" in every county and at the plant quarantine border stations. Fruits were to be "well colored for the variety and locality, virtually uniform in quality, virtually free from insect and fungous pests, rots, bruises, frost injury, sunburn . . . and shall be virtually uniform in size." *Statutes of California: Forty-third Session* (Sacramento: California State Printing Office, 1920), 1222.

13. Minutes of Southern California Fruit Exchange, 10 June 1904, quoted in Rahno Mabel MacCurdy, *The History of the California Fruit Growers Exchange* (Los Angeles: G. Rice and Sons, 1925), 50; Cumberland, *Coöperative Marketing*, 8; William Cronon, *Nature's Metropolis: Chicago and the Great West* (New York: Norton, 1991), 362.

14. Spencer Olin, *California's Prodigal Sons: Hiram Johnson and the Progressives, 1911–1917* (Berkeley: University of California Press, 1968), 105–10; on the tension between modernist and agrarian attitudes, see Cletus Daniel, *Bitter Harvest: A History of California Farmworkers, 1870–1941* (1981; reprint Berkeley: University of California Press, 1982), esp. 15–70; Alfred D. Chandler, Jr., *The Visible Hand: The Managerial Revolution in American Business* (Cambridge, MA: Belknap Press of Harvard University Press, 1977).

15. Quoted in Cumberland, *Coöperative Marketing*, 135.

16. *CC,* December 1920, 66.

17. Ibid.; *CC,* June 1916, 6; on the distinction between markets and market places, see Jean-Christophe Agnew, *Worlds Apart: The Market and the Theater in Anglo-American Thought, 1550–1750* (New York: Cambridge University Press, 1986), 18–19.

18. *Sunset,* March 1907, 464–65.

19. *CC,* December 1920, 67, and April 1938, 239; CFGE, "Twenty-fifth Anniversary of Advertising: Sunkist Advertising and Marketing Plans for 1932–1933" (Los Angeles, n.p., 1932), 3.

20. *Labels,* 36, 9.

21. Leach, *Land of Desire,* 40–41, 48.

22. CFGE, "Twenty-fifth Anniversary," 26; John Kasson, *Amusing the Million: Coney Island at the Turn of the Century* (New York: Hill and Wang, 1978).

23. CFGE, "Twenty-fifth Anniversary," 27; Sunkist Growers, *1927–1928 Sunkist Advertising Plans,* 47–48, quoted in Josephine Jacobs, "Sunkist Advertising" (Ph.D. dissertation, University of California, Los Angeles, 1966), 181; *CC,* February 1937, 149.

24. CFGE, "Twenty-fifth Anniversary," 27; Leach, *Land of Desire,* 41.

25. CFGE, "Twenty-fifth Anniversary," 48; Jacobs, "Sunkist Advertising," 78; CFGE, "Twenty-fifth Anniversary," 48; *CC*, August 1940, 312.

26. Lizabeth Cohen, *Making a New Deal: Industrial Workers in Chicago, 1919–1939* (Cambridge: Cambridge University Press, 1990), 99–120; James Mayo, *The American Grocery Store: The Business Evolution of an Architectural Space* (Westport, CT: Greenwood Press, 1993), 87.

27. *Saturday Evening Post*, 8 April 1939, 68–69.

28. *CC*, July 1939, inside back cover; Francisco, "New Features," 104–9.

29. CFGE, "Twenty-fifth Anniversary," 3, 5; Mark Pendergrast, *For God, Country and Coca-Cola: The Unauthorized History of the Great American Soft Drink and the Company That Makes It* (New York: Scribner's, 1993), 108–24; *Ladies' Home Journal*, July 1918, quoted in Jacobs, "Sunkist Advertising," 96.

30. Jacobs, "Sunkist Advertising," 142–43, 191; *CC*, October 1939, 3; CFGE letter to local managers, 26 July 1916, box 9, Pasadena Orange Growers' Association Papers.

31. Victor Turner, *The Forest of Symbols: Aspects of Ndembu Ritual* (New York: Cornell University Press, 1967), 48, 49, 36.

32. On the social production of space, see Dolores Hayden, *The Power of Place: Urban Landscapes as Public History* (Cambridge, MA: MIT Press, 1995), esp. 15–43.

33. CFGE, "Twenty-fifth Anniversary," 8; *CC*, October 1925, 437.

34. *CC*, October 1925, 437; CFGE letter to local managers, 26 July 1916, box 9, Pasadena Orange Growers' Association Papers; Edward Street, "Don Francisco," *CC*, 1921, 241 ff., quoted in Jacobs, "Sunkist Advertising," 55–56; Jacobs, "Sunkist Advertising," 169; CFGE, "Twenty-fifth Anniversary," 8–11; *CC*, January 1929, 93.

35. Jan Cohn, *Creating America: George Horace Lorimer and the* Saturday Evening Post (Pittsburgh: University of Pittsburgh Press, 1989), 9.

36. Helen Damon-Moore, *Magazines for the Millions: Gender and Commerce in the* Ladies' Home Journal *and the* Saturday Evening Post, *1880–1910* (Albany: State University of New York Press, 1994), 1; see also Jennifer Scanlon, *Inarticulate Longings: The* Ladies' Home Journal, *Gender, and the Promises of Consumer Culture* (New York: Routledge, 1995); Cohn, *Creating America,* 166.

37. The premium offer was a way to assure that consumers bought Sunkist oranges, which would not be stamped with the company name until the mid-1920s; Jacobs, "Sunkist Advertising," 80.

38. *CC*, January 1920, 67; Jacobs, "Sunkist Advertising," 196.

39. Marchand, *American Dream*, 88–89.

40. Jacobs, "Sunkist Advertising," 184–85, 314.

41. *CC*, January 1940, 78; November 1939, 7; September 1940, 351; October 1938, 504.

42. *CC*, December 1920, 66; February 1938, 159; November 1931, 7; May 1931, 315. The opposing images parallel an important scholarly debate over whether advertisers have been all-powerful imperial agents ("captains of consciousness") or ordinary Americans have made creative, even liberatory uses of consumer culture. See Lears, *Fables of Abundance: A Cultural History of Advertising in America* (New York: Basic Books, 1994), 3–5; and Leach, *Land of Desire*, xiv.

43. Don Francisco, "How Sunkist Is Put Over," *CC*, June 1916, 6.

44. Lears, *Fables of Abundance*, 206; Francisco, "Cooperative Advertising, a Social Service as Well as a Powerful Sales Force" (1920), cited in Jacobs, "Sunkist Advertising," 110.

45. The advertisement, sponsored by the Crowell Publishing Company, also appeared in *Country Home. CC*, October 1939, 433.

46. *CC*, January 1939, 99.

47. Elliot Storke, *Domestic and Rural Affairs: The Family, Farm and Gardens, and the Domestic Animals* (Auburn, NY: Auburn Publishing Company, 1859), 162; E. J. Wickson, *The California Fruits and How to Grow Them*, 7th ed. (San Francisco: Pacific Rural Press, 1914), 358.

48. John Muir, *Our National Parks* (1901), in *The Writings of John Muir*, ed. William Cronon (New York: Library of America, 1995), 721.

49. MacCurdy, *History*, 59–62.

50. Gertrude Hobby of Ontario was the author of the poem. Ibid., 59.

51. *CC*, September 1937, back cover, and August 1939, 356.

52. *CC*, April 1918, 131.

53. Don Francisco, "The Story of Sunkist Advertising," typescript of a talk before the apprentice group of the J. Walter Thompson Company, 9 December 1948, box 9, Powell Family Papers, 20.

54. Harvey Levenstein, *Revolution at the Table: the Transformation of the American Diet* (New York: Oxford University Press, 1988), 147–60; *CC*, May 1918, 169; Kenneth Carpenter, *The History of Scurvy and Vitamin C* (New York: Cambridge University Press, 1986), 173–97.

55. *Saturday Evening Post*, 14 January 1922, 103.

56. Sunkist Growers, *The Story of the California Oranges and Lemons* (Los Angeles: California Fruit Growers Exchange, 1931), 25–26.

57. Levenstein, *Revolution*, 154.

58. Sunkist Growers, *The Story*, 26; Robert Berkow, ed., *The Merck Manual of Medical Information* (New York: Pocket Books, 1997); Audrey Ensminger et al., *The Concise Encyclopedia of Foods and Nutrition* (Boca Raton, FL: CRC Press, 1995), 2–6; Lears, *No Place of Grace*.

59. Francisco, "Story of Sunkist Advertising," 18; *CC*, September 1924, 404.

60. *CC*, November 1939, 36; November 1939, 36; August 1942, 272; May 1940, 217.

61. Martha Banta, *Taylored Lives: Narrative Productions in the Age of Taylor, Veblen, and Ford* (Chicago: University of Chicago Press, 1993); Marchand, *American Dream,* 298–99.

62. *CC,* May 1935, 207; *Good Housekeeping,* September 1922, 144.

63. CFGE, "Twenty-fifth Anniversary," 61.

64. Jean Baudrillard, *Jean Baudrillard: Selected Writings,* ed. Mark Poster (Stanford, CA: Stanford University Press, 1988), 172.

65. Jacobs, "Sunkist Advertising," 349; Carleton Beals, as quoted in Carey McWilliams, *Southern California: An Island on the Land* (1946; reprint Layton, UT: Gibbs Smith, 1973), 225. McWilliams noted that this was "a rather good description of Southern California"; *CC,* April 1940, 178.

66. Alfred Crosby, *Ecological Imperialism: The Biological Expansion of Europe, 900–1900* (Cambridge: Cambridge University Press, 1986); Donald Worster, *Rivers of Empire: Water, Aridity, and the Growth of the American West* (1985; reprint New York: Oxford University Press, 1992); Frieda Knobloch, *The Culture of Wilderness: Agriculture as Colonization in the American West* (Chapel Hill: University of North Carolina Press, 1996).

67. Dean Millen, interview by Jackie Malon, 16 July 1981, OHA–CSUF, 88–89; *CC,* October 1941, 371.

PART TWO. INTRODUCTION

1. Karl Marx, *The Marx-Engels Reader,* ed. Robert Tucker (New York: Norton, 1978), 75.

FOUR. THE FRUITS OF LABOR

1. Quoted in Marlene Park and Gerald Markowitz, *Democratic Vistas: Post Offices and Public Art in the New Deal* (Philadelphia: Temple University Press, 1984), 8.

2. For analyses of economics, immigration, and race, see George Sánchez, *Becoming Mexican American: Ethnicity, Culture and Identity in Chicano Los Angeles, 1900–1945* (New York: Oxford University Press, 1993), 17–37; and Matthew Jacobson, *Barbarian Virtues: The United States Encounters Foreign Peoples at Home and Abroad, 1876–1917* (New York: Hill and Wang, 2001). The terms historians use for ethnic and racial groups are inextricably involved in an identity politics. For ethnically Mexican citrus workers in the period before 1940 (some of whom were naturalized U.S. citizens, some of whom were not), I use the term *Mexicano* or *Mexicana.* I use *Mexican* to convey the point of view of a historical actor.

3. Park and Markowitz, *Democratic Vistas,* 139; Charles Stanley Chapman, interview by Nita Busby, 16 October 1975, OHA–CSUF, 19.

4. Chapman interview, 21.

5. Though rare, there were women (especially widows) who managed their own groves. See Grace Larsen, "Commentary: The Economics and Structure of the Citrus Industry: Comment on Papers by H. Vincent Moses and Ronald Tobey and Charles Wetherell," *California History* 74 (Spring 1995): 38–45.

6. CFGE letter, 4 March 1927, box 22, Pasadena Orange Growers' Association Papers, HEH.

7. Los Angeles Chamber of Commerce, *Los Angeles Today, April 1922: Los Angeles, Nature's Workshop* (Los Angeles: Neuner Corp., 1922). During the 1920s, chamber of commerce pamphlets issued by its Industrial Department used this phrase, while the Agricultural Department's publications referred to the city as "The Center of an Agricultural Empire" (and agriculture, it emphasized, was "an industry"). Los Angeles Chamber of Commerce, Agricultural Department, *Los Angeles: The Center of an Agricultural Empire* (Los Angeles: n.p., 1928); Richard White, "'Are You an Environmentalist or Do You Work for a Living?': Work and Nature," in William Cronon, ed., *Uncommon Ground: Toward Reinventing Nature* (New York: Norton, 1995), 173.

8. See Cletus Daniel, *Bitter Harvest: A History of California Farmworkers, 1870–1941* (1981; reprint Berkeley: University of California Press, 1982), 40–44.

9. Frederick Jackson Turner, "The Significance of the Frontier in American History" (1893), reprinted in John Mack Faragher, ed., *Rereading Frederick Jackson Turner* (New York: Henry Holt, 1994), 39; Sánchez, *Becoming Mexican American*, 38–62. Gilbert González notes that "citrus workers were a 'forgotten' people as far as historians were concerned," a status that his own fine study, combined with that of Matt Garcia, makes obsolete. See González, *Labor and Community: Mexican Citrus Worker Villages in a Southern California County, 1900–1950* (Urbana: University of Illinois Press, 1994); and Matt Garcia, *A World of Its Own: Race, Labor, and Citrus in the Making of Greater Los Angeles, 1900–1970* (Chapel Hill: University of North Carolina Press, 2002). The experiences of other workers in the citrus industry awaits the kind of attention González pays to Mexicano workers in Orange County. But see Paul Williamson, "Labor in the California Citrus Industry" (master's thesis, University of California, Berkeley, 1947); and Margo McBane, "The Role of Gender in Citrus Employment: A Case Study of Recruitment, Labor, and Housing Patterns at the Limoneira Company, 1893–1940," *California History* 74 (Spring 1995): 69–81.

10. Varden Fuller, "The Supply of Agricultural Labor as a Factor in the Evolution of Farm Organization in California," in U.S. Congress, Senate, Subcommittee of the Committee on Education and Labor, *Hearings on Senate Resolution 266, Violations of Free Speech and Rights of Labor,* 74th Congress, 2nd Session

(Washington, DC: U.S. Government Printing Office, 1939), 19777–898 (here-after cited as *Hearings*); Carey McWilliams, *Factories in the Field: The Story of Migratory Farm Labor in California* (1939; reprint Berkeley: University of California Press, 2000); Paul Taylor, *Labor on the Land: Collected Writings, 1930–1970* (New York: Arno Press, 1981); Tomás Almaguer, *Racial Fault Lines: The Historical Origins of White Supremacy in California* (Berkeley: University of California Press, 1994), 9.

11. *California Farmer,* 25 May 1854, 164, quoted in Fuller, "Supply of Agricultural Labor," 19802.

12. I follow Peggy Pascoe, who uses the term *racialism* "to designate an ide-ological complex" that held that "race, understood as an indivisible essence that included not only biology but also culture, morality, and intelligence, was a compellingly significant factor in history and society"; in "Miscegenation Law, Court Cases, and Ideologies of 'Race' in Twentieth-Century America," *Journal of American History* 83 (June 1996), 47–48. John Irish, "Labor in the Rural Industries of California," *Official Report of the Thirty-third Fruit-Growers' Convention* (Sacramento: California State Printing Office, 1908), 54; Daniel, *Bitter Harvest,* 64.

13. Charles Collins Teague, *Fifty Years a Rancher* (Los Angeles: Ward Ritchie Press, 1944), 141; McBane, "Role of Gender," 69–81.

14. Dean Millen, interview by Jackie Malon, 16 July 1981, OHA–CSUF; Robert Rydell, *All the World's a Fair: Visions of Empire at American International Expositions, 1876–1916* (Chicago: University of Chicago Press, 1984), 196.

15. Rydell, *All the World's a Fair,* 161; Carlos Bulosan, *America Is in the Heart* (1943; reprint Seattle: University of Washington Press, 1973), 99.

16. Donna Haraway, *Primate Visions: Gender, Race, and Nature in the World of Modern Science* (New York: Routledge, 1989), 9.

17. *Proceedings of the Seventh Western Divisional Meeting, Chamber of Commerce of USA, Ogden, Utah, October 1, 1929* (n.p., n.d.), 7 (copy in Charles Collins Teague Papers, UCLA); George Clements, "Mexican Immigration and Its Bearing on California's Agriculture," *CC,* November 1929, 3; "Labor for Citrus Orchards," *California Cultivator,* 5 September 1931, 208, quoted in Williamson, "Labor," 46. See also Marc Reisler, "Always the Laborer, Never the Citizen: Anglo Perceptions of the Mexican Immigrant during the 1920s," *Pacific Historical Review* 45 (May 1976): 231–54.

18. "Fruit of Men," *Fresno Morning Republican,* 14 February 1910, quoted in Williamson, "Labor," 40.

19. Daniel, *Bitter Harvest,* 15–39; Alexander Saxton, *The Indispensable Enemy: Labor and the Anti-Chinese Movement in California* (Berkeley: University of California Press, 1971); Daniel, *Bitter Harvest,* 55.

20. Steven Stoll, *The Fruits of Natural Advantage: Making the Industrial Countryside in California* (Berkeley: University of California Press, 1998), 154;

Daniel, *Bitter Harvest*, 61; Camille Guerin-Gonzalez, *Mexican Workers and American Dreams: Immigration, Repatriation, and California Farm Labor, 1900–1939* (New Brunswick: Rutgers University Press, 1994), 45–47.

21. Kevin Starr, *Inventing the Dream: California through the Progressive Era* (New York: Oxford University Press, 1985), 475.

22. Sánchez, *Becoming Mexican American;* quoted in Chris Friday, *Organizing Asian American Labor: The Pacific Coast Canned-Salmon Industry, 1870–1942* (Philadelphia: Temple University Press, 1994), 125. On the transition from local to national identities, see Benedict Anderson, *Imagined Communities: Reflections on the Origin and Spread of Nationalism* (New York: Verso, 1991).

23. Sucheng Chan, *This Bitter-Sweet Soil: The Chinese in California Agriculture, 1860–1910* (Berkeley: University of California Press, 1986), esp. 225–64; Sandy Lydon, *Chinese Gold: The Chinese in the Monterey Bay Region* (Capitola, CA: Capitola Book Company, 1985), 24, 68–70.

24. Quoted in Ronald Takaki, *Strangers from a Different Shore: A History of Asian Americans* (New York: Penguin, 1989), 197.

25. For strategies Japanese used to get around the Alien Land Act, see Valerie Matsumoto, *Farming the Home Place: A Japanese American Community in California, 1919–1982* (Ithaca: Cornell University Press, 1993); and Takaki, *Strangers from a Different Shore*, 205–12; Yoneko Dobashi Iwatsuru, interview by Diane Tappey, 19 January 1984, Honorable Stephen T. Tamura Orange County Japanese American Oral History Project, OHA–CSUF.

26. U.S. Bureau of the Census, *The Fifteenth Census of the United States: 1930, Agriculture* (Washington, DC: U.S. Government Printing Office, 1931); Bulosan, *America*, 272.

27. Patricia Limerick, "Disorientation and Reorientation: The American Landscape Discovered from the West," *Journal of American History* 78 (December 1992): 1045.

28. On "social apartness," see Martha Menchaca, *The Mexican Outsiders: A Community History of Marginalization and Discrimination in California* (Austin: University of Texas Press, 1995), 169; Carey McWilliams, *North from Mexico: The Spanish-Speaking People of the United States* (1948; reprint New York: Praeger, 1990), 199. See also Don Mitchell, *The Lie of the Land: Migrant Workers and the California Landscape* (Minneapolis: University of Minnesota Press, 1996).

29. U.S. Senator James D. Phelan, *Merced County Sun*, 11 July 1919, as quoted in Matsumoto, *Farming*, 84–85.

30. U.S. Department of Agriculture, Bureau of Plant Industry, G. Harold Powell et al., "The Decay of Oranges while in Transit from California," *Bulletin No. 123* (Washington, DC: U.S. Government Printing Office, 1908), 9; G. Harold Powell, "The Handling of Oranges in 1908," *Official Report of the*

Thirty-fourth Fruit-Growers' Convention (Sacramento: California State Printing Office, 1909), 61; Powell, "Decay," 20; Roosevelt's comments appear on a small printed page dated 7 May 1903, box 9, Powell Family Papers, UCLA; A. D. Bishop, "The Orange from Blossom to Car," *Official Report of the Twenty-eighth Fruit-Growers' Convention* (Sacramento: California State Printing Office, 1903), 68.

31. On scientific management, see David Montgomery, *The Fall of the House of Labor: The Workplace, the State, and American Labor Activism, 1865–1925* (New York: Cambridge University Press, 1987), esp. 214–56; and Harry Braverman, *Labor and Monopoly Capital: The Degradation of Work in the Twentieth Century* (New York: Monthly Review Press, 1974); *Riverside Enterprise,* 11 February 1904, cited in G. Harold Powell, *Letters from the Orange Empire,* ed. Richard Lillard (Los Angeles and Redlands: Historical Society of Southern California and A. K. Smiley Public Library, 1996), 60.

32. Box 2, folder 4, Powell Papers; quoted in Powell, *Letters,* 60.

33. Powell, "Decay," 26–27.

34. *Pacific Rural Press,* 16 September 1893, quoted in McWilliams, *Factories in the Field,* 71; Paul Wormser, "Chinese Agricultural Labor in the Citrus Belt of Inland Southern California," in Great Basin Foundation, ed., *Wong Ho Leun: An American Chinatown* (San Diego: Great Basin Foundation, 1987), 186–88. For a close look at migration patterns between a region within Guangdong and San Bernardino, see Harry Lawton, "The Pilgrims from Gom-Benn: Migratory Origins of Chinese Pioneers in the San Bernardino Valley," in Great Basin Foundation, ed., *Wong Ho Leun,* 141–66.

35. Williamson, "Labor," 34–36; but note that in the 1930s, U.S. researchers found the handling of fruit in China severely wanting. See Ira Condit, A. N. Benemerito, and Wang Hao Chen, "Citrus Fruits and Their Culture in Kwangtung Province, South China" (typescript, 1937), 13, 37–40, 44.

36. Powell, "Decay," 26; G. Harold Powell, *Coöperation in Agriculture* (New York: Macmillan Co., 1913), 214; Powell, "Decay," 28.

37. Powell, "Decay," 39; Frank Chase, "Biography of the Ethan Allen Chase Family," ca. 1933, holograph, Chase Collection, Riverside Municipal Museum, Riverside, California, 17–21, quoted in Ronald Tobey et al., *The National Orange Company Packing House: An Architectural and Technological History, 1898–1940* (Riverside: University of California, Riverside, Laboratory for Historical Research, 1991), 60; Powell, "Decay," 41–42.

38. Bishop, "The Orange from Blossom to Car," 67; see also B. M. LeLong, *Culture of the Citrus in California* (Sacramento: California State Printing Office, 1900), 121; Powell, "Decay," 28.

39. Martha Banta, *Taylored Lives: Narrative Productions in the Age of Taylor, Veblen, and Ford* (Chicago: University of Chicago Press, 1993), 14, 29;

Richard Lillard, "The 'Powell Era' in the Citrus Industry," in Powell, *Letters,* 7; Powell, "Handling of Oranges," 63.

40. Powell, "Decay," 39; Tobey et al., *National Orange Company,* 44, 92; see also Herman Vincent Moses, "The Flying Wedge of Cooperation: G. Harold Powell, California Orange Growers, and the Corporate Reconstruction of American Agriculture, 1904–1922" (Ph.D. dissertation, University of California, Riverside, 1994), and "'The Orange-Grower Is Not a Farmer': G. Harold Powell, Riverside Orchardists, and the Coming of Industrial Agriculture, 1893–1930," *California History* 74 (Spring 1995): 23–37; and Ronald Tobey and Charles Wetherell, "The Citrus Industry and the Revolution of Corporate Capitalism in Southern California, 1887–1944," *California History* 74 (Spring 1995): 6–21.

41. Powell, *Coöperation,* 214–15, and "Decay," 14.

42. Powell, "Decay," 46, 41.

43. Theodore Norman testimony, in *Hearings,* 20359. Under piecework, some workers could earn relatively high wages, while others would fall below the average amount of daily pay. See also *Hearings,* 20609.

44. Powell, "Decay," 39.

45. Millen interview, 2; on race and workplace hazards, see Andrew Hurley, *Environmental Inequalities: Class, Race, and Industrial Pollution in Gary, Indiana, 1945–1980* (Chapel Hill: University of North Carolina Press, 1995).

46. Alfred M. Boyce, "Insects and Mites and Their Control," in Leon Batchelor and Herbert Webber, eds., *The Citrus Industry,* vol. 2, *Production of the Crop* (Berkeley: University of California Press, 1948), 771–80.

47. Manuel Corona, interview by C. Esther, 1 June 1966, OHA–CSUF, 43; Hoyt Corbit, interview by Tom Peters, 30 April and 6, 10, 17, and 20 May 1968, OHA–CSUF, 54; Boyce, "Insects and Mites," 775.

48. Testimony of J. A. Prizer, manager of the Placentia Orange Growers Association, in *Hearings,* 20365; Alfred Esqueda, interview by Carmen Ressel, 10 June 1971, OHA–CSUF, 2; W. Ray Easton, interview by Vivian Allen, 17 October 1974, OHA–CSUF, 12.

49. Easton interview, 11. For the text of the Fruit Standardization Act, see *Statutes of California: Forty-third Session* (Sacramento: California State Printing Office, 1920), 1222.

50. *Hearings,* 20360.

51. Williamson, "Labor," 87–88.

52. While women have picked oranges in various periods, between 1904 and 1940 they were excluded from the groves and instead worked in the packing houses. Mills reported in 1914 that there was one woman picker in Tulare County, and she was considered a rarity. F. C. Mills, "A Supplementary Report concerning Orange Picking Conditions," typescript (CCIH, 1914), copy in Simon J. Lubin Papers, BL. See also Williamson, "Labor," 78; C. E. Rumsey,

"Packing House Equipment," *Official Report of the Thirty-fourth Fruit-Growers' Convention* (Sacramento: California State Printing Office, 1909); "How to Pick Fruit to Avoid Injuries," *CC,* January 1942, 68; Powell, "Decay," 23; H. O. Easton, "The Careful Handling of Oranges from Tree to Car," *CC,* December 1923, 45; F. G. Webber, "Careful Handling of Lemons from the Tree to the Car," *CC,* May 1923, 224; "Picking, Washing, Storage, Packing of Lemons," *CC,* May 1924, 264; Williamson, "Labor," 119; Esqueda interview.

53. Webber, "Careful Handling of Lemons," 224; Eldon Tackett, quoted in Dan Morgan, *Rising in the West: The True Story of an "Okie" Family from the Great Depression through the Reagan Years* (New York: Knopf, 1992), 174.

54. González, *Labor and Community,* 32.

55. Easton, "Careful Handling of Oranges," 45; Tobey et al., *National Orange Company;* Easton interview, 14.

56. Williamson, "Labor," 77; U.S. Department of Labor, Wage and Hour Division, "Report on the Citrus Fruit Packing Industry under the Fair Labor Standards Acts" (typescript, 1940), 31; Ruth Milkman, *Gender at Work: The Dynamics of Job Segregation by Sex during World War II* (Urbana: University of Illinois Press, 1987), 15–16; Vicki Ruiz, *Cannery Women/Cannery Lives: Mexican Women, Unionization, and the California Food Processing Industry, 1930–1950* (Albuquerque: University of New Mexico Press, 1987), 27.

57. In 1939, 40 percent of packing houses reported that over half of their female workforce was made up of "housewives" (the double entendre suggests that women were married to their workplace, and management certainly treated them as if it had paternal authority over them). U.S. Department of Labor, Wage and Hour Division, "Report on the Citrus Fruit Packing Industry," 15. The association required that single female workers be given permission to work by their fathers; married women needed permission from their husbands. Race segregation was mapped back onto the sex segregation, as white women and Mexicanas working in the same house often would be grouped apart, receiving oranges to pack from separate sizing machines.

58. Easton interview, 15.

59. Dr. G. L. McClelland, "Parts Played by Light, Color and Eyes in Packing House Grading," *CC,* March 1938, 195.

60. Much of Mills's diary (which is otherwise unavailable to scholars) is reproduced, and superbly contextualized, in Gregory Woirol, *In the Floating Army: F. C. Mills on Itinerant Life in California, 1914* (Urbana: University of Illinois Press, 1992), 27–28.

61. Mills diary, quoted in Woirol, *Floating Army,* 29, 28.

62. Quoted in González, *Labor and Community,* 34.

63. F. C. Mills, "The Orange Industry of Central California," typescript (CCIH, 1914), copy in Lubin Papers. Louis D. Brandeis and Josephine Goldmark, *Women in Industry,* as excerpted in Nancy Woloch, *Muller v. Oregon: A*

Brief History with Documents (New York: Bedford, 1996), 129, 124; Katherine Phillips Edson, "Industrial Problems as I See Them," typescript (n.d., n.p.), box 1, Katherine Phillips Edson Papers, UCLA.

64. González, *Labor and Community,* 35, 36. On female "cannery culture," see Ruiz, *Cannery Women,* 21–39.

65. Easton interview, 14, and "Careful Handling of Oranges," 45.

66. On labor, see Michael Denning, *The Cultural Front: The Laboring of American Culture in the Twentieth Century* (New York: Verso, 1996).

67. Tobey et al., *National Orange Company,* 59.

68. U.S. Bureau of the Census, *The Fifteenth Census of the United States: 1930, Agriculture;* Easton interview, 10.

69. On the process through which nature is commodified, see William Cronon, *Nature's Metropolis: Chicago and the Great West* (New York: Norton, 1991), esp. 97–147.

70. U.S. Department of Labor, Wage and Hour Division, "Report on the Citrus Fruit Packing Industry," 17; Carey McWilliams, *Southern California: An Island on the Land* (1946; reprint Layton, UT: Gibbs Smith, 1973), 220–21.

FIVE. "THE FINISHED PRODUCTS OF THEIR ENVIRONMENT"

1. Ellarene MacCoy, Mary Wolseth, and Edith Mills, "Maternal and Child Health among the Mexican Groups in San Bernardino and Imperial Counties," mimeograph (Sacramento: Bureau of Child Hygiene, 1938), 1–6; Michel Foucault, *The History of Sexuality: An Introduction* (New York: Vintage Books, 1990), 140–43.

2. See Daniel Rodgers, "In Search of Progressivism," *Reviews in American History* 10 (December 1982): 113–32; and William Deverell and Tom Sitton, "Introduction: The Varieties of Progressive Experience," in *California Progressivism Revisited* (Berkeley: University of California Press, 1994), 1–11; Kenneth Lockridge, *A New England Town: The First Hundred Years* (New York: Norton, 1970).

3. CCIH, "Wheatland Report," reprinted in Carleton Parker, *The Casual Laborer and Other Essays* (New York: Harcourt, Brace and Howe, 1920), 186.

4. On migratory farmworker bargaining power, see Cindy Hahomovich, *The Fruits of Their Labor: Atlantic Coast Farmworkers and the Making of Migrant Poverty* (Chapel Hill: University of North Carolina Press, 1997).

5. Parker, *Casual Laborer,* 180, 62.

6. Carey McWilliams, *Factories in the Field: The Story of Migratory Farm Labor in California* (1939; reprint Berkeley: University of California Press, 2000), 161.

7. Ibid., 172; Victor Turner, *From Ritual to Theatre* (New York: PAJ Publications, 1982), 70.

8. Parker, *Casual Laborer,* 88.

9. Ibid., 70, 193, 28.

10. Ibid., 88; E. A. Ross, quoted in Rodgers, "Progressivism," 125; Parker, *Casual Laborer,* 194. My interpretation draws on Don Mitchell, *The Lie of the Land: Migrant Workers and the California Landscape* (Minneapolis: University of Minnesota Press, 1996), 81.

11. Parker, *Casual Laborer,* 197; *CC,* March 1919, 129; Parker, *Casual Laborer,* 29.

12. Simon J. Lubin Papers, BL. An early draft also used the term *alien,* which was consistently crossed out and changed to *immigrants.*

13. Spencer Olin, *California's Prodigal Sons: Hiram Johnson and the Progressives, 1911–1917* (Berkeley: University of California Press, 1968), 77; David Herman, "Neighbors on the Golden Mountain: The Americanization of Immigrants in California" (Ph.D. dissertation, University of California, Berkeley, 1981), 320–21; on Roosevelt's views on immigrants, see Gary Gerstle, *American Crucible: Race and Nation in the Twentieth Century* (Princeton: Princeton University Press, 2000); "Labor Day Sermon," Grace United Church, 2 September 1924, printed in the *Sacramento Valley Union Labor Bulletin,* copy in Lubin Papers.

14. Address for the "Lincoln's Birthday International Musical and Folk Festival" before the San Francisco YMCA, typescript, copy in Lubin Papers.

15. In the midst of the Depression, Lubin called for the establishment of a Department of Nation Building in "To Save Capitalism: Our Economic Predicament Involving a Vicious Circle," December 1931, 24 (copy in Lubin Papers).

16. George Sánchez, *Becoming Mexican American: Ethnicity, Culture and Identity in Chicano Los Angeles, 1900–1945* (New York: Oxford University Press, 1993), 4–5; Oscar Handlin, *The Uprooted: The Epic Story of the Great Migrations That Made the American People,* 2nd ed. (Boston: Little, Brown, 1973); John Bodnar, *The Transplanted: A History of Immigrants in Urban America* (Bloomington: Indiana University Press, 1985); Lubin, address for the "Lincoln's Birthday International Musical and Folk Festival."

17. Gayle Gullet, "Women Progressives and the Politics of Americanization in California, 1915–1920," *Pacific Historical Review* 64 (February 1995): 75; Carrie Chapman Catt, "The Home and the Government," *The Yellow Ribbon* 1 (March 1907): 4; on "female moral authority" and the "Christian home," see Peggy Pascoe, *Relations of Rescue: The Search for Female Moral Authority in the American West, 1874–1939* (New York: Oxford University Press, 1990), esp. 32–69; Paula Baker, "The Domestication of Politics," in Linda Gordon, ed., *Women, the State, and Welfare* (Madison: University of Wisconsin Press, 1990), 55–91; see also Nancy Cott, *The Grounding of Modern Feminism* (New Haven: Yale University Press, 1987), esp. 162–65.

18. See Dolores Hayden, *Seven American Utopias: The Architecture of Communitarian Socialism, 1790–1975* (Cambridge, MA: MIT Press, 1976); CCIH, *Ninth Annual Report* (Sacramento: California State Printing Office, 1923), 8.

19. Samuel Wood, "The California State Commission of Immigration and Housing: A Study of Administrative Organization and the Growth of Function" (Ph.D. dissertation, University of California, Berkeley, 1942), 94; Lubin Papers; David Wrobel, *The End of American Exceptionalism: Frontier Anxiety from the Old West to the New Deal* (Lawrence: University Press of Kansas, 1993); CCIH, *A Report on Housing Shortages* (Sacramento: California State Printing Office, 1923), 14, 21.

20. George Sánchez, "'Go after the Women': Americanization and the Mexican Immigrant Woman, 1915–1925," in Ellen DuBois and Vicki Ruiz, eds., *Unequal Sisters: A Multicultural Reader in U.S. Women's History* (New York: Routledge, 1990); Sánchez, *Becoming Mexican American;* Gullet, "Women Progressives"; Vicki Ruiz, "'Star Struck': Acculturation, Adolescence, and the Mexican American Woman, 1920–1950," in Adela de la Torre and Beatríz Pesquera, eds., *Building with Our Hands: New Directions in Chicana Studies* (Berkeley: University of California Press, 1993): 109–29; David Gutiérrez, *Walls and Mirrors: Mexican Americans, Mexican Immigrants, and the Politics of Ethnicity* (Berkeley: University of California Press, 1995); James Barrett, "Americanization from the Bottom Up: Immigration and the Remaking of the Working Class in the United States, 1880–1930," *Journal of American History* 79 (December 1992): 98–120.

21. Herman, "Neighbors"; and Barrett, "Americanization," 1018–19. On the melting pot, see Lawrence Levine, *The Opening of the American Mind: Canons, Culture, and History* (Boston: Beacon, 1996), 105–20; on Ford, see Martha Banta, *Taylored Lives: Narrative Productions in the Age of Taylor, Veblen, and Ford* (Chicago: University of Chicago Press, 1993), 205–15; CCIH, *Ninth Annual Report,* 11.

22. Mary Gibson, "Americanization," in General Federation of Women's Clubs, "A Suggested Program for Americanization" (n.p., n.d.). The Commission reprinted this pamphlet.

23. CCIH, "Americanization: California's Answer" (Sacramento: California State Printing Office, 1920), 9; on Gibson, see Herman, "Neighbors," 372–78; Gullet, "Women Progressives"; and Judith Raftery, "Los Angeles Clubwomen and Progressive Reform," in William Deverell and Tom Sitton, eds., *California Progressivism Revisited* (Berkeley: University of California Press, 1994), 153–58; Mary S. Gibson, "The Immigrant Woman," *California Outlook,* 1914.

24. Raftery, "Los Angeles Clubwomen," 156; CCIH, "Americanization of Foreign-Born Women" (Sacramento: California State Printing Office, 1917), 24.

25. CCIH, "Foreign-Born Women," 20; Amanda Chase, "A Practical Plan for the Home Teacher," in CCIH, "Immigrant Education Leaflet No. 5: The Home Teacher" (n.p., n.d.), 3; CCIH, "Primer for Foreign-Speaking Women, Part 2" (Sacramento: California State Printing Office, 1918), 3; CCIH, *Second Annual Report,* 139–46, as quoted in Gullet, "Women Progressives," 83.

26. Pearl Ellis, "Americanization through Homemaking" (Los Angeles: Wetzel, 1929), 57; see also Suellen Hoy, *Chasing Dirt: The American Pursuit of Cleanliness* (New York: Oxford University Press, 1995), 115.

27. Gilbert González, *Labor and Community: Mexican Citrus Worker Villages in a Southern California County, 1900–1950* (Urbana: University of Illinois Press, 1994), 114–34; Gullet, "Women Progressives," 89; Roland Marchand, *Advertising the American Dream: Making Way for Modernity, 1920–1940* (Berkeley: University of California Press, 1985); Mary Douglas, *Purity and Danger: An Analysis of the Concepts of Pollution and Taboo* (London: Routledge and Kegan Paul, 1966); Hoy, *Chasing Dirt,* 100–17.

28. Sánchez, *Becoming Mexican American,* 102, and "'Go after the Women,'" 257; Ellis, "Americanization," 19; CCIH, "Primer for Foreign-Speaking Women: Part 1" (Sacramento: California State Printing Office, 1918), 19; Ellis, "Americanization," 26, 27.

29. Quoted in Banta, *Taylored Lives,* 111; Ellis, "Americanization," 22–23.

30. Harvey Levenstein, *Revolution at the Table: The Transformation of the American Diet* (New York: Oxford University Press, 1988), 147–60.

31. Ellis, "Americanization," 31.

32. CCIH, *Ninth Annual Report,* 25.

33. CCIH, "Advisory Pamphlet on Camp Sanitation and Housing, Revised 1926" (Sacramento: California State Printing Office, 1932), 5, 16.

34. Ibid., 73, 74.

35. CCIH, *Ninth Annual Report,* 36.

36. CCIH, "Advisory Pamphlet," 74.

37. Wood, "California State Commission," 189; Sacramento Region Citizens' Council, *Community Building Applied to the Sacramento Region* (August 1927, n.p.), copy in Lubin Papers; CCIH, *Ninth Annual Report,* 38.

38. Anthea Hartig, "'In a World He Has Created': Class Collectivity and the Growers' Landscape of the Southern California Citrus Industry, 1890–1940" *California History* 74 (Spring 1995): 106; Kevin Starr, *Inventing the Dream: California through the Progressive Era* (New York: Oxford University Press, 1985), 101; David Shi, *The Simple Life: Plain Living and High Thinking in American Culture* (New York: Oxford University Press, 1985), 189–95.

39. Herman Vincent Moses, "The Flying Wedge of Cooperation: G. Harold Powell, California Orange Growers, and the Corporate Reconstruction of American Agriculture, 1904–1922" (Ph.D. dissertation, University of California, Riverside, 1994), 108–9.

40. George Hodgkin, "Attractive Houses for Employes," *CC,* May 1921, 248; A. D. Shamel, "Housing the Employes of California's Citrus Ranches," part 5, *CC,* October 1918, 294, and part 4, *CC,* June 1918, 177, 176.

41. *CC,* December 1920, 51; J. B. Culbertson, "Housing of Ranch Labor," *CC,* May 1923, 234; Hodgkin, "Attractive Houses," 248.

42. Shamel, "Housing," part 5, 294; Banta, *Taylored Lives; CC,* March 1921, 147.

43. George Hodgkin, "Making the Labor Camp Pay," *CC,* August 1921, 354; González, *Labor and Community,* 118–19.

44. Culbertson, "Housing of Ranch Labor," 232; Hodgkin, "Making the Labor Camp Pay," 354; A. D. Shamel, "Housing the Employes of California's Citrus Ranches," part 2, *CC,* March 1918, 97, 96.

45. *CC,* November 1919, 12, 17.

46. Hodgkin, "Attractive Houses," 249; A. D. Shamel, "Housing the Employes of California's Citrus Ranches," part 1, *CC,* February 1918, 71.

47. González, *Labor and Community;* Matt Garcia, *A World of Its Own: Race, Labor, and Citrus in the Making of Greater Los Angeles, 1900–1970* (Chapel Hill: University of North Carolina Press, 2002), 71, 50.

48. "Coöperation at a Profit," *Fortune* (July 1936). For an account of the strike, see González, *Labor and Community,* 135–60.

49. Text of speech printed in *Sacramento Valley Union Labor Bulletin,* 30 November 1932, copy in Lubin Papers.

PART THREE. INTRODUCTION

1. U.S. Congress, Senate, Subcommittee of the Committee on Education and Labor, *Hearings on Senate Resolution 266, Violations of Free Speech and Rights of Labor,* 74th Congress, 2nd Session (Washington, DC: U.S. Government Printing Office, 1939), 573.

2. Reprinted in John Steinbeck, *Working Days: The Journals of* The Grapes of Wrath, *1938–1941,* ed. Robert DeMott (New York: Penguin, 1989), 151–52.

3. Paula Rabinowitz, *They Must Be Represented: The Politics of Documentary* (New York: Verso, 1994), 11–12.

SIX. A JUNGLE OF REPRESENTATION

1. Upton Sinclair, *I, Candidate for Governor: And How I Got Licked* (1935; reprint Berkeley: University of California Press, 1994), 19, 45.

2. Upton Sinclair, *I, Governor of California and How I Ended Poverty: A True Story of the Future* (Pasadena: by the author, 1933), 5; Einstein cited in Greg Mitchell, *The Campaign of the Century: Upton Sinclair's Race for Governor and the Birth of Media Politics* (New York: Random House, 1992), 176; Sinclair, *Candidate,* 19.

3. For the expulsion motif, see David Wyatt, *The Fall into Eden: Landscape and Imagination in California* (New York: Cambridge University Press, 1986). Sinclair, *Governor,* 3–4.

4. Michael Rogin, Ronald Reagan, *the Movie: And Other Episodes in Political Demonology* (Berkeley: University of California Press, 1987), 83; Sinclair *Candidate,* 5, and *Governor,* 15.

5. Sinclair, *Governor,* 4, and *Candidate,* 79.

6. Sinclair, *Governor,* 5; Upton Sinclair, *Depression Island* (Pasadena: by the author, 1936), 40; Sinclair, *Candidate,* 41.

7. Roland Marchand, *Advertising the American Dream: Making Way for Modernity, 1920–1940* (Berkeley: University of California Press, 1985), 207.

8. Sinclair, *Governor,* 9.

9. Hearst's remark appeared in newspapers across the country on 29 October 1934; Elaine Steinbeck and Robert Wallstein, eds., *Steinbeck: A Life in Letters* (New York: Viking, 1975), 9.

10. Robert Emery, "Thunder over California," campaign pamphlet published in Los Angeles by California's Organ of Democracy in newspaper format. Copy in the Richard Teggart Scrapbook of Republican Campaign Literature of 1934, BL. On Eisenstein's *Thunder over Mexico,* see Upton Sinclair, *The Autobiography of Upton Sinclair* (New York: Harcourt, Brace and World, 1962), 262–67.

11. Mitchell, *Campaign;* Upton Sinclair, *The Jungle* (1906; reprint New York: Penguin, 1985), 120, 145.

12. Rogin, Ronald Reagan, *the Movie,* xvii.

13. Sinclair, *Autobiography,* 126; *Jungle,* 149–50.

14. Sinclair, *Jungle,* 140–41, and *Autobiography,* 159–60.

15. On the relationship of *The Jungle* to the urban environmentalism of Jane Addams, see Robert Gottlieb, *Forcing the Spring: The Transformation of the American Environmental Movement* (Covelo, CA: Island Press, 1993), 65.

16. Cited in James Whorton, *Before* Silent Spring: *Pesticides and Public Health in Pre-DDT America* (Princeton: Princeton University Press, 1974), 104.

17. Reported in the *Pacific Rural Press,* 11 September 1897, 167; William Cronon, *Nature's Metropolis: Chicago and the Great West* (New York: Norton, 1991), 213.

18. Liberty Hyde Bailey, *The Holy Earth* (New York: Scribner's, 1915), 97–98, 100–101, 106–7.

19. Miles Orvell, *The Real Thing: Image and Authenticity in American Culture, 1880–1940* (Chapel Hill: University of North Carolina Press, 1989), xix, 6; Liberty Hyde Bailey, *The Outlook to Nature* (New York: Macmillan Co., 1911), 130; Kellogg cited in Harvey Levenstein, *Revolution at the Table: The Transformation of the American Diet* (New York: Oxford University Press, 1988), 93.

20. T. J. Jackson Lears, *Fables of Abundance: A Cultural History of Advertising in America* (New York: Basic Books, 1994), 137–38, 157.

21. Sinclair, *Autobiography,* 112, 115, 109, 112.

22. On Battle Creek, see Harvey Green, *Fit for America: Health, Fitness, Sport, and American Society* (New York: Pantheon, 1986).

23. Upton Sinclair, *The Book of Life* (Girard, KS: Haldeman-Julius Company, 1921), 8–9.

24. Ibid., 21, 24, 30, 196, 125.

25. Ibid., 195–96, 28.

26. Carey McWilliams, *Southern California: An Island on the Land* (1946; Layton, UT: Gibbs Smith, 1973), 298; Reuben Borough, "Reuben Borough and California Reform Movements," interview by Elizabeth I. Dixon, transcript, 1968, Oral History Program, University of California, Los Angeles, 118.

27. Borough interview, 118; Clarence McIntosh, "Upton Sinclair and the EPIC Movement, 1933–1936" (Ph.D. dissertation, Stanford University, 1955), 143–47; *EPIC News*, 16 July 1934, 6.

28. *EPIC News*, 9 July 1934.

29. *EPIC News*, 17 September 1934; Upton Sinclair, *The Way Out: What Lies ahead for America* (New York: Farrar and Rinehart, 1933), 2.

30. *EPIC News*, 18 August 1934.

31. *EPIC News*, 10 September 1934; Paul Taylor and Clark Kerr, "Whither Self Help?" *Survey Graphic*, July 1934, 328–31; Constantine Panunzio, *Self-Help Cooperatives in Los Angeles* (Berkeley: University of California Press, 1939).

32. Panunzio, *Self-Help*, 12; Clark Kerr and Arthur Harris, "Self-Help Cooperatives in California" (Berkeley: Bureau of Public Administration, University of California, 1939), 4; Panunzio, *Self-Help*, 65, 67–68.

33. *EPIC News*, 10 September 1934.

34. Sinclair, *Candidate*, 13, and *Governor*, 13.

35. Sinclair, *Candidate*, 122, and *Governor*, 16.

36. Sinclair, *Candidate*, 14.

37. On Smyth, see Kevin Starr, *Endangered Dreams: California through the Depression* (New York: Oxford University Press, 1996), 128–29. Thorstein Veblen, *The Engineers and the Price System* (1921; reprint New York: Augustus Kelley, 1965), 58, 1–26; see also William Akin, *Technocracy and the American Dream: The Technocrat Movement, 1900–1941* (Berkeley: University of California Press, 1977).

38. McWilliams, *Southern California*, 294; Robert Glass Cleland, *California in Our Time (1900–1940)* (New York: Knopf, 1947), 218; Akin, *Technocracy*, 151; Rogers cited in Mitchell, *Campaign*, 59–60 (McWilliams lists the pamphlets he collected during this period in *Southern California*, 301).

39. Blanche Greenough, "Towards Humanocracy" (Los Angeles: Winged Cycle Publishing Co., 1933), 37, 60 (this copy held at UCLA).

40. Borough interview, 107.

41. Sinclair, *Jungle*, 408, and *Autobiography*, 105.

42. Sinclair, *Jungle,* 253–60.

43. Ibid., 407–8; Sinclair claimed, "The last chapters in *[The Jungle]* contain everything in EPIC and more" (*Governor,* 33).

44. Upton Sinclair, *EPIC Answers* (Pasadena: by the author, 1934), 3, and *Governor,* 14.

45. Sinclair, *EPIC Answers,* 9.

46. Sinclair, *Governor,* 14, and *EPIC Answers,* 3.

47. Sinclair, *Governor,* 15.

48. Upton Sinclair, *Immediate EPIC* (Pasadena: by the author, 1934), 12–13; letter to the *Los Angeles Illustrated Daily News,* 22 June 1934, reprinted in Upton Sinclair, *The Lie Factory Starts* (Los Angeles: End Poverty League, 1934), 44.

49. This remark from the president's advisor proved damaging to Sinclair's campaign. See Carey McWilliams, "High Spots in the Campaign," *The New Republic,* 7 November 1934, 356.

50. *EPIC News,* 8 October 1934; Sinclair, *Governor,* 52, 15.

51. Borough interview, 118.

52. Reuben Borough, "I Secede: An Argument for a New Frontier," *The Survey* (1934), 353.

53. Ibid.

54. Ibid., 354; Borough interview, 114.

55. Ralph Borsodi, "One Way Out," *The New Republic,* 24 July 1929, 252–53.

56. Myrtle Borsodi, "The New Woman Goes Home," *Good Housekeeping,* February 1937, 52–56.

57. Ralph Borsodi, *The Flight from the City: The Story of a New Way to Family Security* (New York: Harper and Brothers, 1933), 21, 1–2.

58. Ralph Borsodi, *This Ugly Civilization* (New York: Simon and Schuster, 1929), 339, 328, and "Subsistence Homesteads: President Roosevelt's New Land and Population Policy," *Survey Graphic,* January 1934, 11.

59. Mitchell, *Campaign,* 333; David Dunaway, *Huxley in Hollywood* (New York: Harper and Row, 1989), 407; Aldous Huxley, *After Many a Summer Dies the Swan* (1939; reprint Chicago: Ivan Dee, 1993), 168, 278, 167.

60. R. Borsodi, "Subsistence Homesteads," 11. As Sinclair later explained, "Roosevelt had promised me his support, but I didn't feel it was a promise." Upton Sinclair, interviews by John Niven et al., 1963, transcript, Oral History Program, Claremont Graduate School, Special Collections, Claremont Colleges.

61. *EPIC News,* 24 September 1934.

62. Wallace cited in T. H. Watkins, *The Great Depression: America in the 1930s* (New York: Little, Brown, 1993), 193; Devra Weber, *Dark Sweat, White Gold: California Farm Workers, Cotton, and the New Deal* (Berkeley: University of California Press, 1994), 114–23.

63. Sinclair, *Immediate EPIC*, 11–12.

64. See Murray Edelman, *Constructing the Political Spectacle* (Chicago: University of Chicago Press, 1988).

65. Nathanael West, *The Day of the Locust* (1939; reprint New York: Signet, 1983), 192–93; on Los Angeles *noir,* see Mike Davis, *City of Quartz: Excavating the Future in Los Angeles* (1990; reprint New York: Vintage: 1992), 36–38; Borough interview, 107.

66. "C. C. Teague Urges Unity," *LAT,* 11 September 1934; his other comments appear in C. C. Teague, "The Future of American Democracy," Address before the Annual Dinner of Whittier College, 17 December 1934; "The Capitalist System and What Its Destruction Means to the Average Citizen," Annual Dinner of the Santa Paula Symposium, 8 April 1934; and "Government Control of Agriculture," Address at the Eleventh Annual Meeting of the Western Division of the United States Chamber of Commerce, 4 December 1934, all in Charles Collins Teague Papers, UCLA.

67. *LAT* pointed out the uniform position of newspapers in the state in an article titled "Nine-Tenths of State's Papers Oppose Sinclair," 22 September 1934.

68. Mitchell, *Campaign,* 200, 140, 189 (even with the help of BL staff, I was unable to locate the letter dated 11 September to Joseph Knowland cited by Mitchell).

69. John Logan and Harvey Molotch, *Urban Fortunes: The Political Economy of Place* (Berkeley: University of California Press, 1987), 32–33, 62–84; *LAT,* 17 October 1934; *LAT,* 15 October 1934. For a quite different use of photos of Llano ruins, see Davis, *City of Quartz,* 1–14; *LAT,* 17 October 1934.

70. See Kevin Starr, *Material Dreams: Southern California through the 1920s* (New York: Oxford University Press, 1990), 102–3.

71. Teague, letter to Knowland, 20 September 1934, cited in Mitchell, *Campaign,* 201; Mitchell, *Campaign,* 354–55; Don Francisco, "How Sunkist Is Put Over," *CC,* June 1916, 6.

72. On prohairesis, see Wlad Godzich, "Forward: The Time Machine," in Didier Coste, *Narrative as Communication* (Minneapolis: University of Minnesota Press, 1989).

73. *EPIC News,* 30 July 1934; Sinclair, *Governor,* 43.

74. Sinclair, *Candidate,* 22.

75. *Sacramento Bee,* 27 October 1934.

76. Anti-EPIC pamphlets are collected in the Teggart Scrapbook; Mitchell, *Campaign,* 229, 363.

77. Mitchell, *Campaign,* 344.

78. *LAT,* 30 October 1934.

79. Todd Gitlin, *The Whole World Is Watching* (Berkeley: University of California Press, 1980), 7.

80. Teggart Scrapbook.

81. Lears, *Fables of Abundance,* 142, 157.

82. Ibid., 93, 161; Marchand, *American Dream,* 9; Richard Surrey, "Advertising—Arch Enemy of Poverty and Disease," *Printers' Ink* 133 (10 December 1925): 49–52, cited in Lears, *Fables of Abundance,* 161.

83. Sinclair, *Book of Life,* 190–92; *LAT,* 13 October 1934; *LAT,* 4 October 1934; Starr, *Material Dreams,* 102.

84. On rainmakers, see Norris Hundley, Jr., *The Great Thirst: Californians and Water, 1770s–1990s* (Berkeley: University of California Press, 1992), 105–10; *LAT,* 29 July 1905, cited in Hundley, *Great Thirst,* 148.

85. Teggart Scrapbook; *LAT,* 5 October 1934; *LAT,* 20 September 1934.

86. Mitchell, *Campaign,* 511–12.

87. Sinclair, *Candidate,* 181; *LAT,* 5 October 1934; *Sacramento Bee,* 29 October 1934; *LAT,* 2 October 1934; *Oakland Post Enquirer,* n.d., in Belt Collection of Sinclair Material, Special Collections, Occidental College.

88. Sinclair, *Candidate,* 139, 142.

89. Ibid., 156; *Sacramento Bee,* 18 October 1934; *LAT,* 30 September and 24 October 1934.

90. See James Gregory, *American Exodus: The Dust Bowl Migration and Okie Culture in California* (New York: Oxford University Press, 1989), 39, 25, 267–78.

91. Gregory, *Exodus,* 9–10.

92. Ibid., 20.

93. Donald Worster, *The Dust Bowl: The Southern Plains in the 1930s* (New York: Oxford University Press, 1979), 13.

94. *Kansas City Star,* 30 October 1934, Belt Collection.

95. Larry Ceplair and Steven Englund, *The Inquisition in Hollywood: Politics in the Film Community, 1930–1960* (Berkeley: University of California Press, 1983), 92–93.

96. All quotes for *California Election News No. 1* and *No. 2* are from the newsreels themselves. For *California Election News No. 3* I have relied on Mitchell, *Campaign,* 499–501.

97. Mitchell, *Campaign,* 505; Sinclair continued to pursue the idea of making the "End Poverty Picture" (basically, *I, Governor* in film form), but he claimed that the big studios prevented this celluloid dream from materializing. See Upton Sinclair, *We, People of America, and How We Ended Poverty* (Pasadena: National EPIC League, 1935), 26–27; John McDermott, "An Agricultural Army," *Reader's Digest* 11 (June 1932): 92–93, as quoted in James Moore, "Depression Images: Subsistence Homesteads, 'Production-For-Use,' and King Vidor's *Our Daily Bread,*" *Midwest Quarterly* 26, no. 1 (1984): 29; King Vidor, *A Tree Is a Tree* (New York: Harcourt, Brace, 1953), 220.

98. Vidor, *Tree*, 224, 225.

99. Quoted in Mitchell, *Campaign*, 252. Having shown the film in New York in October, United Artists, probably under considerable pressure from the other studios, delayed its release in California until after the election. See Mitchell, *Campaign*, 253, 405–6.

100. *Los Angeles Examiner*, 4 November 1934; *EPIC News*, 22 October 1934, 3.

101. U.S. Congress, Senate, Subcommittee of the Committee on Education and Labor, *Hearings on Senate Resolution 266, Violations of Free Speech and Rights of Labor*, 74th Congress, 2nd Session (Washington, DC: U.S. Government Printing Office, 1939), 25179 (hereafter cited as *Hearings*); see U.S. Congress, Senate, Subcommittee of the Committee on Education and Labor, *Report, Violations of Free Speech and Rights of Labor*, Report no. 1150, 77th Congress, 2nd Session (Washington, DC: U.S. Government Printing Office, 1942), 573–636 (hereafter cited as *Report*).

102. *Hearings*, 20095–107, 20259, 25599; *Report*, 548–49; 610–16; *The United States Census of Agriculture: 1935, Vol. II* (Washington, DC: U.S. Government Printing Office, 1936), 943.

103. *CC*, November 1936, inside back cover; *Hearings*, 24599; *Pacific Rural Press*, 20 October 1934, 360; *Pacific Rural Press*, 27 October 1934, 323.

104. *Hearings*, 24603.

105. *Report*, 585; Richard Neuberger, "Who Are the Associated Farmers," *Survey Graphic*, September 1939, 518.

106. *Report*, 574, 1530.

107. Letter from Guernsey Frazer to CFGE, 11 December 1934, *Hearings*, 20613; letter from Guernsey Frazer to George Clements, 5 January 1935, *Hearings*, 20257; Frazer to CFGE, 11 December 1934, *Hearings*, 20614; *Hearings*, 25130–31.

108. Louis Reccow, "The Orange County Citrus Strikes of 1935–1936: The 'Forgotten People' in Revolt" (Ph.D. dissertation, University of Southern California, 1971), 200. See also Gilbert González, *Labor and Community: Mexican Citrus Worker Villages in a Southern California County, 1900–1950* (Urbana: University of Illinois Press, 1994), 135–60; Clara Engle, "Orange County Citrus Strike, 1936: Historical Analysis and Social Conflict" (master's thesis, California State University, Fullerton, 1975); Gilbert González, *Mexican Consuls and Labor Organizing: Imperial Politics in the American Southwest* (Austin: University of Texas Press, 1999).

109. *Report*, 1543; *Santa Ana Register*, 7 July 1936, and *LAT*, 8 July 1936, as quoted in Reccow, "Orange County," 177.

110. Frank Stokes, "Let the Mexicans Organize!" *The Nation*, 19 December 1936.

111. Ibid.

112. Carey McWilliams, "Gunkist Oranges," *Pacific Weekly,* 20 July 1936, 38–39.

113. John Steinbeck, "Starvation under the Orange Trees," *Monterey Trader,* 15 April 1938.

SEVEN. A RECORD OF EDEN'S EROSION

1. Kevin Starr, *Endangered Dreams: California through the Depression* (New York: Oxford University Press, 1996), 177; *This Land Is Your Land: The Life and Legacy of Woody Guthrie,* Smithsonian Institution Traveling Exhibit; U.S. Congress, House, Select Committee to Investigate the Interstate Migration of Destitute Citizens, *Interstate Migration: Hearings before the Select Committee to Investigate Migration of Destitute Citizens, House of Representatives, Seventy-sixth Congress, Third Session, Pursuant to H. Res. 63 and H. Res. 491* (Washington, DC: U.S. Government Printing Office, 1940–41), 2214; *CC,* September 1937, 492.

2. Recording made in Visalia 27 August 1941, from Voices from the Dust Bowl: The Charles L. Todd and Robert Sonkin Migrant Worker Collection, 1940–1941, American Folklife Center, Library of Congress, cited in James Gregory, *American Exodus: The Dust Bowl Migration and Okie Culture in California* (New York: Oxford University Press, 1989), 21; John Webb and Malcolm Brown, *Migrant Families* (Washington, DC: U.S. Government Printing Office, 1938), 12, 139; "The Prodical's *[sic]* Return," *The Covered Wagon* (Indio), 4 February 1940, cited in Gregory, *Exodus,* 20; John Steinbeck, *The Grapes of Wrath* (1939; reprint New York: Penguin, 1976), 107, 118.

3. Paul Taylor, "Again the Covered Wagon," *Survey Graphic,* July 1935.

4. On "repatriation," see Camille Guerin-Gonzalez, *Mexican Workers and American Dreams: Immigration, Repatriation, and California Farm Labor, 1900–1939* (New Brunswick: Rutgers University Press, 1994); and Francisco Balderrama and Raymond Rodríguez, *Decade of Betrayal: Mexican Repatriation in the 1930s* (Albuquerque: University of New Mexico Press, 1995); Paul Taylor, "From the Ground Up," *Survey Graphic,* September 1936, 537; Taylor "Significant Activities of the Resettlement Administration in the West," 4 March radio address carried by NBC blue network, ca. 1935, in box 23, collection 1243, Carey McWilliams Papers, UCLA. Dorothea Lange and Paul Taylor, *An American Exodus: A Record of Human Erosion* (New York: Reynal and Hitchcock, 1939); letter from E. M. Proctor to Dorothea Lange, 31 December 1936, Roy Emerson Stryker Papers, Farm Security Administration–Office of War Information Written Records, FSA–OWI Collection, PP–LC. The term *social erosion* was first used in 1934. A photograph appeared under the title "Human Erosion" in the Boston Sunday *Herald* on 22 November 1936, the first instance of this usage that I have been able to find.

5. Carey McWilliams, *The Education of Carey McWilliams* (New York: Simon and Schuster, 1979), 74; Victor Turner, *From Ritual to Theatre* (New York: PAJ Publications, 1982), 70, and *Anthropology of Performance* (New York: PAJ Publications, 1988), 75.

6. Lange and Taylor, *American Exodus,* 6.

7. Roy Stryker and Nancy Wood, *In This Proud Land: America 1935–1943 as Seen in the FSA Photographs,* 9, cited in Lawrence Levine, "The Historian and the Icon," in Carl Fleischauer and Beverly Brannan, eds., *Documenting America, 1935–1943* (Berkeley: University of California Press, 1988), 40; Williams cited in Alan Trachtenberg, "Walker Evans' America: A Documentary Invention," in David Featherstone, ed., *Observations: Essays on Documentary Photography* (Carmel, CA: Friends of Photography, 1984), 59; Edward Steichen, "The F.S.A. Photographers," *U.S. Camera* (1939): 44.

8. James Curtis, *Mind's Eye, Mind's Truth: FSA Photography Reconsidered* (Philadelphia: Temple University Press, 1989), 47; Miles Orvell, *The Real Thing: Image and Authenticity in American Culture, 1880–1940* (Chapel Hill: University of North Carolina Press, 1989), 198–239; William Stott, *Documentary Expression and Thirties America* (1973; reprint Chicago: University of Chicago Press, 1986).

9. Roy Stryker, "Documentary Photography," in *The Complete Photographer,* ed. Willard Morgan, vol. 4, 1369, cited in Orvell, *The Real Thing,* 230; Fredric Jameson, *Postmodernism: Or, the Cultural Logic of Late Capitalism* (Durham, North Carolina: Duke University Press, 1991), 8.

10. Stryker quoted in Hartley Howe, "You Have Seen Their Pictures," *Survey Graphic,* April 1940, 236; Henri Lefebvre, *The Production of Space,* trans. Donald Nicholson-Smith (Cambridge, MA: Blackwell, 1991). Though Lefebvre argues that photography often obscured the production of space (97), Lange's exposed it; Alan Trachtenberg, "From Image to Story: Reading the File," in Carl Fleischauer and Beverly Brannan, eds., *Documenting America, 1935–1943* (Berkeley: University of California Press, 1988), 65.

11. James Agee and Walker Evans, *Let Us Now Praise Famous Men* (1942; reprint Boston: Houghton Mifflin, 1960), 12; on the boots, see Stott, *Documentary Expression,* 273; and Jameson, *Postmodernism,* 6–11; Stryker and Wood, *In This Proud Land,* 11, 14, cited in Levine, "The Historian and the Icon," 38.

12. Roland Barthes, "L'effet de réel," *Communications* 11 (1968): 84–89, cited in Christopher Prendergast, *The Order of Mimesis* (New York: Cambridge University Press, 1986), 62; James Guimond, *American Photography and the American Dream* (Chapel Hill: University of North Carolina Press, 1991), 99–148.

13. Charles Shindo has argued that Steinbeck and Lange, among others, "presented the migrants' story . . . to further their own agendas rather than the

goals of the migrants"; *Dust Bowl Migrants in the American Imagination* (Lawrence: University Press of Kansas, 1997), 2. Carol Shloss makes a similar argument about Steinbeck in *In Visible Light: Photography and the American Writer, 1840–1940* (New York: Oxford University Press, 1987), 201–29. Letter from Lange to Stryker, 13 March 1939, Stryker Papers.

14. Taylor, "Covered Wagon."

15. Archibald MacLeish, *Land of the Free* (New York: Harcourt, Brace, 1938), 82–84.

16. Gregory, *Exodus,* 11. Gregory has set the record straight, but I will continue to use the term *Dust Bowl migrants* because it reflects the cultural reality of how those migrants were perceived in the 1930s.

17. *McCall's,* July 1936, copy in Farm Security Administration Scrapbook, FSA–OWI Written Records, FSA–OWI Collection, PP–LC.

18. Donald Worster, *The Dust Bowl: The Southern Plains in the 1930s* (New York: Oxford University Press, 1979), 5, 54–63.

19. Carle Zimmerman and Nathan Whetten, *Rural Families on Relief* (Washington, DC: U.S. Government Printing Office, 1938), 93. Lange's caption can be found in RA 2534-E, FSA–OWI Collection, PP–LC.

20. Lange and Taylor, *American Exodus,* 124.

21. *Pacific Rural Press,* 17 December 1927, cited in Varden Fuller, "The Supply of Agricultural Labor as a Factor in the Evolution of Farm Organization in California," U.S. Congress, Senate, Subcommittee of the Committee on Education and Labor, *Hearings on Senate Resolution 266, Violations of Free Speech and Rights of Labor,* 74th Congress, 2nd Session (Washington, DC: U.S. Government Printing Office, 1939), 19869; Guimond, *American Photography,* 112–16.

22. Henry Adams, *The Education of Henry Adams* (1907; reprint Boston: Houghton Mifflin, 1973), 343; Devra Weber, *Dark Sweat, White Gold: California Farm Workers, Cotton, and the New Deal* (Berkeley: University of California Press, 1994), 180–84; Robert Burke, *Olson's New Deal for California* (Berkeley: University of California Press, 1953), 22.

23. LC-USF34-018383-E, FSA–OWI Collection, PP–LC.

24. Roger Sprague, "The Picture," *The Californians,* April 1996, 39; Dorothea Lange, "The Assignment I'll Never Forget," *Popular Photography,* February 1961, as cited in Milton Meltzer, *Dorothea Lange: A Photographer's Life* (New York: Farrar, Straus, and Giroux, 1978), 132–33.

25. Cited in Meltzer, *Dorothea Lange,* 133.

26. *San Francisco News,* 10 March 1936; *San Francisco News,* 11 March 1936; Milton Meltzer mistakenly thought that the first time the photograph was published was in *Survey Graphic* in September 1936, and this is repeated in Starr, *Endangered Dreams.* Though Starr clearly understands Lange's ultimate commitment to the people she represented, others have taken this (erroneous)

publication date to mean that Lange withheld the masterpiece, and have interpreted that as a sign of her placing art over the people she photographed; *Midweek Pictorial,* 17 October 1936, in FSA Scrapbook.

27. *Survey Graphic,* September 1936; *New York Times,* 23 August 1983; Sprague, "The Picture," 39; Wendy Kozol, "Madonnas of the Fields: Photography, Gender, and 1930s Farm Relief," *Genders* (Summer 1988): 1.

28. *Scholastic,* 26 September 1936, in FSA Scrapbook; R. S. Kifer, H. L. Stewart, and the Bureau of Agricultural Economics, *Farming Hazards in the Drought Area* (Washington, DC: U.S. Government Printing Office, 1938), facing page xvi.

29. Sprague, "The Picture," 38.

30. John Steinbeck, "The Harvest Gypsies," *San Francisco News,* 5 October 1936, and *The Harvest Gypsies* (1936; reprint Berkeley, CA: Heyday Books, 1988), 55; Gary Gerstle, *American Crucible: Race and Nation in the Twentieth Century* (Princeton: Princeton University Press, 2000).

31. Simon J. Lubin Society papers, BL.

32. Steinbeck, *Harvest Gypsies,* 22–23.

33. Michael Denning, *The Cultural Front: The Laboring of American Culture in the Twentieth Century* (New York: Verso, 1996), 265–68; *Grapes of Wrath,* 284–85, 265.

34. Citizens Association, cited in Gregory, *Exodus,* 89; Jackson Benson, *The True Adventures of John Steinbeck, Writer* (New York: Penguin, 1984), 337; Gregory, *Exodus,* 101–2; *California* cited in Walter Stein, *California and the Dust Bowl Migration* (Westport, CT: Greenwood Press, 1973), 102.

35. LC-USF34-000825-ZC, FSA–OWI Collection, PP–LC.

36. Edith Lowry, "They Starve That We May Eat" (New York: Council of Women for Home Missions, 1938).

37. Steinbeck, *Harvest Gypsies,* 24.

38. See Peter Dreyer, *A Gardener Touched with Genius: The Life of Luther Burbank* (Berkeley: University of California Press, 1985), 225–26.

39. Charles Nordhoff, *California: For Health, Pleasure, and Residence* (New York: Harper and Brothers, 1872), 200, 187.

40. Nordhoff, *California: For Health, Pleasure, and Residence,* new ed. (New York: Harper and Brothers, 1882), 97–98; *Pacific Rural Press,* 9 October 1897, 220; J. Parker Whitney, "Educational Orange Growing," *Sunset,* August 1906, 161–70.

41. See Gregory Woirol, *In the Floating Army: F. C. Mills on Itinerant Life in California, 1914* (Urbana: University of Illinois Press, 1992), 32–37; F. C. Mills, "A Supplementary Report concerning Orange Picking Conditions," typescript (CCIH, 1914), copy in Simon J. Lubin Papers, BL.

42. F. C. Mills, "The Orange Industry of Central California," typescript (CCIH, 1914), copy in Lubin Papers; Woirol, *Floating Army,* 29.

43. William Preston, *Vanishing Landscapes: Land and Life in the Tulare Lake Basin* (Berkeley: University of California Press, 1981), 194, 197; Gregory, *Exodus,* 78; Steinbeck, *Harvest Gypsies,* 23–24, 20.

44. See LC-USF34-018875-E, LC-USF34-018874-E, and LC-USF34-018872-E, all in FSA–OWI Collection, PP–LC.

45. See LC-USZ62-38847, FSA–OWI Collection, PP–LC; Preston, *Vanishing Landscapes,* 194; Herbert Floercky and Lee Shippey, *California Progress* (Sacramento: California State Department of Education, 1936), 1, 91.

46. See Paul Taylor, "Central Valley Water Project: Water and Land," and "Reclamation and Exploitation," reprinted in Taylor, *Essays on Land, Water and the Law in California* (New York: Arno Press, 1979); Donald Worster, *Rivers of Empire: Water, Aridity, and the Growth of the American West* (1985; reprint New York: Oxford University Press, 1992), 5; Ickes quoted in *Rural Observer,* 18 November 1939.

47. Steinbeck, *Grapes of Wrath,* 429–30.

48. CFGE, *Sunkist Advertising News* (August 1941), copy in George Clements Papers, UCLA. See also Charles Collins Teague, *Fifty Years a Rancher* (Los Angeles: Ward Ritchie Press, 1944).

49. *Rural Observer,* 2 December 1939.

50. *Rural Observer,* March 1939; Lange and Taylor, *American Exodus,* 127; see negative LC-USF34-19576-E, FSA–OWI Collection, PP–LC. A few months before Lange took her picture of the Bank of America billboard, the La Follette committee had apparently decided to give up its earlier plans to come to California and investigate the Associated Farmers. With his ear tuned to the buzz in Washington, Stryker wrote to Lange about the lobbying efforts he felt were derailing the committee, explaining, "The Bank of America is a powerful organization, and wields much influence outside of the State of California." Stryker to Lange, 2 February 1939, Stryker Papers.

51. The classic statement on simulation in postmodernity is Jean Baudrillard, "Simulacra and Simulations," in *Jean Baudrillard: Selected Writings,* ed. Mark Poster (Stanford, CA: Stanford University Press, 1988), 166–84.

52. Letter from Stryker to Lange, November 1939, Stryker Papers; *Life,* 5 June 1939 and 19 February 1940.

53. Letter from Edwin Lock to Stryker, 28 April 1939, Stryker Papers.

54. John Steinbeck, "The Crop Picker's Fight for Life in a Land of Plenty," *St. Louis Post Dispatch,* 17 April 1938, FSA Scrapbook. This article is the same one that appeared in the *Monterey Trader* under the title "Starvation under the Orange Trees."

55. *Rural Observer; The Grapes of Wrath* (Twentieth Century Fox, 1940).

56. Lot 346, FSA–OWI Collection, PP–LC; on the subsistence farm program, see Shindo, *Dust Bowl Migrants,* 23; FSA–OWI Collection, PP–LC.

57. "The Hub," 22 December 1939, newsletter published by the Visalia Migratory Labor Camp, copy in box 23, collection 1243, McWilliams Papers.

EIGHT. "A PROFIT CANNOT BE TAKEN FROM AN ORANGE"

1. Paul Armstrong, "The Business of Agriculture," *CC,* June 1940, 246; Warren French, ed., *A Companion to* The Grapes of Wrath (New York: Viking, 1963), 106.

2. Carey McWilliams debated AF vice president Philip Bancroft in a "town meeting" radio debate aired on 7 March 1940. Box 5, scrapbook 9, collection 1319, Carey McWilliams Papers, UCLA.

3. See Carol Shloss, *In Visible Light: Photography and the American Writer, 1840–1940* (New York: Oxford University Press, 1987); and Charles Shindo, *Dust Bowl Migrants in the American Imagination* (Lawrence: University Press of Kansas, 1997); Marx cited in Paula Rabinowitz, *They Must Be Represented: The Politics of Documentary* (New York: Verso, 1994), 10.

4. James Gregory, *American Exodus: The Dust Bowl Migration and Okie Culture in California* (New York: Oxford University Press, 1989), 111; Dan Morgan, *Rising in the West: The True Story of an "Okie" Family from the Great Depression through the Reagan Years* (New York: Knopf, 1992), 134.

5. Texas migrant quoted in Dorothea Lange and Paul Taylor, *An American Exodus: A Record of Human Erosion* (New York: Reynal and Hitchcock, 1939), 68; Jackson Benson, "'To Tom, Who Lived It': John Steinbeck and the Man from Weedpatch," *Journal of Modern Literature* (April 1976): 87–88.

6. Tom Cameron, "'Grapes of Wrath' Author Guards Self from Threats at Moody Gulch," *LAT,* 9 July 1939.

7. Ibid.; Jackson Benson, *The True Adventures of John Steinbeck, Writer* (New York: Penguin, 1984), 270.

8. Quoted in Benson, *True Adventures,* 429 (my emphasis); John Steinbeck, *The Log from the* Sea of Cortez (1941; reprint New York: Penguin, 1977), 4, 201, 175–76.

9. James Clifford, *The Predicament of Culture: Twentieth-Century Ethnography, Literature, and Art* (Cambridge, MA: Harvard University Press, 1988), 36.

10. Quoted in Benson, *True Adventures,* 364; *LAT,* 9 July 1939.

11. Benson, *True Adventures,* 359, and "'To Tom,'" 183.

12. Gilbert González, *Labor and Community: Mexican Citrus Worker Villages in a Southern California County, 1900–1950* (Urbana: University of Illinois Press, 1994), 74; Elaine Steinbeck and Robert Wallstein, eds., *Steinbeck: A Life in Letters* (New York: Viking, 1975), 159.

13. Thomas Collins, "From Bringing in the Sheaves by 'Windsor Drake,'" *Journal of Modern Literature* (April 1976).

14. Steinbeck to Lorentz, 6 March 1938, in Pare Lorentz, *FDR's Moviemaker: Memoirs and Scripts* (Reno: University of Nevada Press, 1992), 1.

15. John Steinbeck, "Starvation under the Orange Trees," *Monterey Trader,* 15 April 1938.

16. John Steinbeck, *The Grapes of Wrath* (1939; reprint New York: Penguin, 1976), 566–67. Subsequent cites are given in parentheses in the text.

17. E. Steinbeck and Wallstein, *Life in Letters,* 526; John Steinbeck, *The Long Valley* (1938; reprint New York: Penguin, 1986), 132.

18. Benson, *True Adventures,* 260.

19. E. Steinbeck and Wallstein, *Life in Letters,* 31.

20. Lange and Taylor, *American Exodus;* Richard White, "'re You an Environmentalist or Do You Work for a Living?': Work and Nature," in William Cronon, ed., *Uncommon Ground: Toward Reinventing Nature* (New York: Norton, 1995), 171.

21. Letter from Steinbeck to Carlton Sheffield, quoted in Benson, *True Adventures,* 270; Steinbeck, "Argument of Phalanx," quoted in Benson, *True Adventures,* 268–69; E. Steinbeck and Wallstein, *Life in Letters,* 79–81; Steinbeck, *The Long Valley,* 303.

22. John Muir, *My First Summer in the Sierras* (1911), in *Nature Writings,* ed. William Cronon (New York: Library of America, 1997), 245.

23. On Leopold, see Donald Worster, *An Unsettled Country: Changing Landscapes of the American West* (Albuquerque: University of New Mexico Press, 1994), 82–87; John Steinbeck, *The Harvest Gypsies* (1936; reprint Berkeley, CA: Heyday Books, 1988), 25. Ma and Rose of Sharon also come to this realization of unity, but it is expressed in gendered terms, as a willingness to nurture those who are outside of the family, rather than fight for them.

24. John Steinbeck, *Working Days: The Journals of* The Grapes of Wrath, *1938–1941,* ed. Robert DeMott (New York: Penguin, 1989), 75.

25. Simon J. Lubin Society Papers, BL.

26. E. Steinbeck and Wallstein, *Life in Letters,* 178–79.

27. Carey McWilliams, *Southern California: An Island on the Land* (1946; Layton, UT: Gibbs Smith, 1973), 303.

28. Carey McWilliams, "Steinbeck and the 1930s in California," typescript for talk given at the University of Connecticut in 1969, box 5, collection 1319, McWilliams Papers, 17.

29. State citrus marketing regulations actually began in 1933, and a combination of state and federal statutes regulated citrus by the late 1930s. See Edward Tuttle, "Prorate Status Up-to-Date," *CC,* August 1941, 294–96, 298. For the broader context, see Victoria Saker Woeste, *The Farmer's Benevolent Trust: Law and Agricultural Cooperation in Industrial America, 1865–1945* (Chapel Hill: University of North Carolina Press, 1998), 216–31.

30. U.S. Congress, Senate, Subcommittee of the Committee on Education and Labor, *Hearings on Senate Resolution 266, Violations of Free Speech and*

Rights of Labor, 74th Congress, 2nd Session (Washington, DC: U.S. Government Printing Office, 1939), 20361 (hereafter cited as *Hearings*).

31. H. W. Thompson, "What Prorate on Citrus Fruits Can and Cannot Do," *CC,* April 1940, 180. See also Charles Collins Teague, *Fifty Years a Rancher* (Los Angeles: Ward Ritchie Press, 1944).

32. Armstrong, "Business of Agriculture," 263.

33. Jürgen Habermas, *The Philosophical Discourse of Modernity* (Cambridge, MA: MIT Press, 1987), 203.

34. Carey McWilliams, *Factories in the Field: The Story of Migratory Farm Labor in California* (1939; reprint Berkeley: University of California Press, 2000), 3–7, 249–54.

35. *New York Herald Tribune,* 30 July 1939. This and a large collection of other reviews of *Factories* are in box 56, scrapbook 2, collection 1319, McWilliams Papers.

36. Letter from Alice Harrison to McWilliams, 30 August 1939, box 25, collection 1319, McWilliams Papers.

37. John Watson, "Building Constructive Public Opinion," Address to the Associated Farmers Annual Meeting, 8 December 1939, in *Hearings,* 24755; *Hearings,* 24757.

38. *California Citizens Association Report,* 1 July 1939, from Marshal Hartranft, "The Grapes of Gladness: California's Refreshing and Inspiring Answer to John Steinbeck's *The Grapes of Wrath,*" reprinted in French, *Companion,* 135; George Thompson Miron, *The Truth about John Steinbeck and the Migrants,* cited in French, *Companion,* 135.

39. Confidential News Service of Simon J. Lubin Society (August 1939), copy in box 10, collection 1243, McWilliams Papers; Ruth Comfort Mitchell, *Of Human Kindness* (New York: D. Appleton Century, 1940), 292.

40. Sinclair thought *The Grapes of Wrath* a worthy successor to *The Jungle,* saying, "John Steinbeck can have my old mantle if he has any use for it." Walter Stein, *California and the Dust Bowl Migration* (Westport, CT: Greenwood Press, 1973), 203, 207.

41. Carey McWilliams, "Glory, Glory, California," *The New Republic,* 22 July 1940, 125, reprinted in French, *Companion,* 140–42.

42. The publication of the hearings included a million words of testimony and analysis, as well as charts, photographs, maps, and a wealth of subpoenaed documents from the files of the Associated Farmers, the state and Los Angeles chambers of commerce, and other groups.

43. Kevin Starr, *Endangered Dreams: California through the Depression* (New York: Oxford University Press, 1996), 266–67; Stein, *California,* 209; Jerold S. Auerbach, *Labor and Liberty: The La Follette Committee and the New Deal* (New York: Bobbs-Merrill, 1966), 179.

44. For a discussion of the politics behind the exclusion of agricultural workers, see Devra Weber, *Dark Sweat, White Gold: California Farm Workers, Cotton, and the New Deal* (Berkeley: University of California Press, 1994), 123–26.

45. Roy Pike, *Hearings*, 17686; *Hearings*, 24759. For a provocative and insightful critique of McWilliams's thesis, arguing that "the concept of 'factories in the field' . . . has obscured as much as it has revealed in the history of California agriculture," see David Vaught, "Factories in the Field Revisited," *Pacific Historical Review* (May 1997): 149–84. See also Vaught, *Cultivating California: Growers, Specialty Crops, and Labor, 1875–1920* (Baltimore: Johns Hopkins University Press, 1999).

46. *Hearings*, 17251; Carey McWilliams, *The Education of Carey McWilliams* (New York: Simon and Schuster, 1979), 78–79; U.S. Congress, Senate, Subcommittee of the Committee on Education and Labor, *Report, Violations of Free Speech and Rights of Labor*, report no. 1150, 77th Congress, 2nd Session (Washington, DC: U.S. Government Printing Office, 1942), 161 (hereafter cited as *Report*).

47. *Hearings*, 17215, 17216; Stein, *California*, 206; *Hearings*, 17221; Theodore Thomas testimony, *Hearings*, 20356.

48. *Hearings*, 17224.

49. Ibid., 20361.

50. Ibid., 20629, 20644; *Report*, 307. See also, for example, the testimony of J. A. Prizer, *Hearings*, 20362–68.

51. The connection between Sunkist and the Associated Farmers was established in the Senate hearings (*Hearings*, 20095–107, 20259, 25599) and in its report (*Report*, 548–49, 610–16).

52. Frank Taylor, "California's Embattled Farmer," *Hearings*, 24976.

53. *Hearings*, 24600.

54. Ibid., 20668; Teague, *Fifty Years*, 150.

55. Victor Turner, *Anthropology of Performance* (New York: PAJ Publications, 1988), 75; Starr, *Endangered Dreams*, 266; Victor Turner, *From Ritual to Theatre* (New York: PAJ Publications, 1982), 78; Auerbach, *Labor and Liberty*.

56. Quoted in Stein, *California*, 209.

57. *Life*, 5 June 1939, 67.

EPILOGUE. BY THEIR FRUITS YE SHALL KNOW THEM

1. Charles Collins Teague, *Fifty Years a Rancher* (Los Angeles: Ward Ritchie Press, 1944), 26; Richard Lillard, "Agricultural Statesman: Charles C. Teague of Santa Paula," *California History* (Spring 1986): 2–16.

2. Clippings, Voices from the Dust Bowl: The Charles L. Todd and Robert Sonkin Migrant Worker Collection, 1940–1941, American Folklife Center, Library of Congress, http://memory.loc.gov/ammem/afctshtml/clip2.html.

3. Teague, *Fifty Years,* 148; Dan Morgan, *Rising in the West: The True Story of an "Okie" Family from the Great Depression through the Reagan Years* (New York: Knopf, 1992), 175. On the failure to organize the Southwestern migrants, see Walter Stein, *California and the Dust Bowl Migration* (Westport, CT: Greenwood Press, 1973), 243–78; Martha Menchaca, *The Mexican Outsiders: A Community History of Marginalization and Discrimination in California* (Austin: University of Texas Press, 1995), 88–89.

4. C. C. Teague, "The National Shortage of Agricultural Labor and the Importance of Food Production in Winning the War and Keeping the Peace," Address at the State-Wide Meeting of the California State Chamber of Commerce (ca. December 1942), microfilm reel 14, Charles Collins Teague Papers, UCLA; CFGE, "Advertising Department Special Bulletin No. 7," 11 February 1943, reel 13, Teague Papers; "A Statement by the California Fruit Growers Exchange about the Navel Orange Supply" (n.d.), Teague Papers.

5. Letter from Teague to Paul Armstrong, May 1946, box 2, Teague Papers; Paul Taylor, "From the Ground Up," *Survey Graphic,* September 1936, 537; Gerald Nash, *The American West Transformed: The Impact of the Second World War* (Bloomington: Indiana University Press, 1985); letter from Stuart Strathman, Executive Secretary of the Associated Farmers, to Teague, 13 March 1943, Teague Papers; "Proposal by C. C. Teague for the Organization, Housing and Distribution of Mexican Nationals," 30 April 1943, Teague Papers; Carey McWilliams, *North from Mexico: The Spanish-Speaking People of the United States* (1948; reprint New York: Praeger, 1990), 238.

6. On the varied reactions of Mexican Americans to the braceros, see David Gutiérrez, *Walls and Mirrors: Mexican Americans, Mexican Immigrants, and the Politics of Ethnicity* (Berkeley: University of California Press, 1995), 133–51. Carey McWilliams, "They Saved the Crops," *The Inter-American,* August 1943, 10–14.

7. Letter from Teague to Thomas Robertson, 8 June 1943, reel 14, Teague Papers; Ernesto Galarza, *Merchants of Labor: The Mexican Bracero Story* (Santa Barbara, CA: McNally & Loftin, 1964), 51.

8. McWilliams, *North from Mexico,* 238; Teague, "The National Shortage of Agricultural Labor"; Richard Mines and Ricardo Anzaldua, *New Migrants vs. Old Migrants: Alternative Labor Market Structures in the California Citrus Industry* (San Diego: Program in United States–Mexican Studies, University of California, San Diego, 1982); Woody Guthrie, "Los Gatos Plane Wreck," typescript, 3 February 1948, copy in *This Land Is Your Land: The Life and Legacy of Woody Guthrie,* Smithsonian Institution Traveling Exhibit.

9. War Relocation Authority, *WRA: A Story of Human Conservation* (Washington, DC: U.S. Government Printing Office, 1946).

10. Quoted in Paul Taylor, "Our Stakes in the Japanese Exodus," *Survey Graphic,* September 1942, 373–78, 396–97.

11. LC-USF34-073597-D, Farm Security Administration–Office of War Information Collection, PP–LC.

12. Steinbeck's proposal is reprinted in Donald Coers, Paul Ruffin, and Robert DeMott, eds., *After* The Grapes of Wrath: *Essays on John Steinbeck* (Athens: Ohio University Press, 1995), 27–28; for McWilliams's role, see Carey McWilliams, *The Education of Carey McWilliams* (New York: Simon and Schuster, 1978), 101–8.

13. Taylor, "Our Stakes," 374.

14. Volume 54, section F, WRA no. I-973, War Relocation Authority Photographs of Japanese-American Evacuation and Resettlement, BANC PIC 1967.014–PIC, BL, http://ark.cdlib.org/ark:/13030/ft9k4009b3/. On the novel *Invasion,* see Mike Davis, *Ecology of Fear: Los Angeles and the Imagination of Disaster* (New York: Metropolitan Books, 1998), 298–99.

15. Paul Griffin and Ronald Chatham, "Population: A Challenge to California's Changing Citrus Industry," *Economic Geography* 34 (July 1958): 272; Davis, *Ecology of Fear,* 79–80.

16. Richard Lillard, *Eden in Jeopardy* (New York: Knopf, 1966), 85; Griffin and Chatham, "Population," 275.

17. J. Parker Whitney, "Educational Orange Growing," *Sunset,* August 1906, 161–70; A. J. Wells, "Oranges of the Foothills," *Sunset,* August 1906, 171–73.

18. Shelby Grad, "Packing It In: Landmark Packinghouse, Like Groves, Will Vanish," *LAT,* Orange County ed., 7 February 1997.

19. *CC,* January 1939, 111; Kevin Starr, *Endangered Dreams: California through the Depression* (New York: Oxford University Press, 1996), 343, 349.

20. Diego Rivera, *My Art, My Life: An Autobiography* (New York: Dover Publications, 1960), 151, 152; *Life,* 3 March 1941; Paulette Goddard reportedly gave the tree this name.

21. *Life,* 3 March 1941, 52.

22. The phrase is from William Leach, *Land of Desire: Merchants, Power, and the Rise of a New American Culture* (New York: Pantheon, 1993).

23. Donna Haraway, *Modest_Witness@Second_Millennium: FemaleMan©_Meets_OncoMouse*™ (New York: Routledge, 1997), 66.

SELECT BIBLIOGRAPHY

MANUSCRIPTS AND SCRAPBOOKS

Bancroft Library, University of California, Berkeley:
   Simon J. Lubin Papers
   Simon J. Lubin Society Papers
   Frank Norris Papers
   Richard Teggart Scrapbook of Republican Campaign Literature of 1934
Henry E. Huntington Library, San Marino, California:
   Azusa Foothill Citrus Company Papers
   Jeanne Carr Papers
   Pasadena Orange Growers' Association Papers
   Horatio Rust Papers
   Charles Saunders Papers
   Charles Willard Papers
Library of Congress, Prints and Photographs Division:
   Farm Security Administration–Office of War Information Collection:
      Farm Security Administration–Office of War Information Written Records:
      Farm Security Administration Scrapbook
      Roy Emerson Stryker Personal Papers (microfilm)
Special Collections, Mary Norton Clapp Library, Occidental College:
   Belt Collection of Sinclair Material
   Scrapbook on the 1934 Campaign

Special Collections, General Library, University of California, Davis:
  Paul Nyhus Collection
  James Shideler Papers
  Edward J. Wickson Papers
Special Collections, Charles E. Young Research Library, University of California, Los Angeles:
  California Ephemera Collection
  George Clements Papers
  Katherine Phillips Edson Papers
  Carey McWilliams Papers (collections 1243 and 1319)
  Powell Family Papers
  Charles Collins Teague Papers
Special Collections, Rivera Library, University of California, Riverside:
  Citrus Experiment Station Papers
  J. E. Coit Scrapbook
  A. D. Shamel Papers
Special Collections, Donald C. Davidson Library, University of California, Santa Barbara:
  Romaine Collection of Trade Catalogues

INTERVIEWS

Borough, Reuben. "Reuben Borough and California Reform Movements." Interview by Elizabeth I. Dixon, 1968. Transcript, Oral History Program, University of California, Los Angeles, Bancroft Library, University of California, Berkeley.

Carlson, Elsie. Interview by B. E. Schmidt, 1968. Transcript, Oral History Archives, California State University, Fullerton.

Chapman, Charles Stanley. Interview by Nita Busby, 1975. Transcript, Oral History Archives, California State University, Fullerton.

Corbit, Hoyt. Interview by Tom Peters, 1968. Transcript, Oral History Archives, California State University, Fullerton.

Corona, Manuel. Interview by C. Esther, 1966. Transcript, Oral History Archives, California State University, Fullerton.

Easton, W. Ray. Interview by Vivian Allen, 1974. Transcript, Oral History Archives, California State University, Fullerton.

Esqueda, Alfred. Interview by Carmen Ressel, 1971. Transcript, Oral History Archives, California State University, Fullerton.

Graham, George. Interview by Donna Barasch, 1972. Transcript, Oral History Archives, California State University, Fullerton.

Iwatsuru, Yoneko Dobashi. Interview by Diane Tappey, 1984. Honorable Stephen T. Tamura Orange County Japanese American Oral History

Project. Transcript, Oral History Archives, California State University, Fullerton.

Lange, Dorothea. "The Making of a Documentary Photographer." Interview by Susan Reiss, 1968. Transcript, Regional Oral History Office, Bancroft Library, University of California, Berkeley.

Millen, Dean. Interview by Jackie Malon, 1981. Transcript, Oral History Archives, California State University, Fullerton.

Sinclair, Upton. Interviews by John Niven et al., 1963. Transcript, Oral History Program, Claremont Graduate School. Special Collections, Claremont Colleges.

Taylor, Paul Schuster. "California Social Scientist." Interview by Susan Reiss, with an introduction by Laurence Hewes, 1973–75. Transcript, Regional Oral History Office, Bancroft Library, University of California, Berkeley.

BOOKS, ARTICLES, AND PAPERS

Adams, David Wallace. *Education for Extinction: American Indians and the Boarding School Experience, 1875–1928.* Lawrence: University Press of Kansas, 1995.

Adams, Henry. *The Education of Henry Adams.* 1907. Reprint, Boston: Houghton Mifflin, 1973.

Agee, James, and Walker Evans. *Let Us Now Praise Famous Men.* 1942. Reprint, Boston: Houghton Mifflin, 1960.

Agnew, Jean-Christophe. *Worlds Apart: The Market and the Theater in Anglo-American Thought, 1550–1750.* New York: Cambridge University Press, 1986.

Akin, William. *Technocracy and the American Dream: The Technocrat Movement, 1900–1941.* Berkeley: University of California Press, 1977.

Allende, Isabel. *The Infinite Plan: A Novel.* Trans. Margaret Peden. New York: HarperCollins, 1993.

Almaguer, Tómas. *Racial Fault Lines: The Historical Origins of White Supremacy in California.* Berkeley: University of California Press, 1994.

Anderson, Benedict. *Imagined Communities: Reflections on the Origin and Spread of Nationalism.* New York: Verso, 1991.

Anderson, Kat, Michael Barbour, and Valerie Whitworth. "A World of Balance and Plenty: Land, Plants, Animals, and Humans in Pre-European California." In Ramón Gutiérrez and Richard Orsi, eds., *Contested Eden: California before the Gold Rush.* Berkeley: University of California Press, 1997.

Apostol, Jane. "Horatio Nelson Rust: Abolitionist, Archeologist, Indian Agent." *California History* 48 (Winter 1979/80): 304–15.

Auerbach, Jerold S. *Labor and Liberty: The La Follette Committee and the New Deal.* New York: Bobbs-Merrill, 1966.

Bailey, Liberty Hyde. *The Holy Earth.* New York: Scribner's, 1915.

———. *The Outlook to Nature.* New York: Macmillan Co., 1911.

Baker, Paula. "The Domestication of Politics." In Linda Gordon, ed., *Women, the State, and Welfare,* 55–91. Madison: University of Wisconsin Press, 1990.

Bakker, Elna. *An Island Called California.* Berkeley: University of California Press, 1984.

Balderrama, Francisco, and Raymond Rodríguez. *Decade of Betrayal: Mexican Repatriation in the 1930s.* Albuquerque: University of New Mexico Press, 1995.

Banta, Martha. *Taylored Lives: Narrative Productions in the Age of Taylor, Veblen, and Ford.* Chicago: University of Chicago Press, 1993.

Barrett, James. "Americanization from the Bottom Up: Immigration and the Remaking of the Working Class in the United States, 1880–1930." *Journal of American History* 79 (December 1992): 98–120.

Batchelor, Leon, and Herbert Webber, eds. *The Citrus Industry.* 2 vols. Berkeley: University of California Press, 1943–48.

Baudrillard, Jean. *Jean Baudrillard: Selected Writings.* Ed. Mark Poster. Stanford, CA: Stanford University Press, 1988.

Bauer, John. *The Health Seekers of Southern California, 1870–1900.* San Marino, CA: Huntington Library, 1959.

Beattie, John. *Other Cultures: Aims, Methods, and Achievements in Social Anthropology.* New York: Free Press, 1964.

Benedict, Burton. *The Anthropology of World's Fairs: San Francisco's Panama Pacific International Exposition of 1915.* Berkeley, CA: Scolar Press, 1983.

Benson, Jackson. "'To Tom, Who Lived It': John Steinbeck and the Man from Weedpatch." *Journal of Modern Literature* (April 1976): 151–210.

———. *The True Adventures of John Steinbeck, Writer.* New York: Penguin, 1984.

Berkow, Robert, ed. *The Merck Manual of Medical Information.* New York: Pocket Books, 1997.

Bishop, A. D. "The Orange from Blossom to Car." *Official Report of the Twenty-eighth Fruit-Growers' Convention.* Sacramento: California State Printing Office, 1903.

Bodnar, John. *The Transplanted: A History of Immigrants in Urban America.* Bloomington: Indiana University Press, 1985.

Bogue, Allan. *Frederick Jackson Turner: Strange Roads Going Down.* Norman: University of Oklahoma Press, 1998.

Borough, Reuben. "I Secede: An Argument for a New Frontier." *The Survey,* 1934.

Borsodi, Myrtle. "The New Woman Goes Home." *Good Housekeeping,* February 1937.

Borsodi, Ralph. *The Flight from the City: The Story of a New Way to Family Security.* New York: Harper and Brothers, 1933.

———. "One Way Out." *The New Republic,* 24 July 1929.

———. "Subsistence Homesteads: President Roosevelt's New Land and Population Policy." *Survey Graphic,* January 1934.

———. *This Ugly Civilization.* New York: Simon and Schuster, 1929.

Braverman, Harry. *Labor and Monopoly Capital: The Degradation of Work in the Twentieth Century.* New York: Monthly Review Press, 1974.

Brechin, Gray. "Sailing to Byzantium: The Architecture of the Panama Pacific International Exposition." *California History* 62 (Summer 1983): 106–21.

Brock, Harry Ellington. "Los Angeles, City and County." 23rd ed. Los Angeles: Southern California Printing Company, 1910.

Brook, Harry. "The Land of Sunshine: Southern California. An authentic description of its natural features, resources and prospects." Los Angeles: World's Fair Association and Bureau of Information, 1893.

Brown, Bill. "Science Fiction, the World's Fair, and the Prosthetics of Empire, 1910–1915." In Amy Kaplan and Donald Pease, eds., *Cultures of United States Imperialism,* 129–63. Durham: Duke University Press, 1993.

Bugos, Glenn E., and Daniel Kevles. "Plants as Intellectual Property: American Practice, Law, and Policy in World Context." *Osiris* 7 (1992): 75–104.

Bulosan, Carlos. *America Is in the Heart.* 1943. Reprint, Seattle: University of Washington Press, 1973.

Burbank, Luther. "Evolution and Variation with the Fundamental Significance of Sex." In Race Betterment Foundation, *Official Proceedings of the Second National Conference on Race Betterment.* Battle Creek, MI: n.p., 1915.

———. "The Training of the Human Plant." *Century* 72, no. 1 (1906).

Burbank, Luther, with Wilbur Hall. *The Harvest of the Years.* New York: Houghton Mifflin, 1927.

Burke, Robert. *Olson's New Deal for California.* Berkeley: University of California Press, 1953.

California Commission of Immigration and Housing. "Advisory Pamphlet on Camp Sanitation and Housing, Revised 1926." Sacramento: California State Printing Office, 1932.

———. "Americanization: California's Answer." Sacramento: California State Printing Office, 1920.

———. "Americanization of Foreign-Born Women." Sacramento: California State Printing Office, 1917.

———. "Immigrant Education Leaflet No. 5: The Home Teacher." N.p., n.d.

———. *Ninth Annual Report.* Sacramento: California State Printing Office, 1923.

———. "Primer for Foreign-Speaking Women, Part 1." Sacramento: California State Printing Office, 1918.

———. "Primer for Foreign-Speaking Women, Part 2." Sacramento: California State Printing Office, 1918.

———. *A Report on Housing Shortages*. Sacramento: California State Printing Office, 1923.

California Fruit Growers' Convention. "Hand in Hand Go Horticulture and Civilization: A Short Narrative of Fruit Raising in the United States and Particularly in California." Sacramento: Weinstock, Lubin & Co., 1917.

California Fruit Growers Exchange. *Sunkist Advertising News,* August 1941.

———. "Twenty-fifth Anniversary of Advertising: Sunkist Advertising and Marketing Plans for 1932–1933." Los Angeles: n.p., 1932.

California State Board of Trade. "A Toast, an Introduction, a Few Words, a Tribute at the Banquet in Honor of Luther Burbank." Chicago: Oscar E. Bitmer Co. and Luther Burbank Publishers, n.d.

Carpenter, Kenneth. *The History of Scurvy and Vitamin C.* New York: Cambridge University Press, 1986.

Carson, Rachel. *Silent Spring.* Boston: Houghton Mifflin, 1962.

Ceplair, Larry, and Steven Englund. *The Inquisition in Hollywood: Politics in the Film Community, 1930–1960.* Berkeley: University of California Press, 1983.

Chambers, Clarke. *California Farm Organizations: A Historical Study of the Grange, the Farm Bureau and the Associated Farmers, 1929–1941.* Berkeley: University of California Press, 1952.

Chan, Sucheng. *This Bitter-Sweet Soil: The Chinese in California Agriculture, 1860–1910.* Berkeley: University of California Press, 1986.

Chandler, Alfred D., Jr. *The Visible Hand: The Managerial Revolution in American Business.* Cambridge, MA: Belknap Press of Harvard University Press, 1977.

Channell, David. *The Vital Machine: A Study of Technology and Organic Life.* New York: Oxford University Press, 1991.

Chen, Yong. "The Internal Origins of Chinese Emigration to California Reconsidered." *Western Historical Quarterly* 28 (Winter 1997): 520–46.

Cleek, Patricia. "Santa Barbara Muralists in the New Deal Era." *Noticias,* Autumn 1995.

Cleland, Robert Glass. *California in Our Time (1900–1940).* New York: Knopf, 1947.

Clifford, James. *The Predicament of Culture: Twentieth-Century Ethnography, Literature, and Art.* Cambridge, MA: Harvard University Press, 1988.

Coers, Donald, Paul Ruffin, and Robert DeMott, eds. *After* The Grapes of Wrath: *Essays on John Steinbeck.* Athens: Ohio University Press, 1995.

Cohen, Lizabeth. *Making a New Deal: Industrial Workers in Chicago, 1919–1939.* Cambridge: Cambridge University Press, 1990.

Cohn, Jan. *Creating America: George Horace Lorimer and the* Saturday Evening Post. Pittsburgh: University of Pittsburgh Press, 1989.

Collins, Thomas. "From Bringing in the Sheaves by 'Windsor Drake.'" *Journal of Modern Literature* (April 1976): 211–32.

Condit, Ira, A. N. Benemerito, and Wang Hao Chen. "Citrus Fruits and Their Culture in Kwangtung Province, South China." Typescript, 1937.

Cook, A. J. *California Citrus Culture.* Sacramento: California State Printing Office, 1913.

Cott, Nancy. *The Grounding of Modern Feminism.* New Haven: Yale University Press, 1987.

Cronon, William. "Modes of Prophecy and Production: Placing Nature in History." *Journal of American History* 76 (March 1990): 1122–31.

———. *Nature's Metropolis: Chicago and the Great West.* New York: Norton, 1991.

———. "A Place for Stories: Nature, History, and Narrative." *Journal of American History* 78 (March 1992): 1347–76.

Crosby, Alfred W. *Ecological Imperialism: The Biological Expansion of Europe, 900–1900.* New York: Cambridge University Press, 1986.

Cumberland, William. *Coöperative Marketing: Its Advances as Exemplified in the California Fruit Growers Exchange.* Princeton: Princeton University Press, 1917.

Curtis, James. *Mind's Eye, Mind's Truth: FSA Photography Reconsidered.* Philadelphia: Temple University Press, 1989.

Damon-Moore, Helen. *Magazines for the Millions: Gender and Commerce in the* Ladies' Home Journal *and the* Saturday Evening Post, *1880–1910.* Albany: State University of New York Press, 1994.

Dana, Richard Henry. *Two Years before the Mast.* 1840. Reprint, New York: Modern Library, 1964.

Daniel, Cletus. *Bitter Harvest: A History of California Farmworkers, 1870–1941.* 1981. Reprint, Berkeley: University of California Press, 1982.

Davies, Frederick, and Gene Albrigo. *Citrus.* Wollingford, UK: CAB International, 1994.

Davis, Mike. *City of Quartz: Excavating the Future in Los Angeles.* 1990. Reprint, New York: Vintage, 1992.

———. *Ecology of Fear: Los Angeles and the Imagination of Disaster.* New York: Metropolitan Books, 1998.

Deleuze, Gilles, and Félix Guattari. *A Thousand Plateaus: Capitalism and Schizophrenia.* Minneapolis: University of Minnesota Press, 1993.

DeLong, Lee Rosen. *Nature's Forms/Nature's Forces: The Art of Alexandre Hogue.* Norman: University of Oklahoma Press and Philbrook Art Center, 1984.

Denning, Michael. *The Cultural Front: The Laboring of American Culture in the Twentieth Century.* New York: Verso, 1996.

Deverell, William. "Privileging the Mission over the Mexican: The Rise of Regional Identity in Southern California." In Michael Steiner and David

Wrobel, eds., *Many Wests: Place, Culture, and Regional Identity,* 235–58. Lawrence: University Press of Kansas, 1997.

————. *Railroad Crossing: Californians and the Railroad, 1850–1910.* Berkeley: University of California Press, 1994.

Deverell, William, and Tom Sitton. "Introduction: The Varieties of Progressive Experience." In *California Progressivism Revisited,* 1–11. Berkeley: University of California Press, 1994.

Douglas, Mary. *Purity and Danger: An Analysis of the Concepts of Pollution and Taboo.* London: Routledge and Kegan Paul, 1966.

Dower, John. *War without Mercy: Race and Power in the Pacific War.* New York: Pantheon, 1986.

Doyle, Jack. *Altered Harvest: Agriculture, Genetics and the Fate of the World's Food Supply.* New York: Viking, 1985.

Dreyer, Peter. *A Gardener Touched with Genius: The Life of Luther Burbank.* Berkeley: University of California Press, 1985.

Duflot de Mofras, Eugène. *Exploration du Territoire de l'Oregon, des Californies, et de la mer Vermeille.* Paris: A. Bertrand, 1844.

Dumke, Glenn. *The Boom of the Eighties in Southern California.* San Marino, CA: Huntington Library, 1963.

Dunaway, David. *Huxley in Hollywood.* New York: Harper and Row, 1989.

Dunlap, Thomas. *Nature and the English Diaspora: Environment and History in the United States, Canada, Australia, and New Zealand.* New York: Cambridge University Press, 1999.

Edelman, Murray. *Constructing the Political Spectacle.* Chicago: University of Chicago Press, 1988.

Ellis, Pearl. "Americanization through Homemaking." Los Angeles: Wetzel, 1929.

Emerson, Carline. "Geographical Aspects in the Development of the Limoneira Company, Santa Paula, California." Master's thesis, University of California, Los Angeles, 1968.

Engle, Clara. "Orange County Citrus Strike, 1936: Historical Analysis and Social Conflict." Master's thesis, California State University, Fullerton, 1975.

Ensminger, Audrey, M. Ensminger, James Konlande, and John Robson. *The Concise Encyclopedia of Foods and Nutrition.* Boca Raton, FL: CRC Press, 1995.

Erdman, H. E. *The California Fruit Growers Exchange: An Example of Cooperation in the Segregation of Interests.* New York: American Council, Institute of Pacific Relations, 1933.

Faragher, John Mack, ed. *Rereading Frederick Jackson Turner.* New York: Henry Holt, 1994.

Federal Writers' Project. *California: A Guide to the Golden State.* New York: Books, Inc., 1939. Reprinted as *The WPA Guide to California.* New York: Pantheon, 1939.

Final Report of the California World's Fair Commission: Including a description of all exhibits from the state of California. Sacramento: A. J. Johnston, Supt. State Printing, 1894.

Fish, A. C. "The Profits of Orange Culture in Southern California." N.p.: Semi Tropic Land and Water Company, 1890.

Fisher, Lloyd. *The Harvest Labor Market in California.* Cambridge, MA: Harvard University Press, 1953.

Fitzgerald, Deborah. *The Business of Breeding: Hybrid Corn in Illinois, 1890–1940.* Ithaca: Cornell University Press, 1990.

Floercky, Herbert, and Lee Shippey. *California Progress.* Sacramento: California State Department of Education, 1936.

Fogelson, Robert. *The Fragmented Metropolis: Los Angeles, 1850–1930.* Berkeley: University of California Press, 1993.

Foucault, Michel. *The History of Sexuality: An Introduction.* New York: Vintage Books, 1990.

Francisco, Don. "New Features in Advertising California Agricultural Products." *Proceeding of the Sixty-ninth Convention of California Fruit Growers and Farmers.* Sacramento: California State Printing Office, 1937.

French, Warren, ed. *A Companion to* The Grapes of Wrath. New York: Viking, 1963.

Friday, Chris. *Organizing Asian American Labor: The Pacific Coast Canned-Salmon Industry, 1870–1942.* Philadelphia: Temple University Press, 1994.

Friedland, William. *Social Sleepwalkers: Scientific and Technological Research in California Agriculture.* University of California, Davis, Department of Applied Behavioral Sciences, Research Monograph No. 13, 1974.

Frost, Howard. "Polyembryony, Heterozygosis and Chimeras in Citrus." *Hilgardia: A Journal of Agricultural Science* 1 (May 1926).

Fruit Growers Supply Company. *Annual Report, 1939.* Los Angeles: California Fruit Growers Exchange, 1940.

Fuentes, Carlos. *The Orange Tree.* New York: Farrar, Straus and Giroux, 1994.

Fuller, Varden. "The Supply of Agricultural Labor as a Factor in the Evolution of Farm Organization in California." In U.S. Congress, Senate, Subcommittee of the Committee on Education and Labor, *Hearings on Senate Resolution 266, Violations of Free Speech and Rights of Labor,* 74th Congress, 2nd Session, 19777–898. Washington, DC: U.S. Government Printing Office, 1939.

Galarza, Ernesto. *Merchants of Labor: The Mexican Bracero Story.* Santa Barbara, CA: McNally & Loftin, 1964.

Garcia, Matt. *A World of Its Own: Race, Labor, and Citrus in the Making of Greater Los Angeles, 1900–1970.* Chapel Hill: University of North Carolina Press, 2002.

Garey, Thomas. *Orange Culture in California.* San Francisco: Pacific Rural Press, 1882.

Garner, William Robert. *Letters from California, 1846–47.* Ed. Donald Munro Craig. Berkeley: University of California Press, 1970.

Geertz, Clifford. *The Interpretation of Cultures.* New York: Basic Books, 1973.

General Federation of Women's Clubs. "A Suggested Program for Americanization." N.p., n.d.

Gerstle, Gary. *American Crucible: Race and Nation in the Twentieth Century.* Princeton: Princeton University Press, 2000.

Gitlin, Todd. *The Whole World Is Watching.* Berkeley: University of California Press, 1980.

Godzich, Wlad. "Forward: The Time Machine." In Didier Coste, *Narrative as Communication.* Minneapolis: University of Minnesota Press, 1989.

González, Gilbert. *Labor and Community: Mexican Citrus Worker Villages in a Southern California County, 1900–1950.* Urbana: University of Illinois Press, 1994.

———. *Mexican Consuls and Labor Organizing: Imperial Politics in the American Southwest.* Austin: University of Texas Press, 1999.

———. "Women, Work and Community in the Mexican *Colonias* of the Southern California Citrus Belt." *California History* 74 (Spring 1995): 58–67.

Goodman, David, and Michael Redclift. *Refashioning Nature: Food, Ecology and Culture.* New York: Routledge, 1991.

Gottlieb, Robert. *Forcing the Spring: The Transformation of the American Environmental Movement.* Covelo, CA: Island Press, 1993.

Green, Harvey. *Fit for America: Health, Fitness, Sport, and American Society.* New York: Pantheon, 1986.

Greenough, Blanche. "Towards Humanocracy." Los Angeles: Winged Cycle Publishing Co., 1933.

Gregory, James. *American Exodus: The Dust Bowl Migration and Okie Culture in California.* New York: Oxford University Press, 1989.

———. "Introduction." In Upton Sinclair, *I, Candidate for Governor: And How I Got Licked.* 1935. Reprint, Berkeley: University of California Press, 1994.

Griffin, Paul, and Ronald Chatham. "Population: A Challenge to California's Changing Citrus Industry." *Economic Geography* 34 (July 1958): 272–76.

Gudde, Erwin. *California Place Names: The Origin and Etymology of Current Geographical Names.* Berkeley: University of California Press, 1965.

Guerin-Gonzalez, Camille. *Mexican Workers and American Dreams: Immigration, Repatriation, and California Farm Labor, 1900–1939.* New Brunswick: Rutgers University Press, 1994.

Guimond, James. *American Photography and the American Dream.* Chapel Hill: University of North Carolina Press, 1991.

Gullet, Gayle. "Women Progressives and the Politics of Americanization in California, 1915–1920." *Pacific Historical Review* 64 (February 1995): 71–94.

Gunther, John. *Taken at the Flood: The Story of Alfred D. Lasker.* New York: Harper, 1960.

Gutiérrez, David. *Walls and Mirrors: Mexican Americans, Mexican Immigrants, and the Politics of Ethnicity.* Berkeley: University of California Press, 1995.

Haas, Lisbeth. *Conquests and Historical Identities in California, 1769–1936.* Berkeley: University of California Press, 1995.

———. "San Juan Capistrano: A Rural Society in Transition to Citrus." *California History* 74 (Spring 1995): 46–57.

Habermas, Jürgen. *The Philosophical Discourse of Modernity.* Cambridge, MA: MIT Press, 1987.

Hahomovich, Cindy. *The Fruits of Their Labor: Atlantic Coast Farmworkers and the Making of Migrant Poverty.* Chapel Hill: University of North Carolina Press, 1997.

Handlin, Oscar. *The Uprooted: The Epic Story of the Great Migrations That Made the American People.* 2nd ed. Boston: Little, Brown, 1973.

Haraway, Donna. *Modest_Witness@Second_Millennium: FemaleMan©_Meets_OncoMouse*™. New York: Routledge, 1997.

———. *Primate Visions: Gender, Race, and Nature in the World of Modern Science.* New York: Routledge, 1989.

———. "The Promises of Monsters: A Regenerative Politics for Inappropriate/d Others." In Lawrence Grossberg, Cary Nelson, and Paula Treichler, eds., *Cultural Studies,* 295–337. New York: Routledge, 1992.

Hartig, Anthea. "'In a World He Has Created': Class Collectivity and the Growers' Landscape of the Southern California Citrus Industry, 1890–1940." *California History* 74 (Spring 1995): 100–111.

Harwood, William. *New Creations in Plant Life: An Authoritative Account of the Life and Work of Luther Burbank.* New York: Macmillan Co., 1907.

Hasse, Geraldo, ed. *The Orange: A Brazilian Adventure, 1500–1987.* São Paulo: Duprat and Iboe, 1987.

Hayden, Dolores. *The Power of Place: Urban Landscapes as Public History.* Cambridge, MA: MIT Press, 1995.

———. *Seven American Utopias: The Architecture of Communitarian Socialism, 1790–1975.* Cambridge, MA: MIT Press, 1976.

Herman, David. "Neighbors on the Golden Mountain: The Americanization of Immigrants in California." Ph.D. dissertation, University of California, Berkeley, 1981.

Hine, Robert V. *California's Utopian Colonies.* 1953. Reprint, Berkeley: University of California Press, 1983.

Hoy, Suellen. *Chasing Dirt: The American Pursuit of Cleanliness*. New York: Oxford University Press, 1995.

Hundley, Norris, Jr. *The Great Thirst: Californians and Water, 1770s–1990s*. Berkeley: University of California Press, 1992.

Hurlburt, Laurance. *The Mexican Muralists in the United States*. Albuquerque: University of New Mexico Press, 1989.

Hurley, Andrew. *Environmental Inequalities: Class, Race, and Industrial Pollution in Gary, Indiana, 1945–1980*. Chapel Hill: University of North Carolina Press, 1995.

Hurtado, Albert. *Indian Survival on the California Frontier*. New Haven: Yale University Press, 1988.

Huxley, Aldous. *After Many a Summer Dies the Swan*. 1939. Reprint, Chicago: Ivan Dee, 1993.

Irish, John. "Labor in the Rural Industries of California." *Official Report of the Thirty-third Fruit-Growers' Convention*. Sacramento: California State Printing Office, 1908.

Jackson, Helen Hunt. *Glimpses of California and the Mission*. 1883. Reprint, Boston: Little, Brown, and Company, 1902.

———. *Ramona*. 1884. Reprint, New York: Signet, 1988.

Jackson, J. B. *Discovering the Vernacular Landscape*. New Haven: Yale University Press, 1984.

Jacobs, Josephine. "Sunkist Advertising." Ph.D. dissertation, University of California, Los Angeles, 1966.

Jacobson, Matthew. *Barbarian Virtues: The United States Encounters Foreign Peoples at Home and Abroad, 1876–1917*. New York: Hill and Wang, 2001.

Jameson, Fredric. *Postmodernism: Or, the Cultural Logic of Late Capitalism*. Durham, North Carolina: Duke University Press, 1991.

Julien, Kyle. "Transplanting the Heartland: The Middle Westerner in Los Angeles and Upton Sinclair's Campaign to End Poverty in California." Unpublished paper in possession of the author.

Junker, Patricia. "Celebrating Possibilities and Confronting Limits: Painting of the 1930s and 1940s." In Steven A. Nash, ed., *Facing Eden: One Hundred Years of Landscape Art in the Bay Area*. Berkeley: University of California Press, 1995.

Kasson, John. *Amusing the Million: Coney Island at the Turn of the Century*. New York: Hill and Wang, 1978.

Keller, Evelyn Fox. *A Feeling for the Organism: The Life and Work of Barbara McLintock*. New York: Freeman, 1982.

———. *Secrets of Life, Secrets of Death: Essays on Language, Gender and Science*. New York: Routledge, 1992.

Kerouac, Jack. *The Dharma Bums*. New York: Penguin, 1958.

Kerr, Clark, and Arthur Harris. "Self-Help Cooperatives in California." Berkeley: Bureau of Public Administration, University of California, 1939.

Kevles, Daniel. *In the Name of Eugenics: Genetics and the Uses of Human Heredity.* New York: Knopf, 1985.

Kifer, R. S., H. L. Stewart, and Bureau of Agricultural Economics. *Farming Hazards in the Drought Area.* Washington, DC: U.S. Government Printing Office, 1938.

Kimmelman, Barbara A. "The American Breeders' Association: Genetics and Eugenics in an Agricultural Context, 1903–1913." *Social Studies of Science* 13 (1983): 163–204.

Kling, Rob, Spencer Olin, and Mark Poster, eds. *Postsuburban California: The Transformation of Orange County since World War II.* Berkeley: University of California Press, 1995.

Klotz, Esther H. "Eliza Tibbets and Her Two Washington Navel Orange Trees." In Esther Klotz, Harry Lawton, and Joan Hall, eds., *A History of Citrus in the Riverside Area,* 13–25. Riverside, CA: Riverside Museum Press, 1989.

Knobloch, Frieda. *The Culture of Wilderness: Agriculture as Colonization in the American West.* Chapel Hill: University of North Carolina Press, 1996.

Kozol, Wendy. "Madonnas of the Fields: Photography, Gender, and 1930s Farm Relief." *Genders* 2 (July 1988): 1–23.

Kraft, Ken, and Pat Kraft. *Luther Burbank: The Wizard and the Man.* New York: Meredith Press, 1967.

Labels: Suggestions for the Shipper Who Is Seeking to Give His Pack a Worthy and Effective Mark of Identification. N.p.: Advertising Department of the California Fruit Growers Exchange, 1918.

Lange, Dorothea, and Paul Taylor. *An American Exodus: A Record of Human Erosion.* New York: Reynal and Hitchcock, 1939.

Larsen, Grace. "Commentary: The Economics and Structure of the Citrus Industry: Comment on Papers by H. Vincent Moses and Ronald Tobey and Charles Wetherell." *California History* 74 (Spring 1995): 38–45.

Lawton, Harry. "A Brief History of Citrus in Southern California." In Esther Klotz, Harry Lawton, and Joan Hall, eds., *A History of Citrus in the Riverside Area,* 6–13. Riverside, CA: Riverside Museum Press, 1989.

———. "John Henry Reed and the Founding of the Citrus Experiment Station." In Esther Klotz, Harry Lawton, and Joan Hall, eds., *A History of Citrus in the Riverside Area,* 44–51. Riverside, CA: Riverside Museum Press, 1989.

———. "The Pilgrims from Gom-Benn: Migratory Origins of Chinese Pioneers in the San Bernardino Valley." In Great Basin Foundation, ed., *Wong Ho Leun: An American Chinatown,* 141–66. San Diego: Great Basin Foundation, 1987.

Lawton, Harry, and Lewis Weathers. "The Origins of Citrus Research in California." In Walter Reuther, E. Clair Calavan, and Glenn E. Carmen, eds., *The Citrus Industry,* vol. 5. Berkeley: University of California, Division of Agricultural Science, 1989.

Leach, William. *Land of Desire: Merchants, Power, and the Rise of a New American Culture.* New York: Pantheon, 1993.

Lears, T. J. Jackson. *Fables of Abundance: A Cultural History of Advertising in America.* New York: Basic Books, 1994.

———. *No Place of Grace: Antimodernism and the Transformation of American Culture, 1880–1920.* Chicago: University of Chicago Press, 1983.

Lee, Anthony. *Painting on the Left: Diego Rivera, Radical Politics, and San Francisco's Public Murals.* Berkeley: University of California Press, 1999.

Lefebvre, Henri. *The Production of Space.* Trans. Donald Nicholson-Smith. Cambridge, MA: Blackwell, 1991.

LeLong, B. M. *Culture of the Citrus in California.* Sacramento: California State Printing Office, 1900.

Levenstein, Harvey. *Revolution at the Table: The Transformation of the American Diet.* New York: Oxford University Press, 1988.

Levine, Lawrence. "The Historian and the Icon." In Carl Fleischauer and Beverly Brannan, eds., *Documenting America, 1935–1943,* 15–42. Berkeley: University of California Press, 1988.

———. *The Opening of the American Mind: Canons, Culture, and History.* Boston: Beacon, 1996.

Levins, Richard, and Richard Lewontin. *The Dialectical Biologist.* Cambridge, MA: Harvard University Press, 1985.

Lewis, David Rich. *Neither Wolf nor Dog: American Indians, Environment, and Agrarian Change.* New York: Oxford University Press, 1994.

Lillard, Richard. "Agricultural Statesman: Charles C. Teague of Santa Paula." *California History* 65 (Spring 1986): 2–16.

———. *Eden in Jeopardy.* New York: Knopf, 1966.

Limerick, Patricia. "The Adventures of the Frontier in the Twentieth Century." In James Grossman, ed., *The Frontier in American Culture,* 67–102. Berkeley: University of California Press, 1994.

———. "Disorientation and Reorientation: The American Landscape Discovered from the West." *Journal of American History* 78 (December 1992): 1021–49.

Lockridge, Kenneth. *A New England Town: The First Hundred Years.* New York: Norton, 1970.

Logan, John, and Harvey Molotch. *Urban Fortunes: The Political Economy of Place.* Berkeley: University of California Press, 1987.

Lorentz, Pare. *FDR's Moviemaker: Memoirs and Scripts.* Reno: University of Nevada Press, 1992.

Los Angeles Chamber of Commerce. *Exhibit and Work of the Los Angeles Chamber of Commerce.* Los Angeles: Los Angeles Chamber of Commerce, 1910.

———. *Los Angeles: The Center of an Agricultural Empire.* Los Angeles: n.p., 1928.

————. *Los Angeles Today, April 1922: Los Angeles, Nature's Workshop.* Los Angeles: Neuner Corp., 1922.

Los Angeles Chamber of Commerce, Agricultural Department. *Los Angeles: The Center of an Agricultural Empire.* Los Angeles: n.p., 1928.

Lowry, Edith. "They Starve That We May Eat." New York: Council of Women for Home Missions, 1938.

Lundy, Robert. "The Making of *McTeague* and *The Octopus.*" Ph.D. dissertation, University of California, Berkeley, 1956.

Lydon, Sandy. *Chinese Gold: The Chinese in the Monterey Bay Region.* Capitola, CA: Capitola Book Company, 1985.

Lyotard, Jean François. *The Postmodern Condition: A Report on Knowledge.* Minneapolis: University of Minnesota Press, 1984.

MacCoy, Ellarene, Mary Wolseth, and Edith Mills. "Maternal and Child Health among the Mexican Groups in San Bernardino and Imperial Counties." Mimeograph. Sacramento: Bureau of Child Hygiene, 1938.

MacCurdy, Rahno Mabel. *The History of the California Fruit Growers Exchange.* Los Angeles: G. Rice and Sons, 1925.

MacLeish, Archibald. *Land of the Free.* New York: Harcourt, Brace, 1938.

Madden, Jerome. *California: Its Attractions for the Invalid, Tourist, Capitalist and Homeseeker with General Information on the Lands of the Southern Pacific Rail Road Company.* San Francisco: H. S. Crocker and Co., 1890.

Majka, Leo, and Thea Majka. *Farm Workers, Agribusiness and the State.* Philadelphia: Temple University Press, 1982.

Marchand, Roland. *Advertising the American Dream: Making Way for Modernity, 1920–1940.* Berkeley: University of California Press, 1985.

Marx, Karl. *The Marx-Engels Reader.* Ed. Robert Tucker. New York: Norton, 1978.

Matsumoto, Valerie. *Farming the Home Place: A Japanese American Community in California, 1919–1982.* Ithaca: Cornell University Press, 1993.

Mayo, James. *The American Grocery Store: The Business Evolution of an Architectural Space.* Westport, CT: Greenwood Press, 1993.

McBane, Margo. "The Role of Gender in Citrus Employment: A Case Study of Recruitment, Labor, and Housing Patterns at the Limoneira Company, 1893–1940." *California History* 74 (Spring 1995): 69–81.

McClelland, Gordon T., and Jay T. Last. *California Orange Box Labels: An Illustrated History.* Beverly Hills: Hillcrest Press, 1985.

McIntosh, Clarence. "Upton Sinclair and the EPIC Movement, 1933–1936." Ph.D. dissertation, Stanford University, 1955.

McLung, William. *Landscapes of Desire: Anglo Mythologies of Los Angeles.* Berkeley: University of California Press, 2000.

McPhee, John. *Assembling California.* New York: Farrar, Straus and Giroux, 1993.

————. *Oranges.* New York: Noonday Press, 1966.

McWilliams, Carey. *The Education of Carey McWilliams.* New York: Simon and Schuster, 1979.

——. *Factories in the Field: The Story of Migratory Farm Labor in California.* 1939. Reprint, Berkeley: University of California Press, 2000.

——. "Glory, Glory, California." *The New Republic,* 22 July 1940.

——. "Gunkist Oranges." *Pacific Weekly,* 20 July 1936.

——. "High Spots in the Campaign." *The New Republic,* November 7, 1934.

——. *North from Mexico: The Spanish-Speaking People of the United States.* 1948. Reprint, New York: Praeger, 1990.

——. *Southern California: An Island on the Land.* 1946. Reprint, Layton, UT: Gibbs Smith, 1973.

——. "They Saved the Crops." *The Inter-American,* August 1943.

Meltzer, Milton. *Dorothea Lange: A Photographer's Life.* New York: Farrar, Straus, and Giroux, 1978.

Menchaca, Martha. *The Mexican Outsiders: A Community History of Marginalization and Discrimination in California.* Austin: University of Texas Press, 1995.

Merchant, Carolyn. *The Death of Nature: Women, Ecology, and the Scientific Revolution.* San Francisco: Harper and Row, 1980.

——. "Reinventing Eden: Western Culture as a Recovery Narrative." In William Cronon, ed., *Uncommon Ground: Toward Reinventing Nature,* 132–59. New York: Norton, 1995.

Milkman, Ruth. *Gender at Work: The Dynamics of Job Segregation by Sex during World War II.* Urbana: University of Illinois Press, 1987.

Mines, Richard, and Ricardo Anzaldua. *New Migrants vs. Old Migrants: Alternative Labor Market Structures in the California Citrus Industry.* San Diego: Program in United States–Mexican Studies, University of California, San Diego, 1982.

Mitchell, Don. *The Lie of the Land: Migrant Workers and the California Landscape.* Minneapolis: University of Minnesota Press, 1996.

Mitchell, Greg. *The Campaign of the Century: Upton Sinclair's Race for Governor and the Birth of Media Politics.* New York: Random House, 1992.

Mitchell, Ruth Comfort. *Of Human Kindness.* New York: D. Appleton Century, 1940.

Montgomery, David. *The Fall of the House of Labor: The Workplace, the State, and American Labor Activism, 1865–1925.* New York: Cambridge University Press, 1987.

Moore, James. "Depression Images: Subsistence Homesteads, 'Production-for-Use,' and King Vidor's *Our Daily Bread.*" *Midwest Quarterly* 26, no. 1 (1984): 24–34.

Moore, Jules, and James Moore, eds. *Advances in Fruit Breeding.* West Lafayette, IN: Purdue University Press, 1976.

Morgan, Dan. *Rising in the West: The True Story of an "Okie" Family from the Great Depression through the Reagan Years.* New York: Knopf, 1992.

Moses, Herman Vincent. "The Flying Wedge of Cooperation: G. Harold Powell, California Orange Growers, and the Corporate Reconstruction of American Agriculture, 1904–1922." Ph.D. dissertation, University of California, Riverside, 1994.

———. "G. Harold Powell and the Corporate Consolidation of the Modern Citrus Enterprise, 1904–1922." *Business History Review* 69 (Summer 1995): 119–55.

———. "Machines in the Garden: A Citrus Monopoly in Riverside, 1900–1936." *California History* 61 (Spring 1982): 26–35.

———. "'The Orange-Grower Is Not a Farmer': G. Harold Powell, Riverside Orchardists, and the Coming of Industrial Agriculture, 1893–1930." *California History* 74 (Spring 1995): 22–37.

———. *To Have a Hand in Creation: Citrus and the Rise of Southern California.* Riverside, CA: Riverside Museum Press, 1989.

Mount, Jeffrey. *California Rivers and Streams: The Conflict between Fluvial Process and Land Use.* Berkeley: University of California Press, 1995.

Muir, John. *Nature Writings.* Ed. William Cronon. New York: Library of America, 1997.

———. *The Writings of John Muir.* Ed. William Cronon. New York: Library of America, 1995.

Nash, Gerald. *The American West Transformed: The Impact of the Second World War.* Bloomington: Indiana University Press, 1985.

Nordhoff, Charles. *California: For Health, Pleasure, and Residence.* New York: Harper and Brothers, 1872; new ed., New York: Harper and Brothers, 1882.

Norris, Frank. *The Octopus: A Story of California.* 1901. Reprint, New York: Penguin, 1986.

Norwood, Vera. *Made from This Earth: American Women and Nature.* Chapel Hill: University of North Carolina Press, 1993.

Ohmann, Richard. *Selling Culture: Magazines, Markets, and Class at the Turn of the Century.* New York: Verso, 1996.

Olin, Spencer. *California's Prodigal Sons: Hiram Johnson and the Progressives, 1911–1917.* Berkeley: University of California Press, 1968.

Onda, Tetsuya. "History of Fruit Growing Industry in Japan." In *Japanese Fruits.* N.p.: Japan Mail Times, 1938.

Orsi, Richard. "*The Octopus* Reconsidered: The Southern Pacific and Agricultural Modernization in California, 1865–1915." *California Historical Quarterly* 54 (Fall 1975): 197–220.

———. "Selling the Golden State: A Study of Boosterism in Nineteenth-Century California." Ph.D. dissertation, University of Wisconsin, Madison, 1973.

———. "'Wilderness Saint' and 'Robber Baron': The Anomalous Partnership of John Muir and the Southern Pacific Company for the Preservation of Yosemite National Park." *Pacific Historian* 29 (Summer/Fall 1985): 136–56.

Orvell, Miles. *The Real Thing: Image and Authenticity in American Culture, 1880–1940.* Chapel Hill: University of North Carolina Press, 1989.

Ovid. *Metamorphoses.* Trans. Mary Innes. New York: Penguin, 1955.

Padilla, Victoria. *Southern California Gardens.* Berkeley: University of California Press, 1961.

Panunzio, Constantine. *Self-Help Cooperatives in Los Angeles.* Berkeley: University of California Press, 1939.

Park, Marlene, and Gerald Markowitz. *Democratic Vistas: Post Offices and Public Art in the New Deal.* Philadelphia: Temple University Press, 1984.

Parker, Carleton. *The Casual Laborer and Other Essays.* New York: Harcourt, Brace and Howe, 1920.

Pascoe, Peggy. "Miscegenation Law, Court Cases, and Ideologies of 'Race' in Twentieth-Century America." *Journal of American History* 83 (June 1996): 44–69.

———. *Relations of Rescue: The Search for Female Moral Authority in the American West, 1874–1939.* New York: Oxford University Press, 1990.

Pauly, Philip. *Biologists and the Promise of American Life.* Princeton: Princeton University Press, 2000.

———. *Controlling Life: Jacques Loeb and the Engineering Ideal in Biology.* New York: Oxford University Press, 1987.

Pendergrast, Mark. *For God, Country and Coca-Cola: The Unauthorized History of the Great American Soft Drink and the Company That Makes It.* New York: Scribner's, 1993.

Pisani, Donald. *From the Family Farm to Agribusiness: The Irrigation Crusade in California and the West, 1850–1931.* Berkeley: University of California Press, 1984.

Pitt, Leonard. *The Decline of the Californios: A Social History of the Spanish-Speaking Californians, 1846–1890.* Berkeley: University of California Press, 1966.

Pomeroy, Earl. *In Search of the Golden West: The Tourist in Western America.* New York: Knopf, 1957.

Powell, G. Harold. *Coöperation in Agriculture.* New York: Macmillan Co., 1913.

———. "The Handling of Oranges in 1908." In *Official Report of the Thirty-fourth Fruit-Growers' Convention.* Sacramento: California State Printing Office, 1909.

———. *Letters from the Orange Empire.* Ed. Richard Lillard. Los Angeles and Redlands: Historical Society of Southern California and A. K. Smiley Public Library, 1996.

Prendergast, Christopher. *The Order of Mimesis.* New York: Cambridge University Press, 1986.

Preston, William. "Serpent in the Garden: Environmental Change in Colonial California." In Ramón Gutiérrez and Richard Orsi, eds., *Contested Eden: California before the Gold Rush,* 260–98. Berkeley: University of California Press, 1997.

———. *Vanishing Landscapes: Land and Life in the Tulare Lake Basin.* Berkeley: University of California Press, 1981.

Pulido, Laura. *Environmentalism and Economic Justice: Two Chicano Struggles in the Southwest.* Tucson: University of Arizona Press, 1996.

Rabinowitz, Paula. *They Must Be Represented: The Politics of Documentary.* New York: Verso, 1994.

Race Betterment Foundation. *Official Proceedings of the Second National Conference on Race Betterment.* Battle Creek, MI: n.p., 1915.

Raftery, Judith. "Los Angeles Clubwomen and Progressive Reform." In William Deverell and Tom Sitton, eds., *California Progressivism Revisited,* 144–74. Berkeley: University of California Press, 1994.

Rawls, James J. *Indians of California: The Changing Image.* Norman: University of Oklahoma Press, 1984.

Reccow, Louis. "The Orange County Citrus Strikes of 1935–1936: The 'Forgotten People' in Revolt." Ph.D. dissertation, University of Southern California, 1971.

Reisler, Marc. "Always the Laborer, Never the Citizen: Anglo Perceptions of the Mexican Immigrant during the 1920s." *Pacific Historical Review* 45 (May 1976): 231–54.

———. *By the Sweat of Their Brow: Mexican Immigrant Labor in the United States, 1900–1940.* Westport, CT: Greenwood Press, 1976.

Rice, Harvey. *Letters from the Pacific Slope; or, First Impressions.* New York: D. Appleton & Company, 1870.

Rivera, Diego. *My Art, My Life: An Autobiography.* New York: Dover Publications, 1960.

———. *Portrait of America.* New York: Covici, Friede, 1934.

———. "Scaffoldings." *Hesperian,* Spring 1931.

Robinson, W. W. *Land in California.* Berkeley: University of California Press, 1948.

Rodgers, Daniel. "In Search of Progressivism." *Reviews in American History* 10 (December 1982): 113–32.

Rogin, Michael. *Ronald Reagan, the Movie: And Other Episodes in Political Demonology.* Berkeley: University of California Press, 1987.

Ruiz, Vicki. *Cannery Women/Cannery Lives: Mexican Women, Unionization and the California Food Processing Industry, 1930–1950.* Albuquerque: University of New Mexico Press, 1987.

———. "'Star Struck': Acculturation, Adolescence, and the Mexican American Woman, 1920–1950." In Adela de la Torre and Beatríz Pesquera, eds., *Building with Our Hands: New Directions in Chicana Studies,* 109–29. Berkeley: University of California Press, 1993.

Rumsey, C. E. "Packing House Equipment." *Official Report of the Thirty-fourth Fruit-Growers' Convention.* Sacramento: California State Printing Office, 1909.

Runte, Alfred. *Yosemite: The Embattled Wilderness.* Lincoln: University of Nebraska Press, 1990.

Russell, Edmund J., III. "'Speaking of Annihilation': Mobilizing for War against Human and Insect Enemies, 1914–1945." *Journal of American History* 82 (March 1996): 1505–29.

Rydell, Robert. *All the World's a Fair: Visions of Empire at American International Expositions, 1876–1916.* Chicago: University of Chicago Press, 1984.

Sacramento Region Citizens' Council. *Community Building Applied to the Sacramento Region.* N.p., August 1927.

Sánchez, George. *Becoming Mexican American: Ethnicity, Culture and Identity in Chicano Los Angeles.* New York: Oxford University Press, 1993.

———. "'Go after the Women': Americanization and the Mexican Immigrant Woman, 1915–1925." In Ellen DuBois and Vicki Ruiz, eds., *Unequal Sisters: A Multicultural Reader in U.S. Women's History,* 250–63. New York: Routledge, 1990.

Sánchez, Rosaura. *Telling Identities: The Californio Testimonios.* St. Paul: University of Minnesota Press, 1995.

Saunders, Charles Francis. *Finding the Worth While in California.* New York: Robert M. McBride & Co., 1916.

———. *The Story of Carmelita.* Pasadena: A. C. Vroman, 1928.

Sawyer, Richard. "To Make a Spotless Orange: Biological Control in California." Ph.D. dissertation, University of Wisconsin, Madison, 1990.

Saxton, Alexander. *The Indispensable Enemy: Labor and the Anti-Chinese Movement in California.* Berkeley: University of California Press, 1971.

Scanlon, Jennifer. *Inarticulate Longings: The* Ladies' Home Journal, *Gender, and the Promises of Consumer Culture.* New York: Routledge, 1995.

Schama, Simon. *Landscape and Memory.* New York: Knopf, 1995.

Schoenherr, Allan. *A Natural History of California.* Berkeley: University of California Press, 1992.

Sellers, Christopher. "Placing the Body in Environmental History: From Blind-Spot to Spotlight." Paper delivered at the American Society for Environmental History Biennial Conference, Baltimore, Maryland, 7 March 1997.

Sherwin-Williams Company. *The Story of Sherwin-Williams.* Chicago: Lakeside Press, n.d.

Shi, David. *The Simple Life: Plain Living and High Thinking in American Culture.* New York: Oxford University Press, 1985.

Shindo, Charles. *Dust Bowl Migrants in the American Imagination.* Lawrence: University Press of Kansas, 1997.

Shloss, Carol. *In Visible Light: Photography and the American Writer, 1840–1940.* New York: Oxford University Press, 1987.

Silko, Leslie Marmon. *Gardens in the Dunes.* New York: Simon and Schuster, 1999.

Sinclair, Upton. *The Autobiography of Upton Sinclair.* New York: Harcourt, Brace and World, 1962.

———. *The Book of Life.* Girard, KS: Haldeman-Julius Company, 1921.

———. *Depression Island.* Pasadena: by the author, 1936.

———. *EPIC Answers.* Pasadena: by the author, 1934.

———. *I, Candidate for Governor: And How I Got Licked.* 1935. Reprint, Berkeley: University of California Press, 1994.

———. *I, Governor of California, and How I Ended Poverty: A True Story of the Future.* Pasadena: by the author, 1933.

———. *Immediate EPIC.* Pasadena: by the author, 1934.

———. *The Jungle.* 1906. Reprint, New York: Penguin, 1985.

———. *The Lie Factory Starts.* Los Angeles: End Poverty League, 1934.

———. *The Way Out: What Lies ahead for America.* New York: Farrar and Rinehart, 1933.

———. *We, People of America, and How We Ended Poverty.* Pasadena: National EPIC League, 1935.

Smith, Terry. *Making the Modern: Industry, Art, and Design in America.* Chicago: University of Chicago Press, 1993.

Snyder, Robert. *Pare Lorentz and the Documentary Film.* Norman: University of Oklahoma Press, 1968.

Southern Pacific Company. *Big Trees of California.* San Francisco: Southern Pacific Company, 1914.

———. *California Industries: Personal Testimonies of Experienced Cultivators: How Energy Enterprise and Intelligence Are Rewarded in California.* San Francisco: Southern Pacific Company, 1902.

———. *Catalogue of the Products of California: Exhibited by the Southern Pacific Company, at the North, Central and South American Exposition, New Orleans, Nov. 10th, 1885, to April 1st, 1886.* New Orleans: Press of W. B. Stansbury, 1886.

———. *"Eat California Fruit: By One of the Eaters."* San Francisco: Southern Pacific Company, 1908.

———. *The Lands of the Southern Pacific Railroad Company of California.* San Francisco: Southern Pacific Railroad Company, 1882.

Sprague, Roger. "The Picture." *The Californians,* April 1996.

Stanley, Norman. *No Little Plans: The Story of the Los Angeles Chamber of Commerce.* Los Angeles: Los Angeles Chamber of Commerce, 1956.

Starr, Kevin. *Endangered Dreams: California through the Depression.* New York: Oxford University Press, 1996.

———. *Inventing the Dream: California through the Progressive Era.* New York: Oxford University Press, 1985.

———. *Material Dreams: Southern California through the 1920s.* New York: Oxford University Press, 1990.

Starrs, Paul. "The Navel of California and Other Oranges: Images of California and the Orange Crate." *California Geographer* 28 (1988): 1–41.

Statutes of California: Forty-third Session. Sacramento: California State Printing Office, 1920.

Stein, Walter. *California and the Dust Bowl Migration.* Westport, CT: Greenwood Press, 1973.

Steinbeck, Elaine, and Robert Wallstein, eds. *Steinbeck: A Life in Letters.* New York: Viking, 1975.

Steinbeck, John. "The Crop Picker's Fight for Life in a Land of Plenty." St. Louis *Post Dispatch,* 17 April 1938.

———. *The Grapes of Wrath.* 1939. Reprint, New York: Penguin, 1976.

———. *The Harvest Gypsies.* 1936. Reprint, Berkeley, CA: Heyday Books, 1988.

———. "The Harvest Gypsies." San Francisco *News,* 5 October 1936.

———. *The Log from the* Sea of Cortez. 1941. Reprint, New York: Penguin, 1977.

———. *The Long Valley.* 1938. Reprint, New York: Penguin, 1986.

———. "Starvation under the Orange Trees." *Monterey Trader,* 15 April 1938.

———. *Working Days: The Journals of* The Grapes of Wrath, *1938–1941.* Ed. Robert DeMott. New York: Penguin, 1989.

Stokes, Frank. "Let the Mexicans Organize!" *The Nation,* 19 December 1936.

Stoll, Steven. *The Fruits of Natural Advantage: Making the Industrial Countryside in California.* Berkeley: University of California Press, 1998.

———. "Insects and Institutions: University Science and the Fruit Business in California." *Agricultural History* 69 (Spring 1995): 216–39.

Storke, Elliot. *Domestic and Rural Affairs: The Family, Farm and Gardens, and the Domestic Animals.* Auburn, NY: Auburn Publishing Company, 1859.

Stott, William. *Documentary Expression and Thirties America.* 1973. Reprint, Chicago: University of Chicago Press, 1986.

Streatfield, David. *California Gardens: Creating a New Eden.* New York: Abbeville Press, 1994.

Sunkist Growers. *The Story of the California Oranges and Lemons.* Los Angeles: California Fruit Growers Exchange, 1931.

Synopsis of the proceedings of the eighth Fruit Growers' Convention of the state of California. Sacramento: Supt. State Printing, 1888.

Takaki, Ronald. *Strangers from a Different Shore: A History of Asian Americans.* New York: Penguin, 1989.

Taylor, Paul. "Again the Covered Wagon." *Survey Graphic,* July 1935.

———. *Essays on Land, Water and the Law in California.* New York: Arno Press, 1979.

———. "From the Ground Up." *Survey Graphic,* September 1936.

———. *Labor on the Land: Collected Writings, 1930–1970.* New York: Arno Press, 1981.

———. "Our Stakes in the Japanese Exodus." *Survey Graphic,* September 1942.

Taylor, Paul, and Clark Kerr. "Whither Self Help?" *Survey Graphic* (July 1934): 328–31.

Taylor, Paul, and Tom Vasey. "Historical Background of California Farm Labor." *Rural Sociology* 1 (September 1936).

Teague, Charles Collins. *Fifty Years a Rancher.* Los Angeles: Ward Ritchie Press, 1944.

Tobey, Ronald, and Charles Wetherell. "The Citrus Industry and the Revolution of Corporate Capitalism in Southern California, 1887–1944." *California History* 74 (Spring 1995): 6–21.

Tobey, Ronald, Charles Wetherell, Kevin Hallaran, and Buffie Hollis. *The National Orange Company Packing House: An Architectural and Technological History, 1898–1940.* Riverside, CA: University of California, Riverside, Laboratory for Historical Research, 1991.

Todd, Frank. *The Story of the Exposition; Being the Official History of the International Celebration Held at San Francisco in 1915 to Commemorate the Discovery of the Pacific Ocean and the Construction of the Panama Canal.* 5 vols. New York: G. P. Putnam's Sons, 1921.

Trachtenberg, Alan. "From Image to Story: Reading the File." In Carl Fleischauer and Beverly Brannan, eds., *Documenting America, 1935–1943,* 45–73. Berkeley: University of California Press, 1988.

———. "Walker Evans' America: A Documentary Invention." In David Featherstone, ed., *Observations: Essays on Documentary Photography.* Carmel, CA: Friends of Photography, 1984.

Truman, Major Ben J. *Semi-Tropical California: Its Climate, Healthfulness, Productiveness, and Scenery.* San Francisco: A. L. Bancroft and Co., 1874.

Turner, Laura. "Citrus Culture: The Mentality of the Orange Rancher in Progressive Era North Orange County." Master's thesis, California State University, Fullerton, 1995.

Turner, Victor. *Anthropology of Performance.* New York: PAJ Publications, 1988.

———. *The Forest of Symbols: Aspects of Ndembu Ritual.* Ithaca: Cornell University Press, 1967.

———. *From Ritual to Theatre.* New York: PAJ Publications, 1982.

Tyrrell, Ian. *True Gardens of the Gods: Californian-Australian Environmental Reform, 1860–1930.* Berkeley: University of California Press, 1999.

The United States Census of Agriculture: 1935, Vol. II. Washington, DC: U.S. Government Printing Office, 1936.

U.S. Bureau of the Census. *Thirteenth Census of the United States Taken in the Year 1910.* Washington, DC: U.S. Government Printing Office, 1913.

———. *The Fifteenth Census of the United States: 1930, Agriculture.* Washington, DC: U.S. Government Printing Office, 1931.

———. *The Fifteenth Census of the United States: 1930, Irrigation.* Washington, DC: U.S. Government Printing Office, 1932.

U.S. Congress, House, Select Committee to Investigate the Interstate Migration of Destitute Citizens. *Interstate Migration: Hearings before the Select Committee to Investigate Migration of Destitute Citizens, House of Representatives, Seventy-sixth Congress, Third Session, Pursuant to H. Res. 63 and H. Res. 491.* Washington, DC: U.S. Government Printing Office, 1940–41.

U.S. Congress, Senate, Subcommittee of the Committee on Education and Labor. *Hearings on Senate Resolution 266, Violations of Free Speech and Rights of Labor.* 74th Congress, 2nd Session. Washington, DC: U.S. Government Printing Office, 1939.

———. *Report, Violations of Free Speech and Rights of Labor.* Report no. 1150, 77th Congress, 2nd Session. Washington, DC: U.S. Government Printing Office, 1942.

U.S. Department of Agriculture, Bureau of Plant Industry, G. Harold Powell et al. "The Decay of Oranges while in Transit from California." *Bulletin No. 123.* Washington, DC: U.S. Government Printing Office, 1908.

U.S. Department of Labor, Wage and Hour Division. "Report on the Citrus Fruit Packing Industry under the Fair Labor Standards Acts." Typescript. Washington, DC: n.p., 1940.

Vail, Mary. *"Both Sides Told," or, Southern California as It Is.* Pasadena: West Coast Pub. Company, 1888.

Vaught, David. *Cultivating California: Growers, Specialty Crops, and Labor, 1875–1920.* Baltimore: Johns Hopkins University Press, 1999.

———. "Factories in the Field Revisited." *Pacific Historical Review* 66 (May 1997): 149–84.

Veblen, Thorstein. *The Engineers and the Price System.* 1921. Reprint, New York: Augustus Kelley, 1965.

———. *Theory of the Leisure Class.* 1899. Reprint, New York: Penguin, 1994.

Vidor, King. *A Tree Is a Tree.* New York: Harcourt, Brace, 1953.

Warner, Charles Dudley. *Our Italy.* New York: Harper and Brothers, 1891.

War Relocation Authority. *WRA: A Story of Human Conservation.* Washington, DC: U.S. Government Printing Office, 1946.

Watkins, T. H. *The Great Depression: America in the 1930s.* New York: Little, Brown, 1993.

Webb, John, and Malcolm Brown. *Migrant Families.* Washington, DC: U.S. Government Printing Office, 1938.

Weber, Devra. *Dark Sweat, White Gold: California Farm Workers, Cotton, and the New Deal.* Berkeley: University of California Press, 1994.

West, Nathanael. *The Day of the Locust.* 1939. Reprint, New York: Signet, 1983.

White, Richard. "'Are You an Environmentalist or Do You Work for a Living?' Work and Nature." In William Cronon, ed., *Uncommon Ground: Toward Reinventing Nature,* 171–85. New York: Norton, 1995.

———. "Frederick Jackson Turner and Buffalo Bill." In James Grossman, ed., *The Frontier in American Culture,* 7–65. Berkeley: University of California Press, 1994.

Whitman, Walt. *Leaves of Grass.* New York: Library of America, 1992.

Whitson, John, Robert John, and Henry Smith Williams, eds. *Luther Burbank: His Methods and Discoveries and Their Practical Application, Prepared from His Original Field Notes Covering More Than 100,000 Experiments Made during Forty Years Devoted to Plant Improvement.* 12 vols. New York: Luther Burbank Press, 1914–15.

Whorton, James. *Before* Silent Spring: *Pesticides and Public Health in Pre-DDT America.* Princeton: Princeton University Press, 1974.

Wickson, E. J. *The California Fruits and How to Grow Them.* 7th ed. San Francisco: Pacific Rural Press, 1914.

———. "The Development of California Fruit Industries." *University of California Chronicle,* 20 October 1918.

———. *Luther Burbank, Man, Methods and Achievements: An Appreciation.* San Francisco: Southern Pacific Company, 1902.

———. "The Orange in Northern and Central California." San Francisco: California Sate Board of Trade, 1903.

Williamson, Paul. "Labor in the California Citrus Industry." Master's thesis, University of California, Berkeley, 1947.

Winner, Langdon. *The Whale and the Reactor: A Search for Limits in an Age of High Technology.* Chicago: University of Chicago Press, 1986.

Woeste, Victoria Saker. *The Farmer's Benevolent Trust: Law and Agricultural Cooperation in Industrial America, 1865–1945.* Chapel Hill: University of North Carolina Press, 1998.

Woirol, Gregory. *In the Floating Army: F. C. Mills on Itinerant Life in California, 1914.* Urbana: University of Illinois Press, 1992.

Wolfe, Bertram. *The Fabulous Life of Diego Rivera*. New York: Stein & Day, 1963.

Woloch, Nancy. *Muller v. Oregon: A Brief History with Documents*. New York: Bedford, 1996.

Wood, Samuel. "The California State Commission of Immigration and Housing: A Study of Administrative Organization and the Growth of Function." Ph.D. dissertation, University of California, Berkeley, 1942.

Wormser, Paul. "Chinese Agricultural Labor in the Citrus Belt of Inland Southern California." In Great Basin Foundation, ed., *Wong Ho Leun: An American Chinatown*, 173–91. San Diego: Great Basin Foundation, 1987.

Worster, Donald. *The Dust Bowl: The Southern Plains in the 1930s*. New York: Oxford University Press, 1979.

———. *Rivers of Empire: Water, Aridity, and the Growth of the American West*. 1985. Reprint, New York: Oxford University Press, 1992.

———. *An Unsettled Country: Changing Landscapes of the American West*. Albuquerque: University of New Mexico Press, 1994.

Wrobel, David. *The End of American Exceptionalism: Frontier Anxiety from the Old West to the New Deal*. Lawrence: University Press of Kansas, 1993.

Wyatt, David. *The Fall into Eden: Landscape and Imagination in California*. New York: Cambridge University Press, 1986.

Zeirer, Clifford. "The Citrus Fruit Industry of the Los Angeles Basin." *Economic Geography* (January 1934): 53–77.

Zimmerman, Carle, and Nathan Whetten. *Rural Families on Relief*. Washington, DC: U.S. Government Printing Office, 1938.

Zimmerman, Tom. "Paradise Promoted: Boosterism and the Los Angeles Chamber of Commerce." *California History* 64 (Winter 1985): 22–33.

INDEX

Panama-Pacific Exposition (1915), 62, 65
Pardee, George, 57
Parker, Carleton, 148, 157–58, 176, 239;
    on labor and environment, 157–59
Parsons, Louella, 105
Pasadena (CA), 12, 23, 34, 40, 45, 51
peas, 60–61, 248
pesticides, 53, 76–83, 79, 80, 141–42
Physical Culture (magazine), 192
Pickett, John, 286
Pickford, Mary, 90
Piggly Wiggly window display, 99
Placentia Mutual Orange Association, 146
Plant Patent Act (1930), 54, 63–65
The Plow That Broke the Plains (film,
    Lorentz, 1936), 11, 234, 270
plums and prunes, 60, 84
Pomona (CA), 23, 30, 40
Pomona (goddess), 3, 20, *21*
Port Costa (CA), 38
Porterville (CA), *43, 243, 258, 259,* 261
Portugal, 17
potatoes, 57
Powell, G. Harold, 66, 135–40, 146
Powell Method, 138–39, 141, 146, 151,
    274
Pratt, Richard Henry, 50
Prejudice (McWilliams), 294
Printers' Ink (magazine), 105, 211
Progressivism, 106–7, 149; defined,
    155–56; and housing reform,
    159–71. *See also* Americanization;
    California Commission of Immigra-
    tion and Housing; Lubin, Simon J.
Pure Food and Drug Act (1906), 101,
    190
Purnell, Frank, 64

race, 63, 124, 126–27, 132, 156; and cli-
    mate, 49; and Dust Bowl migrants,
    228, 244–45; and racialism, 128,
    160, 322n12; racialization and natu-
    ralization, 9, 52, 128–31, 135, 182,
    199–200, 242, 244–45; and racial
    nationalism, 242; and whiteness,
    244
Ramona (Jackson), 47–49
The Razor's Edge (Maugham), 65

Reader's Digest (magazine), 283
Reagan, Ronald, 190
Redlands (CA), 6, 45
red scale, 77, 78, 79
Resettlement Administration. *See* Farm
    Security Administration
Richardson, Friend, 176
Ricketts, Ed, 266
Rio Grande, 126
Rivera, Diego, 1–11, *2,* 298
Riverside (CA), 6, 17, 22, 32–34, 40–41,
    49–50, 66, 84
Riverside County (CA), *43*
Rochester (NY), 12
Rockefeller, Nelson, 2
Rockwell, Norman, 209
Roosevelt, Franklin Delano, 123, 200,
    209, 287, 293
Roosevelt, Theodore, 63, 67, 135, 160,
    190–92
Rowell, Chester, 207
The Rural Californian (magazine), 42
Rural Observer (newspaper), 254–55,
    276
Rust, Horatio, 20, 50–52

Sacramento (CA), 6, 60, 175, 196
Sacramento Bee (newspaper), 35, 208
Safeway stores, 100
Salinas (CA), 175
San Andreas fault, 30
San Bernardino (CA), 30, 40, 154
San Bernardino County (CA), 42, *43*
San Bernardino Mountains, 5, 6, 30
San Bernardino National Orange Show,
    115
Sánchez, George, 132, 166
San Diego County (CA), 42
San Fernando Valley, 66, 212–13
San Francisco, 1, 2, 291, 294, 297–98
San Francisco Bay, 38
San Francisco Chronicle (newspaper), 2,
    133, 205
San Francisco News (newspaper), 240–43,
    264, 340–41n26
San Francisco Stock Exchange, 1, 8
San Gabriel (CA), 30
San Gabriel Mountains, 5, 6, 30

Text:	11.25/13.5 Adobe Garamond
Display:	Adobe Garamond
Cartographer:	Bill Nelson
Compositor:	International Typesetting & Composition
Printer and Binder:	Thomson-Shore, Inc.